SOCIOLOGY OF THE ARTS

SOCIOLOGY OF THE ARTS

Exploring Fine and Popular Forms

Victoria D. Alexander

Blackwell
Publishing

© 2003 by Victoria D. Alexander

350 Main Street, Malden, MA 02148-5018, USA
108 Cowley Road, Oxford OX4 1JF, UK
550 Swanston Street, Carlton South, Melbourne, Victoria 3053, Australia
Kurfürstendamm 57, 10707 Berlin, Germany

First published 2003 by Blackwell Publishing

Library of Congress Cataloging-in-Publication Data

Alexander, Victoria D.
　Sociology of the arts : exploring fine and popular forms / Victoria D. Alexander.
　　p. cm.
Includes bibliographical references and index.
　ISBN 0–631–23039–4 (alk. paper) – ISBN 0–631–23040–8 (alk. paper)
　1. Arts and society.　I. Title.
　NX180.S6 A435　2003
　306.4'7—dc21

2002006550

A catalogue record for this title is available from the British Library.

Set in 10.5 on 12.5pt Bembo
by Kolam Information Services Pvt. Ltd, Pondicherry, India
Printed and Bound in Great Britain
by MPG Books Ltd, Bodmin, Cornwall

For further information on
Blackwell Publishing, visit our website:
http://www.blackwellpublishing.com

Contents

Plates

Figures

Tables

Boxes

Preface

I have taught courses on the Sociology of the Arts for quite some time now. Every year, students ask me to recommend a single text that will provide an overview of the materials I cover. I have been unable to accommodate them, despite the existence of a number of excellent books on sociological aspects of the arts, on popular culture, and on culture more broadly speaking. Their constant requests for a single source which draws across different intellectual approaches to the subject while focusing specifically on the fine and popular arts inspired me to write this book.

In setting out the intellectual topography of the field of study, I have drawn on a large body of theory and research. Scholarship is a search for truth, and as such, it necessarily constructs an arena in which combatants from different perspectives battle over each other's claims. My description of the sociology of the arts, then, considers various theories and empirical studies which cluster around central debates that colleagues will find familiar. Nevertheless, this work (inevitably) contains my personal vision of the field. I hope that my presentation is close enough to my colleagues' own understandings of the field to allow them to teach from the book, should they wish, but that it also provides an original argument they will find stimulating. The goal I set for myself in writing the book was to produce a work that would be helpful to undergraduates new to the field, useful to graduate students wishing to launch their research in it, and interesting to colleagues well established in it. How successfully this one modest book has met such a broad goal will be decided by you, its reader.

I have also taught courses on the Sociology of Organizations. One pedagogic lesson I have learned from that field concerns the crucial role that concrete case studies can play in getting students to think about the more abstract theoretical issues. Case studies are almost indispensable in the teaching of work, occupations, and organizational behavior, but are used less often in other subfields in sociology. Convinced of their utility in organizations classes, I subsequently tried them in arts classes, where they worked well. Accordingly, I have written a case study for each substantive chapter in the book. They are intended to spark classroom discussion, and also to exemplify some of the most interesting empirical work within the sociology of the arts.

Structure of the Book

Chapter 1 introduces the issues that underpin the rest of the book. In the first part of the chapter, I set out what I mean by "art." I define the term inclusively to encompass both fine and popular forms; art ranges, as it were, from Rembrandt to rap. In the second section, I discuss paradigms in sociology to highlight the fact that the answers sociologists find in their research are necessarily shaped by the questions they pose. Recognizing that sociologists do not all approach the sociology of the arts with the same types of questions, and that what constitutes an answer varies from scholar to scholar, allows one to develop a richer understanding of the field as a whole. The aim of the second part of the chapter is to provide a primer on social theory for students who may have no background in sociology, although I hope that other readers might find it useful as well.

In the substantive chapters that follow, I map out the currents of thought in the field. I have attempted to balance the requirements of a comprehensive overview (as in a review article of particular interest to scholars) with the need for enough detail on individual studies to make the book useful to readers new to the field. At the same time, I have also worked within my publisher's parameters on the length of the book. I hope that I have struck a balance that will make the book of use and interest to both students and scholars. Inevitably, however, scholars will spot omissions, only some of which will have been intentional on my part.

Part I discusses two approaches to the relationship between art and society: reflection (chapter 2) and shaping (chapter 3). As conceived by these approaches, this relationship can be represented metaphorically as a direct link, a straight line, as it were, between a cultural object and society. These two approaches are intuitive ways to see the connection, and at varying levels of sophistication, they appear in professional research, in student research, and in journalistic accounts about art.

Chapters 2 and 3 will show the benefits, as well as the shortcomings, of these ways of thinking. Though early or naive versions of reflection and shaping are easy to criticize, more subtle elements of reflection and shaping remain important, though often implicit, in many contemporary studies. The final chapter in Part I (chapter 4) outlines a more comprehensive and satisfactory view of the interplay between art and society – the cultural diamond – first formulated by Wendy Griswold (1986, 1994). It adds three other points of interaction – production, distribution, and consumption – to the art-society nexus.

Part II covers approaches subsumed by the cultural diamond. The majority of research reported in the book is presented under this rubric. Part II is divided into (A) the production and (B) the consumption approaches.

The theories that make up the production of culture approach, covered in Part IIA, focus on the "left-hand side" of the cultural diamond. They look at how art is created, produced, and distributed, and examine the relationships among creators, distribution networks, art works, and society. The main idea in this approach is that cultural objects are filtered through – and affected by – the people and systems that create and distribute them.

Chapter 5 presents an overview of the production of culture approach, focusing on Howard Becker's (1982) concept of the art world. Becker suggests that every aspect of the art world comes together to shape the art works produced within it, and he argues that the idea of "the artist" (the special person who is the sole creative agent in art worlds) is a social construct. To understand how art works are created, in Becker's view, we need to include people who contribute to the final product but are not artists in the traditional sense, those whom Becker calls "support personnel," along with the artistic "core person-nel." Indeed, Becker argues that art is a collective activity, not the product of lone geniuses. Chapter 5 also provides a brief critique of the approach.

Diana Crane (1992) argues persuasively that, in place of the traditional division of high culture and popular culture, a better way to understand and categorize the current artscape is to look at the context in which the arts reach the public. They can be disseminated by for-profit cultural industries, non-profit organizations, or local networks. Chapter 6 discusses art forms that are distributed through business firms. For the most part, this category is made up of the popular arts. However, profit-seeking enterprises play a role in the fine arts, too, especially in the sales market for painting, sculpture, and classical music. Chapter 7 looks at art works that are distributed through non-profit organizations or social networks. Fine arts are largely distributed by the former, and both fine and folk arts by the latter, though again, the correspondence between distribution network and category of art work is not absolute. Chapter 7 points out the areas in which nonprofit organizations in the arts face some of the same issues as the commercial sector, but differences between the two systems are also striking and will be discussed. The chapter also briefly looks at art and the nation-state.

Chapter 8 focuses on artists, including visual artists, musicians, and writers. The chapter examines artistic labor markets and careers of artists. Segregating artists from support personnel for the purposes of this discussion might seem a step back from Becker's ideas of the art world, but there are theoretical and empirical insights to be gained. As with many concepts in sociology, demonstrating that the artist is a social construct does not imply that artists are a *fiction* (i.e. something false or inactive). Artists and their actions have explanatory power because our conceptions of artists are real.

Chapter 9 considers the globalization of the arts. Globalization is a production of culture topic because it is primarily driven by international business firms. A debated issue is "media imperialism," defined as the situation in which one nation or region imposes its cultural forms on other nations or regions. The chapter looks at the global circulation of both popular arts and fine arts, and assesses its impact. It also anticipates Part IIB of the book in a brief discussion of how people in local contexts might adapt global products or ideas as they consume them.

The theories that make up the consumption of culture approach, covered in Part IIB of the book, focus on the "right-hand side" of the cultural diamond. They look at how people consume, use, and receive art. The main idea is that audiences are the key to understanding art, because the meanings created from art and the ways art is used depend on its consumers, not its creators. Moreover, if art has any effect on society at all, this effect cannot be direct; it must be mediated by the people who receive it.

Chapter 10 explores the development of the reception approach and explicates the major theoretical strands used by its proponents. Its roots lie in literary theory and cultural studies. It also draws upon an earlier "uses and gratifications" model and the ethnographic style of the Chicago School of sociology. In addition, chapter 10 presents a brief critique of the approach.

Chapter 11 examines a number of empirical studies of audience reception. These studies rest, for the most part, on ethnography or in-depth interviews. They examine how audiences use cultural products for enjoyment and the creation of meaning in their lives. The chapter also reviews studies that examine how different people vary in their use of the same cultural products. Finally, the ways that audiences influence the creators and distributors of art is briefly considered.

Chapter 12 focuses on social class differences in taste and in arts consumption. It looks at Pierre Bourdieu's (1984) theory of distinction, which suggests that cultural capital, including knowledge about high art, reinforces class boundaries, and at recent critiques of this theory. The chapter shows that our current understanding of artistic categories – high, popular, and folk – are relatively recent social constructions. In closing, the chapter considers the general question of social boundaries, and how art plays a role in shoring them up or breaking them down.

Part III returns to art itself. The book starts in Part I with a key question in the sociology of the arts: What is the relationship between art and society? This is the starting point of a *sociology* of art. Part II demonstrates that a fuller, richer understanding of fine, folk, and popular arts comes through examining the roles of creators, producers, distributors and consumers. Part III, in turn, addresses two difficulties that arise with the approaches in Part II.

First, Part II divides the cultural diamond into two sides, production and consumption. This is a convenient strategy for presenting the sociological literature on the arts. It also reflects a genuine division in the literature. For the most part, sociologists have looked at art either from the vantage point of production or from that of consumption. Griswold argued that researchers should examine all the nodes and all the links in the diamond. This is easier said than done, and studies that look at only some of the nodes and links can still enlighten us. But scholars might do well to try to heed Griswold's suggestion and consider more frequently both production and consumption issues in their work.

Second, focusing on either the mechanisms of production and distribution, and their effects on art, or on the reception of art by audiences, often ignores the wider, societal context. More important, it puts the art work aside. While separating art from artists, production systems, consumers, and society makes sense analytically, it can obscure our understanding of both the art itself, and art in its social context. In fact, isolating art as a node in the diamond often renders it epiphenomenal.

In Part III, I move from the discussion of art *and* society, which was presented in Parts I and II, to a discussion of art *in* society, focusing on the interpenetration of art and the other institutions that make up society. As background, chapter 13 presents theories that focus on the analysis of artworks themselves. I review traditional approaches from art history, literature, and music. These theories are important, but are limited in that they consider *only* the art work, rather than how art is constituted in the wider society. Chapter 14 presents work by sociologists who think of the art itself as a central component of their research while also not losing sight of the interpenetration of art and society. These theorists argue that since art is actively constituted within society, artworks, meaning, and aesthetics can be taken as genuine sociological topics.

The conclusion (chapter 15) highlights the multi-stranded nature of research in the arts and calls for more inclusive studies. It presents my own metatheoretical stance – or you could say, my taste in metatheory – and, in essence, it sets out an "aesthetic" of sociological theorizing about art.

Acknowledgments

Although the idea of writing this book came to me fairly recently, the resulting work is, fundamentally, the product of eighteen years of studying and teaching. As a consequence, thanks are due to many more people than I can adequately acknowledge. I owe a great intellectual debt to Ann Swidler. Her ideas have influenced my work since I met her in 1984. I took her seminar on the Sociology of Culture that academic year, a course which provided a strong foundation for my subsequent thinking. Ann has been enormously helpful over the years and it has been my privilege to know her. Also in 1984–5, I took a seminar on Sociology of Literature with Wendy Griswold, whose idea of the cultural diamond frames the presentation of scholarship in this book. My students over the years at Stanford, Harvard, and Surrey, where I have taught courses on the sociology of art and culture, have asked innumerable questions and raised many interesting points. Through them, I have clarified my thinking. I deeply appreciate their input, and the book is better for it.

I met Howie Becker as a student in a photography seminar in Rochester, New York in the late 1970s. I learned a lot, but I had no idea that he was at that very moment researching a book which would so deeply influence my future career. People I have seen regularly at conferences over the years, particularly Vera Zolberg, have shared their ideas. They are too numerous to name individually, but I look forward to seeing them next time. While writing *Sociology of the Arts*, I have also been working with Marilyn Rueschemeyer on a co-authored book, *Art and the State in Comparative Perspective*, and the cross-fertilization between the projects has borne fruit. I would also like to thank the Stanford Women's Culture Project, the FSC Group at Harvard University, Paul DiMaggio, John Meyer, and Dick Scott for invaluable help along the way.

A chance conversation with Bob Witkin got the ball rolling on this project, and two brief conversations with Pete Peterson, on the name of our field and on the cultural diamond, were more influential than he might realize. Anne Bowler, Tia DeNora, Jan Marontate, and Ann Swidler gave useful feedback at an early stage of the project, Geoff Cooper at the end. I would like to thank Anne Bowler for comments on chapter 14, and Sarah Corse for comments on the entire manuscript. Anonymous reviewers provided feedback on the prospectus and the manuscript, for which I am grateful. I regret that my deadline followed closely my receipt of the full reviews, as I was unable to follow through on several useful leads provided by the reviewers. I am grateful to Hilary Underwood for her generous and timely advice on obtaining copyright permission for art works, and to Bernice Pescosolido and colleagues who kindly helped in what proved to be a fruitless quest to reproduce an image from their *ASR* article. Paul Taylor from the Photographic Collection of the Warburg Institute traced information on two problematic images that are now reproduced herein. The University of California Press kindly provided permission to quote from Howard Becker's *Art Worlds*, copyright © 1982 The Regents of the University of California. The professionals at Blackwell Publishing have been wonderful to work with, and I would like to thank Angela Cohen, Anthony Grahame, Susan Rabinowitz, and especially, Ken Provencher.

I would like to thank the University of Surrey, and especially my colleagues in the Sociology Department, for providing me a sabbatical leave in Autumn 2000, which allowed this book to get off the ground. Jim Benson read every word of the manuscript, and I cannot properly thank him.

I dedicate this book to my daughter, Katherine Benson. Without her, the book would have been finished sooner, but my life would not have been as rich.

Plate 1 Comte de Paroy, Engraving after Elizabeth Vigée-Lebrun, *The Artist's Daughter* (*Julie Lebrun*), 1787, © The British Museum, London.

1

Introduction: What is Art?

A colleague of mine was interviewing art students at the San Francisco Art Institute. In a courtyard outside the classroom, a young man dressed in black clothes was standing in the fountain and moving his body in interesting ways. Inside, my colleague found the students discussing whether "Bob" was making art, or whether he was just acting like an idiot again.

This book is about the sociology of the arts. That is evident from its title. Perhaps not clear are what I mean by art and what I mean by a sociology of it. *Art* is a value-laden word, conjuring up images of the best that has been penned into words or brushed onto canvas. This book uses the term in a more mundane, and a broader, sense. Art includes the tangible, visible, and/or audible products of creative endeavor; it includes not only the traditional fine arts but also the popular and folk arts.

Sociology is, among other things, the study of society, the study of human systems, the study of how people create meaning, and the study of social inequality. These aspects of sociology are central to this book. We will examine how groups of people work together to create what we call art. We will look at why some things are called "art" and some people "artists," and why other things and people are not. We will look at the meaning of artistic objects and why interpretations of art vary. We will look at how people use artistic products, for aesthetic pleasure certainly, but also for other reasons. And we will study the intersection of race, gender, and class with art.

Defining Art

Definitions often seem to pin down, in academic phraseology, what seems intuitively obvious. I will not give a formal definition of art suitable for quoting in essays or exams.[1] Instead, I will paint, with a broad brush, a picture of the cultural forms that I intend to cover in this book. Indeed, it is not actually possible to define art in abstract terms, because "what is art" – even broadly stated – is *socially* defined, and therefore subject to many inconsistencies. Why is ballet art but World Federation Wrestling not art? They both are scripted beforehand and performed to a sound track (music or the roar of the crowd and the announcer's voice-over); the performers wear attractive costumes and leap athletically about the stage. We might say that art is not sport (but this begs the question, in this case, as to why the World Federation style of wrestling is considered sport). Family photo albums are not considered art, even the ones in which the pictures are carefully composed and mounted in beautiful books. Family photo albums might be an expressive form, but they are too private to be called art. Nevertheless, most of us would think of the photographer Ansel Adams's private albums as art, and some photographers have created family photos, specifically meant to be considered art, that have been exhibited in museums.[2] If we already think of the creator as an artist, or if we see a work in a museum, we tend to call it art. This points out the importance of the context.

The sociologist Howard Becker (1982) believes that the context is the most important aspect to the definition of art. He says:

> Like other complex concepts, [the concept of art] disguises a generalization about the nature of reality. When we try to define it, we find many anomalous cases, cases which meet some, but not all, of the criteria implied or expressed by the concept. When we say "art," we usually mean something like this: a work which has aesthetic value, however that is defined; a work justified by a coherent and defensible aesthetic; a work displayed in the appropriate places (hung in museums, played at concerts). In many instances, however, works have some, but not all, of these attributes. (p. 138)

Becker believes that a work is art if people say it is. That is, the contents of the category of art are defined socially. Further, art is defined by groups of people organized into art worlds, which we will discuss in detail later. Think back to Bob in the fountain and the students' debate on whether or not his movements were art. If the fountain had been in a theater, his dance would probably be thought of as art (whether it was good art is another question). If he danced in a public fountain, passers-by might think he was mentally ill. Since the context was an art school, the answer was not clear.

Becker also suggests that we think of the definitional problems in relation-ship to art as an opportunity for research rather than as a problem: "Art worlds typically devote considerable attention to trying to decide what is and isn't art . . . ; by observing how an art world makes those distinctions rather than trying to make them ourselves we can understand much of what goes on in that world" (p. 36).

Becker's comments are quite correct and we shall examine them in greater detail later. Assuming that we cannot define art formally and abstractly, there are, nevertheless, some elements that characterize most forms of art:

- There is an artistic *product*. It is tangible, visible, and/or audible. The product can be a physical object, like a book or a CD. Or it can be a performance, like a play or a concert.
- It *communicates* publicly. To be art, the cultural product must not only exist, it must be seen, heard, touched, or experienced by an audience, either in public or private settings. All art is communication. Of course, not all communication is art.
- It is experienced for *enjoyment*. "Enjoyment" can take many forms. Art might be consumed for aesthetic pleasure, for sociability and fun, for mental stimulation, or for escape. Sometimes, however, people are exposed to art because "it's good for them," as in a school trip to a museum.
- Art is an *expressive form*. When art relates to real life, it presents a fiction or an interpretation. Sometimes art claims to tell the "truth," but if it takes this idea too literally, it moves into the area of documentary, non-fiction, or news.
- Art is defined by its *context*, both physical and social. What is art in a museum or theater may be just odd objects or strange behavior in other settings. When different social groups view the same expressive product, they may disagree on whether or not it is art.

It is as important to understand what this book will *not* cover, as well as what it will cover. I *exclude* from analysis (1) popular culture in the broad sense, for instance, youth culture or commodity culture, and (2) the media in their informational, rather than entertaining, formats, for instance news broadcasts and papers, documentaries and the like. Griswold (1994) distinguishes between *implicit culture* and *explicit culture*. Implicit culture is an abstract feature of social life: how we live and think. Explicit culture is a tangible construction, a performance or product that is produced – it is what I am calling "art." The book analyzes culture in the explicit sense, but does not attempt to address implicit culture systematically.

In place of a formal definition, a list of what is "art" and "not art" will help define the scope of the book (see table 1.1). This book will cover: **(1) The fine (or high) arts**. For example: the visual arts (painting, sculpture, drawing, etching, and other works that you might find in an art museum); opera; live symphony and chamber music; recorded classical music; drama; theater; dance (ballet and modern), other performance art (experimental theater, happenings, etc.); literature and serious fiction; and cyber art (art created by computers and visible only in virtual environments). **(2) The popular (or low, or mass) arts**.

Table 1.1 What is art?: Manifestations of culture included and excluded from consideration in this book

Art (as defined in this book)	*Not Art* (as defined in the book)
√ Fine art	× Popular culture (broadly stated)

Opera
Symphony
Painting and sculpture
Experimental performance art
Dance – ballet, modern, etc.
Literature
[etc.]
	Fads and fashions
	Trends in clothing
	The meaning of blue jeans
	Attitudes towards hair coloring
	    or body design (tattoos,
	    piercing)
	Subcultures, as a way of life
	Youth cultures

√ Popular art
Popular music (rock, pop,
    country, etc.)
Popular fiction
Movies & film (Hollywood,
    made-for-TV, &
    independent)
Television drama (series,
    mini-series) and sit-coms
Advertising (print, television)
[etc.]
	Consumerism
	Manufactured products that
	    carry a cultural meaning (e.g.
	    Levi's, Tommy Hilfinger
	    clothes, Coca-Cola, mobile
	    phones)
	Etc.
	
	× Sport

	× Media – in nonfiction and news facets
√ Folk art Folk music Quilting [etc.]	TV and print news Documentaries Current affairs True crime Science shows The WWW, in most of its aspects
√ The art of subcultures (but not how people in them live)	

√ Art products on the web – web
    art, virtual museums, music clips
	× Private expressive forms
	Personal sketches, watercolors
	    doodles
	art therapy

	× Lots and lots of other things

Gray Area
(These fall outside the book's
definition, or at least its
attention, but might have strong
elements with respect to artness)

- High fashion
- Cooking, especially haute cuisine
- World Federation Wrestling
- [etc.]

For instance: Hollywood movies; independent film; television drama (series, serials, made-for-television movies), television sitcoms; best-selling and pulp fiction; popular music (rock, pop, rap, etc.) including recorded music, rock concerts, and performances in pubs and clubs; and print and television advertising. The fine and popular arts are the book's main subjects, but we will also discuss **(3) the folk arts**, that is, artistic activities created in community settings. This includes: quilting (especially in quilt circles), folk music; garage rock music, as performed by teenagers; and graffiti, of the artistic (rather than the public toilet) kind. Note that some types of art do not neatly fall into one of the categories, for instance, jazz can be either popular or high art, and, especially in its early forms, folk art (Lopes, 2002; Peterson, 1972).

This book **will _not_ cover**: (1) Popular culture, in the broad sense. Many people use the term "popular culture" to mean what I refer to as the "popular arts." Other people use popular culture to mean something bigger. They mean "culture" as in Griswold's implicit culture; an anthropological sense − "that complex whole of knowledge, habit and custom" (Tylor, 1871 [1924]: 1). It is this wider component of popular culture that I exclude. For instance, youth culture is excluded (but not the music that young people might enjoy − music is a popular art form); the lifestyles of subcultures are excluded (but not the art forms subcultures enjoy). I will not cover such topics as: trends in everyday clothing; the cultural meaning of blue jeans; attitudes towards hair coloring or body design (tattoos, piercing), consumer culture, and other customs and norms. (2) Sport is not art, and neither are (3) the nonfiction and news facets of the media. Consequently, I will not consider sport or such media forms as television and print news, documentaries, current affairs shows, true crime, and science programs. The World Wide Web has had an important impact on many forms of art, but it is a _vehicle_ for art, like a museum, movie theater, or bookshop. I will not discuss the Web as a media form in and of itself nor will I consider many of its key aspects such as email, information sites, homepages, bulletin boards, chat rooms, and multi-user domains.

There are innumerable things that are not-art. In this list, I have mentioned only those areas which are similar enough to art to cause confusion − mostly cultural forms that are not art. The line between art and non-art is not sharp. How you look at a cultural form, and from where you look, affects your perception of it. For instance, in France _haute cuisine_ is considered to be a part of the national heritage and is supported by the French Ministry of Culture. Gourmets exist in English-speaking countries too, but cooking is not valued in the same way. Similarly, high fashion is a form of artistic expression for designers. But I do not study _haute cuisine_ or _haute couture_ in the book.[3] I also do not cover art therapy or personal art, as in doodles or recreational watercolors. These are important expressive forms for individuals, but they do not communicate in the public sense that art does.

Why do I consider broad categories of art – fine, popular, and folk – together? The full answer lies in the book, but the basic idea is that they all can be understood with the same sociological concepts. These analytic and methodological tools are applicable to arts that appear in some tangible or performative format (although they do not always apply well to related areas in popular culture, broadly stated, or the media, which is why these areas are not covered). Concentrating on the fine, popular, and folk arts makes it possible to cover the topic in some depth. Moreover, the distinctions among fine, popular, and folk art continue to exist, but they have blurred in recent decades and the categories are less powerful than they once were. In fact, these distinctions exist for social reasons, and this is an important topic for discussion.

Terms for art

Since I cover the fine, popular, and folk arts, I need to have a term that includes them all. I will often refer to "the arts," as I have in the title. More simply, I will refer both to the generic concept, and to individual pieces, as *art*. But as I have mentioned, this word can also mean something honorific. For example, an especially good stunt motorcyclist might be described as an "artist" and his demonstration rides as "art" to separate this motorcyclist from ordinary bikers. I shall not use the term art in this sense. Likewise, "art" sometimes means only *good* art and often implies only the fine arts. I shall set aside this honorific use of "art," and apply the term to mean any of the products created within the fine, popular, or folk arts realms. (We shall visit the idea of art and the honor attached to it later in the book, however.)

Other scholars have come to different solutions to the same problem. Griswold (1994) uses the term *cultural object*, which she defines as "A shared significance embodied in form" – it is audible, visible, or tangible and can be articulated (p. 11). I will also use the term "object" (as in artistic or cultural object) or "work" (as in art work) to refer to individual pieces. I tend to use *art*, *object*, or *work* interchangeably. In general, I use these terms to refer to artistic endeavors that produce a product (a painting, a CD, a book, a film) as well as those that produce a performance (a ballet, live music).

Overview of Sociological Theory[4]

Sociology embodies many ways of thinking about society. Sometimes these different thought styles are at odds with each other to such an extent that it may seem that they do not belong in the same discipline. Nevertheless, at least two ideas link the disparate approaches in the discipline. First, sociology endeavors to generate *theory*. A theory is an attempt to describe how society works. One definition of theory is: *an abstract and general set of propositions formally specifying the interrelationships among a defined set of concepts.* Not every sociologist subscribes to this definition, but most sociologists try to surpass "mere" description of the social world and attempt to *theorize* it, that is, to explain how it works.[5]

Second, sociology also looks at systems, structures, and culture; that is, at the connections among individuals, the stabilized patterns emerging from social interaction, and meaning that is shared across individuals. Sociology sees people in relationship to systems, structures, and culture, rather than concentrating on the psychological makeup of particular persons or on the effects of "great men" (or women) who have single-handedly made a difference.

Sociologists do not agree, however, on whether researchers should discuss human action only at the level of individuals or whether researchers can look at aggregates of people and study how groups, organizations, or networks "act" (the issue of "macro–micro translation"). Sociologists also disagree on whether it is possible to separate elements of culture or social structures from the particular individuals who constitute them (the issue of "generalization"). Sociologists' beliefs about these two issues are background *assumptions*; researchers come to hold them independently of their research, as these beliefs cannot be confirmed or refuted through empirical study. There are a number of other crucial assumptions upon which sociologists strongly differ. These assumptions are often called *metatheory*.[6]

Sociology can be divided, for analytical purposes, into four main approaches. An *approach* is a group of theories that look at social phenomena from the same basic perspective, with a similar set of assumptions or metatheories. Though they share metatheories, the specific theories will differ on many details, and may even be contradictory at points. Four key approaches in sociology are positivist, interpretive, critical, and postmodern styles of research (see table 1.2). Dividing the field in this way illustrates important differences among the approaches and highlights the areas where sociologists are likely to disagree.

Table 1.2 Schematic view of the four general approaches to sociology: key focus and goals

Positivists:	**Interpretivists:**
Measurable variables	Meaning
Generalization (and often, Prediction)	Understanding and Explanation
Marxists:	**Postmodernists:**
Conflict	Power-Knowledge
Praxis	Reflexivity and Deconstruction

Further, divisions in sociology as a whole also appear in the sociology of art. The descriptions I provide here are, in Max Weber's terms, "ideal types." That is, they exist at the analytical level and are distinct in the abstract; but in practice, not all theories fit neatly into the four boxes. The description of each approach is necessarily superficial, but will suffice as an introduction.

The "founding fathers" of sociology were Max Weber, Emile Durkheim, and Karl Marx. The general orientations in much of today's sociology were set out by these three theorists. Some sociologists claim that positivistic sociology was started by Emile Durkheim (especially his quantitative study of suicide), that Max Weber's interest in meaning initiated interpretive sociology, and that Karl Marx's work on the conflict between the classes formed the basis of critical sociology (e.g. Gunter, 2000; Neuman, 2000). Though these assertions simplify the contributions of the early sociologists, they do highlight the fact that debates among these three approaches go back to the beginning of the discipline. A postmodern approach has emerged more recently. It draws, in complex ways, on the early sociologists and stands in opposition, especially, to positivistic sociology.

Positivist sociology

This approach to sociology is the most "scientific" in that positivists aim to make sociology a rigorous, empirical discipline analogous to the disciplines in the natural sciences. Durkheim set out many of the precepts of positivism as they relate to sociology in *The Rules of Sociological Method* (1895 [1982]), highlighting the importance of empirical observation and scientific statements of causality. Sociologists in this camp believe in the definition of theory that I gave above: that sociologists are attempting to understand what is abstract and general about society. They try to understand *all* X's, where X is the unit of analysis or subject of the theory. They make theoretical statements along these lines: "All profit-seeking, culture-producing organizations face demand uncertainty. As a result, these organizations are likely to use two particular strategies to overcome this uncertainty."

Positivists shore up their theoretical statements with empirical evidence. They test their theoretical propositions in specific empirical settings by generating hypotheses that relate the abstract theory to the specific setting. Often their research is quantitative, relying on statistical analysis of data sets. Studying a large number of X's allows them to show that most X's do what they say they do. Qualitative data can also be analyzed in a positivistic manner. When authors of a case study (of a single group, network, or organization) try to show how their case is similar to others not studied, they display a positivistic orientation. Since positivists wish to test their hypotheses, a key component of their work involves *measurement of variables*. Measuring a variable well is difficult, but most positivists believe that it can be done. Seeing reality is simply a matter of looking at the outside world.

In relationship to art, Crane (1992: 86) says that positivist sociologists

> tend to view society as a collection of causally related variables. The goal of the social scientist is to produce a set of laws describing the causes of human behavior. This approach leads to a conceptualization of cultural symbols as "black boxes" whose meanings and interrelationships do not require analysis.

The concept of the black box can mean two things with respect to positivist studies of the arts. First, in a mechanical sense, it means there exists a causal relationship that is deterministic (or in more recent positivism, probabilistic), for example that art works reflect – or shape – the general society in direct and unproblematic ways. Second, it implies an unstudied element of art. Some sociologists argue that such things as aesthetics and meaning are not amenable to empirical analysis and thus, must be left to art historians and philosophers. These positivists instead study objective aspects of the art world while leaving meaning and aesthetics aside. They may research, for instance, the demographic characteristics of art museum audiences, the repertoires of orchestras, or the effects on the arts of the cultural policies of various nations.

Positivistic theory often aims to *predict* human behavior, through the general and causal "laws" they contain. Positivistic sociology is more common, and more highly regarded, in America than it is in Europe. In practice, positivists vary in how strictly they apply the criteria of universalness and predictivity to their theories. Most share a general orientation towards gathering data (to build or test hypotheses) and a preference for some degree of generalization. Some critics of positivistic theories look to only the most extreme positivists in their critiques, and therefore overlook some of the benefits of a positivistic analysis. Sociological studies in this tradition have made strong contributions to the sociology of art. There are a large number of topics where the black box approach is useful – for instance, in studying the network structure of culture industries or the labor market for artists. But as Crane suggests, other topics cannot be studied without recourse to meaning.

Interpretive sociology

Interpretive sociology is concerned with the *question of meaning*. How is meaning created and maintained in social systems? How does cultural background (norms, values, unquestioned assumptions) affect the decisions people make? What does a particular art work mean? Interpretive sociologists try to get at these questions by talking to people about how they think – perhaps through in-depth interviews or participant observation – or by closely analyzing an element of culture.

The roots of interpretive sociology lie, in the nineteenth century, in *hermeneutics*. In a hermeneutic analysis, an analyst makes a detailed reading, or interpretation, of a "text" to discover its meaning. A text can be almost anything that carries meaning: a book, a movie, a painting, a billboard, a conversation, or even an interaction between two people.

Max Weber's (1946) theory of meaning, his "switchman metaphor," is a cornerstone of interpretive sociology. Weber believed that people act rationally, based on self-interest, in choosing alternatives. But how they understand self-interest – the meaning interest has – is based on culture or ideas. Weber's idea was that culture is like a railroad switchman: "Not ideas, but material and ideal interests, directly govern men's conduct. Yet very frequently the 'world images' that have been created by 'ideas' have, like switchmen, determined the tracks along which action has been pushed by the dynamic of interest" (p. 280). Studying meaning, therefore, helps us to *understand* people's goals and thereby, to *explain* their behavior.

Some interpretive sociologists try to create a general theory of how meaning is made, and thus, they are closer to the positivists. Other interpretivists try to uncover the meaning of a specific text or the understandings of a group of people. Most interpretivists believe that meaning is particular and that it resides in individuals (although it may be socially structured). Thus, they believe that meaning cannot be abstracted from its particular situation and is, therefore, ungeneralizable. Sociology, in this view, is about understanding subjective experience and, theoretically, interpretivists are interested in explaining particular situations. They do not require that their theories have predictive value. Moreover, they tend not to think of reality as readily observable. They are more likely to believe that reality is socially constructed. They believe, in other words, that the way people perceive the world is strongly shaped by assumptions they hold, and that these assumptions arise from the social groups in which they are embedded. A positivist would be likely to say "seeing is believing" whereas an interpretivist would be more likely to say "believing is seeing."

Interpretive sociologists clearly have a contribution to make to the sociology of art. Their methods and assumptions are particularly helpful in understanding the meaning that might be attributed to art objects and in understanding how people create meaning from them. And indeed, an interpretive approach is often found in studies of audiences and in studies that concentrate on art objects alone.

Critical sociology

Critical sociologists are primarily concerned with class struggles and with the elites' control, both mental and physical, of the masses. Critical sociology maintains the closest links with its founder, Karl Marx. Marx was interested in the relationship between the classes, specifically, the capitalists and the proletariat. Capitalists own the means of production (factories, tools, property, raw materials, money), but they cannot do all the work. Instead, they hire workers for money. These workers are drawn from the proletariat and have nothing but their hands, muscles, and time to sell. The proletariat become "wage slaves" to the capitalists, depending upon them for the income to buy food, clothing, and housing; indeed, for their very survival.

This dependency is a particular problem, because capitalists take advantage of the proletariat. Capitalists try to get as much labor out of workers as possible and pay them as little as possible; certainly less than the value of the labor workers contribute. Marxists call this "extracting surplus value." (Capitalists call it "making a profit.")

There have been many changes in the social structure, in formal organizations, and in industrial relations since Marx's day. Most notable is the fragmentation of the proletariat into a variety of classes – from the urban underclass, through various blue-collar occupations, and continuing onto the middle and even upper-middle class – and the blurring of the roles of top managers and actual owners of businesses (see Edwards, 1979). All of these changes have reduced the applicability of Marx's general descriptions of conflict between two social classes, but it has not negated his underlying insights.

Marx's ideas live on in what is often termed "conflict sociology" in introductory textbooks. It is important to note, however, that not all conflict sociology is Marxist sociology. Indeed, the study of industrial relations and human resources management – both of which recognize a fundamental conflict between workers and management – are key topics in business schools (which rarely harbor Marxists). Marxist sociologists take their concerns about class conflict beyond a recognition of the conflict to the idea that one should do something about it, specifically, something that helps the underdog. Marxists may engage in political activity as part of their academic research. They call this *praxis*. A true Marxist believes in praxis as research. Sociologists who study power relationships among the classes, but who do not engage in political activity, do not fully fit the ideal-type of the critical approach.

Marxist, or conflict, thinking shapes cultural sociology in a number of ways. The first has to do with Marx's idea of *false consciousness*, whereby workers do not see their own exploitation. Marx argued that capitalists have the desire and the power to create stories that legitimize their actions. Indeed, he argues, all elites, throughout history, have created the ideas that support their ascendancy. "The ideas of the ruling classes are in every epoch the ruling ideas," he famously wrote (1846 [1978]: 172). These ideas have been developed by more recent thinkers who talk about *cultural* control – control is the ability of capitalists (or managers) to obtain desired behaviors from workers – and, particularly relevant to this book, how art forms can function as social control.

Second, Marxian analysis informs critiques of mass culture as produced by culture industries. In this view, art forms that are produced by business organizations in capitalist systems are debased. They are not authentic pieces of culture. A third approach to art that draws inspiration from class analysis (if not Marxist, per se) has to do with the uses of culture. Different social classes use art differently, and this may give an advantage to the higher strata. And finally, the critical approach informs the study of how art intersects with other forms of social division, notably, gender and race.

Postmodern sociology

Unlike the previous three approaches to sociology, the postmodern approach has a relatively recent origin. There are precursors to postmodern thought in both interpretive sociology and critical sociology, but postmodernism emerged as a separate way of thinking about society at the time society began to make the transformation from modernism to postmodernism. The term "postmodern," then, refers to both the era of postmodernity (in which we are currently living), as well as an approach to knowledge, to which only a subset of sociologists subscribe.[7]

The easiest way to understand postmodernism is to contrast it with modernism. Modernism, as an era, was the capitalist, industrial society, characterized by a "Fordist" production system. Products were mass produced by workers who earned a wage good enough to consume other mass-produced products. The consumption then pays for the production, the production for the consumption, and so on. Products were advertised in the mass media, and the popular arts were broadcast to large audiences. Moreover, modernism, and modernist theories, were dominated by a mode of thinking – rationalism – which arose during the Enlightenment. Rationalism suggests that society progresses and improves, that science is disinterested and able to build cumulative knowledge, that there exist absolute moral values and universal truths, and that one's individual identity is fixed.

The postmodern era, also called "late industrial capitalism" (see Jameson, 1984) is characterized by "post-Fordist" production. In post-Fordism, manufacturing techniques have improved so that specialized products can be produced for market niches. Consumption and production are still linked in a circuit, but society now values consumption over production. Products are advertised to specialized markets, and the popular arts are "narrowcast" to segments of the population differentiated by "lifestyle." On the political level, nation-states fragment into interest groups, but also agglomerate into supra-national associations. Most observers agree that these changes in industrial society have indeed occurred.

Exactly how these changes have affected cultural ideas, however, is hotly contested. Many observers believe that a series of related changes have occurred in postmodern societies: Cynicism has replaced the old optimism and ideals of progress. Identity politics has called into question the ideas of universal truths and absolute morals. And because people are more geographically mobile and can choose among a wide variety of consumer items, their identities have become fragmented and based on their consuming choices and lifestyles.

Postmodern approaches draw on these ideas to suggest that there can be no such thing as positivistic sociology. (Postmodernism questions positivistic sci-ence, too.) Postmodernists highlight the absolute relativity of all forms of knowledge and reject all forms of generalizing. Some postmodern sociologists eschew empirical research altogether, whereas others try to approach data collection with postmodern tools. Most importantly, postmodern research is reflexive. *Reflexivity* rests on the recognition that research itself is embedded in the social world. Research is said to be reflexive when it looks back at itself to gauge the impact of the researcher and the research process on the subjects and findings.

An important corollary to postmodernism's emphasis on relativity and the unknowableness of reality draws on the work of the poststructural theorist Michel Foucault (1979a).[8] He puts forth idea of *power-knowledge*, a concept which interlinks power and knowledge, emphasizing the inseparability of the two. A modernist might say "knowledge is power." A postmodernist would put power first, and moreover, assert that knowledge is never neutral. Power creates knowledge to serve power's own end. The shape of existing knowledge embodies the power that created it. This power-knowledge is so deeply embedded in the stories we tell that it is not readily evident to us. In order to find the true, hidden meanings of power-knowledge, postmodernists rip away the façade from stories through the technique of *deconstruction*.

Postmodern theories play an important role in the sociology of art, not the least as the mode of thinking that underlies a good deal of work in a related area, cultural studies. Like interpretive sociology, postmodernism appears mainly in studies of audiences and the reception of art. Postmodernism is also the most negative approach, given that its metatheoretical assumptions provide its justification for rejecting all theory in the positivistic vein, and much from earlier critical and interpretive approaches, as well as deconstruct-ing them.

Metatheory

This last point about postmodernism highlights an important aspect of all theories: they all encode (often unstated) metatheorectical assumptions. The four approaches are ideal types that pull together a variety of theories that share similar metatheories. In practice, some theories cannot be neatly pegged into one camp or another because they legitimately mix compatible assumptions from more than one approach (or because they are not well thought out). A number of metatheories, however, are diametrically opposed and thus, fundamentally incompatible. You cannot believe that prediction and generalization are the utmost goals for theory and at the same time hold that prediction and generalization are impossible (your epistemology).[9] You cannot think reality is objective and observable and also think that it is entirely socially constructed (your ontology).[10] Similarly, you cannot think that people are rational, purposive decision makers who control their own destiny and also believe that people are shaped by culture and institutions, act within their roles and are subject to chance, history, and accident (your views of human nature regarding the "problem of action"). These instances of epistemology, ontology, and action metatheories are opposite ends of continuums. You simply cannot be at both poles at the same time, although you can be (and most theorists are) somewhere in the middle. More importantly, metatheories – unlike theories – cannot be tested with data. This is why they are called *assumptions*. It is also why some debates in sociology (as in other disciplines) generate so much heat and so little light: theorists are trying to "prove" the unprovable to each other, and they disagree well before they undertake any research and continue to disagree after they finish.

Theory and maps

Sociological theories can be divided into four basic camps. But what are theories? Some theories are abstract and general, but others are decidedly not. For the purposes of this book, theories are simplifying ideas or models that tell us about society. They are, metaphorically, like maps. Figure 1.1 shows a continuum from infinite complexity to utter simplicity (adapted from Watson, 1995: 26). Reality, whatever that is, is placed near the top; it is complex, ambiguous and unknowable in its totality. "Common sense" is nearer the bottom; it is a simplified model that helps us understand how society works, but is often inaccurate because it is over-simplified. Watson has, optimistically, placed sociological theory above common sense in terms of its complexity. But reality is still much more complex than theory. This is because

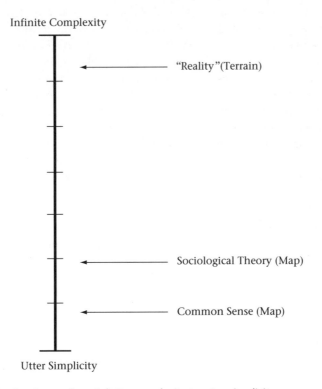

Figure 1.1 Continuum from infinite complexity to utter simplicity
Source: Adapted from Watson (1995), p. 26.

it is necessary to focus on only a few elements of reality, and to simplify their characteristics or relationships in order to tell a story that is clear.

My favorite metaphor for understanding theory, and metatheory, is that theory is a map of a territory (the reality). If you want to get from London to Edinburgh, you might want to find the best route on a road map. If the map were 800 miles long, like Great Britain itself, it would not fit into the car nor be of much help. However, if it were on a scale of 16 miles to the inch, it would fit on one large sheet that most people (or at least some people) could fold neatly like an accordion and put into the glove box. It would be more suitable for the job, even though it would vastly oversimplify the terrain, leaving out things like city streets, farm tracks, and changes in elevation, to concentrate on a schematic representation of the motorways and main highways. But once you get to Edinburgh, a big map with a dot for the city is less helpful. You need a town plan that shows city streets. If you walk in the surrounding countryside, you will want a more detailed map still, one that depicts footpaths and topography.

This metaphor not only shows how helpful simplification can be, it also shows that maps are not completely "true" representations of the territory. The only true representation would *be* the territory. A road map is not any more true than a topographical map. Maps, like theories, are suitable for certain purposes but not others. Of course, maps, like theories can be *wrong*, if they contain errors about the territory. In this case, they should be thrown out or corrected. Many disagreements among sociologists are over which types of maps are true, rather than which contain errors that could be remedied in future research. For instance, proponents of "reception theory" who come from an interpretive framework might rubbish a positivistic study of the "production of culture" merely because it comes from a different perspective. But this is like arguing over whether a town plan or a road atlas is better without asking "better for what purpose?" It is a disagreement at the level of metatheory.

The metaphor of a map is limited, however, as are all metaphors. Social reality cannot be as easily measured as the physical contours and attributes of the landscape. Indeed, as we have seen theorists disagree on the fundamental nature of reality (what we can see and how it should be measured). This means they disagree over what the territory might be, which adds an extra layer of potential disagreement over the purpose of maps (theories) and whether they are "correct."[11]

What theory you use (or develop) depends on two things: (1) The metatheories you hold due to personal predilection or professional training; and (2) the types of questions you pose. Your questions are strongly influenced by your metatheories. Theories are like flashlights, or torches, shining light in a darkened room. Though they illuminate, they also highlight only part of the view. They also cast shadows. Theories are useful, indeed essential, to understanding art. But all theories are, by necessity, limited.

Be critical when you evaluate theory. Look for the metatheory (explicit assumptions and hidden ones), as well as the predictions, descriptions, interpretations, or hypotheses the theory generates. Do reject the theory if it is actually wrong. But also, at least as students, take a flexible approach, and value all research which is excellent within its own perspective.[12] Research uncovers a truth, not the truth. Ask: "Is it *useful?*" not, "Is it right?" This is what I call the *mosaic method* of building sociological knowledge:[13]

> Recognize that there are a variety of approaches and theories about society. Most are partly true, shedding light on various aspects of society and casting shadows on others; therefore, most theories can be helpful some of the time and in some situations. Thus, each theory (and piece of empirical research) is a tile in a mosaic; to get a reasonable picture, you need more than one tile.

Using different theories to understand art can lead to a richer understanding of art.

Structure of the Book

The goal of this book is to give a comprehensive overview of the field of sociology of art. I use the idea of the "cultural diamond" (a metaphor) to structure the chapters. Part I (chapters 2–3) looks at the relationship between art and society, based on metaphors of reflection and shaping. I present these approaches then evaluate them. Chapter 4 introduces the cultural diamond, which challenges the reflection and shaping approaches. Part II is divided into two sections, the first (chapters 5–9) looks at theories about the creation, production, and distribution of art, and the second (chapters 10–12) looks at theories about the consumption of art, that is, how people interact with art. Part III (chapters 13–14) points to a shortcoming of the diamond metaphor, namely that art is part of society and cannot be abstracted from it, and discusses art and meaning. Part IV (chapter 15) sums up the book, and revisits the issue of multiple paradigms in the sociology of the arts.

Each of the substantive chapters is accompanied by a case study which looks at one issue or research project in depth. The cases include questions, designed to stimulate classroom discussion. Some of the discussion questions ask you to apply material from the chapters or to evaluate critically the case, rather than merely to look to the case for their solution. In neither its presentation of cases nor of sociological approaches to art does this book provide "the answers." Rather it aims to raise questions and then to give you enough information to think critically about different – overlapping and conflicting – views.

NOTES

1 Philosophers have grappled with the problem of defining art for centuries. For a useful review of the philosophy of art, see Graham (2000).

2 For instance, Sally Mann and Richard Billingham.

3 On *haute cuisine*, see Trubek (2000), Ferguson (1998), and Fine (1996); on *haute couture*, see Crane (2000).

4 The primary goal of this section of the chapter is to introduce the idea of competing paradigms in social research. Readers who understand this concept will get more out of the rest of the book, as the book is essentially an overview of different approaches to understanding art which proceed from these paradigms. A second goal is to provide some sociological grounding to students who may not have a familiarity with sociology. In working towards those goals, I have covered key paradigms in sociology. I have not attempted to lay out the theoretical foundations of related disciplines such as anthropology, art history, cultural studies, or literature, which also study art.

5   Much has been written about theory in sociology; for reviews at the introductory level, see Cooper (2001) and Gilbert (2001).

6   For useful discussions of metatheory and the consequent divisions in the sociology of organizations, see Burell and Morgan (1979); Astley and Van de Ven (1983). Wuthnow and Witten (1988) provide a helpful division of the sociology of culture, though without discussing metatheory.

7   The term "postmodernism" is problematic for a number of reasons. First, like many terms, it means different things to different people. Second, some theorists who appear to be drawing on postmodern ideas (in one sense of the term) reject a description of their work as postmodern (in another, narrower, sense of the term). I have persisted with the use of "postmodernism," however, because it (a) is commonly used in the discipline and (b) is a generally accurate term at the level of detail in this review. There is a good deal of variation among theorists whom I would place in the postmodern camp (and they might wish me to discuss the finer points of difference in more detail, rather than lumping them together in a single approach), but this is no less true of those theorists in the other three camps.

8   Foucault's work could profitably be discussed in a separate consideration of poststructuralism, rather than in a discussion of postmodernism. But to do so here would bring in more complexity than is required for a brief introduction. Moreover, some theorists would argue that Foucault is not a postmodernist (see note 7). However, I am not alone in linking these two intellectual trends. As Strinati (1995: 218) puts it: "We can see postmodernism as the theory of society and social change which is bound up with the philosophical and theoretical framework of post-structuralism." Nevertheless, Foucault himself has stated that his work is not postmodern. Thus, the "postmodern" category poses a problem in that many theorists whom I place under its umbrella find the term unsatisfactory.

9   An *epistemology* is a belief about knowledge, specifically in this context, a belief about the nature of sociological knowledge (or sociological theory) and how it is acquired.

10 An *ontology* is a belief about the nature of reality.

11 The best statement I have seen of these ideas on metaphors and theories is Morgan (1986, especially chapters 1, 10, and 11). He discusses organizational theory, in particular.

12 I might ask this of colleagues as well, but of course, established scholars are welcome to their favorite metatheory if they want!

13 Watson (1995: 78) would call this "pragmatic pluralism"; also, see Griswold (1992a) and Morgan (1986). Becker (1970) also uses the mosaic as a metaphor.

Part I

The Relationship between Art and Society

Art Object

Society

2

Reflection Approaches

The toothy grin, every politician's gleaming weapon, was considered a sign of dementia until the exhibition of a radical painting [by Elizabeth Vigée-Lebrun, a self-portrait of herself with her daughter; the little one smiling with lips slightly parted] in 1787 . . . .

A study by Colin Jones [2000] . . . uncovers the birth of the modern smile. Until Mme Vigée-Lebrun, icons such as the Mona Lisa had preferred to stay tight-lipped, for good reason. Baring one's teeth was considered rude, lower-class and a possible sign of madness.

Dental care was also of such poor quality that few wished to be depicted with rotten teeth. Professor Jones said: "Teeth quality was at its lowest ebb in the 18th century because all classes were drinking tea or coffee and eating chocolate" . . .

Nevertheless, . . . many significant French figures began to allow their portraits to reveal their teeth. Professor Jones believes that this was due to the radical transformation in the practice of dentistry and a consumer boom in the range of dental products available . . .

(*The Times*, July 19, 2000: 10)

Art contains information about society. Smiles in paintings, for instance, reflect social attitudes and the quality of dental care available (see plate 2). If you wanted to learn about the position of ethnic minorities in society, rather than oral hygiene, you might watch television shows and see how minority groups are portrayed. You might focus on crime shows, counting the police officers of various ethnicities, and coding the ethnic make-up of the criminals and victims (see Oliver and Armstrong, 1998). The *reflection* approach rests on the idea that art tells us something about society. Television crime shows reflect racism; portraits reflect, among other things, beliefs about the best way to smile.

Plate 2 Elizabeth Vigée-Lebrun, *Portrait of the Artist with her Daughter*, 1789, Musée du Louvre, Paris, France, Bridgeman Giraudon.

The reflection approach to the sociology of art encompasses a wide variety of research sharing in common the belief that art mirrors (or is conditioned by, or determined by) society.[1] Research in this tradition looks at art works in order to learn more about society.[2] The approach has a long and venerable history in sociology. This is not surprising, as its main focus is sociological – to learn about society. It has been thoroughly criticized, notably by Albrecht in 1954; nevertheless, it remains an important way researchers approach art.

The Roots of the Reflection Approach

One theory of reflection is found in Marxism, which posits that the culture and ideology of a society (the superstructure) reflect its economic relations (the base). This idea is "the key to Marxist cultural analysis" (Williams, 1973: 3). In 1859, Marx himself wrote:

The totality of these relations of production constitutes the economic structure of society – the real foundation, on which legal and political superstructures arise and to which definite forms of social consciousness correspond. The mode of production of material life determines the general character of the social, political and spiritual processes of life. It is not the consciousness of men that determines their being, but, on the contrary, their social being determines their consciousness.... With the change of the economic foundation the entire immense superstructure [the combination of legal, political, religious, aesthetic or philosophical – in short, ideological – forms] is more or less rapidly transformed. ([1963]: 67–8).

In industrial capitalism, for instance, workers labor in factories doing extremely repetitive, boring tasks. Art, then, will reflect these conditions: mass culture is mindless because it reflects the mindless work of the masses. Theodor Adorno (1941 [1994]), a Marxist cultural critic, argues along these lines with respect to popular music.[3] Storey (1996: 94) summarizes Adorno's thinking:

Work under capitalism is dull and therefore promotes the search for escape, but, because it is also dulling, it leaves little energy for real escape – the demands of "authentic culture"; instead, refuge is sought in forms such as popular music. The consumption of popular music is always passive, and endlessly repetitive, confirming the world as it is. "Serious" music plays to the pleasure of the imagination, offering an engagement with the world as it could be. Popular music is "the nonproductive correlate" to life in the office or on the factory floor. The "strain and boredom" of work leads men and women to the "avoidance of effort" in their leisure time. Denied "novelty" in their work time, and too exhausted for it in their leisure time, "they crave a stimulant": popular music satisfies the craving.[4]

Research Strategies

Researchers embarking on a reflection study can start from different intellectual assumptions and use a variety of research techniques. These will have implications for the conclusions researchers draw. The studies reviewed below each use a different research strategy.

Interpretive analysis

Helsinger (1994) looks at how engravings made by the great landscape painter J. M. W. Turner in the 1820s and 1830s reflected aspects of English national identity. Helsinger situates Turner's engravings, published in *Picturesque Views in England and Wales,* in "the genre of coffee-table books that address readers as travelers" (p. 108). These books show pretty scenes from England that an actual tourist might see while traveling, and through them, middle-class "picturesque travelers" can gain a symbolic possession of the country.

> Purchase these books and you too may gain at least visual access to the land. The prints also . . . provide an analogue for experiences of touristic travel (itself established since the eighteenth century as a means of vicariously possessing England) and for the geographic and social mobility increasingly characteristic of their middle-class, often urban purchasers. (p. 105)

When Turner was creating his views, England was facing particularly unsettled times. Unemployed workers were circulating about the country, generating fears (both justified and unjustified) among the middle and upper classes of mob violence. Turner's landscapes reflect these unstable class relationships in a number of ways, most notably, through his inclusion of figures in the foreground of his paintings. For example, the work

> *Blenheim, Oxfordshire* . . . explicitly asks who shall be admitted to the privilege of touristic viewing. . . . [A] group of middle- and lower-middle-class viewers stand waiting, on the extreme right edge of the picture, at the grand gate of the most visited great house in England, just visible at the upper left. A top-hatted figure holding a brace of hounds and a rifle stands squarely in the left center foreground, confronting the viewer and barring the visitors' way with unknown intent while a riding party from the estate can be seen on the far left. Centered in the distance and lit by the sun emerging from clouds, a bridge (ironically a purely ornamental bridge, built on appropriated land from the town) links the two otherwise tensely separate sides of the picture. Blenheim, financed out of public funds to reward a national hero, was indeed a "sort of national property" that might appropriately stand for the privileges of nationality demanded by the middle classes – and, unsuccessfully in 1832, by the lower classes, who are notably not represented in the party at the gate. . . . These drawings depict English landscape as contested ground (pp. 111–12).

In other engravings, unruly lower class men and women depicted in the foreground stand between the viewer and the landscape painted behind them. They are also, significantly, portrayed at leisure rather than at work. Interestingly, Turner's critics did not like these figures and labeled them as vulgar and incompetent elements in otherwise beautiful works. There is not enough evidence to tell us if the presence of these figures mean that Turner "claim[ed] for them rights of possession" of England and English nationality, or instead expressed a "sympathy with those who felt profoundly threatened by their presence" (pp. 118–19).

Helsinger's work is an *interpretive study*. She has taken a number of art works and examined them in detail in order to extract their meaning, and, thereby, she has shown that elements in the paintings reflect certain aspects of society. Her study shores up the interpretation of the visual objects with a historical analysis, in which she matches the stylistic elements in Turner's work with aspects of the political and economic climate of Britain of the time.

Content analysis

Researchers using a reflection approach might track changes over time, as Lowenthal (1961) did in a study of popular icons in America. He studied magazines from 1901 to 1941 to document a change in the subjects of biographies. Lowenthal argues that biographies celebrate, and thus reveal, society's heroes. Before World War I, heroes in magazine biographies were from "the serious and important professions" (p. 111). They were *idols of production* – captains of industry, politicians, and serious artists. Their biographies reflected the American dream: "This unbroken confidence in the opportunities open to every individual serves as the *leitmotiv* of the biographies. To a very great extent they are to be looked upon as examples of success which can be imitated. These life stories are really intended to be educational models" (p. 113).

After World War I, heroes were different. They were *idols of consumption* – people from the entertainment sphere such as sports figures and movie actors and "people with a more or less normal and typical personal and vocational background who would bore us to death if we did not discover that behind the 'average' front lurks a 'human interest' situation" (p. 116). In addition, Lowenthal adds, people no longer read biographies to obtain general information, as they had before. Instead, biographies "seem to lead to a dream world of the masses who no longer are capable or willing to conceive of biographies primarily as a means of orientation and education. . . . During the leisure in which they read, they read almost exclusively about people who are directly, or indirectly, providing for the reader's leisure time" (p. 116).

The newer biographies focused more on the private lives, rather than the public face, of their subjects, and Lowenthal finds an alarming passivity among the idols of consumption. The older biographies showed how the heroes got ahead through the sweat of their brow, thereby providing models for success that the reader could emulate. In contrast, newer ones contained a dual theme of "hardship" and "breaks." In essence, the newer heroes were just like the rest of us (the "everyman" facing hardships), until at some point a chance occurrence (the lucky break) led to success. The modern individual (in 1943) "appears no longer as a center of outwardly bound energies and actions; as an inexhaustible reservoir of initiative and enterprise; no longer as an integral unity on whose work and efficiency might depend not only his kin's future happiness, but at the same time, mankind's progress in general. Instead of the 'givers' we are faced with the 'takers.' These new heroes represent a craving for having and taking things for granted" (p. 123).

Lowenthal's study, while drawing inspiration from critical analysis, is based on the method of *content analysis* from the positivist tradition. In content analysis, the researcher chooses a sample of materials and then codes them for a variety of factors. Lowenthal chose two popular magazines published in the US from 1901 to 1941 and coded the professions of the subjects of biographies into such categories as politics, business, professional, and entertainment (including actors, sports figures, newspaper and radio figures, participants in the serious arts, and some others). Coding the documents allows the researcher to make quantitative statements about the data. For instance, Lowenthal points out that the eyes of the hero were mentioned in one-third of the stories. The quantitative data can demonstrate that purported changes actually did occur and can bolster the researcher's resulting theory.

Structural semiotics

Wright (1975) also examined changes over time. He looked at an archetypal genre of American movies – the Western – concentrating on financially successful films from 1930 to 1972. He argues that profitability indicates popularity which, in turn, suggests that a film resonates with society. Unlike Lowenthal, who believes that the meaning of art is on its surface (the manifest content), Wright believes that meaning is hidden (the latent content), and can be uncovered through techniques from *structural analysis*.

Wright's argument is based on Lévi-Strauss's (e.g. 1967) structural study of myths. The idea is that stories with quite different "surface" appearances can actually have the same underlying narrative (or mythic) structure. The narrative structure of the traditional romance story, for instance, is: (1) boy meets girl, (2) boy loses girl, (3) boy gets girl. Both *Romeo and Juliet* and *Cinderella* contain this structure, even though the stories themselves appear quite different. Although Wright does not necessarily agree with Lévi-Strauss that structural similarities across types of myths arise from the physical or cognitive structure of the brain, Wright does agree that meaning can be isolated more easily with a structural analysis.

In Wright's method, the meaning of the story can be read in the oppositions within the story. The job of the analyst is to discover the coding of the oppositions, and hence, to discover the structure of the story. Mythic structures can tell us much about a society. For instance, oppositions embodied in myth signal the sources of conflict or contradiction in the society. Myths allow ritual resolution of the conflict. Thus, the analysis of narrative structures yields an insight into the conflicts of a society, and it gives the researcher leverage to overcome the surface differences of structurally similar stories.

Wright identifies four distinct versions of the Western myth – the classical plot, the transition theme, the vengeance variation, and the professional plot – each corresponding to a particular era. Table 2.1 summarizes the narrative structure of the first and fourth versions. Wright relates each version to the particular social structure that existed in American society at the same time. Specifically, he shows how the earliest narrative structure, the classical plot, reflects market capitalism and its ideology (such as an emphasis on individuality), whereas the latest structure, the professional plot, mirrors corporate capitalism (with its emphasis on working in groups). The middle two structures mirror American society in transition from a market to a corporate system. In addition to his intellectual debts to structural theory, Wright has also clearly been inspired by the base–superstructure model from Marxism.

Table 2.1 The narrative structure of western myths: The classical plot and the professional plot

The Classical Plot 1930–1955	The Professional Plot 1958–1970
1 The hero enters a social group.	1 The heroes are professionals.
2 The hero is revealed to have an exceptional ability.	2 The heroes undertake a job.
3 The society recognizes a difference between [itself] and the hero; the hero is given special status.	3 The villains are very strong.
	4 The society is ineffective, incapable of defending itself.
4 The society does not completely accept the hero.	5 The job involves the heroes in a fight.
5 There is a conflict of interests between the villains and the society.	6 The heroes all have special abilities and a special status.
6 The villains are stronger than the society; the society is weak.	7 The heroes form a group for the job.
7 The villains threaten society.	8 The heroes as a group share respect, affection, and loyalty.
8 The hero fights the villains.	9 The heroes as a group are independent of society.
9 The hero defeats the villains.	10 The heroes fight the villains.
10 The society is safe.	11 The heroes defeat the villains.
11 The society accepts the hero.	12 The heroes stay (or die) together.
12 The hero loses or gives up his special status.	
This plot corresponds to: Market society, which values individualism.	*This plot corresponds to:* Corporate society, which values working cooperatively.

Source: Wright (1975), especially pp. 15, 48–9, 113. NB: I have left out the "optional" functions in the classical plot.

Understanding rituals

Goffman (1979) examined advertisements to learn about contemporary society in his well-known study, *Gender Advertisements*. He argues that, in order to make their meaning clear, advertisements contain familiar rituals from everyday life. Rituals "provide evidence of the actor's *alignment* in a gathering, the position he seems prepared to take up in what is about to happen in the social situation" (p. 69, emphasis original). Rituals, then, reveal the structural relationships – the alignments – among people. The depictions in advertising are schematic representations of rituals; they are "hyper-ritualized." Goffman argues that advertisements are an excellent source from which to learn about structural relationships in everyday life, precisely because they present, unambiguously, these hyper-rituals.

Goffman looked at thousands of advertisements to show the structural relationship between men and women. He showed that women are structurally subordinate to men, and we can see this through a variety of displays common in advertisements. For instance, subordination is shown through the height of the participants. Taller participants carry more authority. In the advertisements Goffman examined, men are routinely shown with their heads higher than those of women. While it is true that men are, on average, taller than women, Goffman suggests that this physical difference alone does not account for the way men are shown in advertisements. Rather, advertisements are constructed to make a particular meaning, and it would be possible for advertisers to portray women as taller than men. Moreover, it is actually the height of the head rather than actual height which conveys the authority. So in one picture that Goffman shows us, there are three men, one standing and two seated. The context, and the heights of the heads, show that the men work in an office and the standing man is the boss. It would be easy for advertisers to use images of sitting men and standing women, but it is telling that they almost never do so. Indeed, Goffman finds some exceptions to the "men are taller" rule, but in each of these, there is something else going on which explains the woman's height. In one case, the woman is dressed in upper-class clothing and she stands next to a shorter man dressed as a chef. It is clear that, as his patron, she has more status than he does. In another case, the woman is tall; she is also fat and dressed as an opera singer, complete with a pike and horned helmet! She's powerful, but also ridiculous; the exception that proves the rule.

Goffman describes a number of other displays that similarly reflect the unequal nature of gender relations in society. He posits that a "classic stereotype of deference is that of lowering oneself physically in some form or another of prostration. Correspondingly, holding the body erect and the head high is stereotypically a mark of unashamedness, superiority, and disdain. Advertisers draw on (and endorse) the claimed universality of the theme" (p. 110). He goes on to show that "children and women are pictured on floors and beds more often than are men," (p. 111) and that women are posed with a "bashful knee bend" (p. 115) or with a "cant" of the head or body that "can be read as an acceptance of subordination, an expression of ingratiation, submissiveness and appeasement" (p. 116).

Combining methods

Using a variety of methods in a single study is often more difficult than it first appears. Nevertheless, the use of multiple methods can strengthen the final product, as can triangulation (using more than one source of data). Such strengths are illustrated in Entman and Rojecki's (2001) study of the representation of race in American society. To uncover representations, they do content analyses of a variety of popular arts – American television commercials and prime-time television shows, and top-grossing Hollywood movies.[5] These are supplemented by qualitative analyses of individual television programs, films, and movie reviews, as well as by interviews with media audiences.

Entman and Rojecki treat the media "as a kind of leading indicator, a barometer of cultural change and variability in the arena of race" (p. 205). In general, they show that the media reflect the "polarizing tendencies of racial prototypes" (p. 152). *Prototypes* "encode habitual ways of thinking that help people make sense of a complicated and uncertain world" (p. 60). Prototypes are specific examples typical of a category, as a robin is a example typical of the category, birds. When two categories are invoked (such as black and white people), prototypes of each tend to embody stark contrasts. In television drama, for instance, Entman and Rojecki find that black and white characters are portrayed in hierarchical relationships, but "*in utopian reversal*: over 70 percent of Black characters have professional or management positions" (p. 152, emphasis original). Although this is a positive development over earlier portrayals of blacks as subservient to whites, it reflects a continuation of prototypes of black and white Americans as polar opposites, industrious and responsible on the one hand, and lazy and irresponsible, on the other. Further, depicting black and white characters in hierarchical relationships limits the degree of contact between characters of different races. Television dramas display close interpersonal relationships only between characters of the same race, a portrayal which does not encourage racial comity.

A similar, mixed picture emerges from Entman and Rojecki's examination of Hollywood movies. Movies are more racially progressive than television, in that many movies include black stars in the top billing. Many minor characters and extras are black. And yet, black actors play a more limited range of roles, and black characters are often portrayed in stereotypical ways. For instance, Entman and Rojecki hypothesized that black characters "would be disproportionately associated with an implicitly animal or biological sexuality" (p. 198), as opposed to romantic sexuality or non-sexualized portrayals. This did not hold for black males, who were portrayed as sexualized in equal proportion to white men. All of the black women in their sample, however, were sexualized. White women were portrayed sexually more often than men, but much less often than black women. They conclude that "traditional gender roles, the use of women as sexual objects, continues in Hollywood's top films – but especially so for Black women" (p. 199). The contrast of language use (swearing and speaking ungrammatically) by black and white characters is striking, as well:

> Black males were more profane than White males, though a majority of both used profanity in this sample of movies. All but one of the Black females swore, 89 percent, compared with 17 percent of White females. The disparities in ungrammatical usage were even greater – in fact barely any White characters spoke ungrammatically compared with around half the Blacks. Part of this finding may be due to Blacks tending to portray less-educated characters. Still ... we found examples of Blacks with high education using ungrammatical, perhaps stereotypically "ghetto" speaking styles. And even if occupational differences partially explain the differences in language use, this pattern nonetheless constructs African Americans as occupying a different, quite separate cultural universe from Euro-Americans. (pp. 199–200)

Television commercials tell a more dismal story of the image of blacks.[6] Though blacks appear in commercials in roughly the proportion of their population in the wider society, they often appear in token positions.[7] Moreover, blacks are disproportionately portrayed in commercials for necessities, and rarely appear in those for luxury goods – or for pet food, for that matter. As Entman and Rojecki put it, "only Whites have pets" and in TV advertising, "Whites are the ones that occupy the realm of ideal humanity, of human warmth and connection, as symbolized occasionally by their love for their pets" (p. xv, xvi). Their content analysis of 1,620 advertisements demonstrates that whites were shown in "contact" with the audience (e.g. speaking to the audience or appearing in a close-up) or interacting with each other (e.g. speaking to or touching other characters) three times as often as blacks, and that when hands appeared on the screen (e.g. holding the product) the hand models were five times more likely to be white than black. More chillingly, in a smaller, follow-up study, they find that 55 white children appeared facing the camera for one second or longer, but only four black children do so. This implicit devaluing of black children was highlighted by their finding that white children appeared in advertisements with adults (usually representing parents) much more often than black children, and the white children's parents were more likely to touch or kiss them than the adults shown with black children. Entman and Rojecki also found almost no interracial contact in television commercials.

In general, Entman and Rojecki's work demonstrates what they term the liminality of black people in American society. *Liminality* describes "Blacks' *transition* from rejection toward acceptance" (p. 206).[8] Though the representation of black Americans has progressed beyond "old-fashioned racism," an era of complete acceptance of different racial groups with full integration in society has not yet been reached. As they put it, the "mixture of media images, and of White beliefs, hopes, and fears about Blacks registers the liminality... the media operate both as barometer of cultural integration and as potential accelerator either to cohesion or to further cultural separation and political conflict – or perhaps to both" (p. 206).

Critique

The reflection approach refers to a diverse literature within the sociology of art that shares the core assumption that art is a mirror held up to society. Albrecht (1954) identified six types of reflection in research on literature and society: (1) the notion that literature embodies norms and values of a society, (2) the psychoanalytic variant that literature fulfills shared emotional needs and fantasies, (3) a Jungian view that literature arises from the collective unconscious and thus is similar to dreams, (4) the theory that literature reflects a Hegelian "essential spirit" of society, (5) the Marxian view that forms of literature are a result of the economic conditions of the elite, or of the rising classes, and (6) literature reflects demographic trends. Peterson (1979) suggests a different way of dividing reflection theories: (1) those that focus on how art reflects the whole society, and (2) more modest studies claiming that art reflects only the local milieu of the subculture that consumes it. If we combine Peterson's and Albrecht's schemes, we have at least twelve ways in which art might reflect society, and we could probably think of many more. But which is correct? A major problem with the reflection approach, then, is that its underlying metaphor is defined so broadly that we cannot specify which aspects of society are reflected nor which groups.

Laslett (1976) cautions historical sociologists who would draw conclusions about real life on the basis of literary evidence. Literature, after all, is fiction. There is no way to know whether situations in literature were contrived because they were common in the society or precisely because they were uncommon. Laslett cites several examples where literature and society do not mesh. For instance, literature from the pre-industrial age portrayed British households as large, when in fact they contained, on average, fewer than five people. In essence, Laslett argues that any reflection of society in literature is mediated by literary practices and conventions. For instance, the fiction of large households, with many people from servants to the patriarch living under one roof, creates more dramatic possibilities than the reality of small ones, which explains why so many novels depicted large households. Similar difficulties arise with most other art forms. To overcome them, Albrecht has suggested comparing art to other indices of the "essential spirit" of a society. Using a variety of sources is essentially what Helsinger does in her well-researched and convincing study. Such comparisons will help researchers avoid the *literary fallacy* which is "deducing the 'spirit of the age' from its art and then rediscovering it is its art" (Albrecht, 1954: 431).

In addition to questions of *what* is reflected (norms, values, needs, fantasies, myths, demographic trends, stereotypes, statistical regularities, or unusual events) and *who* is reflected (elites, rising classes, the whole society, or subcultures), there is also the issue of *how* society comes to be reflected. Helsinger's study relies, implicitly, on the assumption that great artists are in touch with the spirit of their times, and with their fingers thus on the pulse of society, they will faithfully perceive and portray the greatest truths of the society in their works. In contrast, Wright and Lowenthal argue that the mechanism of reflection resides in art's popularity.[9] This assumes that a large audience indicates that an artwork resonates with society.

Good practice in reflection studies

Authors using interpretive methods may be open to the charge of bias. They may have, consciously or not, chosen to analyze art objects that particularly support their point of view. Authors using content analysis, ostensibly more objective, face a different issue: content analysis loses the context of the data as a direct cost of systematizing it. To avoid either of these pitfalls, researchers choosing a reflection approach to art must carefully consider their sampling and analysis schemes. They must guard against generalizing to groups other than the consumers of the culture they analyze, and they would do well to examine other data from the society to confirm their findings. Researchers also must be aware that their interpretations of the variations they find can be colored by their own predilections.[10] Most importantly, researchers must keep in mind that any link between art and society is mediated by a variety of factors, as detailed in Part II of this book. (This idea of mediating factors is considered more fully in chapter 4.)

These points may be well taken, but if it is advisable to look at other data one might ask: Why study cultural artifacts at all? Why not study society itself? For instance, Goffman did not need to look at advertisements to learn that unequal relationships exist between men and women. The answer is that most researchers are looking for information more interesting than just the number of people in a household, and that supplemental evidence does not have to come from direct observation of the society. Goffman clearly demonstrated that sexism is reflected in advertisements. But he also uncovered a variety of pictorial styles that portray the unequal relationship between the sexes, and which also, he argues, tell us about real-life rituals.

Often the evidence of the thing we seek is not directly available, either because the evidence has been lost through the passage of time or because there is no direct way to tap the evidence. No time machine yet exists to go back to the seventeenth century. But we can examine seventeenth-century paintings. Dutch artists of that time painted scenes of everyday life. If we assume that the paintings are an accurate reflection of Dutch society, we can get a sense of what life was like through such details as how houses were furnished or how social groups interacted (see Adams, 1994).

Most researchers in the sociology of art believe that art objects can tell us something about the society that produces them, although the picture is much more complex than a single, straight line running directly between art and society. There are many mediating factors, which Part II of this book addresses in detail.

Conclusion: The Fun House Mirror

Art reflects society, but in complex ways. I have identified a number of problems with the reflection approach. In addition, art is filtered through a production system and it is consumed by people who are part of a social system. Both the creators of and the audiences for art shape the artistic product and its meaning in ways that make a simple reflection argument problematic. Indeed, if art reflects society, then the mirror is one of the distorting kind that is found at fun fairs.

In summing up the relationship between art and society, Desan, Ferguson, and Griswold (1988) use a similar metaphor.[11] They tell a story from the Hans Christian Anderson fairy tale *The Snow Queen*. A demon has created a mirror that systematically misreflects (for the worse) people's actions and thoughts. The demon's pupils are very impressed with the mirror, believing that it reveals the truth of human nature. They take it and run around the countryside, holding it up to society, until everyone sees it. One day it breaks and shards of the mirror lodge in the eyes of everyone who had seen it, giving them the same, cynical vision of the original mirror.

Desan, Ferguson, and Griswold point out that each element in the story is analogous to the way art reflects society. The mirror can only reflect one part of reality at any given time (though it can be pointed in the direction of many things); its shifting misreflections are emblematic of art's misreflections. And, indeed, it is *systematically* distorting, which suggests that it is amenable to study. Its distortions and images have been shaped by the Master Demon, its creator, and by the demon pupils, distributors. It has a frame, which suggests that there is an intellectual and institutional context in which art is created. Finally, the mirror's reflections are consumed, as represented by the fragments of glass in the eyes of the beholders, a factor which reminds us that we must remember that art is received by audiences, who are embedded in a social context, and who contribute to the creation of meaning by selectively mispercieving the images they see.

> Like the demon's fantastic mirror, [art] presents structured misreflections, which magnify or diminish certain aspects of reality, twist some or leave others out altogether. The sociology of [art] challenges these mirrors and their inventors, examines their misreflections, their causes and consequences. It shows how and why a particular [art work] or genre or period or [artist] reflects in one way and not in another; it specifies the properties of the mirror that determine its (mis)reflections. (Desan, Ferguson, and Griswold, 1988: 9)

The reflection approach has been an important way of examining art. Despite some serious drawbacks, it remains compelling. It is a common mode of artistic analysis in the popular imagination and the popular press, as the article from the *London Times* quoted at the beginning of this chapter demonstrates. Moreover, it remains a sub-theme in much contemporary research on art, though many of these studies are sophisticated enough to avoid the problems of the "pure," or naive, versions of the approach.

NOTES

1   The reflection approach is often termed "reflection *theory*." This is a misnomer, however, as the approach is neither a formal theory nor a single, unified way of viewing the relationship between art and society. It is more accurately a metaphor for understanding this relationship. I have carefully avoided the use of "reflection theory" to refer to the reflection approach. Individual researchers do, however, create their own, proper theories on how art reflects society.
2   Essentially, reflection studies are a form of documentary analysis, the study of contemporary or historical documents. A *document* connotes something written. In this sense, examples from art include novels, poems, scripts, and printed music. A document, however, can also be visual or aural, as in a painting or a song; or a mix of these, as in a magazine advertisement, film, television show, play, or concert. A useful advantage of documentary analysis is that it enables researchers to study the past, as well as the present; old artworks may offer clues to bygone days. Research

strategies for reflection studies may be found in books and chapters on documentary analysis (e.g. Scott, 1990).

3   We will discuss Adorno, as part of the Frankfurt School, in more detail in chapter 3.

4   This passage can also be found in Storey (1993: 106–7).

5   Entman and Rojecki also consider the portrayal of race on television news. This makes up an important component of their study, but as it is outside the scope of this book, I leave this topic aside. Further, like many studies that draw on the reflection approach, Entman and Rojecki's work is also concerned with the effects that these portrayals may have on society. They also make some suggestions for changes in the media which might encourage racial comity. I have also not considered these aspects of their work here.

6   The portrayal of blacks in television news is more dismal still, with black people commonly shown as welfare recipients, single parents, or criminals.

7   See, also, Seiter (1995) on racial stereotypes in advertisements.

8   As Entman and Rojecki put it, "Liminal people are by their nature *potentially* polluting, disruptive, but not necessarily destructive of the natural order since they are 'no longer classified and not yet classified' " (p. 51). The term was originally coined to refer to the intermediate stage in a ritual whereby the initiates no longer exist in their previous status, but have not been fully integrated into the status the ritual confers.

9   Neither of these reflection mechanisms stands up to scrutiny. It is commonly asserted, especially with respect to the avant-garde, that artists are particularly sensitive to the *zeitgeist* or even to future trends in society. But artists are also sensitive to the artistic conventions and understandings of the art worlds of which they are a part, to other artists, and to potential sales, and not always to the person in the street. They may make powerful statements about the condition of society, they may express intensely personal feelings, they may engage with current aesthetic problems, or they may do something else entirely. The idea that artists have exquisite powers of perception may be an ideology used by artists and their supporters to claim status honor.

On the other hand, it is a truism that art forms would not be popular if people did not like them. But popularity alone does not explain how art reflects society. Do people resonate with art that reflects their psychological needs, their shared societal values, or myths that symbolically resolve unresolvable conflicts in society? Or do they read magazines and go to movies because it seems the least boring thing to do at the time or because their friends are doing so?

Goffman poses still another mechanism: the technical requirements of the form. Advertisements must, he argues, make their scenarios understandable on quick inspection and so they rely on hyper-ritualized depictions of common behavioral displays. Goffman's mechanism, based on advertising conventions, is applicable to the type of advertising he studied. Today's advertisements, however, often use different tropes – they are often purposefully provocative or darkly ambiguous, not instantly clear. Cortese (1999) discusses these tropes in detail and reports (pp. 27–8) that Goffman's findings on the relative height of men and women no longer appears to hold.

10   These issues are discussed in many general methods texts, as well as in shorter pieces on the study of art or visual materials (see, for example, Alexander, 2001; 1994; Ball and Smith, 1992; Banks, 2001; Gunter, 2000; Macdonald, 2001; Neuman, 2000; Scott, 1990; Weber, 1990).

11   Desan, Ferguson, and Griswold write about literature, specifically, rather than art in general, but their conclusions (which are cleverly, as well as clearly, put) may easily be extended to our broader concerns.

Case Study 2.1
The Reflection of Race in Children's Books

Based on Bernice A. Pescosolido, Elizabeth Grauerholz, and Melissa A. Milkie (1997), "Culture and Conflict: The Portrayal of Blacks in U.S. Children's Picture Books through the Mid- and Late-Twentieth Century," (*American Sociological Review*, 62 (3): 443–64).

Points for Discussion

1 How does the portrayal of race in children's books reflect society?
2 In what ways are the reflections indirect or distorted?
3 How can the absence of portrayals of social groups reflect society?
4 The authors' concept of "gatekeepers" adds a production feature to their argument that a "pure" reflection study ignores. How does the inclusion of gatekeepers provide a critique of reflection theory?

Case

Art objects are sites of symbolic struggle among social groups. Because art is created and disseminated by the dominant social groups, its content tends to reflect dominant systems of order. Studies of the portrayal of race (e.g. Dines and Humez, 1995; Dubin, 1987a; Humphrey and Schuman, 1984; Klein, 1985; Merelman, 1992; Thibodeau, 1989; Van Deberg, 1984) have generally shown that disadvantaged groups are depicted less positively than privileged groups. In particular, "the social oppression of Blacks in the United States has been [coupled with], in Tuchman's (1978) term, their 'symbolic annihilation.' Blacks have been ignored, stereotyped, or demeaned in cultural images" (Pescosolido et al., 1997: 443).

Pescosolido, Grauerholz, and Milkie (1997) examine American children's books from 1937 to 1993. During this time, race relations in the United States went through a number of changes. Early in the century, the stereotyping of and discrimination against African Americans was rife. The black civil rights movement, sparked by social changes during World War II, grew in the 1950s and accelerated in the 1960s. It challenged white America's dismissal of black people and black culture, and as an immediate result, it increased interracial conflict in society. This direct, overt confrontation of racial groups declined after the 1960s as white recognition of black claims for racial equality increased. But the degree to which race relations, or the position of black Americans, have improved is debatable: "we can easily sketch a glowing picture of racial progress (e.g. increasing Black voter registration, higher educational and occupational attainment, and a fading of traditional social stereotypes), or with equal persuasiveness, a dismal view (e.g. low college attendance and graduation rates, high Black unemployment, Black-on-Black violence, and new subtle racial stereotypes)" (pp. 444–5).

Pescosolido et al. wanted to know how the change in race relations in American society was reflected in its art. Children's books provide an important source for understanding society. Their stories entail a "moral certainty" and a simplicity of presentation that offer a window into adult belief systems. Moreover, children's books play a role in the socialization of children, thus their content may shape children's views of racial minorities, and of "status arrangements, social boundaries and power" (p. 444).

Pescosolido et al. examined three categories of children's books, *award-winners* (those receiving a Caldecott Medal or Honor for excellent illustrations), the *library market* (those compiled in the *Children's Catalog*, a broad listing from which librarians make purchase decisions), and the *mass market* (the *Little Golden Books*). In total, they coded 2,448 books. They measured the visibility of black characters in each year by counting the number of books which had (1) one or more black characters (African, Caribbean and/or African-American) in the text or illustrations, and (2) exclusively black characters. They also examined the content of the portrayals; quantitatively "by coding geographical and temporal location (e.g. rural versus urban; United States versus other; past versus contemporary), occupational roles, and whether there was interracial contact" and qualitatively through an evaluation of "Black representation and Black–White interactions . . . including the centrality of Black characters and the degree to which interracial contact was central (e.g. whether it involved the main character or background characters), intimate (e.g. brief or sustained interactions), or egalitarian" (p. 447).

The authors were interested in how the portrayals reflected society, specifically, how they reflected the state of race relations. They measured this through data on "racial conflict" based on reports in the *New York Times Index*. They coded three types of events with a racial component as instances of racial conflict, (1) public acts of violence, physical confrontation or arrest, (2) protests, and (3) legal actions.

Pescosolido et al. found that, across the whole sample, only 15 percent of books portrayed one or more black character. Three percent included only black characters. Their statistical results show a strong relationship between the level of racial conflict in society and the portrayals of black characters: "The data indicate a slight rise [in conflict events] beginning in 1945 corresponding to a gradual decline in portrayals of Black characters, a sharp rise between 1955 and 1965 corresponding to the disappearance of Blacks in illustrations and story lines, a sharp decline in the late 1960s paralleled by the dramatic reintroduction of portrayals of Blacks in books, and a return to earlier low levels of conflict corresponding to stabilization in the portrayals of Blacks in overall trends" (p. 457). In other words, portrayals of black characters declines when racial conflict increases, and vice-versa.

Based on these results, Pescosolido et al. (p. 450) divide their sample into four periods: 1938–57 when portrayals of blacks were modest and declining, 1958–64 when black characters were virtually absent, 1965–74 which heralded the reappearance of black characters, and 1975–90 when portrayals stabilized at roughly 20 to 30 percent of books each year. Their qualitative data indicate that two themes dominated the earliest period. First, most books were about white characters, with black characters filling only incidental, subservient, roles. For instance, "a 1952 *Little Golden Book* [depicted] a Black train porter dusting off a White girl's doll" (p. 450). The quality of interracial contact was superficial, and reflected the privileged status of whites. The text of a "1940 Caldecott Medal book . . . is illustrative: 'When my father was very young he had two dogs and a colored boy. The dogs were named Sextus Hostilius and Numa Pompolius. The colored boy was just my father's age. He was a slave, but they [didn't] call him that. They just called him Dick.'" (p. 450). Second, black children were shown in multiracial groups illustrating the theme of the "Family of Man" or "All God's Children." But again, interracial interaction is minimal and the majority of children pictured were white. A few books portraying blacks departed from these themes, but they were rare.

During the second period, from 1958 to 1964, very few blacks were portrayed, appearing in only 12 out of the 384 books studied. A variety of themes appeared among these few portrayals, ranging from a portrayal of "mutuality between a Black girl and her Brownie troop" (p. 452) to a portrayal of "stereotypes that represent symbolic annihilation" (p. 452). *Mutuality* refers to "intimate, egalitarian relations central to the story line" (p. 455) and *symbolic annihilation* refers to the "absence, stereotyping, and trivialization" of minority groups (p. 444). An example of the latter is "a 1958 *Little Golden Book* [which depicts] over 200 Whites and 3 Blacks. The Blacks appear on the top deck of a large paddleboat while Whites socialize below – one Black character is asleep, one plays the banjo, and one eats watermelon" (p. 452).

During the third period, from 1965 to 1974, black characters reappeared in children's books. The numbers of black characters increased and the quality of portrayals improved from the highly stereotypical portrayals in the early period. Books portraying only black characters also increased, and the Caldecott Medal was awarded for the first time to a book written and illustrated by black authors. In the fourth period, the number of portrayals stabilized at a higher level than in the previous times. Pescosolido et al. argue that, while the blatant stereotyping in the early time periods is gone, two features of recent books provide "subtle yet telling [evidence] about a lack of improvement in race relations" (p. 455). First, the portrayal of mutual interracial relationships is very rare. The books "continue to portray mainly surface contact, such as 'crowd scenes' on city streets, playgrounds or in classrooms" (p. 454), or characters from different races appear on separate pages. Second, while the portrayal of black children has increased, black adults – and especially black men – continue to be virtually absent from children's books. For instance, only one out of more than 1,000 *Little Golden Books* included a black male (p. 457). Stories that depict only black characters tend to "focus on historical themes, the depiction of folk tales, or feature social and temporal locations that are difficult to pinpoint" (p. 454); thus, black adults are featured only in "distant, 'safe' images" (p. 456).

Pescosolido et al. also discuss the effect of "gatekeepers" in the children's publishing industry. They explain the disappearance of black characters during the period of increased racial conflict in the United States as due to the reactions of key gatekeepers, the predominantly white publishers. They suggest that publishers avoided portraying blacks as a strategy to avoid "troublesome issues and groups" (p. 460), in essence, to avoid conflict. The civil rights movement made it clear that the old stereotypes were unacceptable, but publishers were unsure about what new images were appropriate to convey to children, so they did not convey any. Two stories illustrate this point. A book of American rhymes, *The Rooster Crows*, which won a Caldecott medal in 1945 "became the focus of controversy when the NAACP contended that [it] portrayed Blacks in an unfavorable light. When a new, revised edition was published in the 1960s, NAACP efforts were finally seen as successful.... But the new edition simply removed Blacks from a book about America. In the face of controversy and with no new rhymes or jingles to replace the stereotyped ones, Black characters were eliminated and [replaced with] blond-haired farm children" (p. 461). In another book, a 1945 *Children's Catalog* title, *Little Fellow*, a black character was shown in a highly stereotyped way: "The most visible (though not central) human character, 'Whitey,' is a stable hand who in the original version is Black, 'exactly the same color as Chocolate' (the horse). His speech is stereotyped: 'An a thororbred ef I evah seed one! De White folks gwine be mighty proud o' yo' baby.' Rather than making Whitey a more positive Black character in the 1975 reissue, he becomes 'Dooley,' White, Irish and speaking with a brogue" (p. 461; see their Plate 3).

The Caldecott awards are decided by an award panel. Thus, the Caldecott books pass through two sets of gatekeepers, the publishers who choose to produce the books and the panel that decides to honor them with an award. The effects of the Caldecott gatekeepers differs from that of the publishers. Black characters were more visible in Caldecott books than they were in the library and mass market samples during all four time periods. Moreover, in the last time period (1975–90) when the general visibility of blacks, measured as the percentage of books with at least one black character, stabilized in the library and mass market books, general visibility continued to increase in the Caldecott sample. An increase in the percentage of Caldecott books portraying exclusively black characters accounts for most of the increase in the general visibility of blacks in these books during this time. Starting in the late 1960s, many Caldecott winners were stories about only black characters, up to 35 percent of books in some years. In contrast, the highest proportion of books with only black characters for the library sample was 9 percent, and just one title from *Little Golden Books* featured only black characters (notably, this was the controversial *Little Black Sambo*). The focus of Caldecott books on exclusively black characters, rather than incidental black characters, however, explains why the books from the other two samples showed a higher degree of interracial interaction. "Ironically, the selection of African folk tales, which are an important part of the African American cultural heritage, rewards books removed from contemporary US society and from Whites" (p. 460).

Is the portrayal of blacks in children's books improving? Pescosolido et al. argue that it is hard to draw firm conclusions one way or the other. On the one hand, the blatantly stereotyped images of the 1930s have disappeared, but on the other, the lack of portrayals of black adults and of positive, mutual interracial interaction "may indicate the continuation of a symbolic status quo in which Black equality is seen as threatening" (p. 462). Along the same lines, the "notable increase in distant and 'safe' images of Blacks in the Caldecott Award books can be seen as a recognition and celebration of Blacks' unique cultural heritage, or it may be seen as a subtle form of 'symbolic annihilation' in which the cultural representations of Blacks do not include contact with Whites or portray contemporary 'real' African American adults" (p. 462).

3

Shaping Approaches

Music soothes the savage breast.
(Old saying)

The Economist reports that in recent decades the portrayal of ventriloquists "dummies," along with dolls and mannequins, have become increasingly sinister in popular culture, for instance in the movie *Child's Play*. "More than sinister, when it was learnt that the killers of Jamie Bulger, an English toddler who was tortured and murdered by two ten-year-old boys in 1993, had been watching videos of this series of films in which a doll called Chucky becomes a vengeful and malevolent spirit. The facial similarities between Chucky and Jamie were unmistakable."
(*The Economist*, December 2, 2000: 145)

In the United States in 1993, a strange and dangerous fad claimed the lives of several young people. To show courage and toughness, you lay down on the center line in the middle of a busy highway. The idea was that cars drive within marked lanes, and so you would be safe on the double yellow line, even when the traffic comes quite close. But, of course, for any number of reasons, cars do not always stay in their lane and some teenagers were run over, two fatally. Why would anyone do something so stupid? Well, characters in a movie (*The Program*, 1993) did it. They were cool. And no one came to harm in the film. After the deaths, the movie's makers faced a public outcry. Accused of corrupting minors, they cut this scene from subsequent releases of the movie.

When people say that an art object affects society in this way, they are subscribing to a "shaping" approach. Shaping theories suggest that art can somehow put ideas into people's heads. The shaping approach encompasses a wide group of theories that share the core belief, or metaphor, that art has an impact on society. As with the reflection approach, the shaping approach presents the relationship between art and society as a simple, straight line. But it reverses the causal arrow (the direction of the effect between art objects and society), so that art is seen as affecting society rather than vice versa.

For the most part, shaping theorists look at the *negative* effects of art on society. Marxists suggest that the popular arts condition workers to accept capitalism and socialize them to be willing to work. Observers of mass culture see many other harmful effects. Their list of accusations is long. Social critics have argued that jazz music leads to a society filled with degenerates drinking in speakeasies (in the 1920s), that pulp fiction corrupts morals (in the 1930s), that the flying of Superman encourages children to jump off rooftops (in the 1960s), that rap music erodes respect for law and order (in the 1980s), and that sensationalist art undermines family values (in the 1990s).

These "evils" are often said to herald the fall of civilization as we know it. But it is not necessarily the case that the effects of art must be negative for an explanation to be of the shaping variety. Art can be seen to shape in positive ways as well. For instance, "green" art might encourage recycling; movies about cancer victims might engender sympathy for those afflicted or encourage donations to medical research charities. Effects can also be morally neutral. For instance, it is said that the *Indiana Jones* movies dramatically increased the number of university students studying anthropology. Or they can be ambiguous or debatable. For instance, advertising can be argued to be bad if it inculcates a mindless consumerism in the populace, but might be argued to be useful when it provides information about products, services, and events.

Art and Uplift

A number of nineteenth-century intellectuals wrote about the uplifting effects of the fine arts. Matthew Arnold (1869 [1960]), a poet and literary critic, was one of these early shaping theorists. He believed that "culture" was made up of the "best that has been thought and said in the world" (p. 6). For Arnold, art included only the fine arts. The fine arts provided uplift due to their "moral, social and beneficial character" (p. 46). Their purpose was "to make reason and the will of God prevail" (p. 42) and they should do this by portraying "sweetness and light" (p. 46). Through their influence, people will be led away from their baser instincts, letting go of envy, spite, hostility, and anger. The fine arts, he believed, should be available to everyone in order to improve the general condition of all humankind. Without their civilizing influences, society falls into "anarchy."

The spirit behind Arnold's work was widespread. The famous art historian and social critic John Ruskin thought that art (and nature) were antidotes to tenement living, and that making art was therapeutic for everyone who did so. These ideas were also a key part in the establishment of museums and heritage organizations in both the UK and the US at the turn of the nineteenth century (see Cintron, 2000; DiMaggio, 1982a, b).

Despite the laudable goals of the social reformer and the spirit of *noblesse oblige* embodied in the actions of these nineteenth-century elites, there were also strong currents of class antagonism in the "culture and civilization approach" (Storey, 1993). In the context of the suffrage agitation of 1866–7 (which resulted in reforms that doubled the electorate by allowing households in the boroughs the right to vote), Arnold (p. 105) wrote:

> the working class . . . raw and half-developed . . . long lain half-hidden amidst its poverty and squalor . . . [is] now issuing from its hiding-place to assert an Englishman's heaven-born privilege of doing as he likes, and beginning to perplex us by marching where it likes, meeting where it likes, bawling what it likes, breaking what it likes.

According to Arnold, the civilizing effects of the fine arts, and culture in general, worked on all classes, but differently for each class. Through education, culture shaped the middle classes as they took up power and leadership and it prepared the aristocracy for its inevitable decline. For the working classes, however, culture inculcated a humbleness and an acceptance of the authority to which they were to submit.

The ideas sewn by Arnold in the 1860s bloomed into the theories of cultural highbrows in the 1930s. These authors – along with many intellectuals – believed that as much as high art was beneficial, mass art was harmful. By this time, the concept of "high culture," especially in its contrast to popular culture, had become firmly institutionalized (the distinction was not as sharply drawn in the nineteenth century, as we shall see in chapter 12). High culture was seen as distinctly different from popular culture, and diametrically opposed. While intellectuals still sung the praises of fine art, they now worried, in addition, about the deleterious effects of the popular arts. For instance, Q. D. Leavis (1932 [1978]) was concerned that the masses were rejecting the great books chosen for remembrance by intellectuals and professors, who knew best, and were instead reading popular fiction, to the detriment of themselves and society. Leavis believed that consuming pulp fiction was like a drug addiction. She was also concerned about the harmful effects of Hollywood movies and advertising. This literature marks the shift from an emphasis on the uplifting effects of fine arts to the "cultural critique" of the mass arts.

Marxism

Some Marxists believe that the cultural "superstructure" reflects the economic "base," as we saw in the previous chapter. A related strand of Marxism sees the superstructure as an instrument of control. The superstructure, created by capitalism, shapes workers to fit better with capitalism.

Hegemony

An important contribution to this line of thinking was made by Antonio Gramsci (1930s [1971]), who wrote about hegemony. *Hegemony* is a form of cultural control. In this view, elites rule through leadership and persuasion, not (for the most part) through force and bald power, as these latter strategies engender resistance. As Marx (1846 [1978]) himself wrote, "The ruling ideas are nothing more than the ideal expression of the dominant material relationships..." (p. 172). But "each new class which puts itself in the place of one ruling before it, is compelled... to represent its interest as the common interest of all members of society, that is... it has to give its ideas the form of universality, and represent them as the only rational, universally valid ones" (p. 174). Hegemony embodies the norms, values, and world views imposed on society by the dominant elites. Importantly, however, while these hegemonic ideals reflect the interests of the dominant elites who created them, they get their power from the fact that they are widely shared by most members of the society. As Strinati (1995: 165) writes, hegemony is

> a cultural and ideological means whereby the dominant groups in society, including fundamentally but not exclusively the ruling class, maintain their dominance by securing the "spontaneous consent" of subordinate groups, including the working class, through the negotiated construction of a political and ideological consensus which incorporates both dominant and dominated groups.

It controls society because people buy into it and come to take it for granted, so they do not question it.

The idea of employment is one such hegemonic idea. Most people reading this book probably either have a job already or are planning to get one, perhaps once their education is finished. We could question the idea of getting a job and contemplate living in simple harmony with the land, hunting or growing all we eat, wearing the same clothes until they fall to rags, having no luxuries like central heat, telephones, or flush toilets. We could question employment, but for the most part, we do not. We want to work, for a whole host of reasons, not the least of which is that we have come to see quite a number of erstwhile luxuries as necessities. The idea of employment is hegemonic; not only do we fail to question it, we actively seek it out. As Marxists point out, however, this plays into the hands of capitalists, who want a source of willing labor to exploit for their own ends.

Hegemony develops through a variety of means, but what is important for the sociology of art is that elites are instrumental in the creation and distribution of cultural products. They are, therefore, able to place into art ideas favorable to their own interests. Movies, television dramas, and sitcoms portray people in occupations. That is, most "normal" people in these shows have some sort of job, even though you may never see them in a work setting. We can think of exceptions, of course. Housewives are shown at home (a different hegemonic idea), the idle rich are shown idling (we envy them and work harder), and down-and-outs are shown in their squalor (we wish to avoid their fate). There is also a "rebel" genre where men or women take to the road to escape (which may soothe our restless fantasies). But the idea that comes across in these cultural forms is that society expects you to get a job. Both fine art and popular art can have hegemonic effects.

The Frankfurt School and critical theory

An important strand of critical theory was written by a group of scholars collectively known as the "Frankfurt School." They wrote about the popular arts produced by the *culture industries*, those business firms which produce cultural products for profit. The mass culture produced by these industries is homogenous, standardized, and predictable. Indeed, they argue, mass culture is a commodity churned out through mass production techniques; it does not differ from other commodities like cars or shoes in any fundamental respect. Marx's concept of *commodity fetishism*, the idea that people value things in monetary terms, is central here. Cultural commodities are tainted by commodity fetishism, and unlike the authentic arts, they are not valued for themselves, but for their exchange value. Adorno suggests, however, that mass culture products are given some surface difference, a *pseudo-individuality* to veil their commodified nature.

This standardized culture is easy to digest, as it requires no critical thinking. In fact, a key function of mass culture is to discourage critical thinking:

> the total effect of the culture industry is one of anti-enlightenment, in which, as Horkheimer and I have noted, enlightenment, that is the progressive technical domination, becomes mass deception and is turned into a means of fettering consciousness. It impedes the development of autonomous, independent

individuals who judge and decide consciously for themselves . . . while obstruct-
ing the emancipation for which human beings are as ripe as the productive forces
of the epoch permit. (Adorno, 1941 [1991]: 92)

As Strinati (1995: 54) phrases it, Adorno "thought that the promise of the
enlightenment, the belief in scientific and rational progress and the extension of
human freedom, had turned into a nightmare [through] the use of science and
rationality to stamp out human freedom."

As we saw in chapter 2, Adorno believed that the mind-numbing work of
industrial capitalism required numb minds. Stimulating the brains of workers,
even outside the workplace, undermines this requirement. Popular entertain-
ments had to be as soporific as daily work. As a result, the popular arts were
"dumbed down" so that workers would not realize just how stupefied they
were and would continue to show up day after day. Adorno also argued that
the purpose of this mass culture was control and conformity – the very vacuity
and banality of commodity culture fools the worker into a passive acceptance
of the world as it is. This demonstrates that Adorno, like other Marxist writers,
saw reflection and shaping working dialectically. The economic base determines ("conditions") the superstructure. In this way mindless art reflects
mindless work. However the superstructure also shapes the base. Mindless art
is passively consumed, so workers do not develop their critical senses. This
inability to evaluate their own conditions hides the true nature of capitalism
from workers, who thus continue their dreary existence with no hope of
release. Authentic art would sharpen their minds, but the workers do not
seek out authentic art, because they are too exhausted from their work to
attack authentic art with the vigor it demands, and so the cycle continues.

Marcuse (1972) suggests that the cultural industries create *false needs* in
consumers. People have true needs to be autonomous – to express themselves
and to make decisions about their actions. The cultural industries substitute the
false needs of consumption, which keeps workers from realizing that their true
needs are not met. Thus, the cultural industries lull workers into a passive
acceptance of capitalism, first, by stupefying them and then by convincing
them that the freedom to buy one brand over another is an adequate substitute
for the true political freedom they would find after casting off the shackles of
capitalist production and wage slavery. The products of the cultural industries
are imposed on workers, but they also act to hide the imposition and, indeed,
encourage workers actually to seek out the distractions proffered.

The arguments of the Frankfurt School are not very flattering to the people
who comprise the masses. Indeed, Adorno was accused in his lifetime of
elitism. His response was to stress "the vacuity, banality and conformity
fostered by the cultural industry. He sees it as a highly destructive force. . . .
To ignore the nature of the culture industry, as Adorno defines it, is to

succumb to its ideology... [which] is corrupting and manipulative, underpinning the dominance of the market and commodity fetishism" (Strinati, 1995: 63).

Writers from the Frankfurt School agreed with Leavis that mass culture was dangerous, but not because it undermined the cultural authority of intellectuals. They worried about almost exactly the reverse. They argued that mass culture strengthened the hand of the elites. Leavis thought that the masses had become strong enough to "outvote" intellectuals on the merits of popular versus quality fiction. The Frankfurt School, on the other hand, saw the masses as powerless and the cultural industries as all powerful. They also agreed that the fine arts are valuable, not because they are fine and uplifting, but because true art is part of an authentic culture that promotes clear and critical thinking, and will allow the masses to comprehend their subjugation, it is hoped, with revolutionary effect.

The Cultural Critique

Mass culture theorists

A number of theorists writing in the 1950s firmly established the cultural critique of mass culture, a critique which continues to the present day. These writers shared the idea that mass culture was standardized, homogeneous, and puerile in its appeal to the lowest common denominator. Mass culture is consumed by an undifferentiated, passive mass audience. The use of mass culture is often compared to drug abuse, suggesting that people are addicted to television (or romance novels, or rock music), going though life foggy-brained and only half-conscious, and continually looking for their next fix. For instance, Marie Winn (1977), in her book *The Plug-In Drug*, suggests that children watch television in a "trance" with a "glazed and vacuous look" in their eyes.

These authors make firm distinctions among types of art:

Folk art grew from below. It was a spontaneous, autochthonous expression of the people, shaped by themselves, pretty much without the benefit of High Culture, to suit their own needs. Mass culture is imposed from above. It is fabricated by technicians hired by businessmen; its audiences are passive consumers, their participation limited to the choice between buying and not buying.... Folk art was the people's own institution, their private little garden walled off from the great formal park of their masters' High Culture. But Mass Culture breaks down the wall, integrating the masses into a debased form of High Culture and thus becoming an instrument of political domination. (MacDonald, 1957: 60)

They suggest that mass culture is "parasitic" in that it feeds off ideas generated by the fine arts, without returning a single new thought to them. At the same time, they argue, mass culture strangles folk culture and displaces it.

These theorists relate the rise of mass culture to changes wrought by the industrialization of society. As Ryan and Wentworth (1999, p. 48) put it:

> By the 1950s, the critique of ... mass culture ... produced the general argument that:

1   Industrialization leads to urbanization because factories and people converge in areas with adequate power, roads, and housing.
2   As people move to these large urban areas they lose their strong ties to community and family of origin.
3   People [disconnected] from community and family have fewer restrictions on their behavior and more readily seek the quick gratifications of permissive sex, crime, and vice.
4   Because of the higher standard of living brought about by industrialization, these unattached individuals also have more money in their pockets.
5   Businesses (including the mass media) spring up in an attempt to profit by nurturing and satisfying these unrestrained urges of the industrial masses.[1]
6   The grand result: Society drifts away from high standards of morality and [from fine] art and is thus opened to and permeated by ... images of sex and violence. Such images appeal to an alienated, debased audience, which, having lost contact with virtue, is easily manipulated by political opportunists, advertisers, and mass media programmers.[2]

These theorists suggest that the mass audience spends too much time on unedifying mass art, and in consequence spends less time on useful, educational and productive pursuits. They develop from this analysis a "Gresham's Law" of culture – the bad drives out the good – whereby mass culture replaces the fine arts and the folk arts. Moreover, they argue that beyond filling time, mass culture actively harms those who consume it by inculcating in them a passivity that erodes their critical faculties and makes them prone to manipulation and exploitation. The similarities of the mass culture critique and the Frankfurt School are evident, especially in their analysis of its pernicious effects.

Media effects

The media effects literature concerns the harmful impact of mass media on society.[3] The media are seen as powerful because they are pervasive. Media present models of behavior that citizens (especially children) might emulate, they set the agenda for political and civic debate, and they do these things in a way that may well be biased. Certain issues, which suddenly become fashionable, are covered with great frenzy. This literature focuses, particularly, on the news aspects of the media, but some of its insights draw from, or can be applied to, the fictional media output that is part of the popular arts. For instance, the majority of Hollywood movie moguls are socially liberal and hold political views to the left of center. As a result, some critics argue, movies are biased toward left-wing politics, and they portray, too often and with too much sympathy, people who lead immoral lifestyles, to the detriment of traditional family life.

Similarly, the media can distort the audience's views of the world when information they provide is biased.[4] For instance, it is well-documented through surveys that people's perception of crime has to do with how much crime is reported in the news. Violent crime may be down, but if coverage of it goes up for whatever reason (usually, a fad in newsrooms) the fear of crime goes up, too. The theme of crime and violence is a strong one in the media effects literature, where fictional violence is seen to increase violence in society. (This debate is presented in case study 3.1.)

It is important to note that media effects can occur at two levels, in single individuals or in society as a whole.[5] For instance, violence in the media might lead to particular violent acts, as when two youngsters murder a toddler after seeing the horror film *Child's Play III* or a father stabs his son after seeing *The Omen*, a movie about an evil child of Satan born to a distressed family. Sensational effects like these resulting from exposure to a single cultural product are rare. Alternatively, fictional violence can be seen to induce a tolerance of violence at the societal level, regardless of whether or not it directly spurs individuals to behave more violently. Or, to take another example, advertisements operate both at the individual level (by convincing people to buy particular products or by encouraging in them a desire for certain lifestyles) and at the societal (by fostering the ethos of consumerism).[6]

The media effects literature, along with the mass culture critique, focuses on what we now think of as the popular arts, art forms that arose during the twentieth century and that are produced by culture industries. There are a number of reasons for this. Most notably, the fact that such cultural forms are new, coupled with the fact that they are created by profit-seeking business people, make them highly suspect to many observers. But it is worth pointing out that cultural objects from the fine arts have also been criticized in the same manner. This has been especially evident in the last decade or so in America when artists, many of them funded by the National Endowment for the Arts, have come under fire for being indecent and contrary to family values. These include such artists as Robert Mapplethorpe, whose homoerotic photographs included images of sadomasochism; Andres Serrano, who photographed a crucifix submerged in urine; and the performance artist Karen Finley, who appeared nude on stage and smeared her body with chocolate.

Critique

The accuracy of the shaping metaphor, as with the reflection idea, is undermined by two facts: art is not monolithic and the audience is not homogenous. These two statements alone remind us that there can be no simple, unproblematic mechanism by which art shapes society. There are, in addition, three main criticisms of the shaping approach. First, there are serious methodological problems in trying to measure the effects of the arts on society. Second, not only are audiences multifaceted, they are made up of thinking human beings, not drugged automatons. Third, the cultural critique is seen by some to be itself a product of elitism.

Methodological issues

As with reflection theorists, many shaping theorists have started – and stopped – with art. These authors do not convincingly link the unpleasantness in the objects they study with the society where the effects are said to occur, as they do not present any data. They merely assert the effect. Adorno and the Frankfurt School are notable in this failing. Other studies have tried to make the link empirically; however, it is extraordinarily complicated to measure media effects. As Abercrombie et al. (1994: 432) write,

> It is notoriously difficult to say how audiences interpret the output of the media, and many studies avoid it altogether simply by assuming that audiences are affected. There are substantial methodological problems in the way of any empirical investigation of the audience. Even if it is clear that people react to, and are influenced by, television programmes in the very short term, it is very difficult to measure long-term changes. Any long-term study will find it awkward to isolate changes in the audience due to the media from those stemming from other social influences. It is not even obvious what is to be measured. For example, is one interested in the influence of the media on the attitudes that people have or on their knowledge?

And research on people's behaviors can be more difficult than on their attitudes or knowledge, as the former cannot be measured by opinion surveys. Abercrombie et al. go on to point out that many media effects studies, especially with respect to violent behaviors, are based on laboratory experiments. These studies are problematic because they are artificial, removing people from their social contexts.

It is also important to point out that studies of media effects have reported inconsistent results. This is because studies differ in how they measure their variables. For instance, a gory murder on-screen clearly counts as a violent act, but does verbal abuse? What about cartoon or slapstick violence? In addition, the media industries have strong incentives to show that their output causes no harm, and they have funded numerous studies. Not surprisingly, studies funded by media companies are more positive about media output than independent studies (Centerwall, 1993).

Audiences

Much of shaping theory talks about the effects of cultural products on society without mentioning the fact that cultural products are consumed by audiences. This way of thinking is called the "injection model" or the "hypodermic needle model" because it suggests that ideas from the arts are injected directly into their audiences.[7] It views the audience as passive and uncritical, as made up of *cultural dopes*. (Or, sometimes, the term is *cultural dupe*, suggesting that individuals are fooled by culture, rather than made stupid by it.)

In contrast to this is the idea of the "active audience" where people who consume culture are seen as competent adults able to make decisions for themselves, to distinguish truth from fiction, and to interpret cultural objects (see chapters 10 and 11). Indeed, some authors suggest that even children are active, competent consumers of the popular arts (e.g. Hodge and Tripp, 1986 [1994]). In addition, not only are audience members competent individuals, they are also embedded in social structure. Thus, their reactions to the popular arts are mediated by those around them. Children, for instance, may learn from television to fight out their disagreements, but when they apply that lesson to life, by hitting a friend or sibling, their parents, teachers or others are likely to sort them out quickly. The active audience approach will be covered in Part II of this book.

Elitism

Other writers reject the critique of popular culture because they reject the elitist purveyors of the theories. They believe that the cultural critique is merely a *moral panic* – the situation that arises when elites worry about other people, couching it in terms of the degradation of the popular arts and therefore society (Cohen, 1972 [1980]). The cultural critique, in this view, is a form of submerged class conflict. Ross (1989) links the cultural critique to the waning of the cultural authority of America intellectuals. No one likes to lose power or authority, and so they look for something to blame, and in so doing they reassert their lost authority. In the cultural critique, intellectuals pin the responsibility on popular culture, arguing that it erodes society, and then claim status based on their superior abilities to "see" that society's problems are caused by popular culture.

Others point out that the cultural critiques of the past are forgotten, and so, in the future, will today's concerns. In the 1930s, for instance, parents worried about the ill effects of children reading too many novels (Starr, 1999). Today, parents worry about too many computer games. Reading books is seen not only as unharmful, but as positively beneficial.

Conclusion

The debate over the shaping approach is often reduced to the question of whether or not art affects society. Shaping theorists, who may be placed on one extreme of this argument, subscribe to an injection model of the relationship. It is easy to reject their ideas, as I have suggested above. On the other extreme are theorists who believe that popular culture has no effect whatsoever on either individuals or society. To them, the popular arts are merely entertainment, and the audience is comprised of competent people able to make up their own minds. The latter ideas are perhaps harder to reject than the former, in the sense that people quite obviously are not automatons who receive art completely unthinkingly or uncritically. But this does not negate the possibility that art influences people. As Seaman (1992: 306) puts it, with respect to television viewing, "It is quite true (one might have thought it too obvious to merit comment) that viewers 'actively' interpret what they see and hear; humans are not computers open to televisual 'programming'. However, [a focus on the 'active audience'] ... simply obscures the ultimate effects which the viewing practices eventually have upon the viewer and, no less important, on other individuals or groups in the viewer's community."

It is debatable whether the viewing of *Child's Play III* led two boys, in any direct way, to murder a toddler (as reported in the epigraph). Many factors beyond just watching a movie enter into an act of such terrible violence. However, it is clear that the teenagers who tried the game of lying down on a lane marker in a busy highway did get the idea from watching the football movie, *The Program*, though the movie did not literally "cause" them to try this stunt. Undershirt sales in America famously declined after Clark Gable took off his shirt in the movie, *It Happened One Night* (1934), to reveal a bare chest directly underneath. And Lieberson (2000: 131–2) shows that the first name Donald, which had been increasing in popularity from 1900, started a steep decline after Walt Disney introduced the cartoon character Donald Duck in 1934. To be sure, many people continued to wear undershirts or to name their sons Donald, but enough people changed their behavior, apparently on the basis of the film or cartoon, for their decisions to show up in the statistics. These effects, measurable if (perhaps) trivial, suggest that art does affect society in some ways. Gunter (2000: 19–20) brings up a different issue with respect to some authors' claims that art has little effect upon society: "The idea of minimal impact can easily become confused... with the maintenance of the status quo. What may appear as zero impact may in fact be profound but not readily detectable."

In sum, it is difficult to imagine that the arts really have no influence on society at all. After all, we live in a media-saturated society where the arts, both fine and popular, form an important component of the wider culture. Since people use ideas from culture to create "tool kits" for daily living (Swidler, 1986), it may make more sense to think of the question as "How much and in what ways does art influence individuals and groups in society?" Just as we have rejected a simple reflection model, but not the idea of a complex relationship between art and society, we cannot reject more nuanced perspectives on shaping, either.

NOTES

1   Here, Ryan and Wentworth suggest that the media are merely suppliers, rather than creators, of the demand. The culture critique, however, can embody either position.

2   For a more elegant summary of these arguments, see Strinati (1995: 5–20).

3   See, for example, research from the Glasgow Media Group (Philo, 1998; 1990; 1982), as well as Bourdieu (1998) and McChesney (2000). Also in this broad tradition are Cohen (1972 [1980]), Critcher (2003), and Thompson (1998) on moral panics. Dayan and Katz (1992) discuss "media events" (special events such as the Olympics or the wedding of Charles and Diana which are scripted so as to attract vast media coverage), and argue that these can have positive effects such as encouraging social integration and relaxing social tensions.

4   Gerbner (1995), for instance, argues that television viewing leads people to feel insecure in their social environment: "Our analysis based on large national probability sample surveys indicates that long-term, regular exposure to television tends to make an independent contribution to the feeling of living in a mean and gloomy world. The 'lessons' range from aggression to desensitization and to a sense of vulnerability and dependence" (p. 73). Morgan (1989), also concerned about the effects of television, suggests that television encourages people to hold contradictory opinions, and supports this assertion with a study of attitudinal data which shows that the more television a viewer watches, the greater the degree of contradictory opinions he or she expresses in surveys. (Along these lines, see Postman, 1986.)

5   The literature is divided, then, between work on individual effects and work on societal effects. A second division revolves around the effects of specific messages within media texts (see, e.g., citations listed in note 3), and those that argue that "the medium is the message" (McLuhan, 1964; see also, Couch, 1996; Diebert, 1997; Eisenstein, 1979; Gellner, 1988; Goody and Watt, 1968).

6   While some studies of advertisements take a reflection approach (e.g. Goffman, 1979; Marchand, 1985), the majority take a shaping approach (e.g. Barthel, 1988; Cortese, 1999; Cronin, 2000; Ewen and Ewen, 1992; Ewen, 1988; 1976; Goldman and Papson, 1998; Klein, 2000; Turow, 1997). This is, clearly, because of all cultural forms advertising most explicitly attempts to shape its consumers. For an excellent discussion of the advertising industry and its ability to influence people (or, rather, its lack of ability to influence), see Schudson (1986). O'Toole (1985) writes about the industry from an insider's point of view.

7   Curran (1990) scathingly attacks the equation of the media effects tradition with a hypodermic model of influence. This, he says, "is a breath-taking, though often repeated, caricature of the history of communications research that writes out a whole generation of researchers. It presents as innovation what is in reality a process of rediscovery. . . . Effects research cannot be said in any meaningful sense to have been 'dominated' by the hypodermic model. On the contrary, its main thrust ever since the 1940s was to assert the independence and autonomy of media audiences and dispel the widespread notion that people are easily influenced by the media. It did this by developing many of the same insights that have been proclaimed afresh in the recent spate of 'reception' studies, albeit in a different technical language and sometimes with less subtlety" (pp. 146–7). Along these lines, Seaman (1992: 306) calls the injection model "the strawman view of television causation."

Case Study 3.1
Violence and Television

Points for Discussion

1 What are the arguments in the case supporting the idea that television causes violence in society? What are the arguments against it?
2 Is the analysis of violence in the vignette convincing? Why or why not? Is it a sociological argument?
3 From your reading of chapter 3, what critiques can you bring to bear on the authors presented in the evidence section?
4 Do you think violence in television causes violence in society? On what do you base your conclusions? Might there be contributory effects on society of violence in movies (whether viewed in the cinema or at home) and in popular music lyrics and music videos? What other factors might contribute to violence in society?
5 What should be done about violence on television?

Vignette

When I was growing up in the USA, I remember hearing, in the context of the 1969 or the 1972 government report on the subject (The National Commission on the Causes and Prevention of Violence, 1969; The Surgeon General's Scientific Advisory Committee on Television and Social Behavior, 1972), that if we did not do something about violence on television, American society would become more violent as children exposed to TV violence grew up. Today, high school students shoot their classmates with semi-automatic rifles before turning the weapons on themselves, and disgruntled workers (disproportionately, for mysterious reasons, in the postal service) fire guns at colleagues. Clearly, the social critics were right. Society has become more violent, so television violence *must* be affecting society.

QED – Argument proven.

Now I live in the United Kingdom, which is a gentler society. But it seems to be getting more violent, too. People do not shoot each other on the freeways, like they do in Los Angeles, but they do succumb to "road rage" and sometimes stab each other as a result. The UK seems to be converging with the US – a result, perhaps, of the Americanization of the British media output as the once staid and placid BBC monopoly was challenged by competing television stations broadcasting imported American fare and of British use of violent new media such as movie videos and computer games.

Evidence

One of the earliest, and most often cited, studies of the effects of televised violence was reported by the psychologists Bandura, Ross, and Ross (1963). In a laboratory experiment, subjects were children 3–5 years of age. They were shown one of three things, (a) a violent act in real life, (2) a film showing a violent act by a real person, or (c) a film showing a violent act by a "cartoon character." A fourth, control group saw no violent acts. Then the researchers examined the child's subsequent behavior to see if they imitated this violence. The goals of the study were "to determine the extent to which film-mediated aggressive models may serve as an important source of imitative behavior" (p. 3). The authors reported that they were motivated to undertake the study after they read in the *San Francisco Chronicle* about a boy who had knifed another after seeing the movie *Rebel Without a Cause* on television.

In the real-life aggression situation, an experimenter served as the model. He or she (the gender of the model was also an experimental variable, which we shall leave aside) punched a five-foot tall "Bobo doll" and then performed the following distinctively aggressive acts:

> The model sat on the Bobo doll and punched it repeatedly in the nose. The model then raised the Bobo doll and pummeled it on the head with a mallet. Following the mallet aggression, the model tossed the doll up in the air aggressively and kicked it about the room. This sequence of physically aggressive acts was repeated . . . interspersed with verbally aggressive responses such as, "Sock him in the nose . . . ," "Hit him down . . . ," "Throw him in the air . . . ," "Kick him . . . ," and "Pow." (pp. 4–5)

For the human film situation, the same experimenters were filmed exhibiting the same behavior as in the real-life situation. In the cartoon situation, a female experimenter dressed as a black cat performed the same behaviors as above, "except that the cat's movements were characteristically feline," (p. 5) and the verbal aggression was articulated in a high, squeaky voice.

After viewing the aggression (or not, in the case of the control group), the children were frustrated (toys were taken away) and they were taken into a room with a different variety of toys including a three-foot tall Bobo doll, a mallet, guns, and some "non-aggressive toys" like teddy bears. Their behavior was coded for its level of aggression. The researchers found that all three experimental conditions provoked levels of aggression higher than that found in the control condition. Indeed, eighty-eight percent of the subjects who saw human aggression, whether live or on film, exhibited some degree of imitative aggression, as did seventy-nine percent of the subjects viewing the cartoon. In addition, boys behaved more aggressively than did girls. Importantly, there were no statistical differences between the amount of violence in children exposed to the real life and the human film situations. The authors concluded, "The finding that children modeled their behavior to some extent after the film characters suggests that pictorial mass media, particularly television, may serve as an important source of social behavior" (p. 9).

This experiment and similar ones that followed have been extensively evaluated. In terms of its "internal validity" – the accuracy, reliability and validity of its procedures and measurements – this study holds up reasonably well. Subjects were assigned to experimental conditions in a way that rendered the four groups comparable, and efforts were made to minimize differences from child to child that were not part of the experimental design. Statistical analysis was applied, demonstrating that the differences found were due to actual differences, not random error. However, as Felson (1996) points out, the aggressive behavior found in experiments may be a "sponsor effect" (where subjects assume that experimenters who show violent fare condone it) or evidence of experimenter bias (where compliant subjects try to help out the experimenter) rather than a true "modeling effect."

The experiment comes under more fire in terms of its "external validity" – how well its lessons might be related to real life. The first question is whether the study measures genuine violence; aggression usually denotes a behavior with the intent to injure a person (Bandura, Ross, and Ross point this out themselves). Moreover, the Bobo doll, also known as a "Punchy Clown," is an inflatable toy resembling an overgrown, fat bowling pin with a protruding red nose. It has a round, weighted bottom, so that when it is tipped over, it rights itself immediately. In other words, it is designed to be a punching bag! So the "violence" measured was directed toward a doll, not a person, and in fact did not damage the toy in any way.

We can also ask if the aggression exhibited by the children might simply be a short-term response, whether this response would obtain in the longer term, and whether it would transfer to social situations or to more serious aggressive acts. Further, while the majority of experiments have supported the findings of Bandura, Ross, and Ross, others have not found a link between televised aggression and subsequent behavior. A few studies have even suggested that televised violence can act as a safety valve for aggressive individuals, helping them let off steam.

Paik and Comstock (1994) performed a meta-analysis on 217 studies of television and antisocial behavior, from both psychology and sociology since 1960. A "meta-analysis" is a relatively new quantitative method that allows researchers to aggregate findings from a number of studies in order to draw stronger conclusions than would be possible for each study alone. Their key finding is that there is a highly significant, positive association between television violence and antisocial behavior.

Paik and Comstock's work demonstrates that experimental studies show a stronger magnitude of effects than those based on surveys, and laboratory experiments greater effects than field experiments or "time-series studies" (which examine naturally occurring situations), but all types of studies showed positive effects in the aggregated analysis. They also found that cartoon violence and fantasies had stronger effects on antisocial behavior than realistic fictional or newscast violence, a finding which might be related to the finding that preschool subjects (who watch more cartoons) demonstrate higher levels of antisocial behavior than adult subjects. Effects were highest in magnitude when antisocial behavior was measured as aggression towards objects and intermediate when measured as verbal aggression. The lowest magnitude of effects were shown for violence towards persons and criminal behavior. The context of the portrayed violence made a difference; cases where violence was rewarded or legitimated had effects of greater magnitude than in the converse situations. Paik and Comstock's analysis also suggests that males and females are equally, and positively, affected by televised violence.

Media executives strongly question these types of findings. They argue that their products do not cause violence, rather television shows reflect it; society, they say, is violent for a host of reasons unrelated to television. Further, they argue, if people wanted to see less violence, they would just turn off their TVs. The media would then switch to more pacific content in order to lure viewers back. Television just gives people what they want – exciting shoot-em-ups and car chases.

Felson's (1996) evaluation of the literature, which looks at both methodological and theoretical issues, would support the media executives in many respects. He suggests that most violent behavior learned from television is likely learned through other sources, too. In addition, audiences are likely to choose shows that match their values and interests. This "selective exposure" provides an alternative interpretation of any correlation between violent audiences and violent television. Further, Felson points out that the story line of most television shows suggests that "crime doesn't pay" and that criminals are punished in the end; indeed, consequences for illegitimate violence on television are greater than they are in real life. This suggests that if viewers are sensitive to the moral of the story, television violence might even reduce real-life violence.

Felson's review finds that many studies lack external validity, they suffer from numerous problems with measurement and data, and are subject to the problems of spurious correlation, where a third variable actually causes the difference the study tries to measure. For instance, longitudinal studies consistently document a relationship between television viewing and antisocial behavior. However, we cannot conclude from this that television viewing *causes* violent behavior, because

> children with favorable attitudes toward violence may be more likely to engage in violence and also more likely to find violence entertaining to watch. Also, children who are more closely supervised may be less likely to engage in violence and less likely to watch television. Intelligence, need for excitement, level of fear, and commitment to school are other possible confounding variables. (p. 109)

A meta-analysis finds strength in numbers and can demonstrate differential effects of different kinds of measurement of key variables. But it is only as good as its constituent analyses. Still, Felson concludes that "exposure to television violence probably does have a small effect on violent behavior for some viewers, possibly because the media directs viewers' attention to novel forms of violent behavior that they would not otherwise consider" (p. 103).

Media executives also dispute the amount of violence that critics find in television. How many violent episodes per hour are found on television depends, clearly, on how it is measured. Ryan and Wentworth (1999) report on a project, funded by the four major American broadcast networks, which revised the measurement of violent incidents:

> Rather than take the traditional approach of simply counting incidents of violence – much objected to by television programmers – the researchers attempted to look at violence in context. They allowed that some violence might, in fact, be appropriate or used for comedic effect in such a way that it would not be taken seriously. (p. 54)

It is worth pointing out, however, that if slapstick and cartoon violence is discounted along with coverage of disasters and accidents, the "incident count" for children's programming would dramatically decrease.

Many commentators mention that the size of the effects of violence found in these studies is so small that it is trivial. Centerwall (1993) vigorously disputes this. He points out that small effects in percentage terms can translate to many more violent attacks when applied to an entire nation. Further, he argues that small perturbations in the middle of a distribution (what these studies measure) can imply quite large effects at the extremes. He estimates that if television had never been invented, "there would today be 10,000 fewer homicides each year in the United States, 70,000 fewer rapes, and 700,000 fewer injurious assaults" (p. 64). Centerwall would also be angered by the television industry's efforts to re-count violence in children's programming, because, he argues, children are powerfully affected by pictorial violence, whereas adults are not, and that small children cannot distinguish between real and cartoon violence in the same way that adults do and that they are less sensitive to the motives of people who are violent.

His article is an impassioned cry for public action. He believes that television violence is a public health issue, like smoking and road traffic accidents. He suggests that parents limit television for their children. But, he says, parental vigilance is not enough.

> Television violence is everybody's problem. You may feel assured that your child will never become violent despite a steady diet of television mayhem, but you cannot be assured that your child won't be murdered or maimed by someone else's child raised on a similar diet. (p. 69)

What is needed is legislation; specifically, he thinks that all new televisions manufactured in the US should be required to have a "V-Chip," which allows parents to lock out violent shows based on a rating system for programs is that quantifies the level of violence and broadcast with them. He finds media executives disingenuous in their declaration that the rights to free speech forbid censorship of television contents; nevertheless, he does not advocate governmental censorship.

Finally, what of the people who watch television? That is us. We are, for the most part, non-violent members of society. Some authors suggest that television does more good than harm, even for children. Máire Messenger Davies, in *Television is Good for Kids* (1989), "describes many positive learning outcomes which have been identified in various academic studies. These include: the development of television literacy skills, such as understanding visual narrative, editing conventions, etc.; improved memory of events due to visual aids, which also stimulate imagination; being able to differentiate different degrees of realism (so-called 'modality judgements') across narrative forms; the acquisition of knowledge, understanding and practical skills; and not the least the play value, usually involving social games in which favourite television programmes are 'remade' or re-enacted" (O'Sullivan et al., 1998: 127).

The media effects literature suggests that other people succumb to television violence, but not ourselves. Most of us are not violent, but might it be that we are more tolerant of violence in society?

4

A Mediated View: The Cultural Diamond

Visual images are made, and may be moved, displayed, sold, censored, venerated, discarded, stared at, hidden, recycled, glanced at, damaged, destroyed, touched, reworked. Images are made and used in all sorts of ways by different people for different reasons, and these makings and uses are crucial to the meanings an image carries. An image may have its own effects, but these are always mediated by the many and various uses to which it is put.

(Gillian Rose, 2001: 14)

As we have seen in previous chapters, it is tempting to view the relationship between art and society as a direct link. Art holds a mirror up to society, reflecting it. Art molds society by providing positive role models and by presenting bad behavior as cool. We have also seen that these approaches are flawed. We do not need to delve too deeply to realize that an art work can only reflect a few aspects of society, and is never a perfect mirror of aspects it does reflect. Similarly, you know from personal experience that you are not a "cultural dope." You might get ideas from television or novels, but you do not uncritically adopt all of them just because you saw or read them. And great painting and great music is more likely to bore than inspire you if it is forced upon you by your parents or your school.

This chapter offers a brief critique of reflection and shaping theories from the point of view of the "Cultural Diamond." This model forms the basis for the sociological work covered in Part II of this book (chapters 5–12). These chapters show the strength of the approach. We will address its weaknesses in Part III.

Wendy Griswold (1994, 1986) developed the idea of the cultural diamond. Put simply, the diamond is a square turned on one end like a kite. It has four corners, representing (1) artistic products, (2) creators of art, (3) consumers of

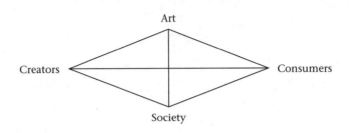

Figure 4.1   Griswold's Cultural Diamond
Source: Adapted from Griswold (1994), p. 15.

art, and (4) the wider society. Each of these four points are linked (with six lines) as in figure 4.1. Griswold argues that to understand art and society, researchers must take account of all four corners and all six links in the diamond. Art is created by an artist or group of artists. It does not spring miraculously into form without human intervention. And art does not reach "society" at large. Instead, it reaches a particular public made up of individuals embedded in a social system. How consumers use art, what meanings it elicits in their minds, and how it eventually penetrates the general society is mediated by these individuals and is affected by their attitudes and values, their social location, and their social networks. "Society" (including wider norms, values, laws, institutions, and social structures) makes up the final node on the diamond. It affects artists, the distribution system, the consumers of culture, and through these, the shape of art.

The cultural diamond is a heuristic device or metaphor that sets out, in general terms, the idea that relationships exist among these points. It strongly suggests that all four points are important in understanding art sociologically. As Griswold states (1994: 15):

> the cultural diamond is an accounting device intended to encourage a fuller understanding of any cultural object's relationship to the social world. . . . a complete understanding of a given cultural object would require understanding all four points and six links.

The cultural diamond is not a theory, however. It does not try to specify in abstract (but specific) terms *what* the relationships among the points on the diamond are, only *that* some relationship exists.

A Better Diamond

The picture of the cultural diamond devised by Griswold has the elegance of simplicity. I modify the cultural diamond in my presentation of research on art

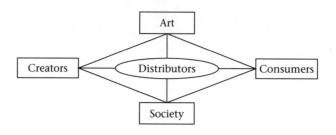

Figure 4.2   Modified Cultural Diamond

worlds, however, to demonstrate some important links that the simple diamond obscures (see figure 4.2). Art is communication. Art has to get from the people who create it to the people who consume it. That is, art is distributed by some person, organization, or network. As we shall see, the shape of the distribution system affects what kinds of art get distributed widely, narrowly, or not at all. The simple diamond lumps the distribution of art objects together with artistic creation. Separating these two allows us to see that the layers intervening between artists and consumption can be many, as in popular music where feedback from the audience to the artist comes via the recording industry mainly in the form of market indicators, or few, as is the case for the consumers of pub music who are more directly in contact with the musicians who perform there. Distinguishing artists (or the production system) from distribution systems also allows us to see that artists can stand apart from the distribution system (as do most novelists), or can be deeply embedded within it (as are many television script writers).

In addition, many forms of art become divorced from the artist after they enter a distribution system. Art museums, for instance, circulate paintings, sculptures, and other works. In some cases, their exhibitions can make or break the reputation of a living artist. But most of the time, the artists have long since died. Even living artists might not benefit directly from museum exhibitions if their canvasses belong to someone else.

A final advantage of a diamond with an embedded distribution node is that it breaks the direct link, in the simple diamond, between art object and society. This link, unlike the others, is not a true link but a metaphorical one, and reminds us of the flaws of over-simplified reflection and shaping arguments. In other words, *the cultural diamond suggests that links between art and society can never be direct, as they are mediated by the creators of art on the one hand, and the receivers of it on the other.* It critiques reflection and shaping approaches by pointing out, from the production side, that artistic conventions and production techniques, not to mention artists, influence the content of art works, and the filtering effects of distribution systems determine which cultural products reach audiences. It critiques reflection and shaping approaches from the consumption side, by reminding us that cultural products are received by a variety of different audiences, not by "society," and that people vary in what types of cultural products they consume and in what meanings they take from them. It demonstrates that sociologists are interested in studying the production and consumption of art. But the new diamond also preserves the society node, to indicate that sociologists continue to be interested in the relationships, albeit mediated ones, between art and society.

Part IIA

The Cultural Diamond

The Production of Culture

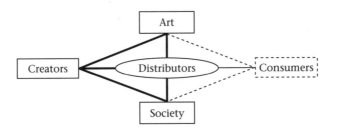

5
Art Worlds

Consider what changing from the conventional Western chromatic musical scale of twelve tones to one including forty-two tones between the octaves entails. Such a change characterizes the compositions of Harry Partch.... Western musical instruments cannot produce these microtones easily, and some cannot produce them at all, so conventional instruments must be reconstructed or new instruments must be invented and built. Since the instruments are new, no one knows how to play them, and players must train themselves. Conventional Western notation is inadequate to score forty-two-tone music, so a new notation must be devised, and players must learn to read it.... Consequently, while music scored for twelve tones can be performed adequately after relatively few hours of rehearsal, forty-two-toned music requires much more work, time, effort, and resources. Partch's music was often performed in the following way: a university would invite him to spend a year. In the fall, he would recruit a group of interested students, who would build the instruments (which he had already invented) under his direction. In the winter, they would learn to play the instruments and read the notation he had devised. In the spring, they would rehearse several works and finally would give a performance. Seven or eight months of work finally would result in two hours of music, hours which could have been filled with more conventional music after eight or ten hours of rehearsal by trained symphonic musicians playing the standard repertoire.

(Howard Becker, 1982: 32–3)

In order to set the stage for a discussion of the production of culture, this chapter concentrates on Howard Becker's (1982) concept of art worlds, and his rich and fruitful description of their effects on art. Production approaches examine factors on the left hand side of the cultural diamond relating to the creation, production, and distribution of art. Key questions addressed by the approach include how art is created, produced, and distributed. It examines the relationships among creators, distribution networks, art works, and society.

The main idea of the approach is that *cultural objects are filtered through – and affected by – the people and systems that create and distribute them.*

Howard Becker's Art Worlds

Becker's book, *Art Worlds*, makes a very important contribution to the sociology of art. Becker is a jazz musician and a photographer, as well as a sociologist. His approach to understanding the arts is deeply rooted in sociology, and somewhat at odds with intuition. He argues that the arts are embedded in what he calls *art worlds*. An art world is "the network of people whose cooperative activity, organized via their joint knowledge of conventional means of doing things, produces the kind of art works that the art world is noted for" (p. x). Some art worlds are small and narrowly defined, say a local poetry circle or an experimental theater group. Others are quite large and broad, such as the art world surrounding Hollywood movies. Becker argues that every aspect of the art world provides a set of resources and constraints for making art. The key point is that art works are shaped by the whole system that produces them, not just by the people we think of as artists.

Becker believes that to understand art sociologically, we should view art as *a collective activity*. To Becker, art is a process – an *activity* – rather than the finished product (an object or performance). This view highlights the creation of art, and the sociological factors that affect this act. Becker emphasizes that making art is a *collective* endeavor. In making this assertion, he does two things. First, he defines art as "a work being made *and* appreciated" (p. 4, emphasis original). If it does not have an audience (a very small one will do), it is not art. Second, he takes issue with the idea, prevalent in Western society, that art is something created by an artist – a creative genius – who works alone. Becker argues that all art forms, from Hollywood movies to poetry, involve the efforts of many people, and that art would neither exist nor be meaningful without their input.

In the simplest terms, Becker's argument is that every aspect of the process of creating art shapes the final results. Many people are involved. Some work directly on the art, others help, and still others (possibly from long ago or far away) have played a role in developing the already existing material and symbolic components upon which the art is built. To help see what he means, Becker invites us to "Think of all the activities that must be carried out for any work of art to appear as it finally does" (p. 2). First, someone needs to conceive of an idea, to decide the kind, and the specific form, of work that will be made. Second, someone needs to execute the idea. For this, the responsible parties will need to obtain materials (paints, musical notation paper, costumes), find equipment (musical instruments, lights, costumes, cameras), find time (work around a day job), recruit other artists (actors, musicians, dancers), and recruit support staff and technicians (cashiers, office staff, printers, welders, paint manufacturers, and if you are Damien Hirst – who has used parts of sheep, cattle, and pig in his work – butchers). The process of conceiving of the idea and then bringing it to fruition is called *production*.

Once people have produced the idea and it is embodied in form, they need to find a way to get their work to an audience. This is called *distribution*. How distribution systems work has profound implications for who will see, buy, or read the movie, CD or poem. Some distribution systems are large and complex, such as the networks that distribute Hollywood movies to an international viewership. Other distribution systems are quite small and local, as when poets photocopy their work for friends or read it in coffee houses or libraries.

But distributing artwork to people is not enough, audiences must appreciate the work as well. Part of the collective activity of art requires that some-one create and maintain the rationale according to which the art is seen to make sense and to be valuable. An *aesthetic system* helps people to understand the work of art. Most art works are situated in standard aesthetic systems that are already available. For instance, they are presented as "paintings" (oil paints on a rectangular canvas, shown in a museum, dealership, or informal "clothes-line" exhibition) or as "rock music" (guitar, electric bass, drums and vocals, usually with a strong beat). Other art works, for instance one using a sheep suspended in formaldehyde (Hirst's *Away from the Flock*) might require that someone elaborate the aesthetic system in order to justify the piece as art. Finally, the activity of artistic creation relies on civic order and stability as well as norms such as the recognition of private property.

This is a long list of things to do, but it is oversimplified compared to what happens in the real world. Becker points out that we take many of these things for granted. But consciously noted or not, each aspect of the process of creating and distributing art affects art. The production system constrains artistic cre-ation and channels art in some directions rather than others. The distribution system constrains artists in that art needs to fit into the system in order for it to reach an audience. Becker does not suggest that these constraints control artists, stripping them of free will. Instead, Becker sees people in the production system as working within a system of constraints: "Available resources make some things possible, some easy, and others harder; every pattern of availability reflects the workings of some kind of social organization and becomes part of the pattern of constraints and possibilities that shapes the art produced" (p. 92).

The division of labor

Nobody does all the work in an art world. All art forms rely on a *division of labor*. This is as true for symphony, opera, plays, and rock music, as it is for painting and poetry. Some people do more of the creative work (or, at least they get the credit for doing so). These *core personnel*, as Becker calls them, are at the center of the making of an artwork and are seen to have the special skills of an artist. Others help design sets or advertising posters for a play, or cast bronze for an artist, or keep track of the finances of an opera house. These *support personnel* are given a lower status. They have skills that are seen as "a matter of craft, business acumen or some other ability less rare, less characteristic of art, less necessary to the work's success, less worthy of respect" (p. 16).

The division of labor varies from art world to art world. Some have a large number of fine distinctions. In filmmaking, for instance, there are many roles; in poetry, fewer. In many art worlds, there is a gradation from core to support personnel, rather than a sharp dividing line. In movies, the director, scriptwriter, and starring actors are close to the artistic center of filmmaking; they are core personnel. The camera operators, score composers, supporting actors, stunt actors, and set and costume designers are further away from the core and can be called support personnel, although important ones. Builders, seamstresses, drivers, and caterers are also support personnel; they seem peripheral, but the creative endeavor relies on their input.

In some art worlds, distinctions are more sharply drawn. In classical music, for instance, there is a sharp distinction between composition and performance. Composers create the idea of the music. Musicians, along with the conductor, produce the actual music. Virtuoso performers generally do not have time to compose (they must continually practice to keep up their playing skills); composers do not practice enough to be superior instrumentalists, as they spend time on composing. Thus, the distinction continues.

Just as tasks are divided differently from art world to art world, they are bundled differently, too. A *bundle* of tasks are those normally done by a single individual. Composing and performing are considered separate tasks in classical music, but in jazz, the activities are merged. Jazz musicians improvise on established songs on the spot rather than planning (composing) their music ahead of time. In rock music, the two activities are viewed as separate, but they are also bundled. Authentic performers play their own music. They may occasionally re-record a great song composed by others, but this must be the exception. Bands that look great on camera, but perform only music written by other people, are often looked down upon.

There is a final aspect of the division of labor. The art world generally agrees that the division and bundling should happen as it does. In other words, the particular division of labor is *conventional*. Most of the time, we do not think about the division of labor. It just makes sense. But divisions are, in some senses, arbitrary and socially defined. For instance, westerners usually think of a poem as a skillful and perhaps beautiful arrangement of words. The words makes the poem. Whether the poem is handwritten or printed in a book makes no difference to its poem-ness. (It may make a difference for sentimental or, in the case of an original manuscript, historical reasons.) We also believe that a poem can exist in multiple copies – the same poem exists in all the copies of the anthology in which it appears, for instance. These statements seem quite obvious to us. But by contrast, in classical Japanese poetry, the physical writing of the poem cannot be separated from the poem-ness of the poem. The calligraphy is an inseparable part of what the Japanese consider poetry. If the words were set in type and printed, the soul of the poem would be torn away. In Japanese poetry, the art object is akin to a painting, whereas in western poetry, it more closely resembles a book of fiction.

Constraints and possibilities

Becker suggests that an art work is affected by the pattern of constraints and possibilities that exists in the art world that creates it. Whatever activities are needed for the art to be created that are not done by the core personnel called "artists" must be done by someone else. Sometimes the cooperation happens easily, and all participants share a common view.

In many art worlds, however, conflict arises because the goals of support personnel differ from those of the core personnel. Becker gives the example of composers versus musicians. Composers are skilled in creating interesting orchestrations, sometimes involving complex or technically difficult playing. In performing such difficult pieces, instruments might squeak or sound off-key, which performers do not want. A composer's wish for complex arrangements, then, can conflict with the performers' desire to sound good. Along these lines, the poet e. e. cummings had trouble getting his poems printed because printers did not want to follow his ideas for layout or his unusual use of capital letters, as it looked to them – and would look to their colleagues – like errors.

Core personnel must liaise with organizations, especially in distributing their work. For instance, visual artists rely on museums to display their work. If an artist makes a sculpture that is too big or heavy to fit inside a museum, then people will not see it, unless there is an alternative site. Sculptors who made industrial-sized pieces in the 1960s had to invent the idea of the sculpture garden, where outsized sculptures stand outdoors, in order to get an audience.

Artists who choose to use materials specifically designed for artistic use or to use conventional materials in conventional ways choose the easy route, as the materials will be readily available and suitable for their purpose (though money to buy these materials can be a problem). If they choose to use unconventional materials, their job will become much more difficult. Harry Partch, for instance, had to build his unconventional musical instruments from scratch, in order to play his unconventional music. Most musicians rely on instruments that are already invented, and are routinely manufactured (by machine or hand) by someone else.

Also, a change in the available materials can change the artistic output. A good example from art history has to do with oil paints in tubes. Before these were available, painters had to prepare the paints themselves, from grinding the pigments to mixing them with the oils. Successful painters could rely on assistants, usually aspiring artists, to do this. Painters without assistants were dramatically slowed in their work. More important, for the history of art, the requirement of making paints as needed meant that it was difficult for an artist to leave the studio where his equipment and assistants were located. With the invention of tube paints, at the time of the Impressionists, artists found it much easier to work on the final canvas (rather than on just a preliminary study) outside, on location. They also found it easier to work by themselves, rather than with lots of assistants. These factors are seen as contributing to the shift from academic to Impressionistic art at the end of the nineteenth century (see case study 5.1).

Available technology, just like available materials, also affects the cultural object. Science fiction films look different since the first *Star Wars* movie was released, and increasingly sophisticated special effects and animation techniques continue to improve the visual impact of these movies. Likewise, music sounds different when played on electrical versus acoustical instruments, and electric guitars are used in very different kinds of music as compared to classical guitars.

As with resources, artists who choose personnel in established ways find their work more easy to complete. Composers who write music for a standard orchestra, and who ask only for sounds that most trained musicians can make will have their works performed more readily than, say, composers who write music that requires an ensemble of three orchestras to perform. And relying on multiple orchestras, conventional arrangements of conventional instruments, though they require an unusually large stage and a larger budget to pay the musicians, is easier than the practice followed by Partch, who not only had to make new instruments to perform his music, but had to train musicians to play them.

Conventions

Becker continues with his theme of how the art world constrains artistic production in his discussion of conventions. He states: "Artistic conventions cover all the decisions that must be made with respect to works produced" (p. 29). Conventions, to Becker's mind, are the "rules of the game" in art worlds, and include the standard ways of dividing core and support personnel and of bundling tasks. They include the usual patterns of linking the personnel together in art worlds, as well as the standard types of materials used by artists.

Conventions also refer to the formal characteristics of the work and what people in the art world expect the art work to say. "Only because artist and audience share knowledge of and experience with the conventions invoked does the art work produce an emotional effect" (p. 30). Emotional response and depth of understanding are enhanced through conventions, so conventions enable, indeed constitute, art as well as constraining it. In other words, conventions create meaning. (Becker, however, was less interested in the particular meanings created by conventions, focusing more on the existence of conventions in art worlds and their contribution to the pattern of constraint and possibility.)

Conventions help mark out the inner circles of an art world, the practitioners and cognoscenti, from the outer circles, the more casual members of the audience. An art world is like an onion, with many layers. At the center of the art world are the professional artists, and support personnel. Moving out from the center are the audience members. Audience members who know the intricacies of the art world (often other artists or art students) are closer to its center than are casual audience members. Outside the specific art world is the more general world which provides art worlds with more general ideas about art and aesthetics. People at the center of the art world understand conventions of the art world at the most detailed level. In some cases, "What serious audience members know about an art . . . conflicts, because of innovative changes, with what well-socialized members of the society know" (pp. 48–9). This is especially the case with avant-garde movements and the leading edge of rock music. Often, "less involved audiences look precisely for the conventional formal elements the innovators replaced to distinguish art from nonart. They do not go to the ballet to see people run, jump and fall down; they can see that anywhere. They go instead to see people do the difficult and esoteric formal movements that signify 'real dance'" (p. 50).

An onion is not a perfect metaphor for an art world, however. An art world is centered on a certain type or genre of art (a genre is form that shares a set of conventions). However, several art worlds can have the same outer layers, or peripheral members. At a broad level, conventions separate dance from opera or rock music. At a more specific level, conventions separate house music from rap. Some sets of conventions are so esoteric that only a few people understand (or want to understand) the art form. Some sets are so widely shared that they can support the worldwide distribution of an art form that is appreciated, or at least watched, by millions of people.

Conventions, like the other factors in the art world, constrain artists, but they also make the art possible. Most artists follow conventions in most aspects of their work. Treading a different path, as the Harry Partch story shows, takes much more effort than staying close to conventional roads. Inventing an entirely new form of art, *de novo*, would be too much effort for a single artist, or even a large group of them. All new forms evolve out of established ones. That said, however, it is also important to recognize that while most artists are mostly conventional, most artists also innovate in some respect. As Becker (p. 63) says,

> Every art work creates a world in some respects unique, a combination of vast amounts of conventional materials with some that are innovative. Without the first, it becomes unintelligible; without the second, it becomes boring and featureless, fading into the background like music in supermarkets and pictures on motel walls.

Distribution systems

The *production* of art, for Becker, involves the activities needed to realize the artistic vision in some form (material object or performance). The *distribution* of art involves the activities that get art to its public. Production and distribution may be distinct or may overlap. Distribution systems act as sets of constraints and possibilities affecting such factors as the size of the audience, the balance of power between the producers or artists and distributors (thus, the degree of control each has over artistic content), and the character of the art work. Becker discusses three types of distribution systems: those based on self support, patronage, and public sale. Most art worlds contain a mix of distribution types.

Self-support occurs when artists distribute their own work by themselves or within small networks. Such artists do not earn much (or anything) from their work, so they rely on a "day job" (not arts related), an arts related job (e.g. teaching or commercial art), an inheritance, or a working or wealthy spouse or partner. But self-supported artists can please themselves. This system offers the most freedom to artists, but at a cost. For instance, self-supported artists buy their own materials and equipment. Unless they are rich, they must use low-cost materials – balsa wood or cement rather than marble or bronze. The most important limitation of self-supported distribution is that the audience will be small.

Patronage refers to support given by wealthy philanthropists to the artists in exchange for works of art.[1] Patrons can be organizations as well as individuals. For instance, the United Kingdom names a Poet Laureate, and corporations commission work for their headquarters and sponsor symphony or dance performances. Patrons are able to control the art that is produced, because the artist must please the patron. Some patrons actually dictate the content (this was true during the Italian Renaissance of the Medici, who specified contracts for paintings in great detail, and of the Soviet Union, which suppressed all styles of painting except the "Socialist Realist"). Other patrons appear to offer more freedom to artists. They support artists whose work they know to be acceptable rather than attempting to control artistic expression. There are also patrons, particularly those interested in prestige among avant-garde circles, who prefer to let artists do as they like. Philistines apart, patrons are often enlightened in their support of art (but they also always control the purse strings).

Public sale refers to market systems of distribution. All market-based distributors are subject to the laws of supply and demand, and they are sensitive to financial concerns. Becker identifies three types of market distributors: dealers, impresarios, and culture industries. Dealers sell physical art objects where each item is unique. Impresarios work in the performing arts. Differences between dealers and impresarios stem from the fact that art objects are purchased after they are seen while performances must be pre-paid beforehand. Culture industries distribute art, books, CDs, videos, and film, in mass-produced copies. The ideas embodied in the copies may be as unique and precious as other forms of art work (perhaps!), but their embodiment, unlike that of the performing and visual arts, is not unique. (The various public sales systems are covered in chapters 6 and 7.)

Becker does not discuss systems like medieval guilds or art academies that are no longer used, nor secondary distributors like libraries and museums. In addition, his book was written before the Internet was invented. The web holds out the promise of reaching a large audience without a formal distribution network. At this point in time, however, most artists' home pages are visited only by friends and family; consequently, in its quotidian operation for unknown artists, the web is a substitution for the photocopier and postal service, rather than a new means of generating attention.

Art and artists

Becker's view of art worlds is a powerful, and indeed a radical, way to view art. He takes aim at the most fundamental view of art that we hold: the idea that art is created by artists. He suggests that art is created by lots of people, by art worlds, not artists. Becker agrees that people have different talents, but he argues that artists are as not special in this regard as the standard ideology of artists suggests. Many people, with diverse talents, contribute to the activity of art – and to the constitution of the final product – but most of them do not get the credit. The idea of giving one special person the credit for the art work is a socially constructed idea – one that we take for granted, and one that, like many social conventions, simplifies the situation. According to the ideology, the artist, and only the artist, creates art. Support personnel do not count.

The Production of Culture

When Becker wrote about art worlds in 1982, his work contributed to a way of seeing art that had already developed into the production of culture approach (Peterson, 1976; Coser, 1978). The approach coalesced in the 1970s as a direct response to problems with reflection approaches (Peterson, 1994).[2] Many of its insights are drawn from the sociology of organizations, occupations, and work. Peterson (1994) identifies four areas in which the production of culture approach has been most fruitful, (1) gatekeepers, (2) reward systems, (3) market structures, and (4) artists' careers.[3] I illustrate the thinking behind each of these and then briefly mention other topics studied under the production of culture rubric.

Gatekeepers

In an influential article, Hirsch (1972) applied ideas from organizational sociology to the sociology of art. He was interested in how the network of *firms* (i.e. profit-seeking businesses) that produce artistic products operate. He focused on firms that produce art for national distribution, noting that the industry system, in which the firms are embedded, stands between suppliers (the artists) and the ultimate consumers of art (the public). A key idea is that only some of the supply reaches the public; specifically which ones depends on *how the system filters objects*. In the book-distributing system, authors write manuscripts and submit them to publishers. The pool of unpublished manuscripts, all of them taken together, is large and varied. Publishers accept only a proportion of these manuscripts, weeding out manuscripts that they think will not sell. This means that the pool of manuscripts selected for publication will be smaller than the pool of unpublished ones. It will also be somewhat more uniform, as publishers reject weak and eccentric manuscripts and choose, more often than not, manuscripts that match their tastes and their ideas of what a strong seller will be. Publishers, then, are biased filters. They take a skewed sample of "what's out there." We may hope that their selection is of high quality, as indeed it may be, but in profit-seeking systems, issues of commercial success tend to override more abstract notions of quality.

A *gatekeeper* filters products (or people) as they enter or leave a system.[4] In publishing, commissioning editors who read and reject (or accept) manuscripts are gatekeepers. They filter at the beginning of the system. Books are filtered as they leave the publishers, when marketing personnel decide on the advertising strategy for each one. Books are again filtered when newspaper critics decide which few to review (Hirsch calls reviewers *surrogate consumers*), and when library and bookstore buyers decide what to put on their shelves. Most books pass through all of these gatekeepers before they come to the attention of potential consumers.

The concept of the gatekeeper has ramifications beyond the profit-seeking cultural industries that Hirsch discussed. As Becker reminds us, all art works whether fine, popular, or folk, must be distributed through some system. All distribution systems are affected in some way by gatekeepers.

Reward systems

Artists, along with support personnel and distributors, are motivated by reward systems inherent in the art world. Crane (1976) suggests that there are four types of reward system: (1) independent, (2) semi-autonomous, (3) subcultural, and (4) heterocultural. In independent reward systems, artists themselves control both the symbolic and the material rewards. (Symbolic rewards refer to such benefits as prestige, but also to the definition of truth and beauty in the field; material rewards refer mainly to financial benefits.) The French Academy (discussed in case study 5.1) is one of the few examples of this type of reward system in arts. Semi-autonomous systems are those in which artists control the symbolic rewards but consumers allocate material rewards. This is the case in many of the fine arts. Avant-garde artists, for instance, gain prestige from their innovations in art, but they become financially successful only when collectors purchase their works. The popular arts show some evidence of this reward system, as in the Oscar and Emmy awards that are given by the industry to its own best artists.

In subcultural reward systems, artists create their work for an identifiable subculture, as in the case of Crane's example of black urban jazz music – or in quilts produced by local clubs or in the fiction written by and for science fiction fans who know each other through the web. Like semi-autonomous systems, artists control symbolic rewards, and consumers material ones. In many subcultural reward systems, however, the creators and audience can merge into one another, and rewards become mostly symbolic. This is the case for most of the folk arts. Finally, heterocultural reward systems are found in cultural industries in which large corporations produce art. Business people, rather than artists, control the financial aspects of the creative process, and also set standards for it. Diverse audiences provide both approval and financial rewards. The rewards, then, come from a variety of sources, but not from artists themselves. Crane's ideas relate to Bourdieu's (1993) concept of *artistic fields* (discussed in detail in chapter 14).

DiMaggio (1987a) discusses the classification of art. Artworks can be divided into "genres" based on the conventions they share – or as DiMaggio puts it, on the similarities they appear to have (p. 441). The emphasis on "perceived similarities" highlights that genre distinctions are generated socially, rather than being inherent in the artworks. On a broad level, the fine, popular and folk arts are genre classifications, though clearly, many more layers of specific genres can be found under each of these rubrics. In fact, the distinctions between fine, popular, and folk arts are examples of "ritual classification" that have been highly institutionalized in society. DiMaggio suggests, however, that the art classification system (at least in America) is "becoming more differentiated and less hierarchical, [with] weaker and less universal" classifications (p. 452). In other words, the strong boundaries among fine, popular, and folk may be breaking down. DiMaggio argues that classification systems are mediated by characteristics of the production system (e.g. its goals): "commercial classification . . . is driven by efforts of culture producers in market systems to sell art for a profit, and tends to yield broader, more weakly framed genres than does ritual classification. . . . [P]rofessional classification . . . results from artists' attempts to develop reputations and, under conditions common to Western democracies, produces narrower, less universal distinctions among genres" (p. 449–50).

Market structures

Production of culture theorists are most noted for their analyses of market structures. As we have seen, Becker points out the different constraints inherent in different distribution systems. In this area of inquiry, researchers have brought in ideas from economic sociology, particularly theories on organizations, industries, and markets, to understand art.

In a fruitful piece, Peterson and Berger (1975) looked at the concentration of the music industry to gauge its effect on innovation and diversity in music (see case study 6.1). DiMaggio (1977) was interested in the type of administrative system that operates in cultural industries. Neither craft nor bureaucratic administration, commonly found in other parts of the economy, seemed to characterize the cultural industries. Instead, DiMaggio posits, they work on a *brokerage* system of administration, in which a person (the broker) acts as an intermediary between the artist and business managers. Artists would prefer to have the freedom of creative expression available under craft administration and managers would prefer the predictability inherent in the bureaucratic model, but neither system of administration would be effective. Examples of brokers include the commissioning editor in book publishing, the Artist & Repertory person in the recording industry, and the producer in television and movies.

Crane (1992) argues persuasively that, in place of the traditional division of high culture and popular culture, a better way to understand and categorize the current artscape is to look at the context in which the arts reach the public. They can be disseminated by for-profit cultural industries, nonprofit organizations, or local networks.[5] For the most part, it is the popular arts that are distributed through business firms. However, profit-seeking enterprises play a role in the fine arts, too, for instance, in the sales and auction markets for visual arts and in the publishing and recording industries' distribution of serious literature and classical music. Nonprofit organizations tend to distribute fine arts, and social networks, both fine and folk arts (though there are exceptions).

Artists' careers

Becker's approach to artists suggests they are not the isolated geniuses of popular imagination, but are talented people working together with a variety of other talented people to generate interesting new objects or performances. Becker suggests that sociologists should focus on the roles that various different "personnel" play in the art world. Other research in the production of culture borrows from organizational sociology, this time from literature on occupations and work (Menger, 2001).

Other factors in making art

Production of culture research demonstrates a number of other ways that features of the creation, production, and distribution systems can shape the art work. Ryan and Peterson (1993), for instance, show how digital technology has altered many aspects of music making, from composition to performance. They point out that, by making it possible to make good sounding music cheaply, albeit with the requisite computer skills, such technology enables musicians to make professional-quality recordings without the benefit of recording studios. They demonstrate how digital devices "threaten a wide range of occupations whose skills are based in playing instruments; foster a new range of, as yet, ill-defined occupations whose skills are based in electronics and programming as much as in music; and shift the balance of creative power between international corporations and independent producers" (p. 175). They conjecture that, as individuals find it easier to create their own music, the ultimate effect of "the digital revolution may be to erode the barrier between performer and audience that heretofore has been built ever higher by each new twentieth-century technology" (p. 195).

Swidler, Rapp, and Soysal (1986) argue that the conventional formats for television shows limit the content of the shows. They were interested in why traditional love stories, in which a man and a woman meet and fall in love, occurred so rarely on television. The answer was not that audiences or script writers did not like such stories, as they remain commonplace in both novels and movies, but rather that the format used by most television series preclude them. The two main formats, used through the mid-1980s, were episodic "series" (such as situation comedies or dramas) and continuing "serials" (such as daytime or evening soap-operas). Neither of these formats were conducive to love stories, which need a clear ending when the couple has come together, with the usual implication that they will live happily ever after. Instead, series require a stable set of characters that reappears each week. The concomitant need, in series, for the interrelationships among the characters to remain the same works against the development of a love story, except as a subplot. In contrast, serials require ongoing changes, so that couples do meet and fall in love, but the need for dramatic tension means that their relationships must always undergo more challenges, as they fall out of love, face up to ex-partners, discover infidelities, or find themselves in some other soap-opera scenario. This is one of many ways that conventions can help shape the content of art.

Critique

The production of culture approach recognizes that art is created, produced, and distributed. Consequently, any art that reaches an audience has been mediated by the core artists, the support personnel, and the gatekeepers in the distribution network. It is shaped by the conventions of the art world, and by the available materials and resources. Art, which we normally think of as somehow sacred or divorced from mundane concerns, is highly tied up with practicality, money, and commerce. This is as true for the fine arts as it is for the "media" arts, and has always been true.

There are three main criticisms of the approach. The first two are inter-related and come from the reception side of the cultural diamond. Individuals with an interest at stake in the art world under study pose similar critiques. The first critique faults the production of culture theorists for ignoring what is special about art; what distinguishes it from the production of automobiles or shoes. The second critique takes the approach to task for ignoring meaning in art.

Proponents of the production view reject these critiques, claiming that the two features in question are strengths (or neutral characteristics), not weaknesses. As Becker (1989: 282) writes, "Sociologists working in [the art worlds] mode aren't much interested in 'decoding' art works, in finding the work's secret meanings as reflections of society. They prefer to see those works as the result of what a lot of people have done jointly." Peterson (1994: 177) argues that one of the strengths of the approach is its "nominalist" stance, which suggests that "for the purposes of the inquiry at hand, there is nothing unique about any specific symbol system that prevents it being studied with standard social scientific . . . methods." However, criticism of the production approach can be passionate precisely because symbols are meaningful, and people feel strongly about the art forms sociologists study with such seeming dispassion. Treating art as "nothing special" can threaten the partisans whose status is tied up with the "specialness" of art. Peterson counters that an opposite threat occurs when researchers become so aligned with the professional attitudes of the art world that they "go native," losing their critical faculties, "obtaining an incomplete and misleading reading of the field under study . . . [and] becoming an unwitting apologist" for it (p. 182). Nevertheless, it remains true that examining production factors demystifies the creative process, rendering it, in critic's eyes, mundane. (This does *not* mean, however, that sociologists of art necessarily devalue art or that they are all philistines; usually quite the contrary, otherwise they would not bother to study art.)

A third critique of the approach comes from sociologists who dislike, a priori, the generally positivist nature of the approach.[6] Peterson replies, "If production studies run the risk of eliminating 'culture' from the sociology of culture, researchers who focus on the content of cultural products run the risk of . . . taking the 'sociology' out" (p. 184). Clearly, these differences are based on metatheoretical tastes concerning the purpose of social theory (see chapter 1). Along these lines, it might be noted that the production of culture approach provides many insights into economic sociology (industries, organizations, occupations, and markets). While not a critique, per se, this comment highlights the fact that the approach engages a particular set of questions, some from other sub-disciplines in sociology, that are not shared by all sociologists interested in art.

Certain questions of meaning cannot be answered well with the production approach. Nevertheless, the production of culture approach has demonstrated convincingly that production factors strongly affect the creation of art works. We will consider these issues at length in the next four chapters.

NOTES

1   The term patronage is often used in the broader sense of any elite support of the arts.
2   This approach has been applied not only to art, but also to news, science, law, and religion.

3 I have collapsed three of Peterson's categories (comparative market structure, market structure over time, and structural conditions facilitating creativity) into "market structures"; he discusses six contributions rather than four.

4 The term gatekeeper is often used in a broad sense to mean any person or organization that filters things, artists as well as art objects. Hirsch employs the term somewhat more narrowly than I do here.

5 Crane divides the artscape into the national cultural industries (profit-seeking organizations orientated towards large audiences) and the urban arts (a variety of organizational forms oriented towards smaller, local audiences). In the latter category, Crane includes the small business that serve a local audience, such as art dealers or pubs and clubs. I have made a slightly different distinction between profit-seeking and not-for-profit organizations in distribution systems. The closeness of the artist to the audience is a crucial variable, however, which I discuss in both contexts.

6 Not all production of culture theorists are hard-boiled positivists. Becker's work, for instance, draws more on the tradition of symbolic interactionism.

Case Study 5.1
From Academy to Public Sale

Based on Harrison White and Cynthia White (1964 [1993]), *Canvasses and Careers: Institutional Change in the French Painting World*, (Chicago: University of Chicago Press).

Points for Discussion

1 List the actors in the Paris art world. Who, in Becker's terms, are the "core artists"? The "support personnel"? What technical, social, cultural, and aesthetic factors affected the production of art at the time?
2 How did the interests of the academicians vary from that of the dealers and of the critics?
3 How did the academic system constrain artists? How did the dealer–critic system free artists from these constraints? What new constraints did the dealer–critic system put upon artists? What constraints existing under the academic system continued into the new one? (Hint: Think broadly, as Becker does, about the concept of "constraint.")
4 How did the change of distribution systems shape the art that was produced?

Case

In their important book, *Canvasses and Careers*, White and White (1965 [1993]; see also White and White, 1964) examine the transformation of the French art world, near the end of the nineteenth century, from an academic system to a dealer–critic system. They tell the story of the fall of the academic system after a successful two hundred years. They ask why it fell and why it fell when it did.

The traditional explanation, by art historians, is that academic art had worn itself out. There was simply nothing new left to say using the academic styles of painting. The decline of the academic system, and the styles of art it supported, coincided with the rise of Impressionism. According to the art historians, Impressionism was fresh; consequently it won out. The Academy withered with the art it supported. Though there may some truth in the description of academic art as staid and inflexible, this story is not very sociological. It relies on the art itself to explain changes in the art. (Many old-style art historians spoke of art this way; it is called *formalism* because it relies on the formal characteristics of the art work.) In terms of the cultural diamond, it looks only at the art node, ignoring creators, consumers, and society. Moreover, this story begs the question: Why did the change occur when it did and not 100 years earlier or later?

A second hypothesis about the change could be called the *zeitgeist* explanation. During the latter part of the nineteenth century, France was changing from a more rigid society, based on upper-class privilege to a more flexible society with a larger middle class. Impressionism mirrored this new form of society, and therefore became more popular than the academic styles which reflected the old order. In terms of the cultural diamond, this explanation is clearly based in the reflection approach.

White and White's story about the transformation is more complete and convincing than either the formalist or the zeitgeist models. Their explanation touches on all four points on the diamond, but emphasizes the production of culture side.

The academic system

The *Académie des Peinture et Sculpture* was established in Paris in 1648 as an alternative to the medieval guild system, which it eventually replaced.[1] It served two purposes, to educate young painters and sculptors and to promote the highest standards in the practice of the fine arts. The Academy itself was a body of distinguished, mature artists who decided what was good in art. They could enforce their ideas because the Academy controlled nearly all the rewards given to artists: artists' apprenticeships and training, exhibition space (and thus the possibility of selling a work), prizes for the best pieces, and eventually, election to an academic chair. There were about 40 chairs in the Academy, and election to a chair was the culmination of a successful artist's career. Young artists, then, were highly dependent on the academicians.

The Academy, located in Paris, provided what we might call secondary education. Young artists all over France started their arts training in the *École des Beaux-Arts*, which had schools throughout the provinces. The best artists from the art schools were sent to Paris to continue their careers in the academic system. They would usually work as an apprentice to one of the academicians and also enroll in the Academy's courses. When they were good enough, they entered a painting into a competition for exhibition space, which was the key to professional success in Paris.

This exhibition, called the *Salon*, was held once a year (see plate 3). The academicians decided which paintings were to be accepted for display. They arranged the exhibition and determined which paintings were hung at eye level (where they are best seen), and which ones were hung in the third or fourth tier up, near the ceiling. They also judged the paintings, giving medals (and prize money) to the most deserving works. The highest prize was the *Prix de Rome*, which provided an artist a stipend to live and work in Rome for three or four years. Huge crowds of people came to the *Salons*, which were important socially, as well as aesthetically. Collectors and purchasers came to socialize and to buy. (Most of the sales went to the national and provincial museums of France, however, and only a few to private collectors.)

The academicians held strong views on the best practice of art, which rested on a clearly articulated aesthetic system. For instance, there was a rigid hierarchy of types of paintings. At the top (good) was history painting, based on patriotic, classical, and religious themes. Figures (people) in these paintings were to be rendered idealistically; figures often stood allegorically for ideas or themes. In the middle was "genre painting" which depicted everyday life. Real life was too messy and ugly to make truly beautiful paintings, according to the aesthetic, but at least genre included human figures. At the

Plate 3   Claude [?] Bornet, *Exhibition at the Salon of 1787*, engraving after Pietro [?] Martini, eighteenth-century print, Cliché Bibliothèque nationale de France, Paris.
The Paris Salons were important socially, as well as artistically, and attracted large audiences. The Academy's juries decided not only which paintings to accept, but also whether they would hang at eye level or be relegated to a place near the ceiling.

bottom (bad) was landscape painting. Paintings were also judged on a number of precepts (see table 5.1).

   Academy rewards were based on individual paintings, not artists, their reputation, or their portfolio of works. As a result, artists concentrated on producing a *masterpiece*, a single great work that had a chance to enter the salon and win prizes. They spent about *two years* working on this one, large canvas. The average artist worked for 22 years as painter or sculptor and entered just 11 works into the Salons over his lifetime. (In most cases, they did complete other, less ambitious works during this time.)

Table 5.1   Precepts of the French Academy

1   Classical and Christian themes are the only proper subject matter.
2   Only the most "perfect" forms . . . should be selected from nature to portray such subjects.
3   Only a certain set of "nobly" expressive positions and gestures . . . are appropriate in the representation of the human figure.
4   The human figure is the highest form and expresses perfect "absolute" beauty.
5   Pictorial composition should preserve classical balance, harmony, and unity: there should be no jarring elements. . . .
6   Drawing [provides the technical, and moral, groundwork for] art.

Source: Quoted from White and White (1965 [1993]), pp. 6–7.

The French Academy worked effectively for more than two centuries. Change in the Academy and in the styles of art that it supported was slow, but it did occur, as can be seen in the shift from the Baroque style of the seventeenth and eighteenth centuries to the Neoclassical, Romantic and then the Realist styles of the eighteenth and nineteenth centuries.

Why did the academic system fail in the end? According to White and White, the Academy's biggest problem was its own success! The academic system was set up to reward and support a community of artists numbering about 200. The Academy drew the best artists to Paris, through the *École* system, and established the fine arts as a proper, middle-class profession that parents would allow their sons to enter. But as more and more artists moved to Paris to commence artistic careers, the Academy failed to expand, and the rewards of the academic system were too few to go around. (*Why* the Academy did not increase the number of prizes and chairs is not quite clear, but in this regard, the academicians focused on their role in maintaining high standards rather than on the competing function of the Academy to train and support artists.) By the late nineteenth century, only one in four artists working in Paris ever earned a medal in the *Salons*, and only one in a hundred artists were ever elected to the Academy. Most of those unsuccessful in the *Salons* and the Academy were quite possibly talented, but the academic system had a limited number of rewards, and these began to go to a smaller and smaller proportion of practicing artists. As the rewards became more scarce, they became more political as well, going to the favorites of the academicians. When the Academy failed them, some artists began to look elsewhere.

The dealer–critic system

As the number of artists in Paris grew, existing dealers became more important as outlets for the work of those who were not succeeding in the Academy. Dealers sell artwork directly to the public, sidestepping the academic system. There were no large-scale dealerships specializing in paintings before 1850, but as a corollary to the Academy's success in generating middle-class interest in the fine arts, this type of dealership emerged in the latter part of the nineteenth century.

Dealers, unable to rely on prizes given by the academic experts to signal great works, had to figure out how to convince the public to buy. The first step was to train potential buyers to appreciate the art works for sale. Critics helped in this by developing ideas on aesthetics and publishing them in books and newspaper articles. This is why the system is called the dealer–critic system. The critics are an important component, a disinterested party whom buyers could trust. Critics and dealers work in concert to draw in an audience for paintings and sculptures that the dealer sells.

Dealers helped fill a gap left by the academic system – enabling artists to maintain an income for the middle-class lifestyle which they expected, and to purchase supplies to create art works. In many ways, the dealers took up the Renaissance role of the patron. They paid the artist a stipend and provided moral support. In exchange, they received art works on which they hoped to make a profit. Dealers, with the help of the critics, encouraged the idea of speculation in paintings. (In this, dealers capitalized on a general "speculation fever" that was sweeping the Continent.) Their message was, "This artist will someday be famous and his works will gain in value." This ideology of the undiscovered genius took hold during the time of the Impressionists and continues on in the art markets of today.

Implications for works of art

In order to understand how the dealer–critic system helped shape the content of art works, consider what dealers needed that the academic system did not. Dealers needed (1) a regular flow of paintings by a small number of artists, unlike the Academy which was set up to receive one painting each from a large number of artists. Consequently, paintings needed to be executed relatively quickly; two years per painting was too long. (2) They needed a way to differentiate their products from those of competitors. The solution was to look for paintings that reflected the personal style of the artist, rather than the uniform, set tastes of the academician. The notion that artists have a unique style, along with a regular flow of paintings, allowed the dealer (with the help of critics) to educate the public as to the particular aesthetic principles used by the artist and inculcate a taste for his style. (3) Paintings needed to appeal to middle-class buyers, as there were not enough elite buyers to go around (and they were mostly captured by the Academy anyway). Paintings that were pretty or decorative fitted well with the dealer–critic system. It was helpful, too, if they were interesting to average viewer – genre scenes and landscapes were more accessible to the middle classes than the highly symbolic history paintings prized by the Academy. (4) Paintings needed to be small to fit in living rooms. This encouraged "easel" paintings. Salon paintings, often very large (floor to ceiling), were meant to hang in museums, mansions, and castles.

All of these needs were well met by Impressionist painting. They used lively colors on small canvasses, often completed outside. They painted landscapes and scenes from everyday life. They worked quickly, using loose brushstrokes, and produced large numbers of paintings. They often painted a whole series of works on the same subject. Most notably, they developed individual ways of seeing the world that they translated into their work. This allowed dealers to encourage buyers to purchase a number of works by the same artist. This is the meaning of White and White's title. In the Academy, the "canvas" (single masterpiece) was the key to success. Under the dealer–critic system, it was the "career" (the artist's special style and his entire *oeuvre*).

It is worth noting that only a small segment of the middle class bought paintings at the end of the nineteenth century. But more did so than before. The Impressionists were successful, but they were laughed at, too, often by the middle classes. It is important, as well, to recognize that White and White's argument is not deterministic. They do *not* argue that the dealer–critic system led inexorably to Impressionism and only Impressionism. Rather, they argue that the constraints of the system shape the art that it produces. The dealer–critic system was conducive to Impressionism in a way that the Academy was not. Other styles also fit well within the dealer–critic system, however, and history could have taken a different turn as the Academy folded, leading to the rise of something other than Impressionism.

Although White and White concentrate on the structure and functioning of the French Academy which worked in combination with the large number of artists in Paris in the last half of the nineteenth century to facilitate the rise of dealers, they recognize the importance of several other factors involved in the rise of Impressionism.

These include the rise of middle class (society node) and the increase in the size of the art buying public (audience). As the audience grew, it also changed in composition, which had implications for the styles of paintings art audiences might prefer to buy. The availability of oil paints in tubes and ready-made canvas (materials, as part of the creator node) made it easier to work outdoors. Artists' tastes were changing (creator node), and some preferred to make smaller paintings of landscape and everyday life, despite the Academy's disapproval. A smaller number began to incorporate scientific findings about the eye, perception, and light in their thinking about painting, which led them to paint with looser brushstrokes and to observe light and shadow directly, perhaps outdoors, rather than recreating it in a planned masterwork composed in the studio from preliminary sketches. Finally, the invention of photography had ramifications for the whole cultural diamond, from formal changes in art works, in the art node, to changes in how audiences and the whole society thought about representation.

Note

1   It was originally called the Royal Academy, and changed names a number of times during its history. (Also, on academies of art, in general, see Pevsner, 1940.)

6

Businesses and Industries

Waterworld may have listed at the box office this summer, but Universal Studios Hollywood theme park is betting $15 million that its newest show, WaterWorld – A Live Sea War Spectacular, will be an explosive success when it opens Saturday. How explosive? Six times every day, eight stunt actors will re-enact the finale of the big-screen movie with... firestorm scenes that Universal officials say have never been done before in live performance.

"The biggest effect is that we fly and crash a full-scale twin-engine airplane over... the atoll wall into the middle of the lagoon a few feet from the audience. It explodes and splashes water all over everybody".... The Water-World arena puts 2,500 visitors at a time into the center of the set... [and the show] is included in the price of daily admission to the park: $33 for adults, $25 for kids.

(USA Today, September 28, 1998)

This chapter focuses on the distribution of art by business firms and cultural industries. A *firm* is a profit-seeking enterprise, and an *industry* is a linked set of firms that work in cooperation or competition in a given arena, in our case, in distributing a particular type of art. The term cultural industries often connotes only firms that distribute the popular arts. Indeed, some authors use the term culture industries to indicate producers of a debased "mass culture."[1] This chapter takes a broader view of the cultural industries. They are clearly relevant in the distribution of a large proportion of the popular arts and, in addition, play a role in distributing many fine arts. For instance, the publishing industry distributes literature and poetry, the recording industry, recorded classical music, and art dealerships and auction houses, works of visual art.

Industry Systems

Drawing on ideas from industrial sociology and economics, sociologists from the production of culture approach have studied how cultural industries shape the art they produce and distribute. Using examples from the publishing and recording industries, we can trace a number of factors, shared across different industries, that affect artistic output. The goal of this chapter is to produce a set of theoretical tools for understanding cultural industries and art, not to produce a full picture of any given industry.[2]

Hirsch (1972) views industries as *systems*. That is, industries are sets of linked organizations each of which draw resources (input) from the environment, transform them in some way (throughput) and then send the result (output) to the next organization or to the market. He studied the industry systems that produce books and musical recordings. Hirsch points out the filtering effects of systems and the importance of gatekeepers. Gatekeeping, either as individual decisions or organizational outcomes, does not shape the content of art objects directly, but it is a crucial determinant of which art objects, from all those created, the public will actually see. In addition, as Becker (1982) argues, artists may create their work with the needs of the distribution system in mind. In this way, the distribution system may indirectly affect the content of art works.

Art products are filtered as they move through the industry, so its structure will affect the pool of works available to the consumer. For instance, the rise of large, chain bookshops, like Barnes & Noble or Borders (in the US and elsewhere), or Waterstone's (in the UK), have cut the profit margins of smaller, independently owned bookshops, driving some out of business (Coser et al., 1982: 336). As a result, the chains, which stock the same titles in all their shops nationwide (and even internationally) have reduced the overall range of titles available to readers.[3]

Input/output strategies

Business managers wish to make a profit. A good way of doing this is giving customers what they want. However, as Hirsch argues, a striking characteristic of cultural industries is how poorly they are able to predict customer desires. In the music industry, ninety percent of album releases fail to make any profit – approximately ten percent of albums make money, ten percent just cover costs, and the rest are loss-making. Sixty percent of singles are never played over the air, on juke boxes, or by consumers (Frith, 1978 [1981]: 147). A similar situation exists in publishing, movies, the visual arts, and indeed, in all cultural industries.

What customers prefer to buy and what they are willing to buy are components of the demand for a product. Cultural industries are characterized by *demand uncertainty*. As a result they often produce too much or too little of the product, and are thus, inefficient. The cultural industries know that a few of their products will make a big splash, that a modest proportion will achieve modest sales, and that the vast majority will sink like a stone. But unfortunately, they are not very good at predicting *which* albums or books will sell.

Hirsch describes the strategies firms use to cope with this situation and to produce reliable revenues. The first strategy is *overproduction*. The cultural industries deliberately produce more books or records than can do well. The success of a few items subsidizes the rest. To be sure, companies do not produce books or records that they actually believe will fail. Countless authors, musicians, and others can attest to the fact that publishers and recording companies are not shy about turning manuscripts and demo tapes away. Rather, in the book and music industries, where production costs are relatively low, firms accept submissions that they believe are good enough to succeed. Yet they know that, in fact, most of those submissions will not. (Denisoff, 1986, calls this the "buckshot" approach.) Cultural industries transfer risk and costs onto artists. They usually pay on a royalty basis, so that artists who do not sell do not get paid.

The industries also try to reproduce hits by copying successful formulas. If a movie that is based on a 1960s cartoon show becomes a blockbuster film, it is a good bet that other movies based on 1960s cartoon shows will start to appear. If television's big hit one season is a medical drama, other medical dramas are sure to appear. In Hirsch's terms, through their strategy of copying what has already been successful, cultural industries process *fads and fashions*. Cultural industries also use a strategy of "recombinant formulae" (Gitlin, 1983) where elements from two or more successful genres are combined into a new offering.

The second strategy, according to Hirsch, is *selective promotion*. Cultural industries do not have unlimited advertising budgets, so they use the bulk of their advertising to support the products that they think are most likely to be successful. They tend to back products that have a history of success. Stephen King's newest novel will get more backing than the first novel of an unknown author. Books in genres or styles that are currently hot get more backing than selections in other genres. Books that are already selling well will get further promotion and those that are not are dropped. Indeed, books that do not sell well in the *first few weeks* are not seen as likely ever to sell well, and no further effort is made to promote them (Ohmann, 1983). In this way, an artist's success in the cultural industry depends quite a bit on luck. In many ways, writing a bestseller can be like winning the lottery.[4]

Recording company executives say that no amount of publicity will make a weak product sell, but that without publicity, even the best products are doomed to failure (Ryan and Peterson, 1982: 19). It may seem unfair, then, to release individual products without promotion or to withdraw promotional support the instant the product fails to sell, but by industry standards it is just good business practice. It may also seem that the cultural objects produced by such industries would become stale, as successful formats are copied and recopied. This certainly can occur, though cultural producers do try to inject something new into the current formula, if only to differentiate their product, if not to maintain customer interest. Moreover, consumers can and do move on when they find something is getting old and boring. When customers move on, firms start looking for the next successful genre. The strategy of overproducing helps in this regard as well by allowing the industries to capture "surprise" hits. Once a product starts to sell well, firms capitalize on this by promoting it more heavily. Selective promotion, then, means not only that the industry initially backs only the products they think will win, but that they are also quick to drop losers and to pick up on successes they had not anticipated.

The final strategy that industries employ, according to Hirsch, is to rely on the skills of *boundary personnel*, whom Hirsch calls "contact men." These are the people who work on the boundary between the organization and its input side (that is, they work directly with authors, bands, their agents or their managers) and on the boundary between the organization and its output (that is, with wholesale distributors or retail outlets; critics, reviewers, disk jockeys, and other "surrogate consumers"; and consumers). On the input side, contact personnel, such as editors and talent scouts, seek out new authors and bands. On the output side, the contact personnel, such as marketing and publicity experts, promote the product. Crucially, they need to elicit reviews and, for popular music, radio airplay. A book review in the *Times Literary Supplement* or *The New York Review of Books* is highly desirable. Interestingly, the fact that the book is reviewed is more important to sales than whether the review is positive or negative (though the former is preferable).[5] Attention is what matters most, as can be seen when controversy (which generates free publicity in the form of news coverage) increases sales. Publicity and promotion is of such importance that most cultural industries allocate a high proportion of their spending to advertising. For a heavily promoted film, for instance, as much as one-third of its costs will be for advertising (Monaco, 1979).

Subsequent research has examined gatekeeping in more detail, showing, for instance, that the personal concerns of book editors – a desire for prestige or a preference for working on projects they initiate rather than following up on inherited projects – can take precedence over the priorities of the organization, the artists, or the audience (Coser et al., 1982).

The cultural industries use market research extensively, but this has not allowed them to overcome the problem of demand uncertainty. Accurate prediction of demand is difficult, not only because of the fickleness of consumers, but also because of uncertainty involved in collecting and analyzing market figures and in evaluating the products themselves, even post hoc (Anand and Peterson, 2000). As Lampel et al. (2000: 264) put it: "Opinions about quality can diverge so strongly that producers find it hard to figure out why some products do well while others do not. . . . This is rarely due to lack of data – plenty of data are usually available – but because the data [are] susceptible to multiple and contradictory interpretations [which] produce ambiguity that impacts on the ability of managers to make well-informed decisions."

Further, businesses may carry out market research, but they also *imagine* their audiences as they choose works to produce. This is Radway's (1988a) point in her study of the editors of the Book of the Month Club. The Club chooses a selection of "high quality" books, one designated as the "book of the month," to offer for sale to members. About twenty people, located in midtown Manhattan, choose the Club's books from typescripts or galley proofs of books soon to be published. Their choices rely on their own sense of cultural and aesthetic excellence, but also their personal opinion of what their readers want: "[B]ecause the membership of the Club is broader, more diverse and dispersed than they are, the editors control or reign in their own preferences and attempt to read as they believe their 'general' readers do. When asked whether they consider their own taste representative of the reader' tastes, nearly all the editors replied that only a small segment of the membership shares their preferences. Their assumption results regularly in a winnowing process based on their perception of the nature of a 'popular,' though again middle-class taste" (p. 160).[6]

Griswold (1992b) shows that stereotypes can influence the gatekeeping process. She argues that British and American publishers assume that Nigerian fiction deals with issues of colonialism and the encroachment of modernity on village life. As a result, a large proportion of Nigerian fiction published in the US and the UK deal with these themes. In striking contrast, the fiction published in Nigeria (in English) is more likely to deal with urban themes. In effect, British and American publishers choose a biased sample of the books available based on their attraction to art that "makes sense" to them.

In earlier work, Griswold (1981) examined the differences between British and American novels. Some authors have argued that the differences reflect differences in the "national character" of the two countries. Griswold traces them to more prosaic effects of the publishing industry. Because copyright law in America did not cover foreign authors until 1891, American firms could publish British works with no copyright fee; consequently, publishers had little incentive to pay American authors for original books unless the books had unusual themes or plots which were not found in British fiction. Griswold demonstrates that the content of American and British novels converge after 1891, when American copyright law began to protect all works, including foreign ones. Thus, Griswold demonstrates a gatekeeping effect of publishers who chose to pirate British work and to publish (and pay for) only distinctive American novels. She also suggests that American novelists might have responded by choosing to write distinctive novels in order to sell their work.

Research on industry gatekeeping is important because it highlights the importance of the firms that take an art work from the creator to the audience. It is not enough to look at just the development of an innovation by the creator or its acceptance by an audience. As Hirsch (p. 640) puts it:

> In modern, industrial societies, the production and distribution of both fine art and popular culture entail relationships among a complex network of organizations which both facilitate and regulate the innovation process. Each object must be "discovered," sponsored, and brought to public attention by entrepreneurial organizations or nonprofit agencies before the originating artist or writer can be linked successfully to the intended audience.

Decision chains

Hirsch focused on the input and output sides of cultural businesses, ignoring the internal workings, or the "throughput." Peterson (1994), on the other hand, highlights the importance of the internal process in his discussion of "decision chains." A *decision chain* refers to all the decisions which affect art objects as they move through the industry system. Thus, Peterson highlights not only filtering processes but also situations where the product is changed, sometimes significantly, as it is produced.

Ryan and Peterson (1982) discuss the decision chains that are common in the production of country music, and how songs are selected, molded, or redrafted at each step in the process. Songs are usually written by songwriters who are represented by music publishers. Some songwriters write under contract to the publishers and others write independently and then submit their work for consideration. Publishers accept only a small number of submitted songs, and they sometimes ask songwriters to revise their works, in major or minor ways. Publishers then place songs in a catalogue for distribution, and they also pitch songs to potential singers, making demonstration tapes ("demos") of a small proportion of new songs for this purpose. How the demo is made can affect the fate of the song. Some demos are simple (a singer and an acoustic guitar); others are more polished, with more complex orchestration. The simple ones allow potential singers to imagine a greater range of possible interpretations, and thus may appeal to more singers, but the polished ones, which already suggest a style, sound better and are more likely to be picked up by one of the (fewer) singers who work in that particular style. Publishers, of course, pitch some demos harder than others.

Singers, their own producers, and their managers are active in the choice of songs. They both select and, less often, rewrite songs. When they rewrite, they demand co-writer credit, and an accompanying portion of the royalties, from the songwriter. One producer, known for routinely making changes on selected songs, says his motives are "purely altruistic and commercial" (Ryan and Peterson, p. 17). By this oxymoron, he means that he insists only on "changes that I think will help the song become a hit," thereby benefiting the songwriter (not to mention himself).

Once chosen by a singer, the recording company produces the song. Many actors are involved in this, and "the meaning of the song is inevitably shaped and interpreted by the way it is recorded" (p. 17). During recording, producers keep in mind that songs need to be less than three minutes long in order to have a shot at radio airplay, where short songs are the norm. After production, records (or tapes or CDs) need to be manufactured and distributed. Major recording companies own such facilities, but independent labels must contract for these services, meaning that recordings made by major companies are manufactured more promptly and efficiently and distributed more effectively.

Songs can be released as album cuts or as singles. Though consumers buy more albums, singles receive more promotion, because in country music, radio airplay is based on singles, and radio airplay drives sales. Recording companies selectively promote these singles, some extensively and others not. They may also decide not to produce a single, thereby killing the potential for the song's commercial success.

A story will clarify this process, as described so far, and its impact. In Ryan and Peterson's words:

> The fate of the song "New York Town," written by James Talley, illustrates some of the ways in which both the content and exposure of a song can be shaped [through decision chains]. As written and performed by Talley, the song recounts in somber tones the observations of a country person viewing all the exotic, fascinating, and frightening people that walk the streets of New York. Johnny Paycheck's manager decided the song would be the perfect lead song for an album that Paycheck was recording live at the Lone Star Cafe, New York's leading "urban cowboy" club. The negative or critical images were all omitted, and Paycheck sang the song in his rousing, up-tempo, honky-tonk style as a city-billy anthem of New York. While the album was called "New York Town," the promoters refused to release the song as a single, explaining to Talley that the song . . . would not be a successful single for national release because it would not be played often by radio stations outside New York. (p. 20)

Most country radio stations are commercial, earning revenues through advertising. This creates an interesting twist in that "more men than women . . . are fans of country music . . . , [but] most advertisers want to attract women between the ages of 25 and 49, and, as a consequence [the country music industry does not] accept songs which portray women in a negative light. . . . Women are portrayed as tempted and long suffering, but only men are played as weak, drunken, guilty bounders. . . . Thus the interests of Proctor and Gamble, Burger King, and the local drugstore impinge directly upon the aesthetics of country music" (Ryan and Peterson, p. 21).

The decision chain model also reminds us that cultural firms are not monolithic. Instead, they are made up of factions. Indeed, publishing is set up on an internal market basis, where editors must "sell" their choices to the editorial board, and subsequently, to the marketing department (Coser et al., 1982). Thurston (1987) argues that gender can be a factor in publishers' decision making. Harlequin romances followed a "sweet" formula when editors were primarily male. As female editors became more influential in the company, they promoted a more erotic "bodice-ripper" genre, but it took them some time to convince the male-dominated marketing department that the largely female readership of these novels would want more explicit story-lines.

Ryan and Wentworth (1999: 185–8) tell the story of how the book manu-script for the bestseller *Jaws* (which was later made into a movie), developed and was dramatically changed from its initial proposal to the finished product. The author was given an advance contract on the basis of a one-page proposal, but the manuscript went through two complete and one partial re-writes before the editor brought it to the editorial board. In addition, the book's title was changed several times, and its cover was altered at the request of district sales representatives. The book went on to break sales records, as did the subsequent movie.

In addition to illustrating the effects of decision chains, this example brings us to the blockbuster phenomenon. Here, publishers seek to find the next mega-bestseller, which will be tied into a television or film version of the book (Coser et al, 1982: 214–22). The search for blockbusters is not limited to publishing, of course, and cultural industries from Hollywood movies (Baker and Faulkner, 1991) to art museums (Alexander, 1996a, b) pursue this strategy. Unfortunately for cultural industries, they cannot reliably predict the actual level of success a potential blockbuster will have despite the extra effort put into shaping them.

While pursuing blockbusters, cultural industries also look for potential synergies between their products and those of other industries. A *synergy* refers to a combination that generates more than the sum of its parts. In business, synergies are links that generate higher profits at little extra cost. A clear example is music videos, which provide content for music television which, in turn, promotes music sales for the companies that produce the videos (Lopes, 1992). Other examples include product spin-offs from children's television and movies such as toys, both for retail sale and giveaways at fast food restaurants. Synergies can affect the cultural product as producers think early on about future possibilities. For instance, characters in children's movies may be designed specifically so they can become toys. Some best-selling authors in the thriller genre seem to write their books as if they were writing movie scripts. The tapping of synergies results both from a refinement of managerial skill in the cultural industries and also from multimedia mergers and conglomerate ownership patterns (Eisenmann and Bower, 2000).

The oligopoly model

Crane (1992), drawing on the important work by Peterson and Berger (1975; discussed in case study 6.1), describes what she terms the *oligopoly model*. The term "oligopoly" refers to a concentrated industry, one which is controlled by a few firms, in contrast to a competitive industry. Economists measure the level of oligopoly as the proportion of the industry's market held by the top four (or eight) largest firms. The idea is that a competitive market allows for more artistic innovation and leads to a larger range of products offered. This is because marketing new, innovative products is risky and firms do not need to accept this risk if they already control a large market share. Big firms compete among themselves for market share using the same set of safe formula, rather than trying to create new markets through innovations. Peterson and Berger demonstrate that, between 1948 and 1973, in periods of competition in the recording industry there was a higher level of diversity in the top selling records than in periods of industry concentration. Similar effects are evident in the film industry (Mezias and Mezias, 2000; Crane, 1992: 51–61).

The oligopoly model has been critiqued by a number of different authors. Frith (1978 [1981]), for instance, argues that the cultural industries cannot be as powerful as some authors suggest, precisely because of the demand uncertainty described by Hirsch. Even an oligopoly of firms cannot dictate their tastes to the public. More recent research (Lopes, 1992) suggests that the level of diversity in the music industry has gone up in recent decades, as has industry concentration. This is because cultural industries, like other firms, no longer try to mass market their product. Instead, they are much more adept at marketing a variety of products to different market niches (smaller, more segmented audiences with specialized tastes).

Recently, many observers have suggested that there is reason for concern about the level of concentration not just within single industries, but across them. Global entertainment companies now have holdings in industries as diverse as television, newspapers, magazines, books, music, movies, internet, and theme parks. A key concern in this area of research relates to the news media and the possibility for freedom of information when all sources of news are controlled by the same few media giants. More relevant to our interests, this strand of research follows the oligopoly model in suggesting that large conglomerates distribute bland and undifferentiated cultural products worldwide, driving out indigenous forms and homogenizing what remains. It also suggests that such conglomerates hegemonically promote the interests of capitalism. (These ideas were anticipated by Adorno and the Frankfurt School, as discussed in chapter 3.)

Herman and McChesney (1997: 1) report that the "global media system is dominated by three or four dozen large transnational corporations..., with fewer than ten mostly US-based media conglomerates towering over the global market." They carefully document this increasing concentration and, relatedly, the deregulation of media industries. From their comparative case studies of several countries (US, Canada, Brazil, Great Britain, Italy, New Zealand, India, and Barbados, Jamaica, and other Caribbean islands), they conclude:

> media globalization effects, while still hard to sort out, are dominated by commercialization and its impact on the public sphere.... There is a strong tendency in the globalizing process for advertiser preferences for light fare to prevail, giving zero weight to the positive externalities of public service programming, and at the same time giving full play to audience-attracting programs featuring sex and violence, all in accord with market logic. Put otherwise, the globalizing media treat audiences as consumers, not as citizens, and they are most attentive to those with high incomes. (p. 188)

McChesney (1999) follows up on this comparative work with an in-depth study of consolidation and its effects on democracy, specifically in the United States. His project is to encourage citizens to mobilize politically to re-structure the media along more democratic lines. In a book on the larger issue of the proliferation of corporate brands, Klein (2000) discusses the invasion of traditionally "unbranded space" by business firms. Not only have corporations increasingly sponsored pre-existing cultural events; they have begun to create their own branded entertainment which allows them a greater ability to place their own interests first. For instance, the Miller Beer company has mounted "Blind Date Concerts" in which the high-profile musicians who play (past acts have included David Bowie, the Rolling Stones, Soundgarden, and INXS) are not named until the audience turns up (Klein, p. 48–9). Here the brand trumps the band.

Not everybody accepts the argument that consolidation has ill effects on either consumers or art. Some argue that current megamergers in the media industries may pose a concern, but not because they will provide a homogenized and narrow range of products. As Hirsch (2000) points out, production, marketing, and management techniques improved during the twentieth century. The "mass culture" produced in the 1940s (when, in America, there were three radio networks, four major record companies, five big movie studios and, of course, virtually no television) began to diversify and segment in the 1950s to the 1970s. Currently, Hirsch suggests, cultural industries produce art that is highly customized to an audience segment.

Differences Among Cultural Industries

The concepts of industry system, gatekeeping, input/output strategies, and decision chains apply to all cultural industries. So far, we have drawn examples largely from the publishing and music industries. The specific dynamics of a number of these effects, especially the strategy of overproduction, apply best to what Hirsch calls the "speculative and entrepreneurial segments" of the cultural industries, especially "adult trade books, popular records, and low-budget movies" (p. 655). A brief comparison with other culture producing industries – Hollywood movies, broadcast television, and art dealerships – will highlight similarities and differences.

Hollywood Movies

The most notable aspect of the Hollywood movie industry is that their products are expensive to make. For instance, *Waterworld*, in 1998 cost a reported $155 million; *Titanic*, even more. Even independent films can be costly to make; for instance, the surprise hit, *Four Weddings and a Funeral* cost approximately $3 million. Unlike publishers and recording companies, Hollywood filmmakers cannot target their products to smaller, specialized audience segments, and they cannot afford overproduction as a primary strategy.[7] Instead, in order to make a profit, they must create a product which appeals to large numbers of people internationally. And they must try to make each expensive blockbuster as successful as possible, and cannot leave much to chance.[8] They do this through a variety of strategies, for instance, heavy advertising and "hype" about a new film, casting known stars in the key roles, and sending the stars out on the interview circuit when the film is due for release. Hollywood also routinely uses market research to gauge the potential of finished films by showing rough cuts of movies to test audiences to see how they will react. If this procedure turns up problems, filmmakers have to consider the expensive prospect of changing the movie's contents, which does occur (see box 6.1). Even films which do not do as well as expected must be milked for all the profits they can yield. *Waterworld*, which was the most expensive film produced at the time it was released, was considered a failure at the box–office because the audience it attracted, while large, was not large enough. The company that produced it went bankrupt as a result. However, it has subsequently made money for its distributors (MCA/Universal) through overseas and video sales and through synergy, for instance, the attraction at the Universal Studios Hollywood theme park described in the epigraph.

Box 6.1   Change in the Film *Fatal Attraction*

The story of the movie *Fatal Attraction* illustrates the effects of decision chains in the movie industry and the lengths to which producers must go in order to maximize the appeal of their product.

The movie was based on a short story, in which an evil, philandering husband seduces a young innocent. She does not understand the terms of the affair – that it is supposed to be temporary and discrete – and is hurt when he drops her. She begins to obsess about him; eventually, he goes to her apartment, where she is about to kill herself with a knife. He takes the knife away from her, but after he leaves, she commits suicide anyway. His fingerprints are found on the knife, however, and at the end of the story, he is taken away by the police. The moral of the story is "you get what you deserve."

The movie cast Michael Douglas as the philanderer. Douglas did not wish to play such a terrible character and, under his influence, the script was changed and his character softened into a nicer guy. The affair with the woman, played by Glenn Close, was changed into his first and only affair, rather than just one among many. Further, Close's character was changed from a *naïve* to a worldly-wise business woman. She appears to understand exactly what a weekend fling is about. The rest of the story was filmed in close approximation to the short story.

When the movie was shown to test audiences before its release, however, the audiences did not like the movie. They thought that Close's actions in stalking him and – famously, in boiling his children's pet rabbit in their own kitchen – was more than sufficient payment for Douglas's single indiscretion with her. Being sent to prison for murder was far too much. So at great expense, the end of the movie was re-shot to show that after his arrest, Douglas was found innocent and released from custody. Even with this change, a second set of test audiences did not like the ending. They still thought that Douglas's character had paid too high a price for a brief affair. So the ending was changed again. This time, after Douglas visits her apartment and takes away the knife, Close does not kill herself. Instead, horror-movie style, she goes to Douglas's house to kill his wife. She is finally subdued and drowned in the bathtub. The movie went on to be a big hit.

Hollywood movies, once mass-produced in the studio system, are now custom made in "network organizations" based on short-term contracts with actors and other talent (Christopherson and Storper, 1989). In the old Hollywood system, the studios kept a stable of actors, and other talent, on exclusive contract and they fully owned distributors and cinemas. The industry was profitable and reasonably predictable. Phillips (1982: 331) estimates that during this time nine out of ten Hollywood movies were profitable. This changed after antitrust law was used to break up the old Hollywood system in 1949. At the same time, film became increasing vulnerable to the competition from television. As a result, the industry became much more uncertain, with only ten percent of releases making money (Phillips, 1982: 331). Hollywood is a concentrated industry, however. Due to the high cost of making a popular movie, there are strong "barriers to entry" – a term from economics that means that competing firms cannot start up easily.[9] Hollywood also has strong links to its well-developed, worldwide distribution system. Movies are thought up, produced, and distributed within the industry; consequently it influences the content of films through decision chains (changing the product), more than through gatekeeping (filtering products).

Television

The television industry faces a different set of constraints, as illustrated by the American television industry (Cantor and Cantor, 1992; Gitlin, 1983).[10] Their products are expensive to produce, compared to books and recordings, but not nearly on the scale of big-budget films. As with movies, relatively high "barriers to entry" exist for competitors, though this has more to do with government regulation of the airwaves (and cable and satellite) than with the cost of production. Cable and satellite television is now said to "narrowcast" to more specialized audiences, as compared to broadcast television. These new television delivery methods have reduced the major networks' share of viewers and changed some of the incentives in the industry (Blumler, 1991). However, television's audience segments are not as narrow as those for music or fiction, and this can be said not only for broadcast, but also for so-called narrowcast television.

Television networks are the most highly regulated of the cultural industries. In addition to legal requirements, such as copyright, that affect all cultural industries, television must also follow government regulations in order to obtain or retain their licenses. Requirements to avoid certain types of violence, sex, and swearing during the early evening, or to broadcast educational programming for children, can directly affect the content of programs. In addition, a large number of special interest organizations, concerned about such issues as the welfare of children, religion and morality, the depiction of violence, or the portrayal of specific social groups, also monitor and lobby the television industry.

Gitlin (1983) shows that the television industry chases fads and fashions, as one successful show spawns both imitators in the same genre and direct spin-offs. New shows are often created by combining aspects of two currently fashionable formulae. Network executives are limited in their ability to over-produce shows because airtime is fixed, but they do overproduce in the early stage of the process by commissioning more pilots than they accept for production. They also selectively promote shows by placing them in beneficial or detrimental time slots. Gitlin also reports that broadcast television shows are created by a very small group of people; only about one-hundred writers work regularly in the industry.

Bielby and Bielby (1994) study the development of series for prime time network television, focusing on the decisions of television programmers (who work for one of the four networks) as to which pilots (made, for the most part, by independent writer-producers) should be developed into network series. Such a decision is "simultaneously a choice about a commercial commodity, an aesthetic endeavor, and a social institution" (p. 1290). It also takes place in the context of uncertainty:

> An experienced programmer can probably distinguish well-crafted from medi-ocre scripts and make informed judgments about the quality of acting, editing, and direction of a pilot. Nevertheless, the programmer has no reliable basis for predicting whether audiences, advertisers, and critics will accept the series. In the words of [one television executive], "All hits are flukes." (p. 1290)

In acting as intermediaries between the networks and the writer–producers, programmers do not weigh commercial and creative aspects equally, however. Commercial interests come first, as this is how programmers are judged by their bosses in the television networks.

Bielby and Bielby examine 112 synopses of pilots provided by the four networks in March 1991. The synopses appear in press kits given to advertising executives in the spring, to promote the (as yet incomplete) programming strategy for the subsequent season. The synopses provide information on all commissioned pilots, only some of which are chosen for broadcast.[11] Bielby and Bielby demonstrate that programmers choose shows based on the track record of the show's producer, strongly preferring shows produced by those with prior successes. The fact that a pilot might be similar in content to previously successful products, in television or in other media, did not affect programmers' choices.[12] Series that were seen as more commercially risky (those that had unproven producers or that deviated from established genres)[13] were more likely to be chosen as midseason replacements, debuting part-way through the winter, rather than as season premieres in the fall.

A major component of broadcast television is advertising.[14] While the other cultural industries may wish to maximize sales, which tends to mean maximizing audience size, commercial television needs to maximize advertising revenues. As a result, television shows must not only appeal to large audiences, but to the "right" audiences. Many advertisers prefer to focus on young consumers in their twenties, who have more disposable income than other age groups. As a result, advertising forces television executives to aim more shows to specific demographic groups at the expense of other groups in society.[15]

Broadcast television has expended a good deal of effort on trying to measure its audience (Gunter, 2000; Ang, 1991), through surveys, diaries, and people-meters. It faces special difficulties in this because it cannot rely on direct market indicators, as can the publishing, music, and film industries. None of the methods devised gives complete data.

Art dealers

Art dealers sell original artworks in varied markets (K. Peterson, 1997; Plattner, 1996; Moulin, 1987). A few important dealerships sell art in an international market, but most are geared towards their local market. The market is divided into two segments, a high price, relatively low uncertainty market selling established (consecrated) works and old masters, and a more uncertain, but lower cost market for contemporary works. There are a large number of art dealers in the latter category, because barriers to entry are low. Art dealers sell more "customized" products than other cultural industries (though fads and fashions are sometimes evident) and sell to very narrow market segments. Contemporary art dealers are speculators. They take on a good deal of risk when taking on a new artist, so they cannot take on too many. As in other culture industries, dealers pass on some of that risk to the artist and request a high commission on sales (from about 30 percent to 50 percent of the sales price). They also selectively promote the artists in their stable, both in choosing which of their artists to exhibit in the showroom and also in subtly steering collectors to the works of certain artists. As the dealership and the number of its artists is small, and the exhibition schedule visible, these tactics often create conflict between the artist and the dealer. But, mitigating this, dealers often provide emotional and intellectual support to their artists.

An important difference between art dealers and other cultural industries is that art dealers are selling products with respect to a long-term horizon rather than a short-term one. Dealers may hold onto paintings while they appreciate in value. They market their products with reference to the investment value of the product, and the deep aesthetic experience it provides, rather than the transitory enjoyment to be had from, say, a book or record. They also cultivate long-term relationships with their customers (Fitz Gibbon, 1987). Since they have a direct relationship with collectors, they rely less on surrogate consumers in the media. Indeed, Simpson (1981) reports that Manhattan dealers specializing in avant-garde art view the art critics as out of date. Nevertheless, art dealers can use the help of other organizations in publicizing their works. Dealers that can afford it advertise in the national arts press. Art museums are especially important to art dealers. When museums have shows of living artists, works by such artists often increase in value. Moreover, artists cannot become established, or remembered by history, without works in museum collections. So dealers, if they possess the right contacts, also cultivate museum curators along with collectors.

The Profit Motive

What all business firms share is the profit motive. To survive, cultural firms need to fit artistic production with the requirements of the marketplace. To some critics, the very idea of generating profits from art makes all cultural firms suspect, and by extension, it debases all commercially produced art. As Fiske (1989: 4–5) points out:

> Behind such arguments lie two romantic fantasies that originate at opposite ends of the cultural spectrum – at one end that of the penniless artists, dedicated only to the purity and aesthetic transcendence of his (for the vision is a patriarchal one) art, and at the other that of a folk art in which all members of the tribe participate equally in producing and circulating their culture, free of any commercial taint.

He concludes, "Our culture is a commodity culture, and it is fruitless to argue against it on the basis that culture and profit are mutually exclusive terms" (p. 4).

Nevertheless, tensions exist between the creation of art and the generation of profit; each of these aspects of a cultural firm requires different resources and is judged by different criteria. The balance between these two varies across industries, and across sectors within industries. Faulkner and Anderson (1987), for instance, show that Hollywood producers, directors, and cinematographers are rewarded for financial success, not artistic integrity. On the other hand, Baumann (2001) illustrates the creation of an intellectual discourse of film and demonstrates that many films are appreciated as expressive art rather than as mass entertainment. Coser et al. (1982) suggest that the publishing industry can be roughly divided into two segments, "production-oriented" publishers who seek short-term profit in the mass market, and "consumer-oriented" publishers whose time horizon is longer and who publish "literature" that is "aesthetically legitimate." Art dealers work very hard to avoid the appearance of commercial interests. They are influenced by the ideal "moral role of dealer" (K. Peterson, 1997; Moulin, 1987), in which dealers altruistically promote artists for the sheer love of art. For instance, most dealers do not post prices (a tactic which not only preserves the symbolic value of the art work, but also which allows dealers to vary the price of works depending on their assessment of the collector who shows an interest). But dealers are *businesspeople* who "work hard to preserve an image of *amateur*. . . . [D]iscretion is at a premium: the aura of art serves the dual purpose of preserving a moral image and of allowing for the backstage handling of 'impure' business matters" (K. Peterson, 1997: 252).

Along these lines, it is worth pointing out that the image of the cultural industries producing bland or derivative objects because of innate philistinism, or cynicism about the general public, is a distorted stereotype. Parts of it may perhaps fit some people in the cultural industries, but one would imagine that the majority of people working in these industries genuinely want to produce good, varied work, even though they are constrained by commercial pressures. As management professors Lampel, Lant, and Shamsie (2000: 263) write, managers "must build creative systems to support and market cultural products but not allow the system to suppress individual inspiration, which is ultimately at the root of creating value in the cultural industries." Cultural firms wish to make a profit, and will go out of business if they fail to do so. They will produce complex, interesting work if that is what sells. But as we have seen, the uncertainty that characterizes most cultural businesses pushes in the direction of safe bets and away from risky ones. Under these conditions, innovative work may be undervalued.

Conclusion

In contemporary society, business firms are at the center of the distribution system for a large range of the arts. The businesses have a profound effect on the art consumed by audiences, both indirectly through their filtering effects as gatekeepers and directly through their impact on products in decision chains. A number of factors are relevant to understanding cultural industries and their effects on art. These include the cost of producing each object, the level of competition in the industry, the amount that the design of a cultural object can change during its production, and the legal and regulatory environment of the industry. In addition, the personal views and assumptions of the gatekeepers at various levels affect their choices of what to pass along to the next step in the process.

All cultural industries can be seen as complex systems, with a variety of different components, that move artworks from their original creators to their ultimate consumers. Many of the same processes occur across industries, but the details obviously vary considerably from industry to industry. The profit motive characterizes the firms in cultural industries; profit takes precedence. This can – and does – conflict with artistic integrity, but as we have seen, both the managers and creative personnel seek to balance these two imperatives. Cultural industries do not purposefully quash creativity or innovation, since these are *the* source of value in the industry. Nevertheless, for many observers, artistic excellence is compromised in many profit seeking businesses and industries.

NOTES

1   This was discussed in chapter 3, on shaping approaches. I will revisit the issue of the distinctions among the fine, popular, and folk arts in chapter 12, and examine some of the reasons that the popular arts are dismissed as "low" or "mass" forms.
2   I give here only a brief overview of a few, important cultural industries. A full description of even these few would be an impossible task for a chapter of this length.
3   Internet-based companies, such as Amazon.com, offer a larger range of titles than the local chain bookstore. However, internet sales are different than store sales, as the customer cannot browse a book's contents as they can in a shop. (They can, however, search for known titles much more effectively on the web.)
4   In an interview on Radio 4's *Desert Island Disks*, J. K. Rowling (author of the *Harry Potter* books) agreed that she felt lucky that her books were recognized and that they sold well. She nevertheless dismissed the idea that her success was like winning a lottery because, she said, she had worked extremely hard to write her books and make them good, implying, therefore, that her success was deserved.
5   See Shrum (1991) on the effects of critics on the performing arts.
6   In relationship to Radway's argument, see Powell's (1988) argument that the Book of the Month Club's main product is not books, but its own middlebrow *taste* in books.
7   They do use overproduction to some extent, however. For instance, some films are capitalized at much higher levels than others; most low-budget films are neither promoted nor find a wide audience.
8   Movie companies do, however, have relationships with independent movie producers that allow them to capture the surprise hits mentioned by Hirsch. They also do make mistakes. Some movies turn out so poor that they are never released to domestic movie theaters, but are instead released straight onto the video market, where the unwary may rent them.

9   On the relationships among the major companies and independent producers, see Aksoy and Robins (1992).

10   See Abercrombie (1996) for a discussion of television starting from a British perspective.

11   As in other cultural industries, television networks whittle down the number of potential series at each step in the selection process:

> Each year, the four networks evaluate thousands of concepts for new series and purchase approximately 600 pilot scripts. From these, the networks select about 20% to be produced as pilots at the networks' expense. About one-third of the pilots eventually appear on the prime-time schedule. For example, of the 112 pilots commissioned by ABC, CBS, NBC, and Fox for 1991, 23 debuted in the fall and another 15 were scheduled as midseason replacements. (Bielby and Bielby, 1994, p. 1288)

12   Note that Bielby and Bielby analyzed the *claims* that a new show is similar to others, as evidenced by the press kit summaries. They did not attempt to investigate independently whether or not shows mentioned as similar actually were so.

13   Shows that deviate from established genres might potentially be the most innovative programs. If so, this would lend some support to the argument that networks quash innovation, as midseason replacements have lower odds of success. These shows are not as strongly promoted as season premieres, nor do they have as much time to build up an audience before spring cancellation decisions are made. Nevertheless, it is important to recognize that Bielby and Bielby did not establish the actual level of innovation in pilots or new series.

14   Advertisers are also important to commercial radio, where they can affect the content of songs played on air, by withdrawing support when controversial songs are played, or more commonly, by requiring that songs be short enough to allow for advertisements to be interspersed with music. Advertisers play a role in movies through what is known as "product placement" in the films.

15   Noncommercial television, such as America's public television and the BBC stations in the UK, face different pressures, most notably their need to secure continued funding, for instance, by the government. Because of this, noncommercial television is often more like the nonprofit organizations discussed in chapter 7 than other cultural industries. However, the rise of corporate sponsorship of American public television has forced the Public Broadcasting System and its local affiliates to attend to commercial concerns, as sponsors make demands for, say, uncontroversial shows, just as advertisers on commercial television do (Hoynes, 1994). (This is a common situation for most nonprofit cultural organizations, as we shall see.)

Case Study 6.1
Innovation and Diversity in the Production of Music

Points for Discussion

1 What is the "Oligopoly Model"? According to Peterson and Berger, how does industry structure affect music? Why does Lopes disagree with Peterson and Berger's findings?
2 What other factors might be important in the changes described by Peterson and Berger and by Lopes? For instance, have audiences changed between 1948 and the present? Have musicians changed? Where does innovation come from?
3 What does the case suggest about current trends towards large media firms buying each other up? Should we worry about the effects of large multinational firms that own television networks, radio stations, book publishing, movie production, and internet access?
4 When you purchase popular music, do you believe that you "get what you want"? Do you "want what you get"? Would you want something different?

Case

Peterson and Berger (1975) tested the idea that the structure of a cultural industry might affect the kinds of art objects it produced. Specifically, they examined the recording industry and its effects on the diversity of records released. They hypothesized that greater competition among the firms in the industry would lead to more innovation in musical styles. This idea has come to be known as the "Oligopoly Model" (Crane, 1992: 49–51).

Their hypothesis was confirmed, using the following methods. They studied a segment of the American popular music industry from 1948 to 1973, firms that released "singles" (a 45 rpm record with just one song on each side). They counted the number of firms that had a hit single appearing on the weekly top ten list during the year. They then calculated the concentration of the industry based on the proportion of hit songs that were released by the biggest four and the biggest eight companies. An industry is said to be *concentrated* when a few firms, an *oligopoly*, control the market. In a concentrated market, the biggest firms own most of the hit songs. In contrast, an industry is said to be *competitive* when a larger number of firms are active and the market is not dominated by only a few firms. Peterson and Berger also looked at the level of *vertical integration*. The entire production process for any consumer product starts with the extraction of raw materials, moving through the processing and assembly of the product, through wholesale distribution and marketing, to retail sales. The more of these functions a firm controls, the higher its level of vertical integration.

Peterson and Berger suggest that the popular music industry goes through cycles of concentration and competition, and that the time period they studied can be divided into five phases. The first, from 1948 to 1955, was characterized by high levels of oligopoly (concentration). Vertical integration was also high as the record companies owned wholesale record distributors. They also shared corporate links with owners of radio stations who helped in the marketing of records by playing songs on the air. Many hit songs came from movies, and the firms had strong links with the movie industry, which itself had a high level of vertical integration at that time.

Peterson and Berger found that during these years popular music was homogeneous, as compared with later periods. Fewer songs made the number one position and fewer new performers appeared on the charts. They also claimed that the content of songs was more homogeneous, as measured by their lyrics. During this time, record sales dropped, even though attendance at live performances (of jazz, blues, gospel, country, and folk music) was strong. They argued, "the total market may be static or even shrink because potential customers, whose tastes are not met by the homogenized product, withdraw from the market. Thus, under conditions of oligopoly, there is hypothesized to be a growing unsated demand" (p. 163).

From 1956 to 1959 (the second period), there was an increase in competition in the industry. National radio stations failed to meet the competition of television, and radio programming shifted from centralized, network broadcasting to local, music-based formats. This loosened the big record companies' hold on marketing. Fewer people went to movies, also because of television. Movie companies stopped making movie musicals, and they expanded into recorded music, becoming direct competitors. Most importantly, small, independent record companies introduced a number of new, very successful performers and flourished as a result. Record sales grew. The strong growth in competition in the second period (1956–9) slowed in the next period, 1959–63. As the industry stabilized, the growth in record sales also slowed, but still, in the third period, the concentration ratios of the largest firms were at their lowest ever, about half the earliest era.

The fourth period, from 1964 to 1969, was a time of renewed growth in the industry, and was characterized by a great deal of innovation, most notably the music of the Beatles. Even though diversity of lyrics was at its highest and sales of singles had soared, after 1964 the industry began to concentrate again. The highest level of competition in the industry occurred during the third period, and since it *preceded* the creative explosion in the fourth one, Peterson and Berger argue that the competition *caused* the subsequent innovation and diversity in music, after a lag time in which artists adjusted to the new conditions.

In the final period studied by Peterson and Berger, 1970–3, the industry continued its trend toward oligopoly. (Specifically, larger companies tended to buy up smaller labels, although the labels retained a separate identity.) Peterson and Berger predicted that, as a result of this trend, music after 1973 would become more homogeneous.

In sum, Peterson and Berger claim support for the oligopoly model, since changes in industry structure came before changes in their measures of diversity. They believe the periods of slowed record sales indicate consumer's boredom with the music on offer.

They conclude: "Assertions that customers necessarily 'get what they want' or 'want what they get' are not supported" (p. 158).

A follow-up study by Lopes (1992) questions the oligopoly model, however. Lopes examined popular music from 1969 to 1990. He shows that music did not become increasingly homogeneous, as predicted by Peterson and Berger. Peterson and Berger use the terms "innovation" and "diversity" almost interchangeably. In contrast, Lopes measured "innovation" as the number of new performers entering the top hits, and "diversity" as the number of different hits at the top (either top ten or number one) each year. He also looks at two "innovative" styles that arose during the eighties: new wave music and rap. Lopes criticized Peterson and Berger for looking only at the sale of singles. Though there was a time when single records were the key to industry sales, by 1973 singles accounted for only 37 percent of recorded music sales, and had dropped to 12 percent of the market by 1988. Accordingly, Lopes examines both top-selling albums and the top ten from the charts (which are based not only on sales of singles, but also on radio airplay and juke box plays).

Lopes finds that, with his measures of both innovation and diversity, recorded music does not become homogeneous. He attributes this to a new strategy of music producers called the "open system." In this model, a few companies own a large number of different record labels. These labels have a high degree of freedom in choosing acts to develop. Once the acts are signed, however, the major companies manufacture and distribute the music (in the form of records, tapes, and CDs) more centrally, which allows for economies of scale. The big firms also buy out, or contract with, new, independent labels which successfully introduce new acts. In this way, "successful new artists and musical styles are quickly incorporated into the popular music market they effectively control" (p. 57). Lopes also suggests that a new format for showcasing popular music, television broadcast of music videos, sparked the interest of consumers in the types of music shown. Indeed, recording companies see music videos as a valuable marketing opportunity, analogous to radio airplay. Music television channels, therefore, play an important role as a gatekeeper in the industry system.

In sum, Lopes argues that "Peterson and Berger's model no longer adequately describes the industry" (p. 65). With respect to Lopes' study, however, Peterson (1994) has written, "there is reason to doubt [his] conclusions. . . . The high rate of turnover of hits on the 'Hot 100' may no longer indicate rapid aesthetic innovation but rather *aesthetic exhaustion* as trivially different songs quickly reach the top of the charts and as quickly fade because they are so derivative" (p. 176, emphasis original).

Neither of these studies measures innovation well. Peterson and Berger do not adequately distinguish innovation and diversity, assuming that (unmeasured) innovation preceeds measured diversity. However, a homogeneous, but changing, system may incorporate innovations more effectively over time than a diverse, but stagnant, one. Lopes does not tap "innovation" either. His measure (the number of new acts each year) is really a measure of turnover. Innovation happens outside, not inside, the industry system through artists in urban music scenes. Take, for example, the two innovative styles mentioned by Lopes, new wave and rap music. As Lopes points out, new wave sales increased after the Music Television Network (MTV) started to broadcast British music videos of new wave artists. MTV relied, in the early stage of its operations, on British artists because American artists and their recording companies had not yet produced a large stock of videos. However, as Hebdige (1979) argues, the commercially successful new wave musicians drew their inspiration from punk, a style which initially developed in urban youth subcultures in Britain. The story of rap music is more striking. As Lopes himself points out, rap "arose in urban 'alternative' music scenes during the late 1970s and early 1980s" (p. 67). Although the first rap hit to make the American charts appeared in 1984, rap did not show a sustained presence on the charts until 1989. Lopes suggests that this is because the playlist of MTV, the only national music video station in the United States, was quite narrow and excluded a large number of acts and music genres, especially music by women and black artists (p. 68). It was not until the development of additional, competing music video stations after 1985 that a wider variety of music was shown in this format.

In other words, the music industry does not produce innovations, although it may tap them. Once the innovations are pulled into the commercial system, the diversity of recorded music may increase as a consequence. The music industry plays a crucial, gatekeeping role in bringing music to the general public, nevertheless – and it can exclude innovations as well as include them. Lopes suggests that the "organization-market perspective" developed in Peterson and Berger's work "rejects the assumption, prevalent in both the mass society and culture industry perspectives, that large culture industries in modern capitalism tend toward the production of homogeneous, standardized cultural products" (p. 56). Nevertheless, Peterson and Berger's work raises concerns about *concentrated* culture industries, if not with competitive ones. The music industry can exert its power in a variety of ways. For instance, in 2000, a US government investigation found that big recording firms had kept the price of CDs artificially high in the US, by paying advertising costs of retailers who agreed not to discount their products. The companies have now paid a fine. A similar investigation is currently underway in the UK.

7

Networks and Nonprofits

[C]an private dollars – donated or earned through sale of services – be substituted for public without fundamentally changing the composition of organizations, programs, and activities that constitute the nonprofit arts sector in the United States? Can culture survive the marketplace?

(Paul DiMaggio, 1986: 68)

Artistic products can be distributed through for-profit business firms, both large and small. As we have seen in chapter 6, this arrangement often pits commercial interests against creative interests. Other ways to distribute art include social networks, on the one hand, and nonprofit enterprises or public trusts, on the other. Networks and nonprofits, by doing away with the profit motive, can be geared more closely to the creative interests of the participants. Indeed, some observers believe that "authentic" art (however that is defined) is produced only in systems with no commercial side. Network forms, those with the tightest links between artists and their audience, most closely approach this ideal, although they often reach only small audiences. Furthermore, while a few art networks may work independently of formal organizations, most are associated with small business firms, such as art dealers or venues such as clubs, or with nonprofit organizations. Nonprofit organizations may not be driven to accumulate an economic surplus, but as we shall see, they must meet other challenges which make it difficult for them to be "pure" in the idealistic understanding of authentic art. Moreover, philanthropists and other funders of nonprofit organizations have ideas about how the organizations should run. Governments often support art through funding nonprofit organizations or establishing public trusts. Government interests in supporting artists and art organizations, however, are tied up with other government objectives such as fostering a national culture.

Artistic Networks

Sociologists often study social networks, that is, the pattern of ties among individuals. Becker's concept of "art worlds" is fundamentally an image of networks, as it highlights the connections among artists, support personnel, producers, distributors, and audiences. Some artists and art forms come closer to approximating *social* networks than others, in that they demonstrate a dense web of connections among individuals.

Crane (1987), for instance, showed that avant-garde artists tend to associate with one another, especially when they work in the same artistic movement. She studied seven different styles of art – Abstract Expressionism, Pop Art, Minimalism, Figurative painting, Photorealism, and Pattern painting – that developed in New York from 1940 to 1985. In order for artists to form a proper avant-garde, Crane argues, they need to belong to a social network of other artists who consider aesthetic innovation as their primary goal. An avant-garde artist "is attempting to paint in a way that no one else has painted before," while at the same time relating to "the body of artistic knowledge that already exists" (p. 21). Networks of avant-garde artists provide a crucible for the sharing of ideas, as well as social support for innovations. Artists outside these networks are likely to produce more conventional works, as they lack access to new ideas and encouragement for experimentation.

The abstract expressionists, the earliest movement Crane studied, had an "intimate face-to-face network" (p. 29), but as the New York art world grew, the networks became more diffuse, with connections crossing among different styles. Nevertheless, the artists were linked through a variety of ties, both direct (friends) and indirect (friends of friends). These networks helped spread new ideas and became the source of information about who was doing what, especially in terms of new work, and the locus of discussions on larger issues such as the nature of the avant-garde itself.

The avant-garde artists did not support themselves within the network, however. They were connected to a variety of gatekeepers, who helped to make or break the style:[1]

> Abstract Expressionism and Minimalism drew their support from academic critics and the curators of New York museums who were committed to the modernist aesthetic tradition, while Pop, Photorealism, and Neo-Expressionism drew theirs from dealers and investor-collectors. The Figurative and Pattern painters appeared to lack a major constituency in the New York art world; their supporters were to be found in regional museums and corporate collections. The Pattern painters were primarily favored by corporate collectors....Consequently, the styles...had varying degrees of success in the New York art market,

as indicated by the extent to which they had access to the auction market and to the collections of the major New York museums. (p. 41)

Many folk art networks form identifiable subcultures which stand in contrast to the dominant culture. As Hebdige (1979) shows for a variety of youth subcultures that produced musical innovations, successful art forms emerging from them are often taken up and tamed by established commercial interests and the art form becomes commodified. Lachmann (1988) shows some aspects of this process, as well as the ways networks work to create and sustain innovation, among graffiti writers in New York.

The graffiti writing Lachmann studied is a good example of a folk art form. The art was, initially, a purely networked-based form. Lachmann distinguished the "mural artists" who painted big pictures on the sides of buildings and subway trains from "taggers" who sprayed their initials, stylized into a "tag," on trains, but also on just about anything. He studied the artistic careers of 25 graffiti writers from Brooklyn, New York. Most graffiti writers started to write while they were in school, and most were male. The majority of writers Lachmann interviewed were black or Hispanic, but a few were white. Networks were located in specific neighborhoods. An interesting aspect of the art form is that it is, of course, illegal. Thus, the police and local gangs were important players in the graffiti writing world.

Novice writers learned their art through a mentor in the social world who shows them how it is done, and teaches them related skills, like how to steal paint. Most started by tagging, and gained some recognition among their peers for having their initials in more places than other writers. The most desirable location for tags were trains that travel throughout the New York subway system and are thus seen by large numbers of the general public. Nevertheless, the writers' main audience was made up of their local peers who recognized individuals' tags. A few writers moved on from tagging to making graffiti murals. In this form, the quality of the piece takes over from the quantity of tags as an indication of the writer's status. These writers sought recognition from an audience beyond their local neighborhood. Graffiti networks still formed the core audience, but for muralists, the audience included networks from other neighborhoods, not just the local one. Muralists met at "writers corners" to discuss ideas and the prestige of writers for the whole of New York City. "Graffiti writers create and sustain a belief in their fame through their ties to fellow taggers and muralists. The nature of those links determines the content and durability of writer's sense that audiences appreciate their graffiti" (p. 242).

Though graffiti, both tags and murals, are still found in New York, and elsewhere, the folk art world studied by Lachmann was active in the 1970s. It was significantly disrupted by police action to close down writers' corners (arresting writers and confiscating the notebooks writers keep with photographs of their work), and by the New York Transit Authority's efforts to clean murals off trains quickly. "As a result, the social and material bases for sustaining their ideology of fame have been lost. Confined to their neighborhoods, muralists cannot determine whether their work merits recognition from the now-shattered muralist art world" (p. 244). A few graffiti artists achieved some fame in the New York avant-garde art world, due to efforts of art dealers and their customers' demands for stylistic innovation. Prices for graffiti art remained relatively low, however, and periods of interest in it were short lived.

Bennett (1997; 2000) discusses the close connection between artists and audiences that arise in network forms. In his study of musicians who play in local pubs, Bennett (1997) shows that listeners often know the performers in the pubs they frequent. They provide feedback to musicians, and to the pub owner, while talking at the bar between sets, and send requests for favorite pieces to the band. Indeed, the musicians value the sociability pub venues provide, rating it alongside the music itself as a reason for playing. Some studies have looked at local pubs as a "training ground" for musicians or a "stepping stone" to recording contracts and professional music careers (p. 97). Bennett shows, however, that for many pub musicians, "performing on the local pub rock circuit [is] an end in itself"; these musicians hold day jobs and lack ambitions for recording contracts and long-distance touring (p. 100). Local audiences actively collaborate with musicians in creating musical traditions in pubs. In choosing their favorite pieces, often by singing along, audiences selectively appropriate music into a "vernacular discourse [in which] popular music is continually being reaffirmed by audiences as *their* music," and thus they transform it into "a form of folk music" (p. 99, emphasis added).

Pubs, then, can serve as a forum for music making which facilitates the contact between creator and consumer. Pubs exist, however, to generate a profit for the landlord. The clash of commercial and artistic interests is illustrated by Bennett's (2000) study of urban dance music, styles such as house and techno, in the city of Newcastle in northern England. Like pub rock music, urban dance music involves close connections between the (dancing) audience and the DJ – who does not merely *play* a dance mix, but actively *creates* the music by mixing "samples" of existing music. In Newcastle, finding venues was difficult. Established clubs there hosted dance music only on weekday nights, reserving the weekends for more standard, and profitable, fare. Consequently, dance music fans have to fall back on DIY (do it yourself) events in private settings.[2]

Some folk art forms are quite stable over long times. Becker (pp. 246–58) discusses quilts. Women on the American frontier created these quilts in community and family groups, passing down techniques and patterns from mother to daughter. Today's quilt circles, comprised of women who enjoy this hobby, continue the tradition. While some quilters innovate, and even sell their quilts as art, many others continue to make quilts for home decoration, using patterns invented in centuries past.

Other forms change over time. Today salsa, a musical style as well as a dance form, is danced by enthusiasts in many countries. Novices take lessons from professional instructors and learn to dance well enough to go to clubs. These clubs are highly stratified, and the best dancers dance only with other top dancers. Weaker dancers are expected to dance only with other weak or new dancers. There are strong norms, which the novice is likely to violate, on when to dance, whom to ask, how to spot an acceptable partner, and what to do when people act incorrectly, for example, by asking a more skilled person to dance (Urquia, forthcoming). Similar rules characterize the tango. Though passive audiences can watch salsa or tango dancers perform, the form is also enacted by individuals who dance it for the pleasure of participating in its production.

Corradi (1997) describes how the tango arose in the barrios of Argentina before the turn of the twentieth century. Because Argentina, due to mass immigration, had many more men than women, the tango started as a "man-dance" in which a single man would dance by himself – it took one to tango. Men also sometimes danced with other men, to practice their steps. As Corradi (p. 194) described the tango of two men, a male dancer's

> male companion was the double of his solitary self, making the absent partner – the woman – all the more vivid in the imagination of each. Those two were not a couple; they were accomplices in a ritual....The two men would concentrate on their steps, on the recognizable patterns of the right. The feet, the hips, the thighs, and the arched backs performed the right. Their eyes were averted from each other. The gaze was fixed, intense and, at the same time, empty of desire. A furtive glance, the mere hint of pleasure, any move that could bring the two males close to what Aeschylus, in a less fastidious age, called "the sacred communion of thighs," provoked a duel, sometimes to the death . . . the tango was an act of elaborate avoidance: it was dancing around something inaccessible.

Women danced the tango with men in bordellos, established in Argentina around 1900. (The men outnumbered the women by a large number, so only the best male dancers were able to attract female partners.) As the women were prostitutes, the tango was shunned by "respectable" people. Then in the 1920s, the tango (along with American jazz music) was imported into Paris where it was a great hit. French laws existed, however, to protect French performers, and made exceptions only for folkloric dances from other countries. Consequently, tango performers had to wear "national" costumes: "Argentine tango players appeared dressed as gauchos – which was tantamount to having jazz players wear cowboy chaps. In exchange for this travesty, Paris gave the tango something more precious: it gave the tango world renown. . . .The tango of Buenos Aires became truly Argentine only after it became the rave in Europe" (p. 204). The tango became a popular form of participatory, rather than spectator, dance when Parisian club managers simplified the dance steps so that beginners could take part.

Network forms, then, can nurture art. The links among artists are often dense, and the distance between artists and their audience is close (as between listeners and musicians in pubs) or blurred (as when spectators are also themselves dancers). Crane (1992) suggests that network forms, such as the early jazz networks she describes (pp. 121–4) which centered on the black bar and the late-night jam session, provide ideal conditions for innovation.

> The combination of a social network and small cultural organizations appears to be especially conducive for the production of culture that is either aesthetically original, ideologically provocative, or both. This is partly because these networks attract the young who are likely to have fresh perspectives on culture and partly because they provide continuous feedback among creators themselves and between creators and their audiences. (Crane, p. 113)

Networks vary, however, in both their access to cultural organizations and the extent to which they wish to innovate. With no organizational involvement, innovations that are developed may be lost to time or may never reach a wider audience. But larger organizations can provide different problems for the art form, either that of commodification (especially with profit seeking organizations) or with the conservative nature of the organization (as with some types of nonprofit organization).

Nonprofit Organizations

Nonprofit organizations, as their name suggests, do not seek to maximize financial returns, nor do they have shareholders, as for-profit firms do. They are bound, by their charters of incorporation, to work toward the public good. In return, they enjoy a number of tax benefits. For instance, gifts from donors are tax free income to the nonprofit and, in many countries, tax-deductible for the donor. Nonprofit organizations have an in-house management, often a director and an administrative staff. They are also governed by an independent board of trustees, customarily, individuals from the social and business elite. DiMaggio (1992) calls the trustee-governed nonprofit cultural enterprise the "high culture model" of organizing the arts. Indeed, many cultural organizations, especially those disseminating fine art, have been set up on a not-for-profit basis. Most art museums, symphonies, and opera houses are set up as nonprofit corporations (or relatedly, as public trusts or charities), as are many theater and dance companies.[3]

Crane (1992) argues that, in comparison to networks, nonprofit arrangements to support the arts are conservative. She argues that nonprofits are less likely to produce artistic innovations because these organizations are subject to fundraising pressures and financial shortages, and because they tend to become bureaucratic over time (Peterson, 1986). For instance, performing arts organizations, like symphony orchestras, must raise substantial revenues at the box office. As a result, they must choose repertoires that will attract a relatively diverse and sizable audience. Consequently, orchestras tend to play a handful of classical composers – Bach, Beethoven, Brahms, and a few others – at most performances, and neglect more innovative contemporary composers (Arian, 1971; Crouch, 1983). The standard repertoire is already well-known to musicians, so it takes less rehearsal time to put together a popular symphony with a guaranteed audience than an innovative one with less certain appeal (Gilmore, 1987). Along these lines, Martorella (1977; 1982) argues that opera houses cannot afford to alienate subscribers (who purchase a series of tickets for the season) with performances they do not wish to see. As a result, smaller companies, especially those associated with universities, are the ones that most often perform contemporary opera. These pieces, however, are unlikely to be performed in more than one or two short engagements.

The level of innovation in nonprofit cultural organizations depends on several factors. In a study of nonprofit theaters, DiMaggio and Stenberg (1985) discovered that smaller theaters – in terms of both the size of their budgets and their seating capacity – found it easier to innovate than larger ones, who have to earn more income to meet their budgets and to find more audience members to fill their auditoriums. Theaters that relied largely on ticket sales for income had more popular and conformist repertoires than those that could count on patrons to underwrite a portion of their budgets. Patrons who value innovation supported innovative theaters, and their donations provided an opportunity for the theaters to experiment, even if the production did not play to a full house. Finally, DiMaggio and Stenberg found that theaters in New York City had more innovative programs than theaters elsewhere in the United States. This was due to three factors: (1) the large audience base in the city, (2) the high concentration of theater professionals there, and (3) a competitive market. Most US cities have only one major theater, but in New York, there are many, including the populist, and profit-seeking, Broadway theaters. Other theaters must compete against the Broadway houses and against each other, giving them incentives to try to find a specialized, and often innovative, market niche.

Nonprofit organizations do not seek money in order to turn a profit. They must, however, find money to support their operations. In their classic study,

Baumol and Bowen (1966) show that performing arts organizations suffer from spiraling cost pressures. Over time the arts become increasingly expensive relative to the cost of living, because the number of personnel needed for performances – the musicians in an orchestra, say, or actors in a Shakespeare play – is difficult to reduce. As a result, the arts do not see the productivity gains realizable in manufacturing industries, so they face increasingly expensive payroll bills. Thus, the performing arts always struggle to find external funding, charge higher ticket prices, or suffer cuts.

In seeking income, arts organizations can rely to some extent on earned income from ticket sales or entrance fees. But as we have seen, this can lead to a standardized, popular repertoire. Many organizations are able to generate significant revenues with perennial favorites. For instance, symphonies play *The Messiah*, and dance companies stage *The Nutcracker* at Christmas, and art museums mount exhibitions of the Impressionists in the hopes of drawing large crowds. Some nonprofit cultural organizations are big businesses and can generate commercial income through shops and restaurants (Alexander, 1999). The Metropolitan Museum in New York City, for instance, had an operating cost of nearly $220 million in 1997 (Metropolitan Museum of Art, 1997). It is funded, as are most nonprofits, by donations, membership and admission fees, endowment income, and also through commercial activities. The merchandise operations alone (excluding income from the restaurant and parking garage) brought in nearly $19 million to the Metropolitan Museum in fiscal year 1997.

Most nonprofit organizations cannot survive only on endowment and earned income, even when these raise significant sums. Consequently, arts organizations must solicit donations from a variety of supporters. Indeed, constant fundraising activities have become the hallmark of most nonprofit arts organizations. The donors and the organizations they fund may share some goals, but donors have goals of their own. Corporate funders, for instance, are interested in the size of the audience for the project they fund, and the "free" advertising that comes with sponsorship. They also seek the prestige associated with the fine arts. The dependency of arts organizations on their sponsors gives sponsors some degree of influence over the organizations they fund (Alexander, 1998; 1996a, b). In art museums, for instance, the number of popular, blockbuster shows has increased as a proportion of the total number of shows mounted by museums. But curators are not passive in the face of funder demands for accessible exhibitions. Instead, they strategically attempt to meet funders' desires while at the same time trying to meet their own goals for scholarly, art-historically important exhibitions.[4]

Cultural organizations often experience a conflict between their artistic goals and business requirements. This is true not only in for-profit business firms in cultural industries, but also in art museums (Alexander, 1986a, b), symphony

120   THE CULTURAL DIAMOND – THE PRODUCTION OF CULTURE

orchestras (Glynn, 2000), public television (Powell and Friedkin, 1986), and indeed, nearly all other types of nonprofit cultural organizations (see case study 7.1). The conflicts in nonprofit organizations have a different flavor than in business firms, however (DiMaggio, 1987b). In nonprofits, artistic and utilitarian perspectives compete, but both views claim a degree of legitimacy. In business firms, the utilitarian side dominates.

Other conflicts can exist in arts organizations alongside the clash of artistic and business needs and the personnel who represent them. Boards of trustees are often a third faction next to the administrative one with a utilitarian outlook and the professional one with an artistic perspective. In addition, different segments of the organization (e.g. curatorial departments in museums or sections in orchestras) may also be at odds over what is best for themselves and their organization. Zolberg (1986) discussed the "tension of missions" institutionalized in art museums from their inception – a conflict between the populist goals of education and outreach, on the one hand, and the elitist goals of collecting and conservation, on the other. It is difficult to meet both types of goals simultaneously, especially in a climate of limited funds. And, until recently, the curatorial departments of museums were decidedly privileged over the educational departments (DiMaggio, 1991a, b).

These tensions suggest that nonprofit enterprises, as with most other organizational forms, are characterized by multiple and conflicting goals. Participants in nonprofit arts organizations spend a good deal of their time thinking about issues not directly related to the art they shelter. And issues such as "what is art?" "what is good art?" and "what should we be doing as an arts organization?" are problematic and contentious.

Government and Art Worlds

National governments are often important funders of arts organizations and of some types of artists. In the United States, many nonprofit arts organizations receive grants from the federal government, often through the National Endowment for the Arts (NEA), and from arts councils at the state and local level. American artists, unless they work in folk styles, jazz, or literature, are not eligible for federal grants, but they may receive fellowships from state and local arts councils, or they may receive payment for works in shows that appear in arts organizations funded by government. In Great Britain, the Department of Culture, Media and Sport funds both artists and arts organizations through a variety of programs and agencies. Some of this money is devolved to arts councils in Scotland, Wales, and Northern Ireland, and to regional arts councils in England. Local city councils may also financially support the arts. In France, the Ministry of Culture oversees a centralized system of funding; in Germany, the federal government plays a minor role and the state and municipal government are the main funders of the arts.

In addition to direct financial support, governments are influential in many other aspects of artistic networks and nonprofits (Alexander and Rueschemeyer, forthcoming; Becker, 1982: ch. 6). For instance, in the United States, gifts to art museums, symphonies, and other cultural nonprofit organizations are tax-deductible, as are gifts to charities. This gives a tax incentive to donors and encourages cultural and charitable giving. Other nations attempt to control the arts to some degree. In France, one of the goals of government funding is to promote French culture and to protect it from outside forces, such as the influence of American popular culture. As a result, arts funding in France has a distinctly nationalistic flavor. Attempts to control the arts are often taken to extremes in authoritarian regimes, as in Fascist Italy (Berezin, 1991), East Germany (Rueschemeyer, 1993; Allmendinger and Hackman, 1996) and the former Soviet Union (Golomshtok, 1985), in which political leaders tried to dictate the style and content of art.

Hillman-Chartrand and McCaughey (1989) distinguish four roles which nation-states play with regard to cultural support, varying by the means with which the state funds art, and the degree to which the state actively shapes the culture it supports. (1) A *facilitator* state encourages private support of the arts through favorable tax policies. (2) A *patron* state funds arts through quasi-independent arts councils. Arts councils rely on peer-review panels, so arts professionals rather than agents of the state decide what art deserves support. (3) An *architect* state relies on centralized ministries of culture to support art. The ministries, an arm of the government staffed by civil servants, attend to social as well as artistic standards in determining funding merit. And (4), an *engineer* state promotes art that fulfills political purposes and suppresses the rest.

The United States has historically served as a facilitator of art, through its tax policies, and has been a patron of the arts since the NEA was founded forty years ago. Since World War II, Britain has taken a patron role, and is now moving to incorporate a facilitator model. France is an architect state. The former Soviet Union was an engineer state.

Nation-states affect the arts in more indirect ways, too. One important way is through laws and policies that promote free trade and encourage a free-market ideology. In most western nations, visual artists sell their works through the market, in the dealer–critic system (see case study 5.1). The market system offers a degree of freedom to artists, but also brings its own set of constraints.

The pressures of the market system are brought into keen focus in the case of East Germany, which was transformed from a state-supported system to a free market one with the fall of the Berlin Wall. As Rueschemeyer (1993) shows, while the German Democratic Republic (GDR) encouraged the "heroic and sentimental" socialist realist style, it also provided secure employment and patronage for visual artists. It existed somewhere in between two extremes – the "Stalinist impositions and total state control of art patronage" at one end of the spectrum, and "the model of the alienated artist without any formal patron or audience, producing for a market that neither directly sponsors nor values the creations" at the other (Rueschemeyer, 1993: 209).

GDR artists did not see themselves as alienated from society as western visual artists often do. Instead, they felt integrated into the society. While many GDR artists disliked the restrictions of the communist system, they found the market system to be more unpleasant. Under the former system, the state proscribed certain types of content, but artists actually focused on their art and got together to discuss ideas. Under the market system, artists were "free" not only in the sense that they could paint what they liked, but also in that they were not paid. Artists complained that their lack of funds distracted them from their ideas. As one GDR artist who had emigrated to the United States said, "I'm not someone who hates the GDR. Actually, I found more people there interested in art and books and not just money. There was also a greater respect for the artist. I miss going into the countryside and painting with a group of people. I don't have much work here; my life is harder" (quoted in Rueschemeyer, 1993: 223). The market appears to be more gentle to expression than systems where the state controls content, but it has a brutal side. Artists may express what they want, but the market encourages some types of content (popular or critically acceptable) over others (those that do not sell well either to the mass market or to the elite). Artists who do not express what the market will buy are left to struggle with little support.

States may affect the arts through financial support, through laws and norms, for instance those relating to free-market ideology, that affect the artist's milieu, and through direct attempts to control artists and their works. Issues of support and control may become tied up with one another, however (see plate 4). In recent arts controversies in the United States, government agencies have withdrawn funding for controversial artists or the art museums that have displayed their work (see Dubin, 1999; 1992). They have also, on occasion, resorted to police or court action, based on anti-pornography laws, when they thought certain works were obscene. Withholding funds is not the outright censorship used in authoritarian regimes; however, it is a punishment and can function as an attempt to control artistic content (Dubin, 1992). These controversies illustrate the conflict, in free societies, between the aesthetic values held by the general public and those held by artists in avant-garde networks (see case study 14.1).

© 1989 MIKE LUCKOVICH—ATLANTA CONSTITUTION

Plate 4 A Wry View of Arts Controversies, a 1989 Cartoon by Mike Luckovich. By permission of Mike Luckovich and Creators Syndicate, Inc.
In 1989, controversy broke out in America over a number of "obscene" art exhibitions which, among other things, displayed male genitalia. The US Congress responded by reducing the budget of the National Endowment for the Arts and restricting its grantmaking abilities.

Conclusion

This chapter has looked at cooperative networks in the creation of art works, both informal networks and those centered around small businesses or nonprofit enterprises. It has also discussed the financing and operations of nonprofit organizations. A key difference between networks and nonprofits is that networks always center on living artists. Nonprofit organizations may benefit living artists, but they also exist to protect and remember artists from the past, as in the collection of old master paintings by museums, the staging of plays by Shakespeare, or the showcasing of the work of classical composers in symphonies and operas. As we have seen, both the orientation of nonprofits toward preserving the past, and the business problems they face, can lead them to be conservative in their actions. Networks can foster artistic innovations more readily than nonprofit organizations, but they do not necessarily do so.

Quilting circles, for example, enact and preserve tradition, rather than striving for ever-changing new ideas.

Nonprofit organizations, while existing to benefit the arts, must raise sufficient funds to break even (or to make a profit, but not to make an unsustainable loss year in and year out). They must also attend to such issues as pleasing donors or finding a "cash cow" (a blockbuster show or performance) to milk for support of other, less fundable aspects of their operations. This discussion of arts funding brings up issues of art and the state, and how states may use art for nation building or other purposes. Consequently, the chapter has reviewed the forms of funding for the arts in an international context.

In western nations, fine arts and folk arts, like the popular arts, exist in a free-market system. A question often asked is, "can culture survive the market-place?" (DiMaggio, 1986). The difficulty is that, compared with the popular arts which enjoys large audiences, fine and folk arts appeal to smaller segments of the population. Moreover, innovative contemporary art and esoteric historical art can have a tiny audience base. The desirability of promoting innovation or preserving history is debated. To the extent that society values these goals, however, it must protect the arts in some manner. Left to itself, the market-place tends to fail in these goals, as the customer base is too small to generate profitable returns. Government support can insulate innovative and historical arts from the marketplace. Networks and nonprofits also play an important part in protecting the arts. Nonprofits organizations shelter art from the market through the legal requirements embodied in their charters of incorporation, and networks protect artists ideologically, by providing social support for innovations not necessarily valued by the wider society.

NOTES

1   As Crane studied seven relatively successful styles, these gatekeepers helped shape the *degree* of success the artists experienced. We can hypothesize that other styles might have failed (and not been available for study), as they were unable to find the support of any key gatekeepers (see Simpson, 1981, ch. 4).

2   Large-scale "raves" in warehouses and farmers' fields were outlawed in Great Britain by the Criminal Justice and Public Order Act of 1994 (Bennett, 2000: 73).

3   This is true in Europe as well as North America; however, some European cultural organizations are state bureaus. For a discussion of the historical roots of the nonprofit form of organization in the arts, see chapter 12 and DiMaggio (1992; 1982a, b).

4   My research (Alexander, 1996 a, b, c) suggests that larger numbers of alternative sources of funds increase the leverage curators have in mounting exhibitions. This is partly a matter of diversity – a large, heterogeneous funding pool enables curators to

mount more varied exhibitions than a small homogeneous group of donors or a single source of funds. But more than that, a large number of funders actually encourages innovation. Funders make demands on museums. These demands do not neatly match what curators have historically done or what curators would like to do. Further, general demands from a variety of funders often conflict with each other. This puts museum personnel in a bind, wanting neither to bow to patrons' pressures, nor to turn patrons away. Curators, then, create solutions to funding problems by mounting innovative art exhibits that satisfy the demands of a variety of funders without sacrificing the curators' own vision of artistic integrity. Since 1965, curators have innovated in three areas of art exhibitions: (1) they have brought new forms of art to museums, such as a variety of postmodern artists, (2) they have rediscovered, and elevated to the canon of high art, old art which was previously ignored, especially old American masters, folk, and ethnic art, and (3) they have brought new scholarly questions to art which is already in the canon.

Case Study 7.1

Piccolos on the Picket Line: A Strike in the Symphony

Based on Mary Ann Glynn (2000), "When Cymbals Become Symbols: Conflict Over Organizational Identity Within a Symphony Orchestra" (*Organization Science*, 11 (3): 285–98).

Points for Discussion

1   In what ways is the Atlanta Symphony Orchestra a "dual identity" organization?
2   What are the structural divisions in the orchestra's organization? How does each group view the goals of the orchestra? What issues are called forth in the conflict that led to the strike?
3   What limitations of the nonprofit form for the distribution of art are evident in the case? (See chapter 7.) Why might it have been important to resolve the strike before the Christmas concert season?
4   Management and musicians hold different views about the functions of the orchestra. Who do you think is right?

Case

Background

The basic structure of symphony orchestras is the same everywhere (Allmendinger and Hackman, 1996; Craven, 1987). They contain, on average, about 100 musicians, rarely having fewer than 70 or more than 130. They have roughly the same range and mix of instruments, and tend to play as their core repertoire the classical French, German, and Italian composers.

Most professional orchestras in the United States are organized as nonprofit organizations. They are funded through philanthropic gifts and earned income; the latter from performances, recordings, broadcasts and sales of programs, refreshments, t-shirts, and the like. Many of these organizations are endowed; that is, they have a pot of money (the endowment) that is designed to provide interest and investment income in perpetuity. The endowment also offers a financial cushion for tough times, but its use in this way is frowned upon because it threatens future endowment income. Though they play the same basic repertoire, orchestras vary in quality and in how often they play more innovative or difficult pieces. The best American orchestras, the "Big Five" including the Boston Symphony Orchestra, the Chicago Symphony Orchestra, the

Cleveland Symphony Orchestra, the Philadelphia Orchestra, and the New York Philhar-
monic, are world-class orchestras.

Orchestras can be divided into four organizational components, the board of
trustees, the administrators, the music director (in common parlance, the conductor),
and the musicians. Musicians are sub-divided into the orchestra section in which they
play (e.g. strings, brass, percussion), and their position (e.g. principle). The administrators manage the business side of the orchestra. They are paid employees of the
orchestra, and most work full-time. The board of trustees is primarily focused on
governance and on fundraising. Trustees work on a voluntary, and usually part-time,
basis subsequent to, or in combination with, a successful career elsewhere. With
reference to money, the "three G's" for boards of trustees, are "Give, Get, or Get
Off"; that is, if trustees cannot donate funds themselves, or leverage funds through
connections, they are not welcome on the board. Traditionally, boards of trustees were
made up of monied philanthropists from the upper crust of society, but today they are
more likely to be made up of wealthy businesspeople, who are steeped in the management culture that gave them their financial success.

Prior to the 1970s, the music director was very powerful in the orchestra's operations.
For instance, he (music directors are overwhelmingly men, even today) was able to
hand-pick musicians for the orchestra from among the best students of his favorite
teachers. But a number of democratizing initiatives in the 1970s and 1980s served to
give more discretion to musicians in the running of the orchestra. Many orchestras, for
instance, have adopted recruitment policies that require openings be advertised and
auditions "blind" to allow artistic merit, rather than personal connections to determine
hiring decisions (Goldin and Rouse, 2000). Nevertheless, the music director's role is an
important one in the running of the orchestra, and he or she acts as a liaison between
the musicians and the board of trustees. Once musicians have been hired, they have a
brief period of probation, after which they are given tenure in the orchestra and their
employment is secure.

Cultural organizations often embody conflicting values, most notably the values of
"normative artistry" and "utilitarian economics" (Albert and Whetten, 1985). This is
true in orchestras, where the musicians focus on how to create the best music possible,
and managers and board members concentrate on how to pay for it. The managers,
and especially the board members, subscribe to a business world logic (Alexander,
1998) in which utilitarian values prevail; they are "governed by values of economic
rationality, the maximization of profit, and the minimization of cost" (Albert and
Whetten, 1985: 281–2). The four main groups in orchestras – trustees, administrators,
musical director, and musicians – must determine the direction the orchestra takes, and
this can be a source of tension. Further, in the United States, orchestral musicians
belong to a union, and herein lies our story.

Conflict in the Atlanta Symphony Orchestra

Glynn (2000) studied the internal disagreements over the identity of the Atlanta
Symphony Orchestra (ASO) that led to a musicians strike in 1996. The ASO, one of
the top ten orchestras in the United States, was founded in 1947. At the time of the

strike, the orchestra consisted of 95 full-time musicians, one conductor, 72 trustees, and 44 administrators (p. 287).

The disagreements reflect deep and long-standing divisions in the Orchestra. The musicians claimed that a rift between management (the administrators and the board) and the musicians had been growing for 30 years. One reason for this was that the board of trustees, once made up of wealthy "music lovers" such as doctors and lawyers, were replaced with businesspeople with a "corporate mentality" that focused on efficiency, costs, and revenues (p. 298). In addition, the external environment of the Orchestra had been changing, with orchestras in general declining due to "a 'graying' audience base, decreasing recording contract opportunities, and diminishing government funding for the arts" (p. 289). These changes made it more difficult for orchestras to bring in money either through gifts and grants or through earned income from concerts and recordings.

The conflict in the ASO embodied disagreements over the balance between utilitarian and musical goals. Though musicians understood that money must come from somewhere, they thought the management were so caught up in their utilitarian models of efficiency and downsizing that they could not understand music or orchestras. As a violinist put it, "[ASO management is] looking at the orchestra like it was a potato chip factory.... A potato chip factory can have a good product with fewer workers, with automation and all. But in an orchestra, the product is the sum of the musicians.... I'm not even sure management knows what quality is" (p. 289). Another musician asserted that music, not management and fundraising, was the core of an orchestra, "I don't know anyone who has ever bought a ticket to attend a board meeting" (p. 289).

The management, both trustees and administrators, for their part thought that musicians were "insular and ignorant" in their refusal to recognize the financial binds which tied the Orchestra (p. 289). As a trustee stated, "Musicians [don't] want to understand the financial picture because then they couldn't make the demands they were making" (p. 290). Further, trustees saw their goal as protecting the endowment for the future benefit of the Orchestra. In a letter to subscribers, they wrote, "Yale Professor James Tobin said it best: 'The trustees of an endowed institution are the guardians of the future against the claims of the present'" (p. 292). This sentiment was amplified in the words of a trustee,

> You're not buying music for yourself. What you're trying to do is provide music for your grandchildren. And the idea that you're just going to invade the trust and go take the money out of the endowment because you want to pay the musicians now is really stealing from the musicians of tomorrow... If you try that (and people have), your orchestra goes out of business. (p. 294)

Before the strike, the board of directors set out three potential strategic options, and their annual costs, for the ASO.

1 *World-market focus*, a 105-member orchestra. This was the most expensive option (more than $100 million)....
2 *Atlanta-market focus*, or the status quo, a 92-member orchestra, with a cost of approximately $30 million.

3 *Fiscally conservative*, with tight fiscal controls, players cut to 80, and reputation enhanced by innovative music and marketing.... The language of the board in framing these issues (as different possibilities for *market* focus, rather than different possibilities for *musical* focus) seemed to reflect its interpretation of the issues. (p. 294, emphasis original)

Musicians believed that the ASO should aim to be a "world-class orchestra in a world-class city." Such quality could be obtained by increasing the number of musicians so that the orchestra could play more challenging and innovative pieces. Musicians argued that it was impossible to play such music with fewer musicians. Management, on the other hand, believed that the ASO should be "the best orchestra *we can afford*" (p. 288, emphasis original). A precipitating event in the ten months before the strike was management's decision to terminate six musicians at the end of their probation, rather than grant them tenure. The reason for the decision was not based on the quality of the musicians – everybody agreed they were good enough to deserve tenure – but due to financial considerations. It seemed tantamount to a decision to reduce the ASO's size. The decision was reversed three months later when community outrage, and a large infusion of grant money, caused the board to reconsider. Nevertheless, seeds of distrust between the musicians and management had been sewn, and two months later management and musicians were unable to agree on musicians' contracts which were about to expire. Management wanted a smaller orchestra and a wage freeze; musicians wanted a larger orchestra and a pay rise. The musicians belonged to the national American Federation of Musicians, and when contract negotiations failed, they voted to walk out.

The strike lasted 10 weeks, from September to December, during which time musicians received union compensation (much lower than their normal salaries), but the administrative staff and the conductor were paid their normal salaries by the Orchestra. Management tried to portray the musicians as "money-grubbing weasels" and to make them look like "union agitators" and troublemakers (p. 290, 292). They cast the disagreement as one about salaries and working conditions, that is, about money.

The musicians, on the other hand, cast the conflict as one over quality. Their slogan was "Keep your symphony world class" (p. 290). The musicians hired a public relations consultant and recruited a support group from the general public. They won the battle of public relations by calling into question the image the board wished to portray of itself as altruistic and public-spirited (p. 289). The musicians also played free concerts in the streets, parks, and shopping malls of Atlanta. "The ASO president [a trustee] said she gave the musicians an 'A' for press, for presenting a very elegant, unTeamsterlike image on the picket line, playing the French horn in fine attire" (p. 292).

The strike was resolved at the beginning of December, just before the lucrative Christmas concert season began. Both sides claimed victory and agreed to: "(1) 95 tenured orchestral positions, (2) outreach to metro Atlanta schools (with no additional compensation), (3) [a] pension plan changed from an ASO managed plan to one managed by the union, and (4) [a] new four-year contract with a wage freeze in the first year, a 2% increase in the second and third years, and [a] 4% increase in the fourth year...; in the final year, the lowest [musician's] salary [would] be $62,500" per annum (p. 296). The tensions between the business and artistic side of the orchestra remain, but the resolution of the strike "created an overall desire for healing" (p. 292).

Interestingly, however, the music director (conductor) did not come out well at the end.

> Albert and Whetten (1985, p. 288) state that "Effective leaders of dual identity organizations should personify and support both identities[;] . . . during retrenchment . . . they must be perceived as the champion of the normative [artistic] as well as the utilitarian values of the institution." In the case of the ASO, the musical director had an independent occupational identity, without strong professional ties to either the musicians or the administrators. He seemed to neither be disclaimed or claimed by either of the competing groups, as he seemed to personify neither identity. His neutrality may have been admirable, but as Albert and Whetten might predict, it cost him his job. (Glynn, p. 296)

The ASO, like other symphony orchestras and nonprofit organizations, has a "plural" identity that is "encoded institutionally, in both symbol and structure" (p. 287). The structural division of the orchestra into trustees, administrators, music director, and musicians reinforces the different points of view these groups hold. "Symbolically, utilitarian values are encoded in the bottom line, and ideological [i.e. artistic] values are encoded in musical icons – cymbals – that are potent reminders of the orchestra's normative identity" (p. 287).

8

Artists

The popular image of the artist is that of an eccentric genius, creating his work in isolation from other artists. This view of artistic activity is widespread among the general public and even among philosophers of aesthetics, art historians, and literary critics. . . . From this point of view, style reflects the individual's personal idiosyncrasies – his character and subjectivity.

(Diana Crane, 1987: 19)

Common sense suggests that artists are at the center of the production of culture. After all, they conceive of the art and bring it into being. Artists are key players in art worlds, and this chapter focuses specifically on them. It looks at the careers of artists, drawing on labor market studies, and at the dynamics of discrimination in art worlds and their effect on female artists and those from ethnic minorities. It examines ways that society might try to control artists. The chapter also discusses artistic reputations and how these are built and maintained. The chapter concludes with a brief look at artistic creativity and genius.

Becker's (1982) work on art worlds is a useful starting point in the study of artists. As we have seen, Becker argues that the concept of "artist," as it is commonly used, is too limited. He believes that many people are involved in the creative process, but that only a few of these are credited as artists (see chapter 5). We will leave aside Becker's powerful idea that the *art world* is the creative agent and focus, in this chapter, on artists in the standard sense, such as painters, writers, and performers.[1]

Artists and Art Worlds

Although Becker focused on the art world itself, he recognizes the existence of the artist's role. Indeed, he notes that the artist's role is very important in western conceptions of art because it has been socially constructed as a privileged and special one. He suggests that artists can be related to art worlds in four different ways. These four types of artists are: (1) integrated professionals, (2) mavericks, (3) folk artists, and (4) naive artists. Recall that Becker argues that art worlds are structured by conventions, or standard ways of doing things. Most artists conform to most of the conventions in their art world because that is the easiest way to get things done and to produce art that audiences will appreciate. They also, however, innovate to some extent as this is the very essence of creativity. Artists, then, must strike a balance between the conventional and innovative aspects of their work. The art world, in turn, judges artists and the balance of innovation and convention in their works. In Becker's (1982: 226) words:

> Wherever an art world exists, it defines the *boundaries of acceptable art*, recognizing those who produce the work it can assimilate as artists entitled to full membership, and denying membership and its benefits to those whose work it cannot assimilate. If we look at things from a commonsense point of view, we can see that . . . art worlds frequently incorporate at a later date works which they originally rejected, so that the distinction must lie not in the work but in the ability of an art world to accept it and its maker.

Integrated professionals, in Becker's terms, include the majority of artists in the fine and popular arts. They are the accepted – or striving – artists who use current conventions, modifying them in acceptable ways. Some of them are highly talented and original, and many of them are neither. *Mavericks* are artists who find their art world's conventions unacceptably constraining and who propose innovations that the art world refuses to accept. It is important to note that, for Becker, most avant-garde artists are not mavericks (though they may wish to see themselves that way), but are in fact, integrated professionals within the avant-garde world. In this way, Igor Stravinsky was an integrated professional from the start, as his innovative music was played and discussed. But his contemporary, Charles Ives, was a maverick whose pieces were rarely, if ever, performed. One of Ives' pieces, his *Universe* Symphony, required "from five to fourteen orchestral groups and choruses, scattered around mountains and valleys," which, for the music world of the first half of the twentieth century, was simply too strange to accept (Becker, 1982: 240). Mavericks, however, are related to an art world, as they tend to start out within it, often receiving their artistic training there before rebelling. They remain oriented toward their art world, even as they reject it (or it rejects them). As a result, it is hard to draw a clear line between integrated professionals and mavericks, as at the edge they blend into one another. Most mavericks remain outside the art world and are forgotten, but a few are accepted back into the art world at some later date, often posthumously. They are seen by the art world as the "unrecognized genius," and although we can think of many examples, they are actually rare.

Folk artists are people who produce creative products completely outside professional art worlds. Many of these artists, of course, work within a social network – quilt clubs, for instance – which act like art worlds, on an amateur basis (see plate 5). These artists also do not try to sell their work at all, or only in amateur venues like county fairs. Becker also considers as folk art the songs sung by church congregations or the dances ordinary people do at clubs or parties. *Naive artists* produce creative products completely outside *any* art world. Becker gives a number of examples of naive works, which are hard to summarize as they are so eccentric, but include such things as large, decorative "houses" made of glass bottles, installations of foil-covered furniture, and rock gardens with 45-foot-high towers.

It is important to note that Becker uses these terms somewhat differently than others do. His point is "not to describe people, but rather how people stand in relation to an organized art world" (p. 228). In this way "naive" does not merely mean a person who is untrained in professional art worlds, but a person who works outside of an art world. Artists working in so-called naive or folk styles, but who sell their works to the public in art galleries, are integrated professionals.

Plate 5 Anonymous (American), *The Quilting Party*, late nineteenth century, Abby Aldrich Rockefeller Folk Art Museum, Williamsburg, Virginia.
Quilting is a folk art, often practiced within social networks rather than professional art worlds.

Becker's work reminds us that artists are not the isolated geniuses of the epigraph at the beginning of the chapter. Rather, they are situated within an art world, and the forms their creativity takes depend on their relationship to the art world. As Becker notes (p. xi), "The dominant tradition takes the artist and the art work, rather than the network of cooperation, as central to the analysis of art as a social phenomenon. In light of this difference, . . . what I have done here is . . . the sociology of occupations applied to artistic work."

Artistic Careers and Labor Markets

Along with Becker, sociologists of work and occupations have recognized that artistic work has much in common with other kinds of work, and they have studied the artistic profession with the same tools used to understand other types of occupations (e.g. Abbott and Hrycak, 1990; Giuffre, 1999). Artists have careers, which can be defined as the succession of jobs they have over a lifetime. Compared to other occupations, however, artists have non-standard careers, produce non-standardized and highly differentiated products, and are difficult to count in a meaningful statistical sense. Social scientists tend to neglect artists in favor of other types of careers and occupations, and aside from case studies of individual artists (the successful ones), artistic careers are understudied.

Social scientists know two things about artists. First, the artistic career is *risky* (Menger, 1999). The odds of becoming even a modest success are low, and only a tiny number of painters, writers, or musicians become well-paid super-stars. Visual artists in New York City say that only one percent of people who make a serious attempt at a career in fine art actually succeed (Simpson, 1981: 58). But no one really knows whether this figure is correct, because no one knows how many striving artists there are or how many give up without having a single painting shown in a gallery or, in other fields, a single short story published, song recorded, or line spoken in a professional performance. Furthermore, success is precarious. "Making it" presages fading away. Finding a publisher or dealer, getting a grant, or selling a song is a step forward, but artists always worry whether their most recent success might be their last. Even highly successful artists can become last year's news as the tastes of audiences shift.

The second thing we can say for sure about artistic careers is that they are *poorly paid*. This goes without saying for the "failed artists" with no successes, but it is also true for most successful artists:

A survey of 4,146 visual, literary, and performing artists conducted by Columbia University's Research Center for the Arts and Culture found that more than half of the respondents earned less than $3,000 from their art in 1988. Gross income [including non-art income] for 85 percent of those surveyed was $30,000 or less. Only four percent reported art earnings of more than $40,000. Ten percent earned between $20,000 and $40,000 from their art. Only 27 percent of those surveyed – from painters and sculptors to writers, musicians and dancers – earned their major incomes as artists: 77 percent worked at other jobs to support themselves. . . . Of the 83 percent who said they earn money through their art, only half earned enough to cover expenses. (Robinson, 1990: 35)

As a result, most artists must rely on second jobs, or on employed spouses or partners for their subsistence. Others draw on unemployment insurance or the dole, as did the children's author J. K. Rowling while she wrote the first *Harry Potter* book. Most artists do without savings and pension plans, and in the United States, without health insurance. Most artists, then, are poor. But the stereotype of the artist literally "starving in a garret" is no longer true. The modern welfare state saves artists, along with other groups, from abject poverty.

In contemporary societies, artists sell their skills in a labor market. They compete with other artists for recognition from buyers, who might be collectors of paintings, Broadway or Hollywood producers, or municipal orchestras. Menger (1999) points out that a common feature of artistic labor markets is *oversupply*. This means that there are more sellers than buyers; that is more artists (painters, dancers, actors, writers, poets, musicians, etc.) than employment opportunities (offered by producers or orchestras) or sales opportunities (offered through publishers, dealers, or collectors). This drives down pay and prices. Artists are paid less than other professionals with similar levels of education and training, they work more often on short-term contracts, and they have a high level of second job holding. As we have seen, most artists do not make a living from their art work, and commonly take a "day job" to support themselves in between gigs or as an ongoing supplement to their income. Some artists are able to find an arts-related job, often in the teaching professions, while others rely on more flexible supplemental work, as in the archetypical example of the waiter who is waiting to make it big.

Menger refers to artists as "professionals," indicating the high level of training many have achieved and the autonomy they have in their work. But they are not "professionals" in one sense in which sociologists use the term. "Profession" often refers to those occupations (classically, doctors and lawyers) in which incumbents have been able to create "barriers to entry" in the field. This makes the professionals more valuable and able to maintain higher salaries. In contemporary, western societies most artistic occupations are open ones in which anyone can try their hand. This is detrimental to most artists, whose pay, prestige, and chances of success are lowered. Art worlds, however, may benefit from the creativity of talented artists who might otherwise be excluded. The arts have at some points in history been more closed as occupations. For instance, medieval guild systems regulated competition among craftsmen, including painters and sculptors, by controlling all access to training and employment. This protected the income of guild members. Strong guilds, however, also tended to suppress innovation "by regulating away the outstanding" (Baxandall, 1980: 117).

An important feature of many art worlds is that they are divided up into two groups, the very successful "superstars," and a large, and mostly undifferentiated "rank and file" of artists who achieve only modest success. Certainly, some artists, actors, or orchestra conductors are more talented than others and this accounts (or we hope it does) for some of the superstar effect. It is reasonable to believe, however, that artistic talent exists on a gradient from the most talented to the least talented. Talent alone can not account for the division of artists into two neat groups of extremely valued artists (who become superstars) and modestly valued ones (who do not). The reason that we see the division between superstars and all the rest in many artistic labor markets is that they work on a "winner take most" basis, as modeled by Rosen (1981). The superstars have what Rosen calls "box office appeal." Rosen does not try to determine *why* some artists have this and others do not. It may be some combination of talent and other characteristics, but whatever creates it, artists who have it have an advantage in the artistic labor market. Buyers seeking the "talent" of superstars are unwilling to substitute for it the labor of someone just slightly less "good." Box office appeal, then, bids up the price of the most desirable artists and leaves the rest scrambling for the crumbs, even though they may be nearly as talented, or even more talented, than the most successful artists.

Artists, on the whole, are poorly paid, but in most artistic disciplines some artists reach celebrity status – they are the superstars – and can earn a great deal. For instance, data from the Actors' Equity Association shows that the median yearly income for employed actors and directors was $30,000 in 1997. However, we all know that the most famous actors can earn multimillions for a single film (Heckathorn and Jeffri, 2001: 324). Though the exact statistics will vary, similar bifurcations in income exist in disciplines from rock music and popular fiction to opera, classical music, and the visual arts.

Some artists work in salaried positions on a long term basis, notably orchestral musicians (Faulkner, 1973; Allmendinger, Hackman, and Lehman, 1996). Most artistic employment, however, is in the *contingent* labor market which relies on "short-term contractual or subcontractual relationships" (Menger, 1999: 546). In a study of French performing artists, Menger (2001) shows that the labor market expanded from 1986 to 1997 but that the supply of workers grew faster than the opportunities for employment, leading to lower average working days per artist per year. That is, the labor market became more contingent. Moreover, the median income for each day worked went up during the time, but because artists worked for fewer days, their average overall earnings from performances were lower.

Identifying artists

One reason that artists are understudied, both in the literature on occupations and in the literature on the sociology of art, is that it is difficult to define clearly who is an artist. As Becker (p. 36) points out, artists themselves, and art world members in general, spend a good deal of time debating this very issue. Jeffri and Greenblatt (1989) suggest three different ways to define an artist: the marketplace definition, the education and affiliation definition, and the self and peer definition (see table 8.1). In a survey of fine artists who had applied for grants in New York State, Jeffri and Greenblatt found that artists rejected the marketplace definition (an artist is someone who earns money from art), and overwhelmingly favored the self and peer definition (you are an artist if you think of yourself as one, and/or if your peers deem you one). This latter definition is a social one, and supports Becker's contention that it is the art world and the artist's orientation to it that determines the status of artist.

The problem with the self and peer definition is that it is hard to measure in statistical surveys. Counting artists is harder than counting plumbers or lawyers. Many attempts to enumerate artists use either Census data or employment surveys, which can be problematic. These surveys, by asking what job respondents held in the week before the survey, rely on the market definition of artist.

Table 8.1 Three definitions of "Artist"

1 **Marketplace**
   - The person makes his/her living as an artist.
   - The person receives some income from his/her work as an artist.
   - The person intends to make his/her living as an artist.

2 **Education & Affiliation**
   - The person belongs to an artists' union.
   - The person has been formally educated in the fine arts.

3 **Self & Peer**
   - The person is recognized by his/her peers as an artist.
   - The person considers him/herself to be an artist.
   - The person spends a substantial amount of time creating art.
   - The person has a special talent.
   - The person has an inner drive to make art.

Source: Jeffri and Greenblatt (1989), p. 10.

As a result, they make both "Type I" and "Type II" errors in counting artists: They include people who are not artists, but who may be working in related areas such as commercial arts, crafts, or arts education, and they exclude people who are artists, but who were not working in art the previous week. These surveys also categorize artists much more coarsely than artists themselves do, mixing commercial, fine, and avant-garde together. As Cantor (1989: 59) says of the Current Population Survey, "striptease artists are counted with ballet dancers, . . . [and the] category for musicians includes church singers."

Purposive surveys of artists, those that set out to survey only people considered artists, are useful but run into similar difficulties. As the researchers lack a "population" of artists from which to sample, they must rely on some selection method for identifying them. Jeffri's work (Jeffri and Greenblatt, 1989; Jeffri, Hosie, and Greenblatt, 1987) samples from a population of artists who had applied for fellowships. The fellowship required applicants to provide evidence of "professional work" in the arts. Though Jeffri's studies are important, they are biased towards successful artists who already have some proof of professional success. This means that we know very little about artists who are just starting out, and about aspiring artists who never make it.

Studies of artistic labor markets need a broad base of data in order to develop a picture of the market's dynamics. A good source of data are artists' labor unions, such as Actor's Equity or the union data drawn on by Bielby and Bielby (1992; 1996), and Faulkner and Anderson (1987). These kinds of statistics are available for only a few types of artistic careers, however. They offer a crucial insight into the work of artists in these occupations and can help us understand artistic careers in general. But the particular dynamics of artistic careers necessarily vary among art worlds. Musicians starting up a band face many of the constraints in achieving success that aspiring visual artists and novelists do, but the particular ways these will play out vary across these disciplines, and also across genres within the discipline.

Simpson (1981) did an ethnography of artists in the Soho district of Manhattan. His project involved situating successful, and notably, striving artists in the local social world. Soho is an interesting case, as the district became associated with artists as a result of complex real estate issues in New York City (see also, Zukin, 1982). Simpson also interviewed art dealers and the spouses or partners of artists, as well as the artists themselves, in order to learn about the experience of working as an artist in Soho. Simpson demonstrates that unsuccessful artists, lacking market indicators of their talent, drew on anti-commercial ideologies about authentic art in order to legitimate their efforts in producing artworks. They tended to live a bohemian lifestyle, working only when inspiration hit them. They also relied on friends, lovers, or spouses, not only for financial help, but for the emotional support necessary for continuing to create. Though they showed disdain for market success, they nevertheless suffered from the lack of external indicators of success that the market (and the critical recognition that comes with it) gives.

Successful artists, in contrast, did not subscribe so strongly to anti-commercial ideals, and more openly talked about how their work meshed with current commercial interests. Let us be clear; successful artists saw themselves as working to solve aesthetic problems they set for themselves, not as pandering to audiences, but they did keep their eyes on the market by regularly visiting dealerships. They also, in Simpson's terms, "rationalized the creative process" by setting up, and sticking to, a strenuous and orderly work schedule, rather than waiting until the mood struck them: "Successful artists compensate for their disbelief in the poetry of inspiration with a commitment to the prose of hard work" (p. 89).

Studies such as Simpson's are invaluable for learning more about artists and the conditions of their work. There are relatively few studies of artists with the encompassing scope achieved by Simpson. Though enthnographies do not provide a statistical picture of artistic labor markets that are standard in studies of other occupations, they provide a rich tapestry of understanding.

Gender, Race, and Age

The effects of racial and gender discrimination is well established in the literature on work and occupations. Artistic labor markets and employment in artistic fields show many of the same outcomes. Tuchman's work (Tuchman, 1989; Tuchman and Fortin, 1984) on nineteenth-century women writers is an important examination of the dynamics of an art world that changed the chances of women succeeding in the field. As Watt (1957) shows, the novel as a literary form was invented in the eighteenth century, and developed alongside increasing literacy rates, especially among leisured women. Tuchman shows that a majority of early novelists in England, before 1840, were women. This was because the art world for novelists was, at that time, a low-prestige "empty field." As the prestige of serious fiction grew, more men wrote novels, and eventually, the art world "edged women out" of the field. Women still wrote and published; however, their numbers were fewer in the late Victorian era than earlier in the century, and they were more likely to be relegated to the areas of popular and romantic fiction, which had less prestige than novels in the "great tradition of English literature" written by "men of letters."

More recently, Bielby and Bielby (1992; 1996) have demonstrated gender effects in the careers of television writers and screenwriters. In a study of television writers, Bielby and Bielby (1992) relied on a data set of 5,157 of these writers all of whom contributed to at least one show between 1982 and 1990. They drew on the work of Faulkner and Anderson (1987;

discussed in case study 8.1), which suggests that the short-term contracting system in Hollywood leads to a "cumulative advantage" in which artists who are successful early on earn the chance to work on future projects, but that those who fail at any stage do not. This creates a small elite of successful artists, and a large corps of mostly unemployed ones. Bielby and Bielby's work concentrated on why women work less and earn less as television writers than do men of similar age and experience. They discovered that women suffered a "continuous disadvantage" in which "the contributions of women writers are uniformly devalued across career stages" (p. 368). The gender barriers that women face are subtle. Though women tend to be overrepresented in certain genres, such as comedies or women's shows, as opposed to action-adventures, at least a few women write in most genres. Consequently, there is no evidence that men are systematically excluding women from the best writing jobs or that women are ghettoized into only certain genres.[2] But, as Bielby and Bielby conclude, "in the male-dominated world of studio and network executives, male writers are better known and are perceived as better risks than equally successful female writers" (p. 382).

These dynamics are evident in other fields. In rock bands, instrumental musicians, unlike singers, are nearly always male. Women instrumentalists often resort to forming a "girl group" in order to play guitar, bass, or drums in a band (Bayton, 1998). And Peterson (1997: 10) writes about country music, "It is not a lack of talent, or motivation, or business sense . . . that explains why so few women played leading roles in the early development of country music. Women were systematically excluded from the business side of the developing industry and for decades were expected to fit into a few stereotyped performance roles." Orchestral musicians have traditionally been men, except for players of a few instruments, notably the harp, that are played almost exclusively by women (Allmendinger and Hackman, 1995). The number of women in symphony orchestras increased when, in the 1970s and 1980s, many orchestras adopted "blind" auditions in which musicians play for employment juries behind a screen designed to conceal their gender (Goldin and Rouse, 2000).

The tone for much of this work on gender and art was set in a fruitful essay by the art historian Linda Nochlin (1971 [1973]), who asked the question, "Why have there been no great women artists?" Nochlin argued that until quite recently, a number of structural constraints made it difficult for women to receive the early training they needed to excel in art. Women were rarely admitted to art schools or art academies. In the few cases where women could attend, they were excluded from life drawing classes, in which artists sketch from nude models. Although men were allowed to draw male (and much later, female) nudes, it was not until the end of the nineteenth century that women were allowed to sketch nude models of either sex, and even then, models had to be partially covered with a drape or other suitable fig leaf. Moreover, in her analysis of the few women artists who did achieve some success before the twentieth century, she found that all, without exception, had close ties to a male artist, usually their father but occasionally a friend, who had been able to provide the technical training needed to be more than just a "lady painter."

Societal attitudes towards a women's place and the level and type of accomplishment seen as ladylike made it difficult, Nochlin argues, for nineteenth-century women to achieve the single-minded focus necessary for great achievement. Women, in the upper classes at least, were encouraged to take up hobbies, perhaps that of a "lady painter," but were strongly discouraged from specializing in, and hence developing deep skills in, a single hobby. Nineteenth-century etiquette books, for instance, insisted "upon a modest, proficient, self-demeaning level of amateurism – the looking upon art, like needlework or crocheting, as a suitable 'accomplishment' for the well-brought-up young woman.... It is this emphasis which transforms serious commitments to frivolous self-indulgence, busy work or occupational therapy..." (Nochlin, p. 27–8).

Artists of color also face discrimination in artistic labor markets and in art worlds. For instance, in their study of 4,093 Hollywood screenwriters active from 1982 to 1992, Bielby and Bielby (1996) found that only 3 percent were from ethnic minorities. Moreover, in their whole sample just 26 writers were minority women, making it impossible for them to analyze statistically the effects of the market on gender and race combined.

Ryan (1985) illustrates the explicit discrimination against African-American musicians early in the twentieth century. The American Society of Composers, Authors, and Publishers (ASCAP), a music-licensing organization, was established after a change in copyright law in 1909 allowed songwriters and music publishers to collect royalties on their works when performed by others. ASCAP's membership policies, based on a procedure of identifying popular songs that undercounted so-called "race" and "hillbilly" music, were use to exclude virtually all black artists, along with white country musicians, from membership in the organization. The few black artists who were admitted to ASCAP received their memberships much later in their careers than white artists of equivalent stature. As a consequence, black musicians did not earn royalties on their music at all or, in a few cases, not until many years after achieving success. It was not until a competing organization, Broadcast Music Incorporated (BMI), was established in 1930 that such musicians were able to protect their work, in practice, from copyright infringement. As a strategy to compete with ASCAP, BMI licensed not only a variety of rhythm and blues styles (gospel, blues, and jazz), but also folk and country music and music from Argentinean, Mexican, Italian, Jewish, and Native American artists.

Not much work has been done specifically on aging artists; however, the evidence available suggests that older artists suffer in such fields as Hollywood television writing (Bielby and Bielby, 1993), the visual arts (Payne, 1989;

Galenson and Weinberg, 2000), and ballet. Symphony orchestras appear to support their musicians until retirement age (Smith, 1988), though of course, starting an orchestral career later in life would be difficult. Western society values both youth and the early revelation of talent; consequently, ageism is a component in many art worlds.

Artists and Social Control

We tend to see artists as special individuals who, because of their creative insights, stand apart from society. This is part of the romantic myth of the artist (see box 8.1). It suggests that artists not only "starve in a garret" but that they also live a bohemian lifestyle that rejects bourgeois, middle class values. Like all stereotypes, this one characterizes only some of the artists some of the time.[3] Nevertheless, it does suggest some difficulties employers of artists might encounter as artists may choose their careers precisely because it gives them some freedom from the norms and values that characterize – and control – members of the general society.

Box 8.1   The Romantic Vision of the Artist

The romantic vision of the artist suggests that artists have not mere skills, but an insight and genius that must be treasured by society. As artists pursue their vision, indeed, as they are driven by it, they do not follow society's strictures. They see through bourgeois norms to the deeper issues in society, and therefore cannot be expected to live by these norms. They must pursue art for art's sake, and be true to their vision. They live a bohemian lifestyle, "starving in a garret," consorting with prostitutes, and otherwise displaying what Adler (1979: 16) calls "anarchistic individualism (eccentricity... and advertisement of personality through flamboyant, spontaneous, and outrageous behavior)," rather than settling down to hold a stable job, marry and have children. Their lifestyle is a consequence of their heightened vision, and it allows them to develop their vision into great art.

Society, to some degree, tolerates their non-traditional lifestyles, in exchange for the fruits of their genius. But society also condemns those who step outside its boundaries, and as a result, artists are often alienated from mainstream society. "It is as if the bourgeoisie [has] given the fine artist a double role: to demonstrate that in this materialistic world it [is] possible for some to devote their lives to work motivated by the most refined aesthetic values, and simultaneously to show that those who [are] imprudent enough to live by this rule would come to a bad end. Thus the patrons of art [can] at once be uplifted and warned by the fine artist's example" (Getzels and Csikszentmihalyi, 1976: 47).

The romantic vision of the artist, as its name suggests, grew out of nineteenth-century Romantic ideology. Its roots, however, are deep in western history. Baxandall (1988) describes the beginnings of the ideology in Renaissance Italy when painters, considered in the middle ages to be possessed of craft skills, began to be seen as having more valuable artistic skills. As Hauser (1951 [1968]: 61) puts it, "The fundamentally new element in the Renaissance conception of art is the discovery of the concept of genius."

The ideology was heightened by developing conceptions in western philosophy and western societies of the ideas of individualism and human rights. The eighteenth-century ideals of the "natural rights of man" included notions of freedom of human expression. The romantic myth came into full fruition with the bohemians of nineteenth-century Paris (Graña, 1964). During this time, and in the preceding centuries, the production of art was transformed from patronage and academic systems, in which artistic expression was closely controlled by individuals or institutions well integrated into society, to market systems where artists were free to pursue their unique vision (White and White, 1965 [1993]). The market system, however, left artists vulnerable to poverty. The philosophy of "l'art pour l'art" (art for art's sake) offered an important compensation to starving artists – creating great art may not pay, but is a higher calling than more mundane pursuits (Graña, 1964; Simpson, 1981).

The romantic ideology is often called the romantic *myth* of the artist. This highlights the fact that, as many authors have pointed out (e.g. Becker, 1982; Bourdieu, 1993; Wolff, 1981), the conception of the starving artist is a product of particular historical circumstances, such as market systems of distributing art, and an historically situated philosophy of the nature of art. This philosophy of artistic genius is widely held in contemporary western society, but does not necessarily characterize earlier historical periods (Belting, 2001; 1994) or other parts of the world (Price, 1989).

Dubin's work (1992; 1987b) has centered on the issues of artists, government, and social control. In the earlier work (1987b), he studied how artists working in programs funded by the American federal government were controlled by their supervisors. The 1930s Works Progress Administration (WPA) programs were plagued with controversy, as artists produced works that were considered too radical or too shocking to be accepted by the wider public. The program's administrators resorted to censoring offending artists. The Chicago Artists-in-Residence (AIR) program, supported by federal funds in the 1970s and 1980s, wished to avoid the same pitfalls the WPA had suffered, and so program administrators instituted a series of bureaucratic controls. For instance, artists employed by the program were required to negotiate explicitly with sponsors about the content of their work. Artists who failed to negotiate were not rehired at the end of their contracts. Visual artists were also required to work in a public library, rather than their own studios, which allowed the program to document the hours the artists spent on AIR activities. More recently, Dubin (1992) has focused on government attempts to control artists, and simultaneously, the various social groups or political positions associated with the artists or reflected in their work, through rescinding or refusing funding.[4]

Adler's (1979) ethnography of an art school illustrates the conflict between artistic freedom and social control in organizational settings. The California Institute of the Arts (Cal Arts) was built in the late 1960s near Los Angeles, and at the same time, it recruited a new faculty. The school was seen, initially, as a "community," steeped in sixties anti-establishment ideology and grounded in "the Bohemian rather than the academic tradition" (p. 104). There was no tenure system for faculty, and no formal academic rankings. Students were not formally assessed or given grades, and there were no course requirements nor any set period within which students had to complete their work and graduate. Cal Arts viewed students as "fully-fledged artists and colleagues" who should be allowed full "autonomy and self-direction" (p. 102, 103), and as a result, teachers were reluctant to teach students any craft skills or to critique their work. Anyone who wanted access to supplies and equipment, teachers and students alike, could have it. In sum, the school was founded on a series of contradictions:

> [Cal Arts] had to assure some people that they would receive a profession for their money and others that they would have students in their classes at a time when vanguardism decreed that boundaries between art and nonart, artists and non-artists, had no further validity. It had to assure trustees that they were respected when vanguard culture required that they be mocked, and it had to provide an impression of efficient and responsible management, of sober and disciplined production, where vanguard culture held such qualities in far lower regard than it did consistent antinomianism and uncompromising playfulness. (p. 46)

The result was a predictable chaos, where some students left early to pursue their careers and others stayed for extended periods, because "by ending their claim on rare equipment ... [graduation] threatened to constitute their occupational retirement" (p. 140). There was no way to prioritize or limit claims on supplies or other resources. Teachers demonstrated the same piece of equipment over and over as individual students demanded, since there were no set times to which demonstrations were limited. Moreover, Cal Arts artists spent vast sums of money, believing that they had put a "joke" over on the conservative trustees who were funding Cal Arts' radical experiment. But a few years later, the joke was on the artists when the trustees reestablished control over the school to reign in budgets, formalize the curricula, and otherwise transform Cal Arts from an art "scene" into an educational institution.

Reputation

Common sense suggests that reputation is built on talent. Great artists have great talent, and people with great talent will become recognized as great artists, so the logic goes. *Talent* refers to the skills of an artist. It can include innate skills like perfect pitch or the ability to "feel" the music, and trained skills, such as reading musical notation or the mastery of music theory, and of course, combinations of the two, as in playing the violin well. Some of these skills can be measured, but in the arts, objective measures of talent itself simply do not exist. *Reputation*, on the other hand, refers to what others think about an artist's work and how widely the artist (or artworks) are known. Reputation is based on judgments made by art worlds or the wider social world. It is not necessarily easy to measure, although indications such as number of engagements played or works published give us some clue, as do the extent to which scholars or critics write about a given artist or teach about him or her in an university course. Reputation is easier to determine than talent and it often stands in for talent.

Reputation is not always a good measure of talent, however, and a strict correspondence between talent and reputation does not exist. Think of popular music. There are many talented musicians who play in the local pub and teach guitar lessons who have not, and will never, make it big. Yet some (though certainly not all!) of rock's superstars seem to have, at best, only modest talents. Why is this? This is a sticky question, but sociological thinking can help provide some answers. First, the tastes of audiences vary, so that one person's talented rock group represents a formulaic and mediocre performance to someone else. Different segments of the population value different manifestations of talent. Second, though some kind of talent is (we hope!) a necessary condition for success, it is not a sufficient one. Many other factors come to play in the building of reputations, and reputation is a crucial key to success in any art world.

DeNora (1995; 1991) studied the art world that Beethoven inhabited, and how he came to possess the strong reputation that he continues to have today. DeNora shows how Beethoven and his patrons worked together in a symbiotic relationship to further Beethoven's career and to teach a wide audience how to appreciate Beethoven's music, which was very different in style than the music that preceded it. No one would argue that Beethoven lacked talent, least of all DeNora, but she does argue that Beethoven's reputation in Vienna, and his reputation today, would not exist without the efforts of his patrons to expose the world to his music and to lionize him. Moreover, DeNora argues that Beethoven and his patrons actively constructed the model of musical genius of which Beethoven is a primary exemplar.[5]

Lang and Lang (1988; 1990) focus on the process by which artists are remembered over the long term. They studied the survival of the reputation of "painter-etchers" who were active in France, Great Britain, and the United States from about 1880 to 1930. Painter-etchers made original artistic statements through their prints, which were reproduced in limited series, and were distinguished from the reproductive etchers of the time who made illustrations or copies of famous works for unlimited reproduction. This style of work found favor among collectors in the early twentieth century, but by mid-century, the style had fallen out of fashion and most of the work was ignored. The style then experienced a revival in the late twentieth century, and some of the work was rediscovered.

Lang and Lang differentiate "recognition" by one's peers within the art world from "renown" (fame in the wider society). They studied a sample of artists, both male and female, from all three societies where the art form was practiced in order to uncover factors which led to the survival of artistic reputation. All of the artists they studied had some degree of professional success, either recognition or renown, during their lives. One explanation of the durability of reputation is that the greatest artists are remembered; those forgotten were not good enough for the critical eye of history. Lang and Lang dispute this idea as oversimplified, and suggest that several other factors affect the survival of reputation. For instance, they show that artists who produced a larger number of works, and those whose works were kept together in collections were more likely to be remembered. Artists who produced few works were less likely to attract scholarly attention, and their small collections were unable to sustain scholarly inquiry. Artists with scattered collections were also harder to study, and therefore, to rediscover. Further, artists who kept careful records, or whose friends or family members did so, were more likely to be rediscovered, as scholars doing a history of the genre needed such records to substantiate the artist's career. Finally, artists who died leaving survivors willing and able to look after their life's work were more likely to be rediscovered than those who did not. This last fact helps explain why more female etchers were forgotten than male etchers. Many male etchers left wives who collected and catalogued their works or saw that they were placed in a museum. Female etchers were more likely to live longer than their husbands, and consequently, were more likely to leave no one to care for their *oeuvre*, which was then either destroyed or dispersed. Female etchers were also more likely to survive well into the twentieth century, when the genre was no longer popular. Etchings of artists who died when the genre was successful were preserved more often than those of artists who died when the genre was ignored, regardless of the quality of the work or the degree of recognition or renown the artist enjoyed during his or her heyday.

Reputation, then, may be fickle. Sheer talent may influence the level of reputation an artist holds, but so do a number of other, unrelated factors (not the least of which is luck). Moreover, as Becker (1982) suggests, the *concept* of artistic reputation is a social construct. It is applied to artists only under certain historical conditions and is present in "societies which subscribe to more general theories emphasizing the individual over the collective" (p. 354). Becker notes that art has been a part of most societies throughout history (at least as decoration and ritual, if not as a separate sphere of activity), but in only some of these are artists written about and remembered. So in many societies, certain individuals may have displayed conspicuous talent, and were perhaps appreciated for it, but this talent did not lead to a "reputation" in the sense we think of it today.

Creativity and Genius

A key aspect of the work of artists is the creativity, even genius, that is reflected in their work. Yet this aspect is often completely set aside in the sociology of art. Studies in the psychology of giftedness examine the talents, or abilities, of gifted individuals. These talents are assumed to be in-born somehow, and part of the hardwiring of an artist's brain. These innate capacities can be recognized and nurtured in childhood – or they can be ignored or quashed. Environmental factors, then, affect the development of genius. Csikszentmihalyi and Robinson (1986) do not dispute these insights. They argue, however, that what is seen as genius is never separable from what the society tries to measure as genius. In this way, their work provides a linchpin for a sociology of genius.

Csikszentmihalyi and Robinson suggest that childhood or youthful genius is more often recognized in fields where there are clear rules as to what is being judged (as in mathematics, classical music, or drawing) as opposed to fields where criteria are more vague (moral action), based on innovation (avant-garde art in various disciplines), or reliant on a store of knowledge learned over a lifetime (most of the humanities). As a result, more child prodigies in chess or mathematics are discovered than are youthful stars in aesthetic innovation or historical scholarship. It is not that more children possess the cognitive abilities in mathematics or chess than whatever cognitive traits might underlie the others. It is just that the former are more easy to measure, and thus, more easy to see.

Moreover, standards of genius can vary over time and place. This means that what we see as talent is never solely an individual trait, but rather, it is an interaction between "culturally defined opportunities for action and personal skills or capacities to act" (Csikszentmihalyi and Robinson, p. 264). That is, the artistic field provides opportunities for genius that individuals with certain kinds of talent are able to exploit. The talents valuable in one artistic field at a given time and place, however, may not be as useful elsewhere. This is clearly shown in a study on the age at which modern painters reached their peak. Galenson and Weinberg (2000) looked at the age at which modern visual artists achieved success. They chose two cohorts of successful American artists, those born from 1900–20 (such as the abstract expressionists Rothko, Pollock, and de Kooning) and those born from 1920–40 (such as the pop artists Stella and Warhol). The artists born in the earlier cohort produced their most important and valuable pieces (as judged by auction prices) later in life as compared with those of the later cohort. Galenson and Weinberg argue that this is because ideas of what constituted great art changed during the century. The earlier cohort of artists worked during a time when artists were thought to develop their personal styles through years of practice. The later cohort developed their styles in an era when new innovations were more highly valued by the avant-garde. Artists needed to innovate early, not develop slowly, in order to succeed in the art world. Thus, the particular talents of each cohort of artists fit well with the requirements of their own art worlds, and the interaction of the talents and the needs of the art world together constituted the genius of these great artists.

Notice that Galenson and Weinberg do not argue that genius, while based on factors external to the artist, is in any sense false. Yet they do show that different criteria for judging genius were in operation in the two time periods. Thus, it is possible to imagine that artists with skills more akin to the first generation American modernists, but who were born late enough to practice in the second generation, would not achieve as great (or perhaps, any) degree of fame as they might have if they were born at the "right" time for their special skills (see Kubler, 1962). In Csikszentmihalyi and Robinson's words:

> it was much easier to recognize artistic talent in the Renaissance than it is in the present, because at that time a child who could draw lifelike pictures had something important to contribute to art of the time. Giotto's gift was supposedly recognized by the Pope's envoy who was riding by the pasture where the young shepherd was sketching his lambs using a flat rock and a bit of charcoal. Most of the [great Italian Renaissance artists] were noted at an early age for their skill at reproducing likeness. By contrast, during the height of abstract expressionism in the 1950s and 1960s, drawing lifelike pictures no longer constituted a valuable talent. Spontaneity and emotionality were considered the key elements in the production of good art. Young people who had these qualities were thought to have talent by the gatekeepers of the domain – the art teachers, gallery owners, curators, critics, and collectors. Then, during the following decades, painting returned to much more controlled styles, such as a hard-edge and photo-realism. The qualities that had identified promising abstract expressionists were no longer in demand. (pp. 267–8)[6]

Today, although we might resist the idea, an artist with Giotto's skills might very well be considered a "mere draftsman."

It is obvious that in order to succeed, potential artists must not give up before they get started. Getzels and Csikszentmihalyi (1976) examine the reasons that artists exit the art world. Although artists might leave the field because they are not "good enough," many of the reasons are unrelated to artists' apparent talent. For instance, a tension exists between the desire to produce and to reproduce. It is difficult to pursue art or music single-mindedly with children underfoot, and difficult to support children on an artist's income. This is true for both male and female artists, but family pressures (or the desire to avoid them) fall disproportionally on women (Simpson, 1981; Bayton, 1998). Successful artists, then, are talented survivors in the field, not necessarily the most talented of all. Further, in order to succeed in art, artists need a number of co-talents to complement their artistic skills. For instance, New York art dealers, who turn away many talented artists each week, look not only for striking artistic accomplishment, but also such factors as an outgoing personality, an ability to talk with potential collectors, and the psychological robustness to weather the storms of fad and fashion that will buffet their careers. In the words of Csikszentmihalyi and Robinson (1986: 279, emphasis added):

> many young people who were good at drawing entered art school because they were attracted to the artist's role: the bohemian life-style of the solitary, independent, unconventional genius without material concerns. Fine-arts students who internalized this role were rewarded in art school.... As the young artist began to move out of his student status and tried to establish himself as a practicing artist, an entirely new set of role requirements, often diametrically opposed to the previous ones, came into effect. To be recognized as an artist in our present culture, a young person has *to turn from being a withdrawn, introspective loner into becoming a gregarious self-promoter* who can attract the attention of the gatekeepers of the fields and who can negotiate advantageous terms with gallery owners and collectors. To make it as an artist, he must learn to banter with businessmen, flatter dowagers, and impress foundations. Many talented young persons succumb to these unexpected challenges that strain the adaptive capacity of even the most flexible among them.

Conclusion

Creativity is notoriously difficult to define. Many authors suggest that the greatest artists work within a set of conventions, adding in just the right amount of innovation in some aspects (Becker, 1982; Griswold 1987a). But how much innovation is the right amount? What aspects are best changed and which left the same? And from where does the creative inspiration to make these innovations arise? Aestheticians and philosophers have not been able to answer these questions satisfactorily. Let me emphasize that the sociology of art does *not* deny creativity or the inborn or trained talents or special capacities of the individuals we call artists. It does, however, look for the ways that social factors interact with creative talents. How society supports, or fails to support, particular types of talent – and how talent itself is defined – is amenable to sociological inquiry.

A key argument of this chapter is that our common-sense views of artists are based on socially constructed ideas about the role of artists in society. More-over, many of the studies in this chapter seem to demystify the creative process. The attribution of genius is viewed as a social act. Innate greatness does not lead inexorably to a well-deserved reputation, but can be hindered by mun-dane considerations and current fashions in art. Artists struggle in their careers and are subject to the same market forces that affect plumbers and lawyers. Racism, sexism, and ageism are as prevalent in the art world as they are in the wider society. This demystification is problematic for many people. To view artists sociologically may seem, to some people, as tantamount to devaluing the art itself. But the two do not have to go hand in hand; we can admire the fruits of genius at the same time as recognizing its social nature.

NOTES

1   It may seem like a step backwards to move away from Becker's art world idea to the everyday concept of the artist. However, as Becker himself notes, artists fill socially constructed and privileged roles. While it is useful to "decenter" the artist, we can simultaneously recognize that the roles are nevertheless real, and are important ones in society and in the sociology of art.

2   Bielby and Bielby's (1996) findings for Hollywood (movie) screenwriters, men-tioned in case study 8.1, also showed gender discrimination, albeit with somewhat different dynamics than in the case of television script writers (Bielby and Bielby, 1992), as discussed here.

3   According to a study of artists by the psychologists Getzels and Csikszentmihalyi (1976: 38–40), "the image of the artist as socially withdrawn, introspective, inde-pendent, imaginative, unpredictable, and alienated from community expectations is not far off the mark."

4   Dubin (1999) extends his work to controversial museum exhibitions.

5   As DeNora (2000: 157) puts it:

Ever since Beethoven uttered the notorious phrase, 'I will not play for such swine' (in response to some aristocratic listeners who talked through one of his performances), Western music has been encumbered with the paraphernalia of 'high art'; 'good' music has become, and been designed as, an object upon which to reflect, an object for rapt contemplation. This ideology has also been projected backward on music that was originally designed to be heard within social contexts . . . even Mozart was often heard amidst cries from sausage sellers.

DeNora's research tells, with rich historical detail, a story of how a particular form of artistic genius arose. "The history of Beethoven's reputation and success among his contemporaries . . . , therefore, is the history of the *representation* of reputation, and not merely of reputation per se" (DeNora, 1995: 188, emphasis original).

6 Nochlin (1971 [1973]: 7) reports that Giotto was discovered by the great artist Cimabue.

Case Study 8.1

Nothing Succeeds Like Success: Careers in the Film Industry

Points for Discussion

1 What are the characteristics of the film industry? How do these characteristics affect careers?
2 What is "cumulative advantage" and how does it work in Hollywood?
3 How might Rosen's model of superstars (see chapter 8) help us understand the careers of people in the film industry? Think not only of actors, but behind-the-camera personnel such as the producer, director, cinematographer, screenwriter, and also those with more "mundane" technical (e.g. art director) and non-technical (e.g. driver) jobs. Which of these jobs fit the superstar model? Which do not?
4 What are some of the dark sides of the production arrangements in film?

Case

People who work in the film industry build their careers by moving from job to job, from one short-term contract to the next, racking up successes. This type of "portfolio career" (Kanter, 1989) is common for artists of all kinds, and is increasingly common in other settings such as businesses organized for "flexible specialization." It stands in contrast to the bureaucratic career, in which individuals work for a single firm, on indefinite (long-term) contracts, and move up through the internal promotion ladder. This case focuses on two studies of careers in the film industry, Faulkner and Anderson's (1987) examination of careers in Hollywood and Blair's (2001) discussion of career structures in British film. Faulkner and Anderson studied three key roles (producer, director, and cinematographer) in 2,430 Hollywood films from 1965 to 1980. Blair concentrates on a case study of the production of a single film in Great Britain. Though the aims and levels of analysis of the studies differ, together they demonstrate how individuals build careers in the industry.

The industry

In the early days of Hollywood, films were made in-house by studios in a mass-production model. "Talent" – producers, directors, actors, and other creative personnel – were either employed by the studios or worked on long-term contracts. Movies were churned out regularly, and by today's standards, cheaply. The studio system fell apart long ago, and for the past fifty years, movies have been made on a project basis

(Christopherson and Storper, 1989). Each movie is made independently, and the producer, acting as an entrepreneur, brings together financial capital and freelance talent in order to produce the product. Moreover, Hollywood now works on a block-buster model in which producers, directors, financial backers, and almost everybody else seek to make a phenomenally successful (i.e. profitable) film (Baker and Faulkner, 1991). The first blockbuster, *The Godfather* (1972), broke all the box-office records. Industry insiders thought that it was a fluke, but then *Jaws* (1975) opened and grossed $8 million in its first three days (Baker and Faulkner, 1991: 288). A string of bigger and better blockbusters has followed to the present day.

Project-based Hollywood is a risky place, as is demonstrated by the not-infrequent production of star-studded, well-financed flops, not to mention surprise or sleeper hits (the occasional success of a lower-budget film). The allure of the blockbuster has served to magnify the riskiness of the business. The structure of the industry poses certain "business problems" to potential movie makers. Investment capital is crucial, and producers seek capital from major studios, banks, and private investors. Audiences are fickle and demand can fluctuate, so producers cannot guarantee a hit by following any set rules or formulae. They must go with their instincts and rely on the talents of the creative people they hire. They generally take the project through a set of six phases while maintaining a schedule and keeping costs under control. These phases are:

> raising the money (finance); hiring the creative and technical personnel (search and acqui-sition); filming the picture within a reasonable schedule (production); editing, dubbing, and scoring [the film] (postproduction); selling [it] to the theaters (distribution); and selling it to the public (exhibition). (Faulkner and Anderson, 1987: 884)

Projects can, and do, fail at each step of the process. As uncertainty is high, and each film is unique, producers do not try to lay out bureaucratic rules or detailed specifica-tions for each job that must be done. (And indeed, they would not have all the technical skills to set out such rules for all tasks in movie-making, even if these could be specified in advance.) Instead, they contract with creative people who are expected to do their jobs well, without close supervision. It is crucial that producers be able to rely on their creative staff, and for the creative staff to be able to rely on each other, in order for the project to proceed smoothly. Everyone has to do his or her job well. Each project is a high-performance system, based on "flexible specialization" (Piore and Sabel, 1984) or "craft administration" (Stinchcombe, 1959). The organization of the British film indus-try is substantially similar to that in Hollywood, though British films are typically capitalized at a lower level than Hollywood films (Blair, 2001).

A Life in the Pictures

The riskiness, high-stakes, and uncertainty in the film industry set the stage for careers there, epitomized by the industry saying, "you're only as good as your last credit." Film workers are employed on short-term contracts connected to the production of a single film, and "a career is a succession of temporary projects embodied in an identifiable line of film credits" (Faulkner and Anderson, p. 887). The freelance contractors in Blair's case study, for instance, had worked on an average of five projects in the year before they were hired for the film, with each project lasting an average of 7.4 weeks (p. 151–2). The risky nature of film careers is heightened by competition. As Faulkner and Anderson put it, there are "armies" of talented people who hope to break into the industry. These include not just actors, but screenwriters, composers, directors, and people working in such technical occupations as photography, sound, lighting, and computers to name a few. Blair (p. 158) quotes the British industry training body, Skillset, as noting that there are sixty-thousand workers in the British film industry, and another sixty-thousand people who aspire to work in the industry. Thus, any type of failure on the part of individuals can be catastrophic for their personal careers, as there are many people waiting in the wings to take their place.

Faulkner and Anderson show that the industry is dominated by an elite corps of workers who work with each other on project after project. Key players who score a success (in their model, measured as the financial success of a film) build their reputation and win the opportunity to try again. Thus, the industry works on a model of *cumulative advantage* in which the rich, as it were, get richer. The "essentials of cumulative performance values" show up in two features of film careers: "(1) each credit in this business increases a person's chances for future work, and each money-earning production increases a person's chances for future contracting with colleagues who themselves are associated with successful ventures; (2) cumulative career attainment is at least partially governed by propensities to contract among equivalent persons" (p. 907). Failures, however, are treated harshly, and a single failure can end the careers of those seen as responsible. The majority of producers and directors, for instance, make only one film in their lives (Faulkner and Anderson, p. 894–5). As Faulkner and Anderson put it, "money 'seeks' money and 'avoids' low earners in this system of contracting. . . . Performance 'seeks' performance. Those with low performance revenues appear to be avoided (or passed over) by those with high cumulative earnings" (p. 901).

Blair's analysis complements Faulkner and Anderson's in that she shows how social networks and on-going working relationships shape careers in the industry. Breaking into the industry is quite difficult. Not only are there hordes of people, talented and not, who wish to work in film, but vacancies are not advertised. Thus, at the early stages of a career, who you know is important, and people get jobs through family and friends who are already in the industry and who will vouch for them. Once in, the work is demanding. The production process is expensive and so work during it is intensive: six-day weeks and 12–hour days are common. Everyone depends on everyone else to do their work correctly and to a high standard. Failure on the part of any individual makes everyone look bad. The work is highly interdependent, and everyone's input, on all levels, is important. For instance, a driver who gets lost while taking a star to a shoot makes the other actors and the whole crew stand around idle, costing time and money. As one of Blair's respondent's put it: "if you've worked with someone for the first time and you've messed something up they . . . wouldn't use you again. Simple as that. So I think there's that sort of fear amongst a lot of people" (p. 166).

A film-making enterprise can be said, then, to be a "high performance organization," albeit a temporary one that creates just one film. Blair shows that producers rely on the talents of their creative departments (e.g. sound, art, camera). Producers delegate many key decisions to the department heads, who then take responsibility for their own successes or failures on a project. Given the high stakes for individuals at every level of the hierarchy, and where failure may portend the end of work opportunities in the industry, people prefer to work with people they know and trust, those that will consistently give their best. As a result, work across projects coalesces into semi-permanent teams of people who have worked together successfully in the past. For instance, the members of the art department on the film Blair studied had all worked together, on several projects, for more than two years. Thus, as individual careers progress, "who you know" remains a key aspect of continuing employment opportunities. "What you know" is also important, however, as no one will continue to work with someone who fails to deliver. One of Blair's respondents describes this:

> there are standards that you have to maintain all the time. You start falling below the standards, you'll get a chance, course he'll [head of department] give you a chance. Give you two chances maybe and then you know he'll pull you to one side and say "what's going on?" and if you don't pull up your socks or get it together, he'll use someone else next time. (p. 166)

The network aspects of film careers can pose difficulties for workers. Successful artists may encounter timing difficulties, as Blair points out. If individuals accept projects with people outside their regular "team," they may be out of synch with the team when a second project arises. Yet, if they are asked to keep themselves free for a project that is expected to materialize in some months, they face the prospect not only of unemployment during that time, but also the possibility the project will fall through before their skills are needed. Moreover, careers themselves are subject to chance. Failures may occur for any number of unlucky reasons unrelated to the skills of individuals, yet damaged reputations are difficult to repair. And certainly, many talented individuals fail to break into the system. They are stopped before the starting line and will never be able to develop the reputation that would enable them to build a career.

In addition, social networks tend to reproduce themselves through "homophily" (McPherson, Smith-Loven, and Cook, 2001; Kanter, 1977).[1] That is, people tend to like and trust others who are like themselves. The basis for similarity can be social class, education level, old boy ties, gender, race, or a combination of these and other factors. This means that discrimination can be a structural feature of networks. While black actors have charted some success in leading and supporting roles, black talent is underrepresented behind the camera. Bielby and Bielby (1996), for instance, find only a tiny number of black screenwriters. They also find that women suffer a "cumulative disadvantage," in which the gender gap in earnings increases over time in individual careers. That is, the longer women work, the less they get paid, in comparison with men having the same level of experience. Interestingly, many screenwriters in the era of silent films were women, but as the film industry grew, and as sound movies allowed storytelling to be more subtle – and more interesting to create – men displaced women in the screenwriting profession. Today, the screenwriting profession is about 80 percent male (Bielby and Bielby, p. 265). Women screenwriters encounter a glass ceiling which they cannot penetrate. Further, many female screenwriters are "typecast," as Bielby and Bielby (p. 266) put it, based on stereotypical views of the writing competence of women. They are hired for writing positions only on films thought to be of interest to women or are relegated to minor roles such as dialogue rewriting. Thus, the patterns

of inequality found in the broader society are amplified by the networking arrangements and the high stakes of film industry.

Note

1   Kanter (1977: 63) called this "homosocial reproduction." "Homophily" is a more recent term,
    but Kanter is usually credited with first discussing the concept.

9

Globalization

Globalization divides as much as it unites; it divides as it unites.
(Zygmunt Bauman, 1998: 2)

This chapter considers the effects of globalization on art. It presents evidence of the circulation of cultural objects across national boundaries as a basis for examining ideas about "media imperialism" and assessing claims of the influence of "the West" on "the rest" of the world. I look at the flow of popular and fine art from the US and other industrialized nations to the developing world, the flow among developing countries, and the flow from developing countries to the West. I consider theories about the interaction between the global and the local. Finally, the chapter briefly examines cultural tourism.

Globalization is discussed as part of the production of culture because a key debate concerns whether global culture is becoming homogeneous, and more specifically, Americanized, due to the actions of multinational cultural industries. An important aspect of the debate, however, concerns the way that people in local contexts use and interpret globalized cultural products and forms. In this way, the discussion foreshadows ideas on the consumption of culture presented in Part IIB of this book.

Globalization refers to the increasing interconnections among the nations of the world, growing world trade, the dissemination of cultural products and the sharing of cultural ideas, links among peoples of the world forged through international travel and through reciprocal communications media (telegraphs, telephones, facsimiles, and the Internet), and the rise of transnational organizations (like the United Nations or the World Trade Organization) and multinational corporations. Held et al. (1999) show the deep historical roots of globalizing processes. Trade was important in antiquity, for instance, and cultural ideas have been shared through the spread of empires and religions, as well as through trade. Various diasporas, voluntary or not, spread people and their cultural ideas across the globe (e.g. Gilroy, 1993). Thus, the process of globalization is not new, although global flows have increased to an unprecedented level. Appadurai (1990) argues that there are five types of global flows:[1] mediascapes (flows of stories, images, and information through the media), ideoscapes (flows of cultural and political ideologies), ethnoscapes (flows of people, including tourists, immigrants, and refugees), finanscapes (flows of money and capital), and technoscapes (flows of machinery, technology, and know-how). Each of these flows produces its own geography, and the relationship among them "is deeply disjunctive and profoundly unpredictable, since each of these landscapes [sic] is subject to its own constraints and incentives . . . at the same time that each acts as a constraint and a parameter for movements in the other[s]" (p. 298).

In addition to examining the process of globalization, many authors have looked at the existence of a global culture – shared understandings that transcend national boundaries. These approaches take many directions, for instance McLuhan's (1964) notion of a global village, Wallerstein's (1974) theories of the world system, and Iyer's (1989) discussion of the cultural montage evident in the existence of video in Katmandu and western-style discos in Bali. Most theorists agree that, despite some sharing of ideas and ideologies, there is no true "global culture" which encompasses a unified – and literal – world-view (e.g. Crane, 1992; Crane, Kawashima, and Kawasaki, 2002; Featherstone, 1990; Hannerz, 1990). Moreover, at the same time that people become more oriented toward the global, they focus more on the local, as nation-states fragment along racial, ethnic, religious, and regional lines, and people cluster by lifestyle preferences (Friedman, 1990; Hall, 1993; Griswold, 1999). People interpret global products within local contexts, which obviously vary from place to place, and they may create new, locally adapted versions of global culture, processes Robertson (1995) calls by the unattractive term *glocalization*.

The International Flow of the Popular Arts

The popular arts, as produced by cultural industries, are available worldwide. The products which enjoy the widest circulation are television programs, movies, and music. America is the largest exporter of products in all three of these media. Hollywood films are distributed worldwide. Action movies, especially, receive the widest distribution. Many people, regardless of background, can relate to heroes trying to escape burning buildings, sinking ships, and evil pursuers. Violence and exciting visual effects translate well across cultures. Comedies and movies about relationships do not work as well in all societies, and are distributed internationally on a smaller scale. According to Giddens (1993: 557), Hollywood's domination started early: in the 1920s, it distributed four-fifths of all films shown in the world. Its influence continues to this day as demonstrated by these statistics: "In Britain, for instance, American films account for 40 percent of all films shown each year in cinemas. . . . In South America the proportion is often over fifty percent, and a similar ratio applies in many parts of Asia, Africa, and the Middle East. In Thailand, as many as 90 percent of all films shown per year are American" (Giddens, 1993: 558). According to Wildman and Siwek (1988, cited in Held et al., 1999: 355), in the 1980s, the USA distributed films to 79 countries, 56 of which count America as their primary source of movies. In comparison, the UK exported to 69 countries, only one of which relied on Britain as its primary source; India exported to 42 countries, six of which primarily consume Indian films, and Japan exported to 46 countries, none of which took Japan as their top source. In addition to exporting new films, movie industries also export videos of previously released films, which can also be quite profitable (see Alvarado, 1988).

One difficulty nations face in making their own feature films is that movies are expensive to produce and distribute. Held et al. (1999: 354) report that

a significant number of nations both inside and outside the West have the capacity to produce feature films. However, it is clear that only a very few nations actually produce large numbers of films. In the 1980s, for example, only the USA, Japan, South Korea, Hong Kong and India were producing more than 150 feature films per year and only another twenty or so nations, mainly Western, were producing more than fifty a year. The main second rank producers were the USSR, France, Italy, Spain, Germany and the UK. The majority of nations, although they had the capacity to produce films, were actually releasing fewer than twenty films per year.

Many countries subsidize their film industries. But the United States has never done so. Nor has the United Kingdom, to any great extent, since the 1970s. As a result, the proportion of new foreign films released in the United Kingdom each year has increased from a low of about 70 percent in the 1960s to almost 90 percent in the early 1990s (Held et al., 1999: 356)[2]. Russian film production has declined since the break-up of the Soviet Union and the end of subsidies. Regional and colonial ties are important in the export of films. France, for instance, distributes films to francophone nations in the Caribbean and North Africa. India is a major supplier to South East Asian, Gulf, and African countries.

The international diffusion of television depends not only on the supply of television programs, but also on the availability of broadcasting capacity and television sets in importing nations. The USA is unique among nations in its extremely low import of television from abroad, with nearly all of its few imports coming from the UK.[3] The success of American television in its home market is matched by the strength of its export market. The US distributes television programs to nearly every nation on earth, both to the major markets in Latin America and Western Europe and to the smaller and developing markets in Asia, Africa, and the Middle East (except Arab nations). The UK has a strong export market for television, but as Giddens (1993: 558) points out, the British export market consists largely of the United States, so even though the earnings for British and American television exports are on parity, the American exports have a larger influence in the wider world. France and Germany also have export markets (mostly to French- and German-speaking nations) and exports from Brazil, Mexico, Egypt, Hong Kong, Spain, and Australia are growing (Held et al., 1999: 362). For instance, the Mexican soap opera *The Rich Cry Too* (*Tambien Los Ricos Lloran*) became a global phenomenon, and was broadcast throughout Latin America and the Pacific, including China (Lull, 2000: 172).

As in film, one of the limiting factors in the local production of television programming is its expense. Broadcast television has a schedule to fill each day, and imports are often cheaper than local programming. For example, Zimbabwe Television (ZTV)

> can only afford to produce about twelve hours of indigenous drama a year, albeit incredibly cheaply with the actors also doing day jobs and providing their own costumes. Drama series like *Ziva Kawakaba* (*Know Your Roots*) are very popular with the majority black audience, but the advertisers know they are going to get better value for money from imported programmes that appeal to the more affluent white or middle-class black audiences. And ZTV know that they can acquire an episode of *Miami Vice*, say, for the special "Third World" rate of $500 – a fraction of the already minimal budget of an episode of *Ziva Kawakaba*. (Dowmunt, 1993: 6–7)

There exist strong regional markets in television, especially because of the number of hours to be filled. For example, Mexico is an important distributor of television in Spanish to Latin America and Spain (McNeely and Soysal, 1989). And recently Brazilian television has been successfully exported to Portugal (Held et al., 1999: 372). Further, many nations see television as a way to extend their own national interests. For instance, McNeely and Soysal (1989: 137) report that the Bangladesh Ministry of Information, which controls television, stated that "programmes shall be formulated on the basis of state policies and...there shall be expression and development of Bangladeshi nationalism..., efforts shall be made to reflect Muslim culture, heritage and ideologies." Varis (1985: 21) also suggests that while third world countries might import up to fifty percent of their television content, a relatively small proportion of the population watches these programs.

Popular music, especially Anglo-American music, has enjoyed the greatest worldwide success. Held et al. (1999) argue that music is more suited to international distribution than other cultural forms, as it does not rely on language for its primary impact. (Although this is belied by the fact that American and British listeners do not tend to buy popular music that is not in English. Other countries are not as chauvinistic about the language of the lyrics; nevertheless, most countries record local versions, in the vernacular, of the popular international styles.) Held et al. state that "Rock 'n' roll and its various descendants found their way to Europe via the radio as much as the concert hall and the record shop. . . . [But] the radio has also been an important instrument of localism and the maintenance and re-creation of local identities within special ethnic stations" (p. 351).

As with other forms of popular art, the distribution of music internationally is dominated by large firms from the first world, particularly American firms. But small recording companies exist in greater profusion around the world than film or television producers. First world producers of music contract with local companies across the globe, and the latter distribute local products alongside the international ones (Crane, 1992: 169–70). Pirate radio and music based on western rock genres have been influential in solidifying national resistance movements. For instance, in Lithuania, rock music helped foster popular solidarity against the Soviet Union in 1980s. In the 1990s, a rap singer celebrated intergenerational links and encouraged Lithuanians of all ages to work together to rebuild the country after the Russians left (Lull, 2000: 176–9). Indeed, popular music has encoded resistance since it solidified American resistance to the Vietnam war; indeed, since Elvis first swung his hips (Bennett, 2001).

A global market for books also exists, although for the most part it is limited to best-selling novels (both literary and pulp fiction), and literary prize winners. The flow of books is smaller than that of music, television, and film, and is limited mostly to the first world countries (see Crane, 1992: 167–68; Held et al. 1999: 346). American publishers share the market with the UK, France, Germany, and Spain. America imports more books than it exports with respect to eight different countries. In this way, the global market for books is unlike that for any other form of popular arts.

Media Imperialism

The thesis

The media imperialism thesis suggests that when first world countries, and especially the United States, export their cultural products to the rest of the world, especially to the third world, indigenous art, both folk and popular, is threatened and replaced by foreign products. This leads to an unfortunate homogenization of the world's art forms. Moreover, the culture industries are becoming increasingly concentrated in the hands of a few very large media conglomerates, who are interested solely in making a profit (see, e.g. Herman and McChesney, 1997; Schiller, 1969; 1989). The media imperialism argument is couched in concerns about more general international homogenization, for instance, the ubiquity of the fast-food chain McDonald's (e.g. Ritzer, 1993) and the domination, not just of the art produced by capitalist enterprises, but of capitalist ideology and consumerism (e.g. Baudrillard, 1970 [1998]; Ewen, 1976). The global media are seen as emissaries of these ideologies and of homogenization (Herman and McChesney, 1997). An ongoing metaphor of colonialism is employed: the cultural products of the first world "invade" the third-world and "conquer" local culture. In the stronger variants of this approach, world domination (in a cultural form) is the explicit goal of the nation-states, or the corporations, that export the culture. (See Tomlinson, 1991, for a critical analysis of theories and debates that surround the issue of media and cultural imperialism.)

Assessment

The media imperialism thesis has a number of flaws. In the first instance, theorists from this point of view sometimes conflate "American" with the multinational corporations that are headquartered in the United States. Americans, as a people, are not attempting to dominate the world with their cultural ideology. Instead, corporations are attempting to make a profit using cultural forms that have a broad appeal worldwide. Equating the dominance of American firms in the global distribution of popular arts with American cultural hegemony is inaccurate, although, arguably, these corporations do foster the ideals of capitalism and consumerism that are prevalent in American society. Nevertheless, economic control does not necessarily imply cultural control. More importantly, the media imperialism thesis implies a strong model of the center and periphery, and a one-way flow (Varis, 1974) of materials from "the West" to "the Rest." As Hannerz (1989: 67) put it, the thesis posits that "When the center speaks, the periphery listens, and on the whole does not talk back." This idea is contradicted by ample evidence of the intra-regional distribution of television (McNeely and Soysal, 1989), local production of music in popular styles (Held et al., 1999), and strong centers of film production outside of the United States, e.g. in France (Scott, 2000), and in third world countries, e.g. Bollywood in India (Penkakur and Subramanyam, 1996). In addition, some exported shows have been modified for local consumption (McNeely and Soysal, 1989: 142):

In Israel, Big Bird of *Sesame Street* has been replaced by a tougher character regarded as more suitable to the local temperament – a giant porcupine named Kipi (Shipler 1983). In the Spanish language version of the show, "Big Bird" has become a green-and-orange parrot named Montoya, with a macho character (Meislin 1983).

Hannerz (1989: 67–8) speculates that the motives of the various first world countries in distributing popular arts vary importantly, too.

> By and large, Americans may not expect that the meanings and the cultural forms they invent are only for themselves; possibly because they have seen at home over the years that practically anybody can become an American. The French may see their culture as a gift to the world. There is a *mission civilisatrice*. The Japanese, on the other hand, – so it is said – find it a strange notion that anyone can "become Japanese", and they put Japanese culture on exhibit, in the framework of organized international contacts, as a way of displaying irreducible distinctiveness rather than in order to make it spread.

Katz and Wedell (1977) argue that nations go through different phases in their reliance on imported culture. It is too expensive for many countries to fill their television broadcast schedule, for example, so they import television from abroad. However, as they develop their local capacity, they rely less on imports. The export of television from the United States peaked in the 1960s (Giddens, 1993: 559), and the international viewership of the spectacularly successful *Dallas* has not yet been matched by subsequent shows. Some authors have argued that *Seinfeld* was the last American television blockbuster at home. Due to expanding choice of television channels in America, they suggest that it is likely that national audience figures for individual programs will continue to decline (see Lull, 2000: 125). In the future, the ability of audiences to choose among a large variety of shows, including a stock of locally produced programs, may come to characterize television of all nations.

The concern that the worldwide distribution of the popular arts have eclipsed indigenous forms is asserted but rarely investigated: "Much of the evidence that is offered is merely anecdotal or circumstantial. Observations of New Guinean tribesman clustered around a set in the sweltering jungle watching *Bonanza* or of Algerian nomads watching *Dallas* in the heat of the desert are often offered as sufficient proof" (Lealand, 1984: 6–7). Moreover, much research has shown that people consume cultural objects in different ways. Access to movies, television, and music varies by country and region, as do patterns of viewing and listening (e.g. Lull, 1988). People also interpret imported cultural objects in relationship to their own backgrounds, so that the meanings derived from art differ from place to place (e.g. Liebes and Katz, 1993). Bennett (2000), for instance, shows how music is re-cast in local communities, as for instance, in white Britons' use of rap and hip-hop styles in their own music. Along these lines, Griswold and Bastian (1987) show how Nigerian authors re-work western formulas for romance novels as they adapt them for local publication.

The media imperialism thesis posits only deleterious effects of imported culture. Hannerz (1989: 70–1), however, questions whether the import of cultural forms is necessarily bad:

> Current conceptions of cultural imperialism exemplify on the largest imaginable scale the curious fact that according to the economics of culture, to receive may be to lose. In that way, they are a useful antidote to old "white man's burden" notions of the gifts of culture from the center to periphery as unadulterated benefaction. But perhaps a closer examination allows us to see more shades in the picture. In the areas of scholarship and intellectual life in general, we hardly take a conflict for granted between the transnational flow of culture and local cultural creativity the way we do with popular culture. Without a certain openness to impulses from the outside world, we would expect science, art and literature to become impoverished. . . . [T]here would not have been a Nigerian Nobel Prize winner in literature in 1986 if Wole Soyinka had not creatively drawn on both a cosmopolitan literary expertise and an imagination rooted in a Nigerian myth-ology, and turned them into something unique. . . . Why, then, are we so quick to assume that in [the transnational diffusion of popular culture] the relationship between local and imported culture can only be one of competition?

The media imperialism thesis, then, shares much in common with other writings on media effects, and with shaping approaches in general (as discussed in chapter 3). As with shaping approaches, the media imperialism argument is thrown into question by works on the reception of culture (see chapters 10 and 11).

The concern about the homogenization of cultural forms is not entirely unfounded, however. In a study of American and Canadian literature, for example, Corse (1995, 1996) shows that the content of best-selling fiction in the two countries is virtually the same, unlike literary prize winning novels and canonical novels (those on university syllabi for Canadian and American literature), which show more variation between the countries. She argues that the similarity between the two countries in terms of popular novels is due to the fact that the novels are produced by the same set of publishers using the same type of mass-market techniques to reach similar audiences.[4]

Held et al. (1999: 346–50) discuss the consolidation of multinational media companies. They show that about twenty to thirty multinational corporations control a large proportion of the entertainment and communications market in virtually every part of the world. All of these corporations are located in first world countries. Their portfolios include film and video production, television production, ownership of terrestrial, cable, satellite, or digital television channels, recorded music, radio, newspapers, magazines, book publishing, internet access, and online publishing, as well as other business interests. Ownership patterns are complex, however. Firms from one country often have a stake, through stock ownership, in firms based in another country. In this way, many large American conglomerates are "owned" by Japanese, German, and Dutch companies. Furthermore, many of the products associated with these firms are not produced solely by one conglomerate, but are made in conjunction with other media companies through joint ventures. Most have connections with national and local organizations for both the production and distribution of products.

A different, and in fact opposite, concern for theorists is not homogenization, but fragmentation. This can be traced at least as far back as Durkheim, who "pointed out the paradox that in a society with a highly advanced division of labor, the only thing people have in common is their individualism" (Griswold, 1994: 149–50). Lull (2000) discusses the division of audiences into niches, which leads to segmentation, or even "hyper-segmentation" (Turow, 1997), and discusses the possibility that "such media audience fragmentation leads to fewer common experiences for any society, resulting in a harmful loss of commonality, and the creation of a possible social polarization" (Lull, 2000: 124). While Lull does not dismiss this concern out-of-hand, he does suggest that it applies particularly to first world nations with a long history of market segmentation in industry and a highly articulated division of labor. He suggests that the popular arts, especially broadcast television, may do more to bring people together in places like Mexico and China, at least in the short term, than to drive them apart. Nevertheless, in studying the output of the culture industries, it seems that while homogenization is bad, so too is diversity.

The International Flow of the Fine Arts

Fine arts circulate internationally in patterns considerably different from those of the popular arts. One obvious difference is that the markets for fine arts are smaller and more decentralized. Moreover, the global context is highly commercial, and while noncommercial art is part of the global economy, it plays a relatively minor role in it. As Held et al. (1999: 368) write:

> [globalizing systems are] intensively used for business and commercial communications as well as for the production, transmission, and reception of popular culture. Elite cultures, high cultures, academic and scientific cultures, while obviously making use of these technologies, and occasionally featuring as content within them, are drowned in the high seas of business information systems and

commercialized popular culture. No historic parallel exists for such intensive and extensive forms of cultural flow that are primarily forms of commercial enrichment and entertainment. This includes the explosive growth of international travel and mass tourism since 1945. Once again, this phenomenon has historic predecessors in the elite tourism of nineteenth-century Europe, but in scope and scale that era is dwarfed by today's industry.

Many forms of fine art draw on conventions that are shared across nations. Crane (1992: 170) points out that symphony orchestras and opera companies are just such international art forms. They exist widely in western and post-communist societies, and they play a similar classical repertoire based on European composers.[5] (There are a few symphonies in Latin America, but for the most part, they are absent from the third world and from Eastern countries.) The visual arts also exemplify an international form. Works ranging from the cave paintings of prehistory to the cutting edge of contemporary work are appreciated by viewers and collectors worldwide. Art museums, as a cultural form, also exist worldwide, though the contents of their collections vary to a great degree. Crane (p. 171) suggests that the world's great encyclopedic museums, such as the Metropolitan Museum in New York or the Louvre in Paris, epitomize world culture through their collections, which include objects from every corner of the map.

Much of the circulation of fine arts occurs among first world nations. There is an international flow of drama, especially between the West End in London and New York's Broadway. Art works circulate on a global level in international blockbuster exhibitions, though again, these are mostly exhibitions shared among developed nations.[6] The art market, especially for old masters sold at auction, is an international one. Prices are high and only the world's wealthiest people or institutions join in the bidding. Private bidders have tended to be western, but notably, many works of fine arts were sold to Japanese corporations in the 1980s and 1990s. Most of the world's museums are priced out of the market, leaving only a few, rich institutions, such as the Getty Museum, able to bid for rare, older works. As a result, many nations have implemented laws prohibiting individuals from selling old works to interests outside the national borders without giving first right of refusal to a national museum, and have implemented tax incentives that encourage heirs to donate art to museums rather than sell them to pay death duties. The most famous contemporary artists also sell their works at high prices (but not as high as rare old masters) to an international clientele, either through dealerships or through auctions.

High prices have encouraged an underground market in stolen art and antiquities, as well as in forgeries (Meyer, 1973; Dutton, 1983). Countries such as Italy, Greece, Turkey, Thailand, Mexico, and Guatemala, with antiquities still in situ at archeological sites, are the most frequent targets of theft (Elia, 1995; Tubb, 1995). These uncatalogued works are stolen and smuggled out of the country. A "provenance" (ownership history) is sometimes forged, but other times, the works are sold without documentation to unscrupulous dealers, who in turn sell them to collectors and museums. If artifacts are discovered to be stolen, the nations that properly own them can make a compelling legal case for their return.[7] In many instances, however, it is difficult to prove the theft, as the works may have been unknown to authorities at the time they were taken. Moreover, an international agreement to protect stolen artifacts was not created until 1970[8] (and not all nations subscribe to the agreement; Bator, 1982). Works that were stolen before that date are not covered by this agreement, nor are works that were collected by previous generations in ways we may now consider ethically dubious (see case study 9.1).

Well-known works are sometimes stolen from museums. Occasionally, they are held for ransom, but more often simply disappear. They cannot be sold on the open market, but may be used as currency by members of the underworld. As with stolen antiquities, stolen fine arts can create tensions between nations. The American police, for instance, focus on catching the thieves whereas Italian authorities focus on retrieving the art work, even if it means letting the villains get away.

Artworks have moved across national boundaries as a result of wartime plunder. Napoleon famously stole art objects as he crossed Europe, notably from the Vatican, but was forced to return them after his defeat at Waterloo. Nazi forces plundered a good deal of art from the nations they occupied, and stole, either directly or indirectly, art works from Jewish collectors (Nicholas, 1994). Much of this art has been repatriated, but the claims of many Jewish victims are still pending, given the difficulties of substantiating claims in the absence of records, which were destroyed during the war. More recently, art that went missing during World War II has turned up in the Hermitage Museum in St. Petersburg and has yet to be returned (Simpson, 1997).

Price (1989) examines the flow of art objects from the third world to the first world. Specifically, she looks at the collection of "primitive" art by westerners. She shows how the meanings of the art works change as they are imported. They are fetishized as "dark" and "sexual." Moreover, westerners tend to believe that such works represent the spirit of the community or tribe that created them. This belief stands in contrast with western views of western art which is associated with individual, named artists. The identities of artists of older "primitive" works may have been lost; contemporary creators are known, but often not noted. This can create difficulties, as when the work of a living Aboriginal artist turned up on Australian currency notes, without attribution or payment (Bennett, 1980; see box 3). Price believes that art dealers have driven up the price of non-western art in the interests of their own profit margins, but that just as collectors have misconstrued the nature of non-western art, so too dealers have failed to treat non-western artists in the same manner financially as they would treat western ones.[9] She also believes that western use of the art of third world people is an example of unjustified cultural appropriation.

It is clear, then, that fine arts flow across national boundaries, and that this brings up a number of difficult issues. As we have seen, the concerns about the flow of fine arts are of a notably different character than those relating to the flow of the popular arts. In contrast with fine and especially popular arts, folk arts – by definition more closely tied to local cultures – play a small role in the globalizing economy. Occasionally, folk art groups such as dance troupes travel to various countries to display their art. Folk art can also be taken up and commodified by the culture industries, as in the "world music" phenomenon (Robinson et al., 1991). In a similar way, large media conglomerates seem destined to play a greater role in the fine arts. For instance, Microsoft's Bill Gates has purchased copyrights on the display of images from a number of picture libraries and museums across the globe.

Box 9.1   The Australian One-Dollar Bill

Westerners may hold unexamined cultural assumptions of so-called primitive art. These may be illustrated by the following, extraordinary story.

Malangi, an artist from Arnhem Land in Australia specialized in paintings on bark. His paintings were admired by a Hungarian collector who bought a number of them and brought them to Europe. In 1963, the collector donated one of Malangi's bark paintings to the Musée des Arts Africains et Oceaniens in Paris. Later that year, a museum curator sent a number of slides of Australian Aboriginal works to an official who was working on the conversion of Australian currency to the decimal system, and the resulting redesign of banknotes. This individual sent the portfolio on to designers on his team. They created the one-dollar bill, illustrating it with an Aboriginal motif – in fact, using Malangi's design without alteration.

Fortunately for Malangi, when the bills were released, a school teacher recognized the design as his work and contacted a journalist. A lawsuit was mentioned, but not carried forward, and Malangi received both compensation and, in the form of an inscribed medal, recognition for his art work. The banknote continued to carry the white designer's initials, however. When asked how the design team could have, in effect, stolen someone else's image, the governor of the Reserve Bank replied that everyone simply assumed "that the designs were the work of some traditional Aboriginal artist long dead" (Bennett, 1980: 45).

Cultural Tourism

As tourism has grown dramatically since the close of World War II, it has come increasingly under the scrutiny of scholars, many of whom are interested in such issues as the time–space compression of the world. There are many important issues in tourism not considered here, for instance, the unequal distribution of tourists in regard to their countries of origin and their chosen destinations, the economic impact of tourism, and its potential for overcrowding and polluting delicate ecologies and quaint villages. Instead, we briefly consider the relationship of tourism to fine art and heritage.

Does "cultural tourism" affect the way that art is housed, displayed, or experienced? Certainly, cultural tourism plays an important role in generating audiences for certain forms of culture. Forty percent of the audience of London's West End shows are foreign tourists (Urry, 1990: 51). Art museums, especially those in large cities, also rely to a great extent on tourists, both foreign and domestic. Three-quarters of foreign visitors to the United Kingdom visited at least one museum or gallery during their stay (Urry, 1990: 106). The commercialization of high culture, especially in the form of museum restaurants and shops, can be traced, in part, to the increase of tourists. Tourism has also played a part in the rise of international blockbuster exhibitions. Exhibitions that bring together the *Treasures of Tutankhamen* or Monet's *Water Lilies* encourage travelers, both foreign and domestic, to come to museums. Visitors to blockbusters, both local audiences and tourists, consume the art in such shows as an event or spectacle, rather than in the quiet contemplation preferred by connoisseurs (Alexander, 1996a, c).

Boorstin (1964) argues that tourists seek an "environmental bubble" when they travel, in order to shield them from the unexpected and unpleasant. As a result, tourists seek the "pseudo-event" in place of a real experience. Disneyland is the emblem, *par excellence*, of this protected bubble. MacCannell (1976) draws upon Boorstin's ideas, but suggests that tourists do not purposefully seek out pseudo-events. Instead, they actively seek the authentic. But as authenticity is difficult to find, and is intrusive, the tourist industry creates "staged authenticity." In this regard, tourists experience repackaged, commodified folk arts, and purchase "airport" or "tourist" art, rather than viewing authentic folk performances and buying local crafts. Urry (1990) believes that the very experience of art – and heritage, and landscape – is changed through tourism. The tourist "gaze" changes the object viewed from a sign of something to a "sign of itself" (p. 3). Tourists go to see the Eiffel Tower because it is famous and because it is there. They take photographs of it and themselves in front of it. "The gaze is constructed through signs, and tourism involves the collection of signs. When tourists see . . . Paris what they capture in the gaze is 'timeless, romantic Paris'. When a small village in England is seen, what they gaze upon is . . . '[ye] olde England' " (p. 3). Places like Niagara Falls in the US or Gretna Green in Scotland "become a signifier now emptied of meaning, a thoroughly commercialised cliché" (p. 11). Thus, even authentic settings become, under the tourist gaze, a simulacrum (a substitution of the pseudo for the real) just as inauthentic as Disneyland. One may wish to question how much tourists actually experience the gaze in this latter way, but the idea is captured in the popular phrase "been there, done that."

Conclusion

The literature on globalization is diverse. Often, it shares assumptions with theories from the shaping approach. In this way, globalization, especially of the popular arts, is seen to promote homogenization of art at the lowest levels of artistic merit. The products of the cultural industry are seen as driving out more worthy indigenous art. These concerns can be countered by looking at how popular forms are shaped to local conditions. Nevertheless, the concentration of a large variety of media concerns in a few, large, multinationals based, for the most part, in first world countries, remains an issue. Art and aesthetic forms do not stand still, but must be open to new influences. What goes into the mix affects the aesthetic outcome, as is argued by the production approach in general. Observers do not agree on what constitutes authentic versus derivative art, however, and the ultimate effects of the incorporation of popular forms (both high-quality and "debased," low-quality works) on local art (which itself can encompass both creative art and "junk") is a matter of considerable debate.

Globalization theory also draws inspiration from the interpretive or consumption approaches, focusing on the reception of global products and the myriad ways individuals cobble together the cultural objects at their disposal into unique patterns. It draws on postmodern thinking as it concentrates on the fragmentation of the world into smaller niches and as it thinks about simulacrum and spectacle. Other research is more positivist in focus, trying to measure global flows of art works. This latter research has shown that core–periphery models of diffusion (from the first world to the third world) are too simple. Enormous methodological issues are hidden in their measurements, however. Different countries collect data on cultural flows in different ways and for different purposes, and information from the culture industries involved can be in short supply – and is reported for business, rather than research, purposes.

The fine arts are affected by globalization, but the dynamics of increasing international links play out differently for them than for the popular arts. Tourism changes the orientation of such tourist attractions as theaters and museums, leading many observers to blame tourism, at least in part, for their increasing level of commercialization. More people see more art than ever before, as works travel to local venues and as tourists travel abroad, but high prices encourage the flow of the very best art to wealthy countries and individuals. This benefits the financial elite, just as the international flow of popular art appears to benefit capitalists. High prices limit the ability of museums to acquire the best (i.e. most expensive) works that come to market, and also drive the international trade in fakes, forgeries, and stolen objects. Thus, while the international circulation of fine and popular works produces a deeper and more widely shared familiarity with the varied arts from all over the world, globalization clearly has the potential to produce deleterious results.

NOTES

1   Appadurai appears to leave out the global flow of goods, both for consumers (from food to clothing), and for business (raw materials, parts, and commodities besides machinery). His reminder that different types of flows exist is more important than the jargon he invents to describe them.

2   The proportion of American films screened in the UK, as reported by Giddens, is much lower than the proportion of new foreign films, including American ones, released in the UK, as reported by Held et al. It is not clear whether this reflects a difference in what is measured (American versus all foreign films, but also new films *released* versus *screened* films, whether new or old) or different measurement techniques. Giddens does not provide a source for his statistics.

3   Most of the British television shows imported to America appear on the Public Broadcast System (PBS), leading some to joke that its acronym stands for Primarily British Series (Abercrombie, 1996: 99).

4   Corse does not argue that the novels she examines are homogeneous. Rather, the popular novels of the two countries are similar in their variation. She also argues that literature continues to play a role in creating ideas of national culture and both prize-winners and canonical works are used by elites in this manner. This point also argues against ideas of global homogeneity, in that nation-states are far from defunct.

5   As part of the flow of classical music, symphonies go on tour. One would imagine, however, that "world tours" include mainly first world counties, and, much less commonly, large cities in other regions.

6   Lai (2002) considers international traveling exhibitions, including those traveling to and from Taiwan.

7   In addition to unwittingly buying stolen goods, many museums and collectors have been taken in by forgeries (WGBH Educational Foundation, 1991). As with stolen objects, they are often supplied with a fake provenance. When forgeries are unmasked, however, no one wants them back, and objects which once held a venerable position in a museum and, often, withstood critical scrutiny and received

critical acclaim, are relegated to storerooms. This brings up interesting questions about how art acquires both aesthetic and financial value (see Zolberg, 1990: 85–92).

8   This is the 1970 *UNESCO Convention on the means of prohibiting and preventing the illicit import, export, and transfer of ownership of cultural property.*

9   The situation may have improved to some degree since Price wrote. For instance, while prices do not yet match those of western artists, they have increased, and named living artists working in traditional styles have become well known in art circles (see *The Economist*, 1998 on Aboriginal art).

Case Study 9.1

The Return of the Elgin (or Parthenon) Marbles?[1]

Points for Discussion

1 What are the arguments for the return of the Elgin/Parthenon marbles to Greece? What are the arguments for keeping them in the British Museum?
2 To whom do the marbles belong? The British Museum, the British people, the Greek people, the people of the world? What difference might each of these answers make to the debate about where to house the marbles?
3 Should the marbles be returned to Greece?

Case

Background

The assembly of Athens decided in 448 BC to build a temple to the goddess Athena on the highest point of the Acropolis, a citadel situated on the highest hill in the city. An earlier temple to Athena had been demolished a few years before by occupying Persians. The new temple, called the Parthenon, was finished sixteen years later, in 432 BC. It was built in the Doric style, having a rectangular shape (about 70 meters by 30 meters) and surrounded on all sides by Doric columns to support the roof. Between the tops of the columns and the cornice on the edge of the roof was a frieze, which portrays a continuous scene running all the way around the building. On either end, there was a triangular pediment above the frieze, which was also adorned with carved figures. In most Doric temples, the pediment is supported by six columns, but the Parthenon's pediments are supported by eight columns, which allowed the pediments to be particularly large and spectacular. The entire building was made of white marble. Each stone was individually carved to fit perfectly with its neighbors. The frieze was carved in low relief (the figures stand out somewhat from the background) and the pediments in high relief (the figures are almost free-standing sculptures, although they remain attached to the pediment). The marble was not left white. Instead, the figures were painted in brilliant colors.

Some 800 years later, in the fifth century AD, the temple was converted into a Christian church. It remained in use as a church until 1458 when the Ottoman Turks conquered Greece. The Acropolis became a fortress for the occupying Turks, and the Parthenon was converted into a mosque. In 1687, in an attack on the Turks by the Venetian army, the Parthenon was seriously damaged when a mortar bomb was shot into the gunpowder stored inside by the Turks. Some bits of the sculpture that had been blasted off were removed by the Venetians after their victory over the Turks, who returned two years later. The Venetians also attempted to remove some of the sculptures from the west pediment, but succeeded only in smashing them as they fell to the ground. In the late eighteenth century, a French ambassador to Turkey acquired part of the east frieze and some other pieces of sculpture, which presumably were lying on the ground after the gunpowder explosion, and these are now in the Louvre.

After successful lobbying to be ambassador to Ottoman Turkey, Thomas Bruce, seventh Earl of Elgin, was appointed in 1799. This set in motion a series of events that were to produce one of the most important controversies in the international flow of arts. Lord Elgin started by hiring an artist to sketch the Parthenon sculptures. He turned down J. M. W. Turner, the famous English landscape painter, and instead hired Giovanni Battista Lusieri. The Turks, it was reported, were grinding down the Parthenon marble to make mortar and had little desire to protect the ancient work. Elgin was able to get a writ, called a *firman*, from the Turks (who needed Britain's help in their conflict with France), which gave him permission to sketch and make plaster casts of the Parthenon sculptures, to excavate around the building, and to collect objects with inscriptions or figures. The *firman* was written in vague language and Elgin interpreted it in the broadest possible way as giving him permission not just to make models and sketches, and to claim small fragments that had already broken off, but to preserve the works by taking the most important ones away. Back in England, Elgin claimed to have removed the sculptures for their own protection. In any case, his men had begun removing sculptures six months before Elgin's only visit to Athens in which he saw what he described as their deteriorated condition.

At Elgin's behest, in 1801 and 1802, Lusieri began to divest the Parthenon of its adornments for shipment to England. The frieze was chopped off the building, and the backs of many stones were sawn off in order to make it easier to ship their sculpted portions by sea. Lusieri wrote to Elgin in 1982,

> I have, my Lord, the pleasure of announcing to you the possession of the 8th metope [part of the frieze], that one where there is the Centaur carrying off the woman. This piece has caused much trouble in all respects, and I have even been obliged to be a little barbarous. (Quoted in Hitchens, 1987: 30)

The barbarity, in this case, was the damage to the marble surrounding the section of the frieze, which came down in a hail of fragments as the metope was removed. In the end, Elgin caused the removal of about half of the surviving sculptured parts of the Parthenon itself (including metopes, frieze panels, and sculptures hacked from the pediment), and a caryatid (a column in the shape of a woman) from an adjoining building. One shipment of sculptures sank off Kythera, but most of the pieces were rescued by local fishermen. At least one frieze broke in half as it was transported. After these pieces were carried off, Lusieri continued to send vases, marble fragments, and other objects that Elgin used to decorate his house at Broomhall. Finally in 1819, Elgin, citing financial problems, dismissed Lusieri, who died two years later. In a sad footnote to this story, all of Lusieri's drawings and paintings of the Parthenon and Athens, twenty years of work, were lost at sea when the ship carrying them to England went down in a storm.

Elgin sent the main sculptures and friezes to London, where, facing financial difficulties, he tried to sell them to the British government. Many smaller pieces of marble, however, were brought to his estate in Scotland and were incorporated there as decoration. It took him a number of years to convince Parliament to buy the marbles, partly because one classical scholar inaccurately declared the marbles to be Roman rather than Greek, and partly due to a dispute over how much they were worth. Eventually, in 1816, Parliament agreed to buy them for the sum of £35,000 (about half of what Elgin wanted) and to house them together in perpetuity in the British Museum where they would be known, by statute, as the Elgin Marbles.

Just ten years after they were removed from the Parthenon, even before Parliament purchased them, Lord Byron called for the return of the marbles to Greece. He was one of the first in a long line of both eminent and ordinary people who have argued for the repatriation of the marbles. Others, however, fiercely disagree.

Point: the Elgin Marbles should remain in Britain

Return the sculptures to Greece? Have you lost your marbles? The British Museum, with Elgin's help, has preserved the marbles for posterity. Had the marbles remained in Greece, they might have been destroyed by the Turks, who seemed to pay them scant regard. They have been kept in proper, museum conditions for two hundred years and are now in much better condition than the marbles remaining in Athens, which have succumbed to the elements and, until recently, neglect. And they have been spared the assaults of environmental pollution, especially auto exhaust, that attacked the marbles in Athens until they were removed to the new Parthenon Museum where they are now kept in cases pumped full of inert gas.

The Elgin Marbles are beautifully displayed in the British Museum, in galleries designed specifically for them. Large numbers of people come to see the British Museum (more than five million per year, many of them tourists from abroad) and, arguably, more people see them in London than would do so if they were in Athens.

By today's standards, the techniques of removing and transporting the marbles were poor. However, by the standards of the time, Elgin did his best. His heart was in the right place in attempting to preserve the marbles. Furthermore, Elgin sought and received permission for his actions from the legal government (Ottoman) of Athens at that time. He did not steal the marbles, nor did he smuggle them out of Greece. The removal of the marbles, therefore, was legal, and their purchase and deposit into the British Museum was also legal. Parliament decreed in 1816 that the marbles must remain together, and remain forever in the British Museum. It is not possible to reInterpret old acquisitions which were legitimate at the time by today's standards. It would be an assault on British law, and on the principles of museum acquisition, to deaccession works accepted in perpetuity.

More importantly, if the Elgin marbles are returned to Greece, what else will the Greek government wish to reclaim? What other governments will want back antiquities found originally on their soils? Greece may now have the technology and political stability to give proper care to their antiquities, but will other nations? Giving the marbles to Greece would set a dangerous precedent and open the floodgates to claims for "repatriation" of all sorts of art and artifacts. The world's great museums could be emptied.

The British Museum acquired the marbles legally, and their legal ownership continues to this day.

Counterpoint: return the Parthenon Marbles

About half the surviving sculpture from the Parthenon resides in the British Museum, and about half in Athens. A major section of the frieze is in the Louvre, and a small number less important fragments are scattered among a number of countries. As Hitchens (1987: 37) puts it:

> Since the sculptures were carved to adorn a building which still . . . survives, and since they were carved (most especially the friezes) as a unity of action and representation, this state of affairs seems absurd. . . . [T]o keep them in two places, one of them quite sundered from the Parthenon and its context, seems bizarre and irrational as well as inartistic.

The Parthenon marbles – to call them the Elgin marbles is a travesty which celebrates their desecration – are particularly important for Greece. In addition to their archeological and artistic import, they are an important symbol for Greeks of the greatness of their nation and their history.

Moreover, Elgin did not take the sculpture legally. He had permission to sketch and cast, not to saw and hack. He looted the Parthenon and sent the spoils to a foreign country while another foreign power occupied Greece. Greeks could only watch and cry. The Turks had no right to allow anything with regard to the Parthenon, and Elgin far exceeded the permissions that Turks illegally gave to him. In prizing the sculpture off the facade of the Parthenon, Elgin not only damaged the integrity of the building in its artistic impact, he badly damaged the remaining structure. The tiny chips and fragments his men knocked off with their clumsy removal efforts can never be recovered or replaced. They also removed the cornices to get to the frieze, and broke up the entablature underneath it. The least the British can do to repay this damage is to return the pieces of the building that still remain intact. Furthermore, Elgin claimed to have saved the marbles for the (British) nation, but when he carted them off, he may have planned to keep them for himself. Only financial ruin forced him to try to recoup his costs by selling them off.

Returning the Parthenon marbles would not set a dangerous precedent. Of all the antiquities and archeological objects in the world's museums, only a few belong to surviving buildings, and of those, none has the importance to their country of origin as the Parthenon does to the Greeks. The Greek government itself has made it clear that they relinquish claims to all other Greek antiquities, except the Parthenon marbles. In addition, Greece is a modern country, and although not rich, it is quite capable of maintaining museum collections to world-class standards. And the British museum has not taken as good care of them as it has professed – in 1937–8, it "cleaned" the sculptures with carbolic acid and wire brushes, in order to whiten them, thereby removing the outer layers of marble, a fact which the British Museum took pains to cover up.

Most importantly, the feelings of the Greek people must be respected. Their wishes were disregarded then, and continue to be disregarded now. The Parthenon symbolizes

Greek national identity, and the connection of its people to its past. They have always cared highly for it, to the best of their abilities. For instance, in 1822, Turks in the Acropolis, under siege by the Greeks who were fighting for their independence, broke into the walls of the Parthenon to make bullets from the lead that was inside. So deep was the feelings of the Athenians about the Parthenon that they sent bullets to the very Turks they were trying to oust, to prevent them from further damaging the building.

The marbles are special, and different from all other antiquities in their importance to their country of origin. The marbles were specifically designed to be seen as a unit, from below. The Parthenon marbles should be together to be seen where they belong, up high on the Parthenon.

Reply: The Elgin Marbles should stay put

The Elgin Marbles cannot be put back on the Parthenon. If they were returned to Greece, they would have to reside in a museum, and would not have any greater an impact than they currently do in the British Museum. The Greek restoration projects can, and do, rely on casts taken of the marbles. The three caryatids remaining on the Erechtheion (next to the Parthenon) were recently removed to a museum and replaced with replicas. The fourth caryatid is in the British Museum. The replica made of it is of higher quality than the other three copies, because it was less damaged by time and pollution than the ones from Athens.

And who is to say what is "important" and "special"? Removing the most special set of objects in the British Museum would indeed open the door to claims by other peoples, and perhaps even the Greek people, for the next-most-special objects, and so on. The foundations of the world's museum collections must not be chipped away.

Note

1   Quite a lot has been written on the Elgin/Parthenon marbles. Good references are Chamberlin (1983), Cook (1997), Hitchens (1987), Lowenthal (1985), Merryman (1985), and Meyer (1973).

Part IIB
The Cultural Diamond
The Consumption of Culture

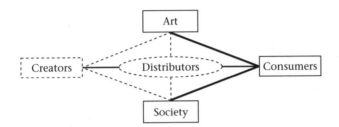

10

Reception Approaches

[A] text's unity lies not in its origin but in its destination.
(Roland Barthes, 1969 [1977]: 148)

Theories which constitute the consumption of culture approach focus on the right-hand side of the cultural diamond and look at how people consume, use, and receive art. The main idea is that *audiences are the key to understanding art, because the meanings created from art and the ways it is used depend on its consumers, not its creators.* The approach also critiques simplistic shaping approaches by denying that art has a direct impact on society. Rather, art shapes society through audiences, who are for the most part quite capable of intelligent reaction. All of the studies presented in this chapter share the idea, as Griswold (1993: 457) puts it, of the "reader as hero."

This chapter briefly explores the roots of this idea, then turns to a discussion of early writing in reception that looked at how people use the arts (especially popular ones) and what gratifications they draw from them. A number of approaches developed subsequently from this, including models of how people decode texts, and more recently, studies of the active audience. Other research in the consumption of culture draws on reception aesthetics, first developed in literary criticism, which suggests that people receive culture in relationship to their personal "horizons of expectations." The implication is that art never stands alone, but must be understood in relationship to the people who consume it. Specifically, the meanings people take from art, and the type of art that they choose to consume, are based on their backgrounds and their social networks.

Roots of Reception Approaches

Many sociologists, especially those from an interpretive framework, are interested in the question of how people create meaning in their lives. In order to uncover meaning, a researcher needs to talk to people, and to study their social relationships and their milieu. This interest in meaning has deep roots in sociology, going back to the works of Max Weber. In post-war America, the "Chicago School" of sociology produced a number of studies of social groups and the meanings they generate (e.g. Whyte, 1943; Becker, 1963; Liebow, 1967). Most of these studies did not look at artists or art works,[1] but the spirit of their research pervades much interpretive work on the uses of culture, especially in American research (e.g. Press, 1991).

As discussed by Press (1994), studies in the reception of culture draw on two key traditions, cultural studies (especially in the United Kingdom) and literary criticism (especially in the United States). These two strands of research have led to a variety of theories that all emphasize the importance of the receiver in the creation of meaning. I will set out an important precursor to these two approaches, one that came from media research. Then I will review the British cultural studies that led to the development of the "active audience" approach. I will return to the influence of literary theory on the sociology of reception later in the chapter.

In the 1970s, a new model of understanding the consumption of culture, the *Uses and Gratifications* perspective, arose from media studies. It suggests that audiences are *active* in consuming culture. Shaping approaches assume a passive audience, and as a result are often called the "mass manipulation model" by the new theorists. The uses and gratifications approach asks how and why people use culture, arguing that an important clue is that people consume culture to gratify their own needs. Blumler and Katz (1974), for instance, argued that people watch television to meet four needs: (1) *diversion*, (2) *personal relationships*, both with on-screen characters and with friends and family while watching together or discussing shows, (3) *personal identity*, reinforcing one's own values, and comparing one's circumstances and personal problems to those presented on television, and (4) *surveillance*, to gain information on what is happening in the wider world.

Lull (2000: 109–110) gives a fuller list of the uses of television:

> How people use media to gratify their needs is limited only by their imagination. They can use television, for example, to illustrate their experiences and feelings, establish common ground with others, enter conversations, reduce interpersonal anxieties, set the agenda for talk, clarify, promote, and transmit values, establish physical and verbal contact . . . develop family solidarity . . . reduce conflicts,

maintain relationships, learn social behavior, make decisions, model behavior, solve problems, support opinions, disseminate information, enact and reinforce roles, exercise authority, filter experience, and facilitate arguments.

A number of studies have looked at the ways people watch television. For instance, Tuchman et al. (1978) claimed that television is an "electronic hearth" that has replaced the fireplace as the area where families gather for companionship and conversation. They argued that the television might pro- mote more family sociability than, say, reading books because people talk about what they watch. Morley (1986), in a study of eighteen families in South London, showed that men tend to decide what to watch when the family is watching together. Many men actually held onto the remote; wives and children only got to flip the channels when their husband or father was not in the room. Morley also found that the London men watched television more deliberately than women, choosing their viewing ahead of time from the television listings and watching programs with relatively close attention. Women were more likely to do other activities, like housework, while looking at the television and were more likely to talk to others during the shows. Collett's (1987) research showed that people do not stare constantly at the television screen, in fact when they are in front of the set, they look at it an average of only 65 percent of the time. They also eat, sleep, or do homework or chores while the television is on, and spend a good deal of time talking to others in the room, using the television as part of socializing. Lull (1988) reports considerable cross-national variation in these patterns. For instance, he says, in Venezuela, women control the viewing of television. In India, the television has helped increase women's power in the family.

The uses and gratifications perspective viewed the audience as active in their interactions with popular art and proposed that people can meet their needs through its consumption. It focused on audiences, rather than the art object itself or its negative effects, and thus was influential in casting the audience as powerful.

British Cultural Studies

British cultural studies (which finds its own roots in such work as Hoggart, 1957, and Williams, 1959) takes an explicitly Marxist approach to culture.[2] But instead of decrying the loss to society implied in the growth of the popular arts, as did the mass-culture critics, scholars in cultural studies have examined, and celebrated, the oppositional use of the popular arts by marginal, subcultural, and working-class groups. As summed up by Storey (1993: 67), theorists in the cultural studies approach examine "cultural texts and practices in order to reconstitute or reconstruct the experiences, values, etc. – the 'structure of feeling' – of particular groups or classes or whole societies, in order to better understand the lives of those who lived the culture. . . . [They do so] because they believe that popular culture (defined as the lived culture of ordinary men and women) is worth studying."[3] As with the uses and gratifications approach, researchers in cultural studies believe that people are active in their consumption of culture.

Research by Hall (1980) provided a key building block in cultural studies. This work, which draws on semiotics (discussed more fully in chapter 13), focuses on the *encoding and decoding* of cultural texts. Art objects are seen as "texts" which embody meanings. These meanings are presented in verbal or visual codes. The creator of the art object encodes meaning into it. In order for the audience to make sense of the art object, it must decode, or *read*, the message. The meaning that the author of the text intends is called the *preferred meaning*. However, people can take different meanings from the text by decoding them in different ways. Hall (1980) suggests that there are four basic categories of decoding. (1) The *dominant-hegemonic* position, which occurs when receivers read the message as it was intended. (2) The *oppositional* position, a stance in which receivers understand the intended meaning, but nevertheless, take an alternative meaning that was not intended by the creator of the art object. (3) The *negotiated* position, in which receivers mix the first two positions. The final type of decoding is called (4) the *aberrant* position, which occurs when the receiver does not understand the encoding, and consequently, interprets the text in an idiosyncratic or bizarre manner.

A classic study of the audience's decoding of the media was conducted by Morley (1980), who showed focus groups a recording of the British news/current affairs program, *Nationwide*. He was interested in whether such programs enforced hegemonic ideas in society. He discovered that the readings produced by the discussion groups did fall into the categories of dominant, negotiated, and oppositional, but that the readings were not based solely on social class, which was his original hypothesis. He found that bank managers, not surprisingly, produced dominant readings of the news program, but so did young, working-class apprentices. University art students and students learning to be teachers took an approach that mixed negotiated and dominant positions. Finally, both white shop stewards and black further-education students took oppositional stances, but the readings of the shop stewards differed greatly from that of the black students. Morley concludes that viewers of the program decode it based on their social position, not their class position, because the social position gives different groups access to different kinds of discourses to draw upon in discussing the portrayal of world events. Bank managers and shop stewards take a dominant and an oppositional stance, respectively. Their class interests and their social position coincide. But the apprentices take an uncritical, dominant reading because they have learned the dominant model in school; they do not yet have access to alternative discourses. By extension, we would expect Morley's findings to help us understand how people decode art forms as well.

Subcultures

A key focus of cultural studies involved research on subcultures (Hall and Jefferson, 1975). In an influential study, Hebdige (1979) examined the succession of youth subcultures in Britain that center around music. His work draws on the ideas of Gramsci (see chapter 3), and considers how people resist hegemonic messages. Youths in oppositional subcultures create meaning for themselves by actively reworking the arts, fashion, and commodities available from cultural and consumer industries. Young, working-class men symbolically resist both adult culture and middle-class values, through a process called *bricolage*. They pick and choose products and combine them in unexpected ways that adults find shocking, and they develop new musical styles, also shocking, that help define them as a group. The new styles express the resistance of the youth subculture, but are eventually adopted and cleaned up by the culture industries, which strip the styles of their oppositional power. Thus, a new generation of youth must develop its own, original expressions of resistance, which will also, eventually, be captured by hegemonic forces.

Willis (1978) used an ethnographic approach in his study of two subcultures, "bikeboys" and hippies, and the music that structures their lives. He argues that the "best ethnography does something which theory and commentary cannot: it presents human experience without minimizing it, and without making it a passive reflex of social structure and social conditions" (p. 170). Moreover, he argues that the meaning of art works is actively constructed in use: "objects, artifacts and institutions do not, as it were, have a single valency. It is the act of social engagement with a cultural item which activates and brings out particular meanings" (p. 193). Willis looks at how the hippies and bikeboys themselves connected music and social life, looking for the "homologies" between musical choice and group lifestyles.[4]

Bikeboys preferred music that had a strong, fast beat; classic rock of the late 1950s. The music gave them a sense of "security, authenticity and masculinity" (p. 63) and actually got them to move. As one bikeboy put it, "if you hear a fast record you've got to get up and do something, I think. If you can't dance any more, or if the dance is over, you've just got to go for a burn-up [a fast motorcycle ride]" (p. 73). They listened to the music while dancing, and then heard the beat in their heads while riding. Hippies, on the other hand, preferred progressive rock, and liked to listen to long, uninterrupted albums.

Music did not encourage movement, or anything else, but was seen as another sensual experience, which could be heightened by the use of drugs. According to hippies, "straights" could not adequately appreciate progressive rock because they lacked the mind-expanding experience of being high.

The active audience

Contemporary research in cultural studies takes what is called an active audience approach. This research is epitomized by the work of Fiske (1989). Fiske suggests that people take their own meaning from cultural texts, attributing almost full autonomy to receivers in creating meaning. Fiske examines the popular arts.[5] He starts with the idea that these are produced by elites and their intended meaning is to dominate, either economically or intellectually. Fiske calls the ability to create meanings *semiotic power*. In the US, the UK, and Australia, the contexts that Fiske examines, the main hegemonic forces are white, capitalist, and patriarchal. Fiske asks why people consume the popular arts if the goal of these products is to dominate? As Fiske puts it, "There is no lasting pleasure in being a cultural dope" (p. 116).

The answer, according to Fiske, is that people resist these messages by creating messages of their own. People create their own social identity, in social systems. They make their own identities; they do not accept one proffered through the media by the dominant elites. Meaning comes from "circulation," the interaction of texts and their reception. The meanings of texts are appropriated and subverted in the interests of those who consume the text. Generating meaning by subordinate classes in opposition to the dominant message is an act of defiance, it is *semiotic resistance*. The creation of meaning is a constant, and political, process. Meaning is a contested terrain. For instance, the "girl fans" of Madonna resist patriarchal messages about their sexuality, by constructing more active, and oppositional, views of female power and desire.[6]

Fiske does not test his ideas through empirical research, however. Ironically, though he gives more weight to the readings taken by audiences with respect to the text, he focuses much of his own analysis on texts themselves, and the broader popular culture. For instance, he "reads" the activity of shopping and he "reads" the beach, without interviewing shoppers or surfers. He does, however, assess a range of texts and the way that they interrelate "intertextually." In the realm of the popular arts, Fiske analyzes the narrative of Madonna's music videos. In *Material Girl*, Madonna is not the passive recipient of jewels, as is Marilyn Monroe in the musical number, "Diamonds are a Girl's Best Friend," on which part of the video is based, but instead controls the riches, the chorus boys, and the video's hero with whom she runs off at the end. Monroe used her attractiveness to get men to give her diamonds, singing that diamonds will provide security as she ages. She needed the attention of the men. Madonna, on the other hand, does not need men or their gifts. She makes it clear with puns in her lyrics that she herself is already wealthy, a fact we know anyway. Indeed, all Madonna "lacks is the *need* for men. She relates to them in order to assert her independence of them. Men [are] objects of feminine pleasure and subjects of feminine power" (p. 129). Madonna's work, in particular, uses irony to play with the patriarchal images of women and employs visual and verbal puns to "undermine the dominant ideology while wryly recognizing its presence in the representation" (p. 110). Fiske concludes, "Madonna's popularity is a complexity of power and resistances, of meanings and countermeanings, of pleasures and the struggle for control" (p. 113).

Fiske suggests that semiotic resistance supports people in their daily lives. It is a tactic for dealing with subjugation, a way of making do. It does not foment social change or revolution, and in this way the gains of semiotic resistance are "progressive rather than radical" (p. 11). It makes life more pleasant.[7] But economic hegemony still wins out. The young women who take strong messages of resistance from Madonna – or of "girl power" from the Spice Girls – still go to the shops to buy the music, and to buy the clothes to support the style and image they wish to project. They might, or might not, act differently with their boyfriends, but they certainly do not go out and demonstrate against sexism or patriarchy. But as they spend their money, they build self-esteem and identity through the meanings they have taken from the videos.

Power and Ideology

The active audience approach posits a "semiotic democracy" in which receivers of texts are able to create empowering messages by drawing on the materials that the culture industry has to offer. It has given all the power in the relationship between art and audiences to the audiences. Theorists who draw on Marxist ideas of hegemony, as well as those who draw on poststructuralist ideas of power-knowledge, revive the notion that art can have power, either through its encapsulation of ideology or in its role in discourses that work to the advantage of elites. McKinley, for instance, is interested in how girls and young women talk about a television show, *Beverly Hills, 90210* and how they use it to discuss issues such as identity. She is also, however, concerned about how readily they accept ideologies, for instance, those about gender roles (see box 10.1).

Ang (1991) is interested in how the television industry and other institutions associated with it discursively construct a conception of "the" audience. Drawing from the work of Foucault, Ang argues that the audience exists

Box 10.1 *Beverly Hills, 90210*

McKinley (1997) studied how viewers spoke about the television show *Beverly Hills, 90210* in order to understand how their "talk" positioned them as viewers and served to construct their identities. She begins by taking viewers, literally, at their word, in their account of the pleasures they obviously took from viewing the program. But she also draws on the idea of hegemony and shows how it works, through the program, to perpetuate certain dominant ideologies in society.

In 1990, *90210* was first broadcast on the American Fox network. It is a show about posh high school students (in subsequent seasons, the main characters go to university) in wealthy Beverly Hills. Their zip code, which appears in the show's title, indicates they are from one of the most exclusive neighborhoods in southern California.

McKinley's study took place during the height of the show's popularity, in 1994–5. The participants in the study were 36 girls and young women ranging in age from 11 to 22. She viewed the show with small groups of participants, consisting of friends who often watched together. They were regular viewers and considered themselves fans of the show. The study took place in the girls' living rooms, bedrooms, or dorm rooms, and McKinley watched three episodes, of either live broadcasts or videos of shows taped a few days earlier, with each group. She tape-recorded the spontaneous discussion that occurred during the show, and the transcriptions of this "talk" made up her data. Her analysis blends a perspective which emphasizes "language as constitutive of our understanding of reality – of talk as action" with an approach which highlights how the girls "discursively constructed themselves and others within situations and contexts" (p. 65). As McKinley puts it, "nearly every statement implies identity, and talk that discursively constructs identities for 'I,' 'me,' 'us,' and 'them' in one situation is . . . valid as an indicator of the potential to construct subject positions" (p. 66).

More specifically, McKinley was interested in the "enculturation process" by which girls take on hegemonic cultural messages that have been "naturalized," or made to seem normal and inevitable. She is careful to point out that she was not trying to uncover what the girls "really" thought. Rather, she was interested in the discursive practices they used in identity construction. These are evident in the way we use language. Studying them allowed McKinley "to examine whether viewer talk constructed alternate subject positions (discursive agency) or worked to perpetuate dominant notions of female identity" (p. 66).

The first thing to notice about the talk is that, on the surface, it sounds banal. Indeed, the girls would say that their comments were trivial. But McKinley suggests that just this banality reveals the power of the discourse and of the enculturation process. Here, I show how McKinley interprets the girls' talk on appearances. (The italics indicate what is happening on the screen while the talk occurs.)

Show comes on.
Katey: Didn't she used to have brown hair? It looks red.

* * *

[*Show plays.*] ... *Brenda (talking about eating meat): "We might as well eat our own young."*
Both: Snigger.
Karey: I actually like Cindy's hair right there. It looks good compared to other episodes.
Marion: Yeah. It doesn't look like a helmet anymore.
Karey: Uh-uh.

* * *

... *Donna and David talking about his music. Donna persuades him to take piano lessons.*
Kaitlin: I like her sweater.

(pp. 68–9)

These quotes show that talk positioned the speakers as experts, who were equal, or even superior, to the characters. Being an expert in matters such as aesthetic judgements (who is pretty) offered pleasure to the viewers. The talk also positioned the viewers as

active, as authors of their meanings and behaviors ... Never did
they suggest that their definition of "pretty" came from anywhere except
themselves, that this particular combination of height,
weight, features, body shape and hair color available to only a
fraction of women on this planet came with any value implications.
As they expertly "authored" their opinions, they perpetuated this
system in which, as feminists have pointed out, we set ourselves impossible
standards, then denigrate ourselves when we don't
measure up. (p. 73)

McKinley also suggests that the girls connected beauty with niceness, using the terms almost interchangeably ("G" is McKinley):

Maddy: I like Kelly.
G: Yeah? What do you like about her?
Maddy: She's, uh, she's nice.
G: Uh huh.
Colleen: She's pretty.

* * *

G: Yeah. What about Donna?
Sandy: I like her.
Maddy: She's nice.
Colleen: Yeah, yeah.
G: Do you?
Maddy: She's pretty.
...

> **Jane:** I like, like the most characters, my favorite one is like Kelly. I like how she dresses. I like how she acts on the show.
> **G:** Really? Do you um – like how she acts – you mean her acting or how she is, the character?
>
> **Jane:** How she is.
> **G:** Like can you give me an example what she does?
> **Jane:** She's just so nice, that's all.
> **G:** Yeah.
> **Jane:** And I love how she dresses.
>
> (p. 74)
>
> In sum, McKinley concludes that the girls' talk "vibrantly perpetuated cultural norms and stereotypes" (p. 11). The fact that only one group took an oppositional reading, commenting on the "skinny woman thing" and its relationship to anorexia, gave McKinley reason for concern.

only as an imagined entity (though certainly, actual viewers exist) and that television defines the audience in ways that meet television's needs. For instance, the industry constructs the audience in terms of consumption, specifically, of the products their advertisers sell. Viewers become, in Ang's terms, the audience commodity. Thus, the audience research conducted by the television industry seeks to construct the audience in order to control it, if only symbolically. The audience is difficult to measure, however, for a variety of reasons. The industry's response has been to adopt a series of ever more sophisticated methods, from diaries to people meters. In Ang's words,

> the move towards more scientific ways of knowing the audience within television industries is not simply a sign of progress from ignorance to knowledge, from speculation to fact, from belief to truth. Rather, what is at stake here is a *politics of knowledge*. In the way television institutions know the audience, epistemological issues are instrumental to political ones: empirical information about the audience such as delivered by audience measurement could become so important only because it produces a kind of truth that is more suitable to meet a basic need of the institutions: the need to control. (p. 10, emphasis added)

The television industry, then, treats viewers as objects of discourse. The industry uses the knowledge it generates from audience surveys and the like to draw viewers more effectively into viewership. It is Ang's idea that television controls the discourse and that viewers are the subjects of this discourse, they are constantly "objectified" and "othered"; thus it is the industry that has power over the viewers. The institutional view of the audience created by the industry serves symbolically to silence actual audiences, and their myriad uses of television. The discourse has infected academic research, as well, so Ang argues that if we are truly to understand the "infinite, contradictory, dispersed

and dynamic practices and experiences" of actual viewers of television (p. 13) –
a task more easily said than done – we need to step outside the discourse
provided to us by the industry.

Reception Aesthetics

The theory of reception aesthetics (also called, for short, reception theory) was
developed in literary criticism and is situated in a debate about where the
meaning of a text lies (Jauss, 1982). In the model of literary analysis that was
dominant during most of the twentieth century, the meaning of the text was in
the text itself and the role of the literary critic was to explicate the text, based on
what it said and, as determined by research, what the author intended to say. So
a professor would study a work, say a poem by Emily Dickinson or Mary
Shelly's novel *Frankenstein*, and tell us what it meant. If a student took a different
meaning from the text, then the student had mis-read it and was wrong.

Under the influence of postmodern theorizing, literary analysts began to
question the idea that a preferred meaning resided in the text, and began
to suggest that *readers* create meaning from the text. This is what Barthes
meant by his famous quote on the unity of the text. As Eagleton (1983: 89)
puts it, "the meanings of a text do not lie within them like wisdom teeth in a
gum, waiting patiently to be extracted." Instead, readers actively create meaning. With this insight, reception theory has shifted the core question of literary
analysis from what the text really means to what meanings and interpretations
audiences create, and under what circumstances.

Reception theory assumes that readers come to a text with a "horizon of
expectations," all their background characteristics, which include their demographic profile (nation of origin, gender, age, race, sexuality, etc.), their social
networks, and personal idiosyncrasies. They read the text against their horizon
of expectations. As a result, the meaning they attach to the text will be
influenced by their own background.

In a study of how interpretations of a television show vary in accord with
the characteristics of the audience, Vidmar and Rokeach (1979) looked at
the effect of racist attitudes amongst audiences and their readings of *All in the
Family*. This television comedy, which was broadcast in North America in
the 1970s, centered around a conservative, bigoted, white, working-class
character, Archie Bunker, his long-suffering wife, and his leftist daughter and
son-in-law. Archie often said outrageous things, including deeply offensive
racist comments. The show was popular with a large segment of the American
and Canadian population. But as Vidmar and Rokeach show, viewers who
were not prejudiced, according to their survey's indicators, and those who were
members of ethnic minorities saw the show as satirizing Archie and his racist

and parochial views (as did the producers of the show). But viewers who shared Archie's bigoted views took the show seriously and appreciated the fact that their views were being aired on TV. This study highlights an important idea in reception theory – that texts are "multivocal" or "polysemic." Both of these terms mean that texts have multiple meanings; that is, they can support more than one reading.

Readers belong to "interpretive communities" (Fish, 1980). These are groups of people who share similar horizons of expectations. A sociologist can learn what the text might mean, with respect to certain categories of people, by studying such groups. This is what Radway (1984) does in her important and well-known study of a group of women who read romance novels (see case study 10.1). Reception theory implies, at its logical extreme, that every person who comes to a text will take her own, unique reading of it, so that there are as many readings as there are readers. While this is undoubtedly true, it is not very sociological. The idea of an interpretive community, which shares a cognitive style or a set of conventions in approaching art, helps to make reception ideas amenable to sociological research. Many studies of reception focus on either genuine interpretive communities (e.g. subcultures or an identifiable group) or on differences in readings taken by different social groups.

Long (1986) examined women's reading circles. In studying the upper-middle-class women who comprise these groups, one of her central aims was to examine the "diversity within the cultural mainstream." The reception of art by middle-class, or even upper-class people, had not been well studied, due to the concentration on oppositional subcultures by British cultural studies, and the influence of this approach on subsequent research. Long focuses, in particular, on how literary cultural authority affected the women's reading. She showed that the views of the literary establishment affected the choice of books read by the circles. They often chose canonical "great works" and, even when choosing contemporary works, eschewed popular works from genres such as romance, mystery, or thriller for reading-group discussion. (The women might pick up "light, summer reading" for their personal consumption, however.) Although they sometimes disliked a modern work chosen by one of their members, wondering why it had been published or why they had bothered to read it, they never criticized the canonical works in this way. Instead, they always tried to understand why such books were considered great, even when they had difficulty with some of the characters (as in Hawthorne's *The Scarlet Letter*).

When it came to their reading strategies and interpretations, however, the women did not rely on cultural authority. They rarely read what literary critics had to say about the classics, and they did not rely on literary publications (like the *New York Review of Books*) for understanding their contemporary titles. The women were interested in each other's personal experience of the books and

were content with the idea that different women might have different interpretations. They did not try to dissect these differences, or argue about them,
but instead merely shared them. Moreover, despite recent theorizing on the part
of literary analysts about the ambiguous nature of language, the women used a
"realist" strategy to understand the books. They wanted a clear story-line,
believable characters, and vivid descriptions. Although they were well-aware
that the books were fiction, they related to the characters as if they were real
people. As Long puts it, "discussants seem to have a positivistic understanding of
words as a neutral or transparent veil over objective reality. . . . [They] appear to
be informed by an older 'mimetic' understanding of literature as an imitation or
representation of reality, an understanding . . . that is now under sharp attack in
literary and philosophical circles" (p. 604–5). As a result, readers' "conception[s]
of the ontological status of the text makes 'people' in books the equivalent of
people, and their knowledge about the first can have the same certainty as their
personal and experiential knowledge about the second" (p. 608). In other
words, readers spent their time discussing which characters were believable,
and which ones they best related to. They also talked about how clearly they
were able to imagine characters and scenes. They did not discuss the structure of
the book, unless it created problems with the plot, and they did not discuss the
aesthetic dimension of the writing, except to the extent that certain books were
seen as "beautifully written." What constituted beautiful writing was never
specified; instead the women would, almost invariably, read passages aloud to
support their assertions.

In a study which nicely complements Long's work, Reed (forthcoming)
studies men's fiction reading. A key theme in Reed's work is reading rapture,
the *pleasure* involved in consuming art, a theme reported by both Radway
(1984) and Ang (1985). Reed studied the Henry Williamson Society, an
association of fans of the late British author. The men in Reed's study enjoyed
reading, and in doing so, they related to "Henry," the image of the author that
they extracted from his *oeuvre* of about fifty works. Their reading was a private
activity, and yet their appreciation of the books was, in part, a social act,
highlighted by their discussions of the books – always conducted with proper
British, and masculine, reserve – during the Society's conferences. The men
experienced the act of reading as a surrender to the consciousness of the book's
author. In an interesting contrast to women romance readers, Reed's respondents read to escape their position of power. In Reed's words: "While Radway's
women readers start from a position of disempowerment, too little agency, in a
patriarchal home, and use reading to recover a space and time for themselves,
Society members claim to suffer from *too much agency*, the constraints of men to
act and assert themselves, and therefore seek relief in reading. For these men,
one of the pleasures of fiction reading is precisely the sensation of being acted
upon, having 'Henry' invade or possess you" (p. 4, emphasis original).

Cultural Explanation

Griswold (1987b) draws on insights from reception aesthetics and applies them to sociological theorizing about art and culture. She proposes a methodological framework that situates cultural explanation, and the sociology of art, in a positivistic framework.[8] She suggests, first of all, that cultural explanation is a way of connecting art objects to the wider society. In order to do this, a researcher may well start with the art object itself and attempt to comprehend it. A useful way of comprehending art objects is to study a group of objects that share some structural aspects and draw on the same set of conventions; these groupings are commonly seen as a *genre* of art.

Once the genre of art objects has been identified, the researcher can look at the agent. Griswold argues that cultural objects connect to society only by means of individuals, or agents. In her model, these can be either the creator or the receiver of the art. If the agent of interest is a creator, the researcher reconstructs his or her *brief*, the probable factors that come into play in creating the work. If the agent is a receiver, the researcher reconstructs his or her *horizons of expectations*, or the probable factors that affect the agent's reading of the art object. Griswold also points out that agents and their briefs or horizons change over time and place. Consequently, this leads us to produce different cultural explanations for the same art object when it is received in different times and places. From an understanding of the agent, the researcher can then infer the mentality of people in the creative community, and can then use this to connect the cultural object to more general social and cultural experience.

Griswold shows how her framework applies to Geertz's (1983) interpretation of Moroccan poetry, to Goldmann's (1964) study of seventeenth-century French writing, and to her own work (1986) on Renaissance plays as they have been revived over the subsequent centuries.[9] An important difference between Goldmann and Geertz, however, is that Goldmann set out explicitly to create an analytic framework for understanding "masterpieces," whereas Geertz's cultural anthropology does nothing of the sort: "Geertz is not willing to generalize from one 'local' result to another; Goldmann is" (Griswold, p. 23).[10] Griswold has shaped Geertz's "thick description" of Moroccan poetry to fit into her analytic scheme.

Critique

Theories from the reception approach are subject to a number of critiques. At the broadest level, some positivist sociologists question the usefulness of sociologists studying something subjective, like meaning. They dismiss all interpretive sociology as unfalsifyable and therefore not worthy of consideration. Less extreme positivists may value the interpretive approach as a general aim, but still question the reliability and validity of particular studies. Most ethnographies and many interview studies are not based on random samples and, as a consequence, are not generalizable. Some interpretive studies make an attempt to study a large number of respondents, chosen in relatively unbiased ways, or to make comparisons among respondents from different backgrounds. Some ethnographies study a coherent group as a case study, explaining the particular group's ideas in a specific way, but theorizing (in effect, generalizing) the social processes involved. These studies are more acceptable, on methodological grounds, to positivist sociologists than studies that choose their sample in highly biased ways (for instance, recruiting respondents through newspaper advertisements) or "merely" describe a specific group. Meaning is unique to individuals, reception theorists might counter, so does sampling matter? This question goes to the heart of meta-theoretical debates in sociology over both the purpose of theory and the possibility of generalizing across time and place. If all social processes are historically situated and contingent, as phenomenologists might argue, then generalization is not possible. Or if all "grand narratives," including sociological theory, are constructed out of power, as postmodernists might argue, then generalization is to be questioned and, when encountered, deconstructed.

The flip side of this debate comes from the key question posed by reception approaches, "what meaning does the audience create from art?" Some reception theorists think that this question is the *only* question worth asking. This leads them to devalue studies which ask a different set of questions, such as the production approach's emphasis on what art objects look like and how they are filtered before they reach audiences. These reception theorists lodge a similar complaint against the uses and gratifications approach, which looks at what people might get from art, but not what the art might mean to them. A more serious critique of the functionalist basis of the uses and gratifications approach is summarized by O'Sullivan et al. (1998): "At its crudest, it implies that audiences comprise individuals whose conscious search for gratification elicits a media response which supplies their needs. This *laissez faire* market concept overlooks the extent to which audience needs are partly a product of media supply (learning to enjoy what's available), and the social context from which an audience originates" (p. 131).

On a more prosaic level, some reception scholars theorize audiences, but fail to examine them, as in Hebdige's study, which is based on a semiotic analysis of the elements of the styles created by youth subcultures, rather than on an ethnography of, or interviews with, members of the subculture. Hall's model of encoding and decoding and Fiske's work on resistance are also susceptible to this critique.

The benefit of an ethnographic approach is shown in its sensitivity toward the meaning generated by oppressed groups or by countercultures, as in Willis's study of subcultures and music. However, the Marxist orientation of researchers who employ this technique can cause them to ignore or dismiss middle-class or elite groups. A researcher's more sophisticated, postmodern orientation may prove problematic in the examination of middle-class groups, as demonstrated by Long's study.[11] Long's subjects subscribe to what she sees as an outmoded, modernist way of reading novels. On the one hand, she faithfully describes their reading strategies as different from those of the literary establishment, but on the other, she has trouble in valuing their approach. Long argues that the women's "tenacious adherence to a vaguely defined 'realism' obscures the provenance of the text, and confers on it a false innocence. These readers may be indulging in what Lyotard calls 'fantasies of realism,' which leave unquestioned the received rules of narrative and genre, and the limits of representation itself" (p. 609). If the goal of reception studies is to learn about the audience response to a text, the question for Long is, why is it problematic that the women have an allegiance to realism? Saying that they are wrong about the nature of texts harkens back to a style of research which privileges the researcher's voice over that of her subjects.

A central debate in reception studies is the degree to which the text structures the meanings receivers take from it. The active audience approach moves away from the media effects literature with its focus on the influence of media texts, and views the power in the creation of meaning as a property of audiences. Reception aesthetics also moves away from the authority of the text and authorial intention, though it posits a partnership between text and reader. The extreme privileging of the text is seen as either crudely Marxian (in the case of the dominating hegemonies in media effects and shaping approaches) or unforgivably elitist (in the case of authorial intention). Some theorists see the creation of meaning as an interaction between reader and text. Others see it, essentially, as the receiver's free choice. This latter view is certainly extreme, being either pointlessly populist or strikingly naive about power relations.[12] The semiotic materials available within a single art object are not unlimited and, moreover, audiences can choose only among those art objects that they can access or that are made available to them. As Seaman (1992: 306) puts it, the metaphor that audiences "interact" with television does not actually change television, or the capitalist ideology or racial stereotypes they may portray. Yet as Strinati (1995: 258) points out, a balance is needed between views that focus on the pernicious effects of, especially, the popular arts, and the populism of the active audience view. The former "has patronised the audience by calling it stupid [and the latter] has patronised the audience by calling it subversive," whereas, on the whole, they are neither.

NOTES

1   For exceptions, see Becker (1951; 1963, chapters 5–6) and Gans (1962).

2   For some theorists, the term "British cultural studies" implies, narrowly, the work done at the Centre for Contemporary Cultural Studies (CCCS) in the 1970s and 1980s when it was directed by Stuart Hall, work collectively known as the "Birmingham School." However, this does not capture the whole of cultural studies in Britain. The CCCS was founded in 1968 by Richard Hoggart, who was more critical of contemporary culture, for instance of rock music, than his colleagues and students. The school was influenced not only by such European Marxists as Antonio Gramsci and Louis Althusser, but also by the French structuralists. These and other developments led to what Storey (1993: 67) calls the "disunified" field of British cultural studies.

3   It may be worth noting that cultural studies, as the name suggests, encompasses popular culture broadly defined as lived culture. I review only those aspects of the work that relate to the reception of popular arts.

4   Frith (1978 [1981]: 269) points out that the homology metaphor is really only a fancy name for a reflection approach. While Willis's work is both rich and evocative in its descriptions of the use of music by the subcultures he studied, he does not adequately explain their choice through his recourse to the homologies between the music and the subcultures. In the end, it says no more than that the music each group prefers reflects their lifestyles.

5   More accurately, Fiske is concerned with popular *culture*, not just the popular arts. For Fiske, "Culture is the constant process of producing meanings of and from our social experience, and such meanings necessarily produce a social identity for the people involved" (p. 1). Popular culture, then, "is the culture of the subordinate who resent their subordination" (p. 7). Fiske is interested in the use of the popular arts, but also in language and consumer goods such as clothing, as resources for meaning creation.

6   One might like to ask if the girls themselves are creating the oppositional meanings of sexuality, or if they are uncritically adopting Madonna's portrayals. Moreover, as Seaman (1992: 308) points out, "Reading the concert or video performances of the mega-opportunistic pop star, Madonna, as 'empowering' for young women does nothing to decrease the staggering risk of date rape and other all-too-common forms of sexual assault and harassment. The fact that such 'inflected' readings are possible or even probable for young women has exactly zero implications for the odds that profoundly sexist interpretations will be made by young men."

7   Fiske notes that some theorists would like the subordinate classes to experience their misery in the fullest, making them more likely to revolt. Fiske says that wretchedness may indeed have revolutionary potential, but it is hardly humane to wish it upon people.

8   More accurately, Griswold does not entirely dismiss postmodern ideas on discourses and how they structure knowledge. However, she suggests that, as a research strategy, sociologists adopt a "provisional, provincial positivism" (1990; 1992a).

9   In an amusing example of taking a good metaphor too far, Griswold argues that as the plays she studied were revived and re-revived the cultural diamond becomes, over time, a cultural parallelepiped (i.e. a long 3–dimensional "bar" that is square in cross-section).

10 Geertz (1973) advocates a particular type of interpretive (or symbolic) ethnography, which finds the idea of generalization unnecessary or suspect. In ethnography, a researcher spends a great deal of time with his or her subjects in order to understand their meaning systems and way of life. Geertz believes that researchers can translate the symbol systems of one culture into those of another, so that members of the second can more fully understand the first. Postmodern researchers are suspicious of this type of ethnography, seeing in it hubris on the part of researchers who set themselves up as experts with respect to their subjects, presuming to study them as objects that can be theorized. They advocate a more reflexive research style that involves the researcher studying his or her own role in the creation of the ethnography and actively involving informants as participants in the research process.

11 See also Radway (1991).

12 The "pointless populism" in active audience research has been sharply criticized by Seaman (1992); also see Herman and McChesney (1997: 194–5). Curran (1990) critiques the active audience theorists, whom he calls the new revisionists, on other grounds, faulting them for overlooking the similar contributions made by an earlier generation of researchers (see note 7, chapter 3). He writes, "In short, the research of the new revisionists is only startling and innovative from a foreshortened perspective of communications research in which the year AD begins with textual analyses of films and TV programmes in the journal *Screen*, and everything before that is shrouded in the eddying mists of time" (p. 150). It is unfortunately true that some sociologists have a peculiar habit of judging a work's scholarship by calculating the average date of citation in their bibliographies; the more recent, the better. This leads them, however, to undervalue the important contribution of those in whose footsteps they follow.

Case Study 10.1
Romance Novels as Combat and Compensation

Based on Janice A. Radway (1984), *Reading the Romance: Women, Patriarchy and Popular Literature* (Chapel Hill: University of North Carolina Press).

Points for Discussion:

1 Why are the literature professors concerned about romance novels?
2 What do romance readers learn from their books? Why do they believe that the novels are not formulaic?
3 In what ways do the novels fulfill the readers' needs? How do the narrative structure of the books and the women's reading strategies help in this?
4 In what ways is reading romances a compensation for patriarchy? In what ways is it a means to combat patriarchy?
5 How might you critique Radway's study?

Case

The puzzle

Radway (1984) studied women who read romance novels.[1] She started out with a puzzle. Many people, when they think about romances, dismiss them as light-weight and formulaic "womens fiction." Literature professors have harsher comments, worrying about readers of romances in general and the "Harlequin" brand in particular:

> Because readers are superior in wisdom to the heroine at the same time that they emotionally identify with her, the reading process itself must lead to feelings of hypocrisy. Since we know the outcome of the story, we feel pleasure in those episodes which further the desired and expected ending. We tend to doubt from the beginning the heroine's avowed dislike of the hero, and, moreover, we are pleased whenever her expressions of this aversion have effects contrary to what she intends – that is, whenever they excite the hero rather than alienate him. . . . We consider most of the heroine's emotions important only insofar as they subvert themselves. Reading Harlequin Romances, one has a continual sensation of being in bad faith. (Tania Modleski, Professor of English; quoted in Radway, p. 4)

> Harlequins . . . are consumed not only by schoolgirls but by "normal" active women in their 30s, 40s, and 50s. . . . [T]his statistic hardly assures us that the Harlequins are harmless, . . . but provokes instead serious concern for their women readers. How can they tolerate or

require so extraordinary a disjuncture between their lives and their fantasies?...[T]he women...are enjoying the titillation of seeing themselves, not necessarily as they are, but as some men would like to see them: illogical, innocent, magnetized by male sexuality and brutality. (Ann Douglas, Professor of English; quoted in Radway p. 4)

These academics dismiss the readers as being dumb, naive, or victims of false consciousness. Readers are purely passive and purely receptive – powerless to resist the books' ideology. The professors imply that the "true, embedded meaning of the romance is available...only to trained literary scholars who are capable of extricating the buried significance of plot developments, characterizations, and literary tropes. It is their specialized training that enables them to discern the nature of the connection between these tacit meanings and the unconscious needs and wishes that readers have" (p. 5).

But romance novels sell very well – in the US, up to one-third of paperback titles released each month are romances (p. 44). Radway wanted to know why women read these books, given that they seem to offer them so little. Why would women spend time – and money – on books scorned by their husbands and the media, as well as by academics? After all, who would enjoy being a hypocrite? To answer her question, Radway decided to go out and ask romance readers themselves.

She discovered that the assumptions of the literary critics were wrong. They believed that since romance novels are formulaic, they are interchangeable and their meaning can be deduced by analyzing a random sample of releases. Radway's work relies, instead, on *reader-response criticism*, a type of literary analysis that suggests that meaning is not found in a text. "It is, rather, an entity produced by a reader in conjunction with the text's verbal structure. The production process is itself governed by reading strategies and interpretive conventions that the reader has learned to apply as a member of a particular interpretive community" (p. 11). Her study has become a cornerstone of the reception approach because she took seriously what reader-response criticism implies and actually talked to ordinary people about reading. She did not depart entirely from literary analysis, however. She analyzed the narrative structure of romance. She argued that books are always read in some context, and agreed with the professors that a key context for romances is patriarchy.

To set the stage for her research, Radway explains the publishing context of romance novels. She reminds us that novels are not only written by authors, but are also shaped by the production and distribution process. As in other cultural industries (Hirsch, 1972), publishers attempt to reduce uncertainty by relying on formulae. Publishers provide "tip" sheets to new authors, giving them advice on such things as the types of names suitable for male and female characters, the personalities and backgrounds of the hero and heroine, appropriate settings, level of sexual experience of, and contact between, the hero and heroine, and the length of the manuscript. (Manuscripts which do not adopt a publisher's suggestions are usually rejected.) Romances are divided into several categories, or genres. For instance, Harlequins are "sweet" (the heroine is reserved and shy and there is no explicit sex in the books), whereas Historicals are "bodice rippers" (their heroines are plucky, the sex more explicit). Romances are sold in bookshops (especially the chains), but also in drugstores and supermarkets, places where women shop.

The study

Radway had already started her research when she fortuitously learned of a woman named "Dorothy Evans" (Dot) who worked in a bookstore. Dot was the unofficial leader of a group of romance readers living in "Smithton." She started to read romances when, as a housewife, she began to suffer considerable stress. Her doctor's orders were to do something for herself every day, and she chose to read. She began to read quite a lot – eventually, as many as a hundred books per month. At her daughter Kit's urging, she took a job in a bookstore and found herself giving advice to customers on which romances to read. She began to publish, first informally, and then more formally, a newsletter about recent releases. When Radway met Dot, she had become known to publishing houses, and was playing a gatekeeping role (as a surrogate consumer, in Hirsch's terms) in the industry by reading manuscripts and galley proofs of soon-to-be published books.

A core group of regulars talked to Dot about books. Radway calls these women the "Smithton readers," and they became her subjects. Radway gained in-depth knowledge of their reading choices and strategies. Her research is based on 60 hours of interviews and three surveys. The women were all lower-middle to middle-class married women, who lived in the suburbs and owned their houses. Most were housewives or worked part time, and nearly all had children (though not tiny babies). About half had completed high school, and half had some further education or had completed university. On the whole, they were religious, and regularly attended church services.

The findings

The women insisted that reading romances was a positive experience for them, one that gave them a sense of well-being and produced a hopeful, upbeat mood. Not surprisingly, then, the Smithton women read a lot. One-half of the women read 1–4 books per week, one-third read 5–9, and the rest read ten or more. Radway found that, although the novels were formulaic, they were not identical. Indeed, the women did not see the formula, but instead focused on the differences among the books. One reader asserted that there is no typical heroine, as "they all have to be different or you'd be reading the same thing over and over" (p. 63). They chose novels differently than the professors mentioned above. A random sample would not do. The women knew what they liked in a romantic tale, and tried to find the books that best suited their expectations.

Radway's respondents were proud of their status as wives and mothers. They did not think in terms of "patriarchy," which would have implied a feminist outlook they lacked. Nevertheless, patriarchy did play a part in the women's reading strategies, as we shall see.

Their general practice was to read a book straight through to the end in one sitting. A two-hundred page book, a "thin book," took the women about two hours to read. They saved "thick books" for the weekend, to read in several sittings before the start of the next week. Radway explains this in terms of the women's psychological needs: they need to get to the (happy) ending to get emotional gratification from a book. A good romance cheers up its reader, and the Smithton women often re-read their favorite books in times of stress or depression. The women explained that though most romances are "safe" (i.e. they have a happy ending), at times when they feel particularly sad or upset, they choose a proven product. A romance with a bad ending or unacceptable plot elements (e.g. brutal rapes, torture scenes) makes them feel miserable.

The women wanted to identify with the heroine, and when they did, the story created in them a tension and anticipation. The hero and heroine slowly grow to love each other and surmount obstacles together, and the hero begins to pursue the heroine. Finally, at the end of the story, the heroine finds herself enfolded by the strong arms of the hero, and the tension is resolved. Many women read the ending of new novels before purchase, or before they started to read, to convince themselves that the book will end well. They rejected books whose endings they did not like. They also relied on advice of friends or on the reviews in Dot's newsletter in choosing books. Furthermore, Radway argues that the romance "is never simply a love story, [it] is also an exploration of the meaning of patriarchy for women. As a result, it is concerned with the fact that men possess and regularly exercise power over them in all sorts of circumstances. By picturing the heroine in relative positions of weakness, romances are not necessarily endorsing her situation, but examining an all-too-common state of affairs in order to display possible strategies for coping with it" (p. 75). The romance suggests that women can reinterpret the downsides of patriarchy as minor misunderstandings on the road to true love. A happy ending in the story reassures the women that their place in patriarchy is a secure and beneficial one.

The Smithton women reported that they read for two reasons, for *escape* and for *education*. The books helped them get away from their daily problems and gave them a chance to relax. The books, they believed, also helped them learn more about the world. They found that they encountered new words which helped them build their vocabularies. Moreover, though the women knew the books were fiction, they believed that the descriptions of historical periods and foreign countries were accurate. So they saw their reading as a way to learn about these things in a more entertaining way than reading history or geography textbooks.

In this way, the readers displayed a "textual strategy" of realism. They believed that words are used only to describe. As a result, women liked stories to be written with a clear plot and vivid characters. They liked detailed descriptions of clothes, furnishings, and surroundings. Following Eco (1979: 166), Radway describes the technique authors use to do this as the "aimless glance" (p. 194), in which the book's narrator looks around a room or a landscape and describes what she sees.

The realistic convention gives the appearance of uncertainty as the story unfolds – the hero and heroine could be separated forever, or fail to overcome the problems that keep them apart. But, as Radway points out, the reality of a romance novel is that the separation will be overcome, as the heroines find fulfillment in patriarchy. The ending always unites the couple, usually in marriage, and hints that they will live happily ever after.

Radway learned that the women had distinct tastes in the books they read. First and foremost, they wanted the story to end on an upbeat note, with the hero and heroine coming together. They also enjoyed reading about the process of the hero and heroine falling in love, and they preferred depictions of slowly growing love rather than love at first sight. The women had strong preferences for what they liked to see in the heroine: intelligence, a sense of humor, and independence. The heroine is extremely important, as her character differentiates the book from all the others and masks, for the women, the formulaic nature of romances. Radway examined novels that were successful with the Smithton women and those that were failures. She argues that successful novels had a particular narrative structure not shared by the others. They provided the readers with depictions of nurturing that may have been missing in their lives, and also assuaged any fears they may have had about their role in patriarchy. The failed romances, however, exacerbated their fears. If they accidentally read a bad romance, many women threw the book into the garbage to rid themselves symbolically of the unpleasant feelings it engendered.

Radway "attempted to infer from the women's conscious statements and observable activities other unacknowledged significances and functions that make romance reading into a highly desirable and useful action in the context of these women's lives" (p. 9). In doing so, she concludes that reading these novels served two purposes other than those of education and escape claimed by the women themselves. First, the romance offered a *compensation* for patriarchy. The Smithton women were proud of the roles they play in patriarchal society. They were wives and mothers first and foremost. They found in romance novels an affirmation that patriarchy does, indeed, work. Romances promise that sensitive and tender men who will give up everything for their women really do exist. The women knew that the novels are not real life. They did not apply the lessons in the book directly to their own lives. They did not try to become the naive, passive (or plucky!) heroines they read about, nor did they wish to leave their husbands and live a romance story of their own with another man. But in romance stories, they found a symbolic resolution of the tensions involved in patriarchy: True love is real, but the everyday nature of marriage is hard work, and meeting the daily needs of husbands and children and keeping up with housework is exhausting.[2] In other words, romances function as *myth*. Myth here does not mean that the ideas in romances are false; rather, myth means a re-telling of a story already familiar (p. 198). Myths resolve in fiction tensions that exist, and are unresolvable, in society.[3]

Radway also looks at how the women used their reading time – the meaning of the act of reading – as well as the meanings they took from the stories. The reality of their lives as homemakers involved spending most of their time nurturing others. They had little time for themselves and no one was responsible for nurturing them. Women used reading as a time for themselves. Many women saw reading as a "declaration of independence" (p. 14). In reading romances, they carved out part of the day and reserved it for themselves and they claimed part of the family budget to buy books for themselves. Many of their husbands looked with disdain at romance novels and thought their wives should not waste time on them. Dot suggested to women whose husbands react this way to draw an analogy to sport. If their husbands can claim time on the weekend to watch football, or spend money on going to games or buying team shirts and caps, then it is only fair that women be able to choose a hobby for themselves. In asserting their right to spend time and money on the books, Radway suggests that women used the act of reading *combatively*, "in the sense that it enables them to refuse the other-directed social role prescribed for them by their position within the institution of marriage. In picking up a book, as they have so eloquently told us, they

204 THE CULTURAL DIAMOND – THE CONSUMPTION OF CULTURE

refuse temporarily their family's otherwise constant demand that they attend to the wants of others" (p. 211).

In sum, by actually talking to romance readers, rather than guessing what they think, Radway discovered that the romances offer a number of benefits to the women. The novels are read in the context of patriarchy, but they do not lead their readers to reject this institution (as some feminists and literature professors might prefer). Rather, they offer the women both a compensation for and method to combat the demands of patriarchy.

Notes

1   Radway's book is now available only in a revised edition (1991) with a new introduction, titled "Writing *Reading the Romance*." In it, Radway takes a reflexive look at her study, strongly criticizing herself, while she situates her research in a "newer," broader literature. Radway appears to view her initial introduction as not just out-of-date but a little naive. However, her second, more sophisticated version loses some of the benefits of the first, most notably, the clear statement of the research question, why women read romances when the form seems so debased, and the critique of literary analysis that purports to say what books mean without ever asking receivers their own opinion. The more mature, recent Radway no longer has confidence in ethnography as a mode of inquiry, in that she now says that she has produced merely an interpretation of the interpretation that her readers gave to her about what they were up to (1991: 5). I preferred the first version. Nevertheless, Radway's work is excellent and I highly recommend reading either edition – which, aside from the introductions, are identical.
2   See Swidler (2001) on the different cultural understandings of love that exist in western societies, and how people mobilize these different understandings to explain different parts of their relationships with their partners.
3   In her explanation of myths, Radway relies on Eco (1979). Similar ideas are explicated by Cawelti (1976) and Lévi-Strauss (1967).

11

Audience Studies

My opinion of *Dallas*?...WORTHLESS RUBBISH. I find it a typical American programme, simple and commercial, role-affirming, deceitful. The thing so many American programmes revolve around is money and sensation. Money never seems to be a problem. Everyone is living in luxury, has fantastic cars and loads of drink. The stories themselves are mostly not very important. You never have to think for a moment: they think for you.

(A Dutch viewer)

My leisure reading consists 90 percent of feminist books, but when I'm watching *Dallas* with my girlfriend and Pamela comes down the stairs wearing a low-necked dress, then we shout wildly: just look at that slut, the way she prances around, she ought to be called Prancela....Jock is like my father, so I can hate [him] intensely too...J. R. laughs just like Wiegel [Dutch right-wing politician] and that has me jumping with rage...I like to let it all hang out, a sort of group therapy, mostly together with friends.

(A second Dutch viewer)

I notice that I use *Dallas* as a peg for thinking about what I find good and bad in my relationships with others....We also sometimes try to get an idea of how the Ewings are all doing. Sue Ellen has postnatal depression and that's why she is so against her baby...J. R. is just a big scaredy-cat, you can see that from that uncertain little laugh of his.

(A third Dutch viewer; quoted in Ien Ang, 1985: 91, 100, 108)

The previous chapter looked at how theorists have thought about audiences looking at art, illustrating the general approach with a few empirical studies. This chapter concentrates in more depth on studies of audiences themselves. It draws on a variety of enthnographic and interview studies. Audience surveys are mentioned, but they are used more extensively in debates over art and social boundaries, the topic of the following chapter. The chapter closes with a discussion of recent thinking about the nature of audiences, and on the ways that audiences might influence distributors and artists.

Art in Private Settings

Halle (1993) studied how people live with art in their homes. He looked at fine arts (original paintings and reproductions) as well as family photographs and religious iconography. He interviewed people, and viewed their homes, in four different neighborhoods: two elite (upper-middle to upper class), and two working-class neighborhoods, one of each in urban New York City and in suburban Long Island. Halle interviewed a random sample of forty households in each neighborhood. His goal was to find out what art people had inside their houses and what meanings they took from the works.

Respondents in all neighborhoods filled their homes with an assortment of visual images.[1] The most common of these in the households Halle studied were landscapes – about one-third of all pictures displayed in each of the neighborhoods fell into this category. And regardless of social class, people preferred "calm" landscapes (instead of stormy ones), and, in depictions of contemporary American scenes, unpopulated ones. The reasons for this preference were the same across social classes. People found that landscapes helped them feel peaceful and serene. In this preference, respondents displayed a "modern orientation to nature" (p. 71) in which the great outdoors is valued as a site for leisure pursuits and for its unspoiled vistas.

A few of the very wealthy respondents had original landscapes by such artists as Monet and Corot. More of the respondents in the elite neighborhoods than in the working class ones knew the name of the artists of the works they hung (in original or reproduction). Also, the well-to-do had more landscapes of other countries (especially Japan, England, and France) and more historical landscapes. Working class respondents rarely had foreign scenes, except when they depicted their country of origin (particularly Italy or Poland).

Nearly all households had family snapshots, but only the working-class Catholic households displayed religious iconography like busts of the Virgin Mary. Both abstract art and so-called primitive art appeared only in a sub-set of upper-middle-class homes. Halle finds that most working-class respondents disliked abstract art. Although the taste for such art is, indeed, an elite taste, Halle points out that even a substantial minority of the wealthy Manhattan respondents disliked abstract art. Further, the majority of elite respondents who liked abstract art said they did so because of its decorative effects, most of these citing color, form, or line and a few citing how the art complements their decor (p. 129). Others who liked abstract art said that it set their imaginations free, but most of these, when asked what they imagined, then said that their abstracts reminded them of landscapes. Halle concludes from this that while abstract art is enjoyed only by the elite, their reasons for liking it are quite similar to the general reasons all social classes enjoy landscapes.[2]

Halle also looked at the display of "primitive" art from "tribal" societies in Africa, the Americas, and Oceana. (He included an additional sample of upper-middle-class households in a predominantly black area to supplement his examination of this issue.) For the most part the displayed items included masks, statues, and faces, but not textiles or basketry. Halle attributes this focus on the person in "tribal" art to the meanings that their owners find in the art, namely that persons represented in masks and statues suggest a connection to the peoples of Africa or South America. Interestingly, many owners of "primitive" art described their masks and figures as "ugly," further highlighting Halle's suggestion that the art is displayed for reasons beyond the aesthetic. African Americans display art to assert "some ancestral connection, however distant, between the 'tribal' art and their own culture" (p. 158). However, the display of primitive art, especially from Africa, in white households has ironic overtones because neighborhoods in America are largely segregated by race. White respondents who owned primitive art were, for the most part, from the left-of-center politically and displayed the art to symbolize their inclusive attitudes towards American blacks. But this art "is a sign that both *gestures toward* African American culture and residents and, at the same time, *distances from* actual contemporary African Americans by the very unlikeliness of the Africans depicted in the image. Thus 'primitive' art is also an example of an imaginary achievement [of social integration]" (p. 201).

In sum, Halle found that different types of art are displayed in the homes of people from different social classes, but he suggests that the meanings taken from these art works are more similar across classes than one might expect. Halle did not find any differences between men and women in his sample, but he did notice differences between adults and adolescents. Although he focused on adults, who tend to make the decisions on how to decorate most rooms of the house, teenagers are less likely to display art in their rooms and instead preferred posters of rock stars or album covers.

Reception and Horizons of Expectations

A number of studies focusing on television examine the different ways that different groups receive the same cultural object. These studies have demonstrated differences across ethnicity and national origin, interpretive community, class, race, and gender. Not all studies refer explicitly to the different horizons of expectations (the background characteristics of people and groups and the assumptions that shape their reading of art objects), but they all suggest, in effect, that these different groups have different horizons which lead them to take different meanings from the objects or to use different reading strategies when consuming them.

National origin

The American prime-time soap opera *Dallas*, the story of a Texas oil million-aire (J. R. Ewing) and his extended family, achieved the largest international viewership on record in the 1980s, and was broadcast in more than 90 countries (Abercrombie, 1996: 161). In addition to being widely popular, it provoked fears of Americanization; the French Minister of Culture Jack Lang, for instance, called it "the symbol of American cultural imperialism" (quoted in O'Sullivan et al. 1998: 292). So it is not surprising that the reception of *Dallas* received a good deal of scholarly attention.

In a well-known set of studies Liebes and Katz (1993) showed an episode of *Dallas* to focus groups in six different communities. Four were distinct com-munities in Israel: Russian immigrants, Moroccan immigrants, kibbutz dwellers, and Arabs who lived in Israel. The other two communities were made up of Americans (where the program originated) and Japanese (where the program failed). They interviewed 65 groups, of about six people each, for a total of around 400 participants. Each of these groups talked about *Dallas* in different ways. For instance, the Russian Jews criticized the program for glorifying capitalist values, whereas Arabs thought almost the opposite, that the program showed how wealth did not bring happiness. The Arabs believed that *Dallas* illustrates how American materialism leads to the breakdown of families and the loss of respect for tradition, resulting in chaos for families and individuals alike. Moroccan Jews thought the show was primarily about family relationships and how difficult it is to negotiate the bonds of kinship.

The groups also differed in how they discussed the program. Most evalu-ations were based on a "realist" frame (talking about the characters as if they were real people), but some used a playful or "ludic" frame, as well (for instance, imagining how you would behave if you were the character). Americans and kibbutzniks used the ludic frames about a quarter of the time when referring to the characters or situations, whereas the other groups did this less often (about ten percent of the time). Groups differed in how much they mentioned certain kinds of referents, for instance Americans and kibbutzniks referred to self and family most often, whereas Russians referred most often to abstract groups (such as businesspeople in general). Arab groups talked about national and ethnic classifications, the only group to do so, and made moralistic references much more often than the other groups. Groups also differed in the "critical" frames they applied to the show, that is, how they perceived the show as a construction made by television producers, writers, and actors. (Critical here is used in the sense of literary criticism, rather than as Marxist criticism or simply as complaining.) Russians were most likely to see *Dallas* as promoting an ideology (of capitalism) through a series of messages embedded in the show. Americans, however, talked the most about the genre and narrative schemes used in the show (repetition, ongoing plot complications to keep viewers tuning in, and other characteristic aspects of soap operas), perhaps because they were most familiar with the conventions of American programs, and were, overall, the most "media skilled" community.

Liebes and Katz's study also included an evaluation of the reception of *Dallas* in Japan, where the show failed (it was canceled after six months). Very few studies examine the question of what audiences dislike (for an important exception, see Bryson, 1996, discussed in Chapter 12). The focus groups were shown the first episode, and unlike the respondents in other countries, most of the Japanese respondents were unfamiliar with the show. On the whole, they did not like it, many saying that they would have stopped watching had they not been part of a research project. Their response to the show was to refuse "the multidimensional invitation to involvement in the program. The Japanese willfully deployed their critical ability to stay away. . . . They refused to let themselves get hooked" (p. 131).

The Japanese respondents found the aesthetic form of the show to be grating. It did not fit into the genre of "home drama," the closest television format to American soap opera in Japan, and thus it violated their sense of symbolic boundaries, failing to "fit" into any symbolic category. The respondents found that many of the characters and situations simply did not make sense to them, and they also found the show to be lacking in the subtlety they expected from drama. As Liebes and Katz put it,

> a central theme, perhaps *the* central theme, in Japanese reactions to *Dallas* has to do with inconsistency. *Dallas* is inconsistent within itself, with its title, with the genre in which it presumes to belong, with the romantic expectations the Japanese have of this genre, with their aesthetic criteria for the construction of a television narrative, with their image of post-war American society, with their image of themselves, and with their image of men. Some of this is internal inconsistency and apparent contradiction; some of it is incompatibility between the cultural product and this audience. (p. 138, emphasis original)

Interpretive stance

Ang (1985) also studied the reception of *Dallas*. She looked at how women took different readings of the show in the Netherlands, where at the height of its popularity it was watched by half the Dutch population (p. 1). Ang placed an advertisement in a Dutch women's magazine asking for letters on why their writers liked or disliked *Dallas*. She received forty-two replies which make up her data.[3] Her research takes aim at the uses and gratification approach. She agrees the people watch television because they enjoy doing so, but she does not think that *Dallas* fills some pre-existing needs. Instead, she is concerned with how the show elicits pleasure in its viewers.

Ang argues that the best way to understand *Dallas* is to focus on its "emotional realism." On a "denotative" level, the show is completely un-believable – three related, very rich families would not live under the same roof, for instance, and would not face the swirl of soap opera situations that the Ewings confront in each episode. But on the "connotative" level, the charac-ters make sense to a lot of people who know individuals in real life who bear a resemblance to the characters.[4]

Ang finds three different *reading positions* taken by her letter-writers: true fans, ironical viewers, and haters of the program. The respondents who disliked the program drew on the "ideology of mass culture" and dismissed the show as rubbish produced by the culture industry (worse, the American culture industry) to make a profit for itself. They saw the show as banal, stupid, and repetitive. They criticized, from a feminist point of view, the female stars for being too skinny, too beautiful, and too subservient, and the men for being too macho. Their criticisms were often quite heated. While Ang does not question the sincerity of those who condemn *Dallas* from an anti-capitalist or feminist position, she points out that their argument is simply, "*Dallas* is obviously bad because it's mass culture and that's why I dislike it" (p. 95–6). This point is highlighted by the stance taken by the ironical viewers, who argue that the show is, in fact, trash, but it is fun to watch anyway. These viewers stand at a distance to the show and can laugh at its excesses at the same time that they might enjoy the characters and the story. Their pleasure comes from their mockery of the program and the ironical stance they take with relationship to it. They place themselves in a superior position with respect to the show, as do the haters, but they still enjoy it.

The women who love *Dallas*, true fans who watch without apparent irony, also have to contend with the ideology of mass culture. They know that others cast the show as "bad" mass culture, and they find themselves having to defend their enjoyment of the show against the implied criticism. They counter the critique in a variety of ways, none of which draws from a stance as powerful as the critique itself.[5]

Corse and Westervelt (2002) study the ways that interpretive strategies can change over time (see also Corse and Griffin, 1997). For Corse and Westervelt, *interpretive strategies* "are intellectual resources, varying across environments, that create new readings of texts and therefore new audiences" (p. 141). They studied the reception, by literary elites, of Kate Chopin's novel *The*

Awakening at three points in time. To discover interpretive strategies, they analyzed published reviews. In the initial period, just after the book was published in 1899, the majority of reviews (61 percent) were unfavorable. At that time, the reviewers read the book from within Victorian conventions of Christian piety that shaped the belief that novels should portray spiritual redemption. The "dominant interpretive strategy of reviewers in 1899 was built on assumptions of reading as moral instruction and of women as selfless nurturers. Such interpretive strategies could make little value out of *The Awakening*, constructing a narrative that was objectionable at best and virtually unintelligible at worst" (p. 141). Reviews from the second, "liminal" period (1950–79) demonstrated that interpretive strategies were in transition. In the third period (1980–94), the meanings the reviewers created from their reading of the text were quite different. By this time, the novel had been accepted by the literary establishment and elevated to the category of great American fiction. "Late twentieth century feminist interpretive strategies . . . constructed *The Awakening* as a compelling and socially resonant narrative of the search for the female self and patriarchal limits to women's lives that . . . provided rich material for critical and pedagogical investigation" (p. 141).

The interpretive communities in which reviewers are situated provide tools for interacting with a text that produce or enhance certain readings of it. For instance, just one of the initial reviews mentioned self-discovery as a theme in the book, but two-thirds of the recent reviews did so. Similarly, no early review mentioned sexuality or sensuality, but these themes were discussed by the majority of the later reviews. In contrast, several of the early reviewers cast the book as an unpleasant tale about a women seduced by a morally corrupt "bad love," whereas none of the later ones saw it that way. Quite the reverse. They cast the heroine's burgeoning passion as a liberation from the bonds of marriage and patriarchal expectations.

Social class

Leal and Oliven (1988) examined how Brazilian families from different social classes gave different descriptions of a soap opera, *Sol de Verão* ("Summer Sun").[6] In an ethnographic study, they watched an episode of the *novela* with informants (ten families from the working class, and ten from the upper class), in the families' own homes. They analyzed each family's home, and the place of the television in it, as well as their reception of the soap opera. They asked the participants to tell them about the show. The participants varied by social class in their styles of narrative interpretation.[7] Working–class respondents used a realistic frame and described the story as if it were real. For instance, they referred to the characters by their names in the stories. Upper-class respondents, on the other hand, used a framework that viewed the soap opera as a constructed story. Their view of the story was more detached, and they referred to the characters by the names of the actors who played them, discussing how well they played their roles.

The contrasting narratives can be seen in these two accounts of the soap opera (p. 86):

> *Working Class*: In the soap opera there is Abel who is deaf and doesn't talk, but he doesn't talk because of a problem and also there is everything mixed from all the families and from the father who left the son and we didn't know why – yesterday when we were watching we found out about it . . . .

> *Upper Class:* It's a *novela* where the feminist issue is presented in a different way – it's very interesting. The story takes place in a southside neighborhood of Rio de Janeiro [– an] upper-class neighbourhood and everything happens there: in an old mansion, an empty lot and an apartment building . . . .

The upper-class respondents were also aware that upper-class people were not "supposed" to like *novelas* (as they are seen as a form of working-class culture). Even though they watched, they kept a distance from the soap opera through their critical stance and ironic comments.

Press (1991) found that working-class respondents in America also employed a realistic frame in evaluating the television they consume. She studied the ways that both working-class and middle-class women talked about television, and how closely they identified with the characters. Press suggests that

> middle-class women more often identify with television characters, in particular with their situations and dilemmas vis-à-vis family and other relationships, than do working-class women. Paradoxically, . . . middle-class women generally seem to like television less overall but to identify with its characters and situations more than working-class women. . . . Working-class women, on the other hand, while overall claiming to value television more highly, are often critical both of television shows themselves and of the characters on them, primarily for their lack of realism. Working-class women's lack of identification with television characters is perhaps not surprising when one considers the middle- or upper-class bias of most television content. (p. 175)

Press was also interested in how television might work, hegemonically, to transmit dominant values to viewers. She argues that television provides messages that are based on capitalist and patriarchal values and that these values contribute to the oppression of women and the working class. Women do resist these messages, at least partly, in their viewing. However, Press finds evidence for both class-based and gender-based hegemony. Middle-class women were more susceptible to a gender-based hegemony in their reception of television. For instance, they were "vulnerable in a deplorably direct way" to culturally prescribed notions of femininity (p. 96). They subscribed to presentations of how women should look and dress. Middle-class women also used television characters and situations to help understand the pressing issue of work–family conflict in their own lives. Working-class women, in contrast, were more susceptible to class-based hegemony. They did not find the depictions of working-class life realistic, but they accept portrayals of middle- and upper-class life, with all their material accoutrements, as accurate. In consequence, their "television watching may contribute . . . to a degree of alienation from the reality of their own material experience and . . . may contribute to a sense of personal failure women experience for not achieving this media-defined norm and may thereby confound working-class women's oppression in our society" (p. 138).

Age

There are quite a number of studies of the popular arts and youth, but virtually no attention has been paid to popular arts and older people.[8] Press's study is unusual in that it examines the reception of television by women of varying ages. She compared the reception of television by older women (aged 60–78) to that of younger women (aged 17–29). She discovered that older women engaged with female characters who worked outside the home in a way that Liebes and Katz would describe as "ludic." They found it interesting that women can juggle career and babies, and reflected on how their own lives might have been different had they the same opportunities for employment as women today do. Younger women were more likely to use a realist frame, questioning the portrayals of television women who easily handled work–family conflicts. The older women were less sensitive to sexist portrayals of women (for instance, the scantily clad *Charlie's Angels*), but were more likely to be offended by explicit references to sex between characters and promiscuity on the part of female characters. The younger women were exactly the opposite, finding sexist portrayals offensive, but not commenting on portrayals of sexuality.

Race

Jhally and Lewis (1992) studied the different perceptions by white and black Americans of *The Cosby Show*, an American situation comedy about a well-to-do African-American family, the Huxtables.[9] They conducted 52 focus groups (23 groups comprised of black participants, 26 white, and 3 Hispanic) where each was shown the same episode as a springboard for discussion. White respondents tended to see the show in a context of "color blindness." They saw the show as depicting an ordinary but successful family who just happen to be black, and as affirming the idea of the "American Dream" in which anyone, regardless of skin color, can be upwardly mobile and achieve economic success. Black respondents, on the other hand, were much more sensitive to the portrayal of black culture in the show. For instance, they noticed the anti-apartheid posters on the wall of the Huxtables' home that the white viewers ignored. They also had a more mixed response to the show. On the one hand, they were largely supportive of the show, given how few positive representations of African Americans appear on television. On the other hand, they were concerned that the show lacked social realism – it "sugar coated" the black experience by leaving out depictions of the racism and economic oppression that plague African Americans in real life.

Jhally and Lewis start from a different interpretive perspective than their respondents, however. Their critical perspective leads them to a very negative assessment of *The Cosby Show*. They argue that the show illustrates and reinforces the ideology of the American Dream. But, they argue, this notion that anyone who works hard enough, even if they are black, can become successful is false. They argue that the individualizing hegemony embedded in the show serves to obscure the fact that most people in America do not become even comfortably well off, let alone rich. The class-based stratification system is hard on white Americans and is harder still on black Americans, as a greater proportion of blacks are born into the lower social strata from which it is difficult to escape. On television, a disproportionate number of characters are wealthy; this is presented as normal. To be working class or poor is to be abnormal.

Furthermore, Jhally and Lewis are critical of white viewers who think of themselves as racially tolerant because they watch *Cosby*, at the same time as they readily express negative, and even racist, opinions on the topic of affirmative action. They suggest that the myths presented through the show encourage inaction on the part of whites with respect to racial (not to mention, class) inequality. They are also critical of black viewers, whom they see as victims of false consciousness. The show, they say, is "flattering to deceive." They suggest that black viewers would do better to engage their critical faculties, rather than sit back and enjoy the show for its positive portrayal of a wealthy black family. Passively accepting the show's message, Jhally and Lewis argue, means that black viewers must either buy into the ideology that to be working class is to be marginal, or they must come to believe a fiction that the Huxtables are representative of black people and thus, deny the reality of black disadvantage. In consequence, *Cosby* and its showcasing of a black American's success story has hidden, but pernicious effects, both on individuals (as they are cast as failures when they are unable to climb the social hierarchy) and on race relations in society.

Modes of Reception

People from different interpretive communities bring different horizons of expectations to the art objects they consume; therefore, they often interpret the same cultural object in different ways. In addition, there are a variety of strategies that people can bring to the art objects they consume.

People can attend to art with differing *levels of attention*. For instance, a number of studies suggest that women are more likely than men to do other activities (talking to others or doing housework) while watching television (Morley, 1986; Gray, 1992). For instance, Hobson (1982) found that women often listened to television, rather than actually watching it. They looked at the screen only when something important was happening. Modleski (1984) terms this *distracted viewing*. Turnstall (1983) divides the levels of attention into *primary* (close attention to the object), *secondary* (the object is attended to, but relegated to the background), and *tertiary* (the object is not consciously noticed). Watching movies in a cinema and reading books usually require primary attention, whereas television, radio, and music can be consumed in all three modes. Advertisements in magazines and billboards on the highways are, for the most part, attended to in the tertiary sense. Some theorists suggest that hegemonic messages are most successful at the tertiary, and even the secondary, level of attention because the viewer's critical and resistance skills are not engaged.

Abercrombie (1992; cited in Abercrombie, 1996) argues that there are two modes of the reception of cultural objects, the *literary mode* and the *video mode*. The literary mode requires primary attention, and is like reading serious fiction. The object must be consumed seriously (perhaps through evaluating or analyzing it), and in the proper order (often, beginning to end) and proper manner (in silence). The video mode can be used with both primary or secondary attention, but consumers can skip around within an object or dip in and out, and relate to it playfully, like they might with something recorded on videotape. They can consume several objects at once.

Abercrombie suggests that the literary mode is more often applied to the fine arts and the video mode to the popular arts, and that the former is more highly valued in our society. But he also argues that audiences can use either mode to relate to any cultural object. He points to studies of television use to illustrate this (Abercrombie, 1996: 183). For instance Mace (Laurence and Mace, 1991; Mace, 1992) argues that early television audiences used only the literary mode, because they did not have other models available. They related to television as if it were cinema or theater. But eventually audiences learned to treat television in a different way, and paid it less attention.[10] And Ang (1991) argues that contemporary television viewers are difficult to pin down precisely because they use this video mode. For instance, remote control devices allow people to change the channel conveniently (zapping or channel surfing), and so "graze" through proliferating channels on air, cable, and satellite. Along these lines, research on museum audiences suggests that most viewers walk through the galleries, stopping to look at only a proportion of the paintings on view, and chatting with companions as they do so. They also appreciate contextual information about works, although they do not read all the didactic information available on the wall labels. They do not look at art the way curators suggest, studying the painting in a silent room with no visual or social distractions.

Liebes and Katz (1993), as mentioned above, distinguish between referential frames and critical frames. Viewers of *Dallas* use both types of frames, relating television to real life and treating the characters as if they were real in referential statements, but evaluating the construction of the television program in critical statements. This ability to switch between these two frames is suggested by a number of other studies. For instance, Taylor and Mullan (1986) suggest that television audiences can be simultaneously detached and involved with television. They talk about soap operas, for example, as if the characters were real, and they can be moved to tears by the stories. Yet they also talk about the plot, the acting, and the special effects. They notice the use of stock footage and dramatic conventions, and the lack of reality, as for instance, the fact that no one ever works in the offices portrayed in *Dynasty* and *Dallas*. (The British respondents in this study also found American soap operas to be less realistic than British ones.) In other words, they never forget that the stories are fiction. A similar point is made by Buckingham (1987; 1993), who notes that children "enjoyed playing the game of make-believe" (1987: 180) in relating to the stories they watched, but they were also very willing to critique the shows. They also knew a lot about the process of production; for instance, they understood that an actor might die on the show because his contract expired.[11] These studies demonstrate that audiences can be active in their consumption of art, keeping a distance from the story and, at the same time, being receptive to some of the messages in it. Thus, these studies demonstrate a fruitful middle ground between shaping approaches and those that give audiences almost total power in receiving art objects.

Conceptions of the Audience

Recent work has addressed the nature of the audience, through both the development of theoretical understandings of the concept of audiences and the study of practices of real people. These theories take us away from the consideration of sociology of the arts into a discussion of culture more generally. They are important however, and although they fall somewhat outside the scope of the book, they merit brief examination.

Abercrombie and Longhurst (1998) point out that there are three kinds of audiences: simple, mass, and diffused. A simple audience is physically present at the event, say a play. The art is experienced directly and publicly. A mass audience, as in broadcast television viewers, experiences mediated communication in private settings. Diffuse audiences relate to mediascapes in ways that constitute a very different type of "audience-experience," as outlined below. All three types of audiences exist in contemporary society, although in the past, there were only simple audiences. The commonsense notion of "the audience" is based on a model of simple audiences. Theorists have developed more sophisticated ways to understand mass and diffuse audiences, as they came into existence through changing technology.

Abercrombie and Longhurst suggest that initial attempts to understand audiences, established as the mass audience arose, drew from a "behavioral" model. This line of research corresponds to the media effects literature in which the audience is conceived of as individuals who receive stimuli (messages) from the media, and are positively or negatively affected by them. A second approach, growing out of the problems discovered in the first, is referred to as "incorporation/resistance," and is illustrated by the encoding/decoding model of British cultural studies. In it, audiences are seen as socially structured, by class for instance. They interpret texts in ways that either reinforce or resist hegemony. In the third model, "spectacle/performance," fragmented audiences are seen as socially constructed and reconstructed through spectacle and narcissism. The idea of *spectacle* is that the world is to be looked at. "The people, objects and events in the world cannot simply be taken for granted but have to be framed, looked at, gazed upon, registered and controlled" (p. 78). The concept of *narcissism* suggests that "people act as if they are being looked at, as if they are at the centre of attention of a real or imaginary audience," (p. 88) and relates to the social face, or *performance*, that people must construct in daily life in the interactions with friends and strangers in widely different contexts. "Audience-experience" is a product of the interaction of these two processes: "People simultaneously feel [that they are] members of an audience and that they are performers; that they are simultaneously watchers and being watched" (p. 75).

One key aspect of this model concerns the process of identity formation and reformation in relationship to "mediascapes" in everyday life. The term *mediascape* refers to the fact that we are surrounded, everyday and all the time, by a host of different types of media. As with the experience within simple and mass audiences, the experiences of people within diffused audiences are shaped by their location within those audiences. As Abercrombie and Longhurst put it,

"The essential feature of this audience-experience is that, in contemporary society, everyone becomes an audience all the time. Being a member of an audience is no longer an exceptional event, nor is it an everyday event. Rather it is constitutive of everyday life. . . . [The] experiences [of people as simple audiences or mass audiences] are as common as ever, but they take place against the background of the diffused audience" (p. 68–9). In this way, because people spend so much time consuming media in a "media-drenched society," media and everyday life have become fused.[12]

Audiences, Creators, and Distributors

A large proportion of research on the consumption side of the cultural diamond focuses almost exclusively on audiences and their relationships to works of art, sometimes incorporating their social context. Some research, however, does look back toward the production side of the diamond to consider the interactions among distributors and audiences. Gunter (2000) explores different techniques of researching media audiences, and reviews a large number of studies on media exposure and the affective and cognitive responses of audiences to the media. He points out that the research on audiences can be divided into academic studies and industry studies.

> The study of media usage has been closely tied with the needs of media industries to collect data, relevant to their business purposes, about their consumer markets and the performance of the publications and productions in attracting those markets. Hence, much research effort has been expended on the development of methodologies that are technically proficient at measuring audiences and their consumption of media, often on a large scale. (p. 133)

The existence of this research reminds us that audiences can affect the actions of the producers and distributors of art.

In a study of the relationship between romance readers and publishers, Thurston (1987) shows both the difficulty encountered by publishers in trying to understand their audience and the effects of the changing tastes of audiences on the production of romance novels. She traces changes in the genres of romance novels, from "sweet" Harlequins (called Mills and Boon romances in the UK), where sex is not mentioned, to "bodice ripper" Historicals, where sex is more explicit (but often portrayed as near-rape where the heroine resists but is overcome by the hero's desires), and then to contemporary novels which appeared in 1980 in which sex is erotic, mutually chosen, and not violent. The heroines in romances have also shifted, from young ingenues to more mature, experienced career women.

Thurston connects these changes to changes in the readership of romances. In 1984, about one in four American women read some sort of romance regularly (p. 113). The readership is heterogeneous and is not characterized by the "bored housewife" stereotype. The views of romance readers have been influenced by the women's movement of the 1960s and '70s, and the influx of women into the labor market. Thurston's model is not a simple reflection argument, however. Instead, she traces the changes through a complex set of interactions among readers, publishers, and authors. "Sources of feedback [to publishers] included sales figures, letters from readers, promotional activities of booksellers, and reports from booksellers to publishers, consumer research data, informal reader networks, and eventually a number of parasite enterprises [magazines and newsletters, writers' organizations and conferences, and instruction manuals for authors]" (p. 212).

In some art worlds, the distinctions among creators and consumers dissolve. This is the case in fan cultures in which fans engage in a variety of creative activities based on characters from their favorite series or genres (see Jenkins, 1992; Bacon-Smith, 1992). For instance, science fiction fans might watch and re-watch episodes from the various *Star Trek* series (their source material), but then write stories about the characters. These can evolve into story trees in which the inventions by one fan are used in a story by another fan. Some branches may stay close to the original personalities of the characters, others might bring characters from different science fiction shows together (e.g. Luke Skywalker and Captain Picard), still others rewrite the characters or their relationships extensively. In one branch, for instance, Captain Kirk and Mr. Spock are lovers. Many of these works are posted on the web. The communities that support this culture are often close-knit, sometimes locally, but also across distances through the Internet. In this way, the stories created by fans resemble folk art.

Conclusion

The research presented in this chapter suggests that audiences actively engage with the cultural objects they consume. They employ a variety of "reading strategies" in confronting a cultural object, at some times treating a story as if it presented real people and situations (and relating to them as they might to their friends and neighbors), and other times treating it as a construction (and evaluating the plot, writing style, acting, or intentions of the creators). People also interpret cultural objects in the context of their horizons of expectations, and the meanings taken from cultural objects vary by social groups and interpretive communities. Consumers do not take any meaning they like from an art object, however. Instead, they are constrained, to some degree, by the content of the art work. (The theorists presented in this chapter agree that receivers interact with the text, but would disagree, however, on the exact balance between textual input and personal input in the generation of meaning.) People are also constrained by the range of cultural objects available. They cannot consume what is not available. Nor can they consume everything that is. Instead, people consume only those cultural objects they prefer. Choice in consuming culture is considered in the next chapter.

NOTES

1   That people should include photos, paintings, posters, prints, knickknacks, and statues in their homes seems so obvious that Halle does not even comment upon it. But this fact is worthy of study, perhaps in comparison to other societies or other historical times, or to art forms that engage other senses, like music.

2   Halle uses this argument to refute claims made by proponents of the theory of cultural capital, as we shall see in chapter 12. However, it is hard to imagine how his respondents might answer questions of why they like a work, without reference to color, form, or line, whether they consider the entire effect "decorative" or not (see note 1, chapter 12).

3   Three letters were from boys or men, the rest from girls or women; most letters were written by individuals but three were written by groups (p. 10).

4   Along these lines, Swidler (2001) argues that people enjoy stories that help them exercise the cultural skills that they need in everyday life, and evaluating a person's character and motives is a crucial skill.

5   For lack of a better term, I have called these different reading strategies "interpretive stances." Ang does not attempt to link the different readings of the text to any characteristics of the readers. Consequently, more research would be needed to determine if the different readings are internally linked, and whether the different interpretive stances described by Ang are produced by women who are in fact part of different interpretive communities.

6   *Novelas*, as these shows are called in Brazil, only approximate the American genre of prime-time soap opera, just as American prime-time soap operas only approximate Japanese "home drama," as described by Liebes and Katz, above.

7   Leal and Oliven also analyzed the life story of each family member, and found that it was a factor in the individual's horizon of expectations and that, in some way or other, it affected his or her reception.

8   To be sure, age is a variable in audience surveys, both those conducted by industry and academic researchers. Stacey (1993) interviews older women about their memories of the Hollywood films they enjoyed during World War II, but she was interested in how women had related to the films in their youth. Blaikie (1999) discusses the image of older people within the wider society, but not how they might consume fine or popular art.

9   Also see Lewis (1991).
10 Root (1986) makes a similar point.
11 See Swidler (2001) on how people switch cultural frames in more general settings.
12 See also McQuail (1997), who discusses different kinds of audiences, and how audiences fragment as new technologies arise, and Ang (1991), whose work was discussed in chapter 10. Silverstone (1994) provides an exemplar of the spectacle/performance paradigm. Radway's discussion (1988b) takes the view of diffused audiences to an extreme.

Case Study 11.1
Cowboys, Indians, and Western Movies

Based on JoEllen Shively (1992), "Cowboys and Indians: Perceptions of Western Films among American Indians and Anglos" (*American Sociological Review*, 57 (6): 725–34).

Points for Discussion

1   Why did both the Indians and the Anglos living on the reservation like Western movies? How did the narrative structure of *The Searchers* shape their reception of it?
2   What interpretive strategies did the respondents use when discussing the movie?
3   What differences did Shively find between the two groups in their reading of Westerns? How did the horizons of expectations of the groups affect their reception of the film?
4   How did the readings of Westerns by university students differ from that of reservation residents? What might account for this difference? Why did the students fail to identify with the cowboys?

Case

Shively (1992), a Chippewa who grew up on a reservation, noticed that Western movies and books were quite popular with the Indians who lived there.[1] This popularity seemed odd because in Westerns, Indians are usually presented as the bad guys. Shively wondered whether this fact affected the way Indians understood Western movies. Did Indian viewers identify with the Indians presented on the screen? Did the tribe of the movie Indians make a difference to the viewers? For example, did they like Westerns only when the Indians portrayed were from a different tribe?

To answer these questions, Shively showed a Western movie to twenty Indians and twenty "Anglos" (white Americans), all males. The two groups were matched by age, education, and occupation, and all lived on a reservation. (Many Indian reservations in the United States contain land owned by both Indians and Anglos. The town where Shively did her study was comprised of equal numbers of the two ethnicities.) The Indians were all "full-blood" Sioux, and none of the Anglos were from a bi-racial background. The movies were shown to Indians and Anglos separately. After the movie, respondents were given questionnaires to fill out individually and were then interviewed as a group.

The movie *The Searchers* (1956) was a top-grossing film starring John Wayne. Shively summarizes the plot: It "is about Indian-hating Ethan Edwards's (John Wayne) and Martin Polly's (Jeff Hunter) five-year search to find Debbie Edwards, Ethan's niece (Natalie Wood), who has been kidnapped by Comanche Chief Scar (Henry Brandon). In the end, Scar is killed, and Debbie, who was married to Scar, is taken back to the white civilized world" (p. 727).

Shively expected to find that the different backgrounds of her respondents would affect their understanding of cultural objects. Instead, her most striking finding was the similarity with which both Anglos and Indians experienced the movie. All of the respondents liked the movie. Both groups identified with the good guys, either John Wayne or Jeff Hunter. None of the Indians (and none of the Anglos) identified with Scar. Both groups entered the movie's world as the narrative structure suggested, rooting for the good guys to win over the bad guys. They accepted at face value the movie's justifications for the heroes' actions and the portrayal of the savagery of the villains. At the same time as they enjoyed the story, they also related to it as a construction. All respondents referred to the characters by the actors' names rather than the story names, and they all liked the actor John Wayne and cited his starring role as one of the reasons they liked the movie. When asked in the focus groups why Ethan Edwards hated Indians, both Indians and Anglos responded something to the effect that John Wayne hated Indians in this movie because they had killed his brother's family, but he does not hate Indians in all of his movies and in some of them, he is on their side. In other words, they saw John Wayne as the sum of all his movie roles, always the hero and the embodiment of the cowboy ideal.

The Anglos and Indians did differ strongly, however, on which elements of the movie they thought were "authentic" and which were "fictional." Indians liked this movie, and Westerns in general, because of the portrayal of the cowboy way of life – living outdoors on the range, connected to the land, and not tied down to a boss and the workaday world. They also related to the physical beauty of the settings. "What makes Westerns meaningful to Indians is the fantasy of being free and independent like the cowboy and the familiarity of the landscape or setting" (p. 729). For Anglos, on the other hand, the movies represented authentic portrayals of the historical West and of their own past. "What is meaningful to Anglos is not the fantasy of an idealized lifestyle, but that Western films link Anglos to their own history. For them, Western films are like primitive myths: They affirm and justify that their ancestors' actions when 'settling this country' were right and good and necessary" (p. 729).[2]

The two groups also looked for different qualities in the hero. Indians chose "toughness" and "bravery" as the two most important traits, whereas Anglos ranked "integrity/honesty" and "intelligence" most highly. Shively suggests that people may choose character traits in heroes that they would like to see in themselves. One Indian respondent summed up the attitudes towards the cowboy lifestyle by saying "Indians today are the cowboys," meaning that "contemporary Indians are more like cowboys than Anglos are, in the sense that it is the Indians who preserve some commitment to an autonomous way of life that is not fully tied to modern industrial society" (p. 730). These attitudes also relate to personal values: "To live free and close to the land like Indians wish to live, exceptional bravery and toughness are necessary. Because Anglos do not want to live like cowboys, bravery and toughness are not as important" (p. 731).

Indians and Anglos agreed that the three most important elements in a Western were: "a happy ending," "action/fights," and "authentic portrayal of the Old West." The first two of these are simply part of the Western formula. Good and evil meet and come to blows. In the end, good wins out. Both groups also valued authenticity, but as we have seen, Anglos thought the portrayal of the history of the Old West was authentic. Indians did not find any historical value in the portrayal, but instead valued as authentic the portrayal of cowboy ideals and the cowboy way of life.

In a pilot study for her interviews with men living on a reservation, Shively tested her survey and focus group questions on a group of Native American university students. This group was made up of both men and women, the majority of whom were "mixed bloods" with bi-racial backgrounds. The diversity of this group made direct comparisons with the reservation groups problematic. However, Shively's pre-test brought out some important issues, which she discusses under the heading, "the politics of perception." As Shively says, "Ethnicity was a salient issue for the majority of the students. The narrative of *The Searchers* did not 'work' for the students and they were unable to fully enter the drama" (p. 732). A majority of the students rooted for Scar or for Debbie, the kidnapped girl. They did not think that Debbie, who was happy living with the Comanche tribe, should be forced to go back home. They were quick to point out and deplore stereotypical portrayals of Indians, and noticed a number of inaccuracies. For instance, Scar's tribe was said to be Comanche, but many of the actors were Navajo who spoke in Navajo on screen. They also wore Sioux war bonnets, not only when they were on the warpath, but also at inappropriate times, as when fishing. The students said that they liked Westerns in general, but only those that pitted cowboys against cowboys, or Indians against Indians. They did not like plots involving cowboys versus Indians, unless the Indians were cast as the heroes. The students also did not like John Wayne, citing racist comments he made in a number of off-screen interviews. Shively concludes, "The heightened ethnic awareness of the college students interferes with, or overrides, their responses to the Western so that they do not get caught up in the structure of oppositions in the narrative.... Education increases their awareness of anti-Indian bias in the film, producing a 'revised eye' that frames these films in ethnic terms" (p. 732).

Notes

1   Shively uses the term "Indian" to refer to Native Americans, and I follow her in this.
2   Myth, here, in Malinowski's (1948: 84–5) sense: "The *myth* comes into play when rite, ceremony, or a social or moral rule demands justification, warrant of antiquity, reality, and sanctity" (quoted in Shively, 1992 p. 729).

12

Art and Social Boundaries

There is no such thing as an immaculate perception.
(Marshall Sahlin, 1985: 147)

This chapter turns from the consideration of how audiences find meaning in art works to how social systems create boundaries among different social groups on the basis of taste and aesthetic choice. Boundaries can exist in both physical and symbolic form. This chapter is concerned with the latter. "Symbolic boundaries are conceptual distinctions that we make to categorize objects, people, practices, and even time and space.... [They] presuppose both inclusion (of the desirable) and exclusion (of the repulsive, the impure) [and] imply a third, gray zone made up of elements that leave us indifferent" (Lamont, 1992: 9). Symbolic boundaries can divide objects, for instance, when elites say that fine arts are "high" and popular arts are "low" forms of culture. They can also create distinctions among social groups. In this way, they serve as invisible barriers to inclusion that can be as effective as visible barriers such as fences and walls, or the explicit exclusion of certain social groups (historic- ally, women, foreigners, immigrants, and ethnic minorities) from membership in clubs, attendance of universities, or participation in elections (see Lamont and Fornier, 1992).

The creation of symbolic boundaries is important in social life because, as Lamont (1992: 11–12) puts it:

Boundary work is...a way of developing a sense of group membership, it creates bonds based on shared emotions, similar conceptions of the sacred and the profane, and similar reactions toward symbolic violators. More generally, boundaries constitute a system of rules that guide interaction by affecting who comes together to engage in...social acts [and which social acts are enacted].

They thereby also come to separate people into classes, working groups, professions, species, genders, and races. Therefore, boundaries not only create groups, they also potentially produce inequality because they are an essential medium through which individuals acquire status, monopolize resources, ward off threats, or legitimate their social advantages, often in reference to a superior lifestyle, habits, character, or competencies.

High and Low Art Forms

Are fine, popular, and folk arts fundamentally different? This is an important question in the sociology of art given the pervasive view of the arts as being divided into distinct categories. On the one hand there are the "high" arts, made up of various categories of fine arts, and on the other the "low" arts, composed of the "authentic" folk art of the masses and the commercialized "mass" or popular arts. Some writers have suggested that the distinction between the two categories is "natural" and does not require sociological analysis. But efforts to explain differences between the categories based on the intrinsic characteristics of the art forms are largely unconvincing. For instance, one common argument is that high art is richer and more complex than popular art. While it is undoubtedly true that many high art objects are more complex and somehow "better" than many low forms – Mozart's work clearly embodies genius and is richer than, say, nursery rhymes – this argument underestimates the complexity of many low forms. Opera and Shakespearean plays, for instance, were popular forms in their original setting. The cultural objects themselves did not change with their status. One might argue that a change in the setting has "changed" the art form. Opera is often sung in a foreign language, for instance, and Shakespeare's speech is now so archaic that, for many people, the plays might as well be in a foreign language. But as we shall see, Shakespeare remained popular in America throughout the nineteenth century, and the English language had already changed quite a bit by then. And this argument does not explain why operas sung in English are thought of as high culture alongside those in Italian or German. Jazz music, to take another example, changed in status from a folk to a popular to a fine art style in a much shorter time span (Peterson, 1972; Lopes, 2002). Further, once they started to study popular forms, scholars found a good deal of complexity in them, for instance, in the movies of Alfred Hitchcock or Frank Capra (Carney, 1986). Along these lines, Baumann (2001) documents the development of the art film, a genre which came to stand in contrast to the popular movie.

A second argument that is made about the distinction between high and low art is that high art takes more training to understand. It is opaque without this training. This is also sometimes true. However, young fans often know much more about their favorite musical style than their parents, and the music remains inaccessible to the older generation who do not learn how to appreciate it. In other words, the ability to enjoy all art forms is enhanced by, or sometimes even requires, a familiarity with the conventions used in that form. Furthermore, many items from high art are "popular" items. Leonardo's *Mona Lisa*, Van Gogh's *Sunflowers*, Monet's *Water Lilies* and Botticelli's angels are but a few examples from the visual arts, and, as Storey (1993: 8) reports, Luciano Pavarotti's recording of Puccini's "Nessun Dorma" shot to number one on the British pop charts when it was chosen as "The Official BBC Grandstand World Cup Theme." Halle (1992; 1993) suggests that when elites decorate their houses with abstract art, they consider the decorative qualities of the works rather than their art-historical import. In this way, Halle argues, abstract art – in its actual use in people's homes – is not much different from the display of landscape paintings or other decorative motifs, such as patterned curtains, in the homes of ordinary folks.[1]

A third explanation is that high art sustains serious intellectual–aesthetic experience whereas mass culture "merely" entertains (see Gans, 1982). This argument moves away from the content of art objects, and concentrates on the ways that people use them. It suggests that the use of high culture is "creator-oriented" and popular culture is "audience-oriented" (Gans, 1974). In creator-oriented art, audiences must adjust to the art form and attend to the artists' intentions; in contrast, in audience-oriented art, the artist must attend to the audiences requirements and make the meaning in their work clear. This argument holds up under scrutiny better than the first two arguments. Still, one can listen closely to Beethoven while following along with the full orchestral score (certainly an intellectual–aesthetic experience, if you have the musical training to do so) or one can listen to Beethoven as background music while doing housework or studying. The argument suggests that enjoyment that is hard work (eliciting intellectual or aesthetic responses) is better than enjoyment that is fun and easy (serving as entertainment or escape), and thus, it still begs the question as to why fine art is high and popular art is low.

Rather than viewing the distinction between high and low forms of art as something that is inherent in the art itself, scholars have proposed a number of more convincing alternatives. These suggest that the distinction comes from class relationships in society and differential tastes for and uses of art by different social classes. It has to do with who uses art forms, and for what purpose they use them. Most importantly, sociologists have suggested that the division is a historically situated concept that has been institutionalized by powerful groups who have wished to enhance their own status through assertions that their art forms are better than those of other people.

Consumption of Art and Social Class

Popular stereotypes suggest that different social classes consume different types of art. The highbrow looks at visual art in museums and listens to classical music at the symphony. The lowbrow looks at television and listens to popular music on the radio. In between, as Lynes (1954) suggests, is the middlebrow. According to my dictionary (*American Heritage*), a highbrow is "one who has or affects superior learning or culture" whereas a lowbrow is "one having uncultivated tastes." Apparently, no one wants to pretend to have uncultivated tastes! Only people with the right level of refinement can understand the high arts, and these people are found in the higher classes in society. This assertion relates to the origin of the term *highbrow* (Levine, 1988: 121–2).[2]

The origins of terms that describe tastes are telling. The highbrow/lowbrow description is based on the nineteenth-century idea of phrenology, which promulgated the theory that people's cognitive capacities were indicated by the shape of their skulls. Highbrows had a large forehead (as did William Shakespeare) and this showed that they had a well-developed cerebral cortex. They were, in other words, smart. Lowbrows, correspondingly, had flat or receding foreheads (as do apes) and were stupid. The social Darwinism implicit in the idea that the upper classes are smarter than the lower classes is now discredited, of course, but the classification scheme lives on. Along these lines, the term "philistine" indicates "a person who is hostile or indifferent to culture and the arts, or who has no understanding of them" (*The New Oxford Dictionary of English*). The Philistines were the enemies of the ancient Israelites, suggesting that taste differentiates *us* from *them* (see plate 5).[3]

Stereotypes of arts consumption are more sharply drawn than is its actual pattern in contemporary society (DiMaggio, 1987a);[4] nevertheless, empirical studies consistently find associations of social class and patterns of arts consumption (e.g. DiMaggio and Useem, 1978). To explain this robust finding, sociologists have created, as DiMaggio and Ostrower (1990: 755) put it, a "theory of cultural participation (DiMaggio 1987[a]; and see Bourdieu 1984; Collins 1979; Douglas and Isherwood 1979) that views artistic taste and consumption as a means of establishing social membership and constructing and maintaining social networks that provide access to material and symbolic goods."

Distinction

Bourdieu (1984) formulated the theory of *distinction*. He suggests that just as social groups vary in the amount of economic capital they control, so too do

Goliath, the World's Biggest Philistine, at the Gath Art Gallery

Plate 6 Social Boundaries in Action, a *New Yorker* Cartoon by J. B. Handelsman.
© 1989 J. B. Handelsman from cartoonbank.com.

they vary in the amount of their cultural capital. *Cultural capital* is a currency based on taste. It involves knowledge about high art and culture, a high degree of sophistication and of know-how, and an appreciation of knowledge in general and of speaking knowledgeably. Elites in society are able to use this capital to do two things, first, to maintain an invisible boundary between themselves and lower classes, and second, to perpetuate class distinctions intergenerationally.

They are able to do the first by being able to recognize other members of upper classes by their taste. They are able to do the second because they are in positions of power and can structure other institutions – school systems, for instance – to favor themselves. That individuals from poor backgrounds may get ahead through education gives the impression that society is fair and open. But the odds are stacked in favor of children with higher levels of cultural capital, that is, the offspring of those who already occupy the higher positions in society (see DiMaggio, 1982c; Bourdieu and Passeron, 1977).

Bourdieu demonstrates that there are differences in the tastes of people based on their social class. For instance, when asked which of three pieces of music people preferred, upper-middle-class respondents preferred Bach's *The Well-Tempered Clavier*, middle class respondents chose Gershwin's *Rhapsody in Blue*, and those who were working class chose Strauss's *The Blue Danube*. Respondents also chose different items (from a list provided by Bourdieu) in answer to a question about which objects would make a good subject for a beautiful photograph. Working-class respondents chose conventional items, like "a sunset," whereas upper-class respondents eschewed the sentimentality of the conventional subjects and chose more challenging objects, for instance, "a cabbage" or "a car accident," or they asserted that any object could make a beautiful photograph.

Bourdieu showed that people's knowledge of art in general was also related to taste and to social class. The higher the social class of the respondent, the more likely he or she would be to know twelve or more classical composers, and to affirm the proposition "Abstract painting interests me as much as the classical schools." Different social classes talked about art in very different ways:

> Confronted with a photograph of an old woman's hands, the culturally most deprived express a more or less conventional emotion or an ethical complicity but never a specifically aesthetic judgement (other than a negative one): "Oh, she's got terribly deformed hands!...Funny way of taking a photo. The old girl must've worked hard. Looks like she's got arthritis....I really feel sorry seeing that poor old woman's hand, they're all knotted, you might say" (manual worker, Paris). With the lower middle classes, exaltation of ethical virtues comes to the forefront ("hands worn out by toil"), sometimes tinged with populist sentimentality ("Poor old thing! Her hands must really hurt her. It really gives a sense of pain"); and sometimes even concern for aesthetic properties... "That reminds me of a picture I saw in an exhibition of Spanish paintings, a monk with his hands clasped in front of him and deformed fingers' (technician, Paris)....At higher levels in the social hierarchy, the remarks become increasingly abstract, with (other people's) hands, labour and old age functioning as allegories or symbols which serve as pretexts for general reflections on general problems....An aestheticizing reference to painting, sculpture or literature, more frequent, more varied, and more subtly handled, resorts to the neutralization and distancing which bourgeois discourse about the social world requires and performs. "I find this a very beautiful photograph. It's the very symbol of toil. It puts me in mind of Flaubert's old servant-woman...That woman's gesture, at once very humble...It's terrible that work and poverty are so deforming" (engineer, Paris). (pp. 44–5)

Bourdieu connects cultural capital with the concept of habitus. *Habitus* is "the internalized form of class condition and the conditioning it entails" (p. 101). In other words, it is the way people think. Bourdieu suggests that as children are socialized they develop characteristic ways of thinking, a world-view or habitus, based on their class position. They internalize this habitus, and consequently, they carry a mode of thought with them throughout their lives that betrays their social origins regardless of where they end up.

Critiques of distinction

Bourdieu's work has been extremely influential, and it has also received a correspondingly great amount of critical attention. Many authors have criticized Bourdieu's idea that habitus is internalized. Swidler (1986; 2001) argues that people can and do learn different cultural repertoires throughout their lives. People vary in the contents of their cultural "tool kit," but they can both add to this kit and can choose among repertoires according to the situation. Many authors have suggested that Bourdieu's ideas might describe France, a country which is relatively homogeneous and where social mobility is relatively low. But they question the degree to which it applies in more heterogeneous and mobile societies. Lamont (1992), for instance, studied upper-middle-class men in four cities, discovering that the type of cultural capital described by Bourdieu, based on cultural sophistication, was central only in Paris, but not in a provincial city in France nor in two American cities. She also found that American men had broader cultural repertoires than French men, and consequently drew weaker boundaries between themselves and other social groups.[5] Nevertheless DiMaggio (1982c; DiMaggio and Mohr, 1985) has shown that, even in America, the possession of cultural capital influences marks received in school, educational attainment, and marital choice.[6]

Peterson and colleagues (Peterson and Simkus, 1992; Peterson and Kern, 1996) have demonstrated that, in America at least, "cultural omnivores" – people who consume a selection of art, both high and popular – have replaced the traditional highbrow who enjoyed only high art. Peterson and Simkus (1992) use a survey which reports detailed occupational categories, measures of taste (answers to questions about favorite music, and the range of musical genres enjoyed), and participation in cultural activities (kinds of artistic events attended). They discovered that higher classes (based on occupational titles) did prefer, as their favorite, musical genres that could be considered of higher status. However, when asked about the range of musical styles they enjoyed, people from higher classes reported a larger range of styles than those from lower classes. From this, they suggest two modifications to Bourdieu's work.

First, Bourdieu proposes a hierarchy of tastes, with high art on the top, and low art on the bottom, and some intermediary forms in between. Peterson and Simkus suggest that this model resembles a column, with an equal number of forms at each level of the hierarchy. But because only a few highbrow forms exist while there are many low- and middlebrow forms of art, Peterson and Simkis suggest the column metaphor should be replaced with one of a pyramid: a few agreed "high" forms are at its apex, but there are an increasing number of popular forms as one moves toward its base. Second, Bourdieu suggested that class segments consume cultural products from the column that are directly analogous to their class position. The highbrow "snob" consumes high art, the middlebrow, middling forms and the lowbrow "slob" low forms. Peterson and Simkus suggest that this distinction between snob and slob be replaced with omnivores and univores. Omnivores consume a variety of cultural objects from both fine and popular forms and participate in more cultural events, whereas univores (who have lower socio-economic status) tend to specialize in only a few popular forms.

DiMaggio (1987a) also noted the larger cultural repertoires of higher status people. He suggests that this is a result of increasing social and geographic mobility in American society. Taste and the ability to discuss cultural objects and events are useful status markers in a mobile society: "artistic experience, described and exploited in conversation, [is] a portable and thus potent medium of interactional exchange" (p. 443). He argues that people deploy their artistic experience in a variety of ways. Knowledge of high arts is used as a buffering strategy related to class solidarity – to recognize the location of individuals in the class hierarchy, and to include people from the same social class and exclude those from other social positions. For instance at a cocktail party one might continue to talk to people who can discuss literature or ballet, but move along after meeting others who cannot. In DiMaggio's words, "Consumption of art gives strangers something to talk about and facilitates the sociable intercourse necessary for acquaintanceships to ripen into friendships ... conversations about more arcane cultural forms – opera, minimalist art, breakdancing – enable individuals to place one another and serve as rituals of greater intensity" (p. 443). Knowledge of popular arts, in contrast, is often used as a bridging strategy – to make links with people from other social classes. For instance, a high status manager can comfortably chat with the cashier at the supermarket till or the childminder about a movie or television show. As DiMaggio puts it, "Some cultural consumption, notably of television, provides fodder for least-common-denominator talk" (p. 443).

Moreover, DiMaggio (1987a) points out that "our cultural stereotypes of different social strata ... are more vivid than the images portrayed by survey data on [cultural] consumption" (p. 445). He argues that this is due to the number of social contacts individuals have, and the fact that they use different cultural repertoires in different social circumstances. People with higher socio-economic status (SES), that is, the middle and upper classes, find themselves in a wider variety of settings, thus, filling a variety of social roles. DiMaggio suggests that "social roles replace persons as the bearers of status cultures. When individuals occupy many roles and participate in several status cultures, consumption surveys portray little pattern but for the ubiquitous associations between SES and, first, taste for high culture and, second, the number of kinds of culture in which persons participate" (p. 445). Thus, tastes tend not to cluster in individuals, but they may still cluster in roles.

In an innovative study, Bryson (1996) looked at musical *dislikes*. She argued that although Bourdieu's work is about social exclusion, his work and most of the subsequent work looked at inclusion by looking at forms of culture that people liked. Bryson discovers evidence that higher status people are more omnivorous in their cultural choices, in that they disliked fewer forms. However, the forms that they disliked the most were precisely those forms preferred the most by lower status people. Omnivores particularly disliked rock, country, and gospel music. Bryson argues that this indicates exclusion based on social class. That is, she suggests that higher status people, who in general like more styles, particularly dislike the music favored by the working class precisely because this distinguishes them from the lower classes.

Interestingly, the racial roots of the music did not affect the dislikes of the high-status omnivores. Three styles that were disproportionally preferred by African-American and Hispanic survey respondents (latin/salsa, jazz, and blues/rhythm and blues) were the least disliked by omnivores, whereas two other styles enjoyed by minorities (rap and reggae) fell into the middle of the range of omnivores' disliked styles, and only one style (gospel) fell at the most-disliked pole. In contrast, white respondents who scored highest on a racial intolerance scale disliked all of the styles preferred (and often created) by minorities.[7]

Bryson suggests that there may be different kinds of arts-related cultural capital that people can draw upon. Bourdieu describes what could be termed "high-cultural capital" whereas Bryson finds "multicultural capitalism." (Other forms of cultural capital could include counter-cultural capital or techno-cultural capital.) With this concept, Bryson suggests that "cultural breadth, or tolerance, could itself be a source of cultural capital" (p. 888).

Most of the studies that examine issues of distinction focus on social class, but a few offer clues about distinctions based on gender, age, or race. Peterson and Simkus (1992), whose key variable was social class as measured by occupational classification, found no differences in taste in listed musical styles between men and women in the same occupations, although they suggested (without elaboration) that men and women might have different musical tastes in general. They also discovered that, even when controlling for occupational category, the two genres historically created by black musicians (in this survey, jazz and soul/blues/rhythm and blues), were, perhaps not surprisingly, more strongly preferred by black survey respondents. Older people were more likely to choose classical, hymns/gospel, and big band, whereas younger people were more likely to choose rock music.

Some studies suggest that taste differences by gender can lead to gendered distinctions in which the genres preferred by women are devalued with respect to those preferred by men. For instance, "women's culture" (romance novels, "chick flicks" that focus on relationships, daytime soap operas) is devalued (e.g. Radway, 1984; Modleski, 1984). Hebdige (1979) and Frith (1978 [1981]) suggest that teenagers and young adults use rock music to create boundaries between themselves and the older generation. The use of taste to demarcate age and gender boundaries, however, has not been studied in the systematic way that status markers based on class have been.

DiMaggio and Ostrower (1990) examine racial differences in cultural participation and choice, explicitly tying their results to theories of cultural capital. Participation in a variety of high art forms could occur in three ways: public attendance (going to a museum or opera), watching a fine arts program on television, and privately participating in the arts (painting at home, taking arts classes, playing an instrument, or taking part in amateur productions). Taste was indicated by which musical genres the respondents said they liked. DiMaggio and Ostrower showed that by far the strongest predictor of participation in, and taste for, the fine arts for both black and white survey respondents was educational attainment. Black participation rates, however, were slightly lower than white participation rates, and the difference was more sharp for public performance than for avocational participation or television consumption of the fine arts. DiMaggio and Ostrower attribute these differences to the historical exclusion of African Americans from public participation in the high arts that did not abate in the United States until the 1960s, and to the possibility that, in some circumstances, investments in cultural capital by blacks will not pay off (e.g. in occupational attainment) to the extent that they might for whites, as a direct result of racism.

African Americans were more likely to report they enjoyed jazz and soul/blues/rhythm and blues than white Americans, even controlling for education (although well-educated whites enjoyed these styles, jazz, especially, more than whites with less education). DiMaggio and Ostrower suggest that this reflects the desire of "upwardly mobile minorities to maintain credible membership claims in both dominant and minority cultures. The complexity of the roles that black Americans, especially those in the middle class, must play, demands a bicultural competence that Americans with more limited role sets need not achieve" (p. 774). In sum, they conclude:

Our findings demonstrate . . . the applicability of the notion of cultural capital, developed by Bourdieu in research on historically unicultural France, to the multicultural U.S. They also suggest that the concept must be refined . . . for work on culturally heterogeneous societies. The extent to which black Americans share artistic-consumption patterns of white Americans, the absence of taste segmentation, and the fact that black participation in Euro-American high culture is predicted by the same status measures that influence white participation, indicate that the Euro-American high-culture arts operate as a cultural standard for the U.S. as a whole. At the same time, high and undiminished levels of black participation in historically Afro-American art forms demonstrate that supplementary cultural resources provide additional, but not alternative, foci of social membership. (p. 774)

The Institutionalization of High Art

The distinction between high and popular culture is socially constructed. We have already seen that intrinsic differences between the different cultural forms cannot fully explain the distinction between high and low art, and we have seen that taste or cultural capital can serve as a status marker, especially for elite groups. Moreover, the strong distinction between high and mass forms is a particular social construct situated historically, specifically from the late nineteenth century through the late twentieth century. However, the distinction has blurred in recent decades and continues to break down in the twenty-first century.

DiMaggio (1982a, b) shows how the idea of the high arts was institutionalized in nineteenth-century Boston. The social and political elites of the city, the Boston Brahmins, faced a political challenge from increasingly numerous immigrant groups, especially the Irish Americans. As the Brahmins lost political power, they asserted a cultural basis for their higher status through establishing the Boston Museum of Fine Arts (1870) and the Boston Symphony Orchestra (1881). These organizations showcased the fine arts and classical music.[8] The Brahmins asserted that these forms of art were better than the forms favored by the immigrants, and an explicit purpose of the new organizations was to educate the masses. Through education, the elites could be sure that their views about the cultural hierarchy could be spread to the populace: "As Weber noted, mastery of the elements of a status culture becomes a source of honor to group members. Particularly in the case of a dominant status group, it is important that their culture be recognized as legitimate by, yet be only partially available to, groups that are subordinate to them" (p. 303).

DiMaggio shows that before the institutionalization of high art in Boston, museums displayed an eclectic mix of fine arts and popular curiosities and orchestras played a range of music, from popular to classical, in the same concerts. He concludes that the distinction between high and mass forms of culture was not well established at this time, but gradually became so as the concept of high art was institutionalized. Similar processes were occurring at this time in England (Wolff and Seed, 1988; Tuchman, 1982; Weber, 2000).

DiMaggio suggests that drawing a distinction between the high and the low was one step in the creation of a "high culture model." The process also required that art be separated into a sacred sphere (Douglas, 1966), and removed from the profane (both unappreciative audiences and popular forms of culture). The instrument for effecting this separation was the nonprofit organization, the organizational form used by both the Boston Symphony Orchestra and the Museum of Fine Arts. DiMaggio (1992) shows that ballet, theater, and opera companies also adopted the institutionalized "high culture model," although this occurred somewhat later (from 1900–40) than was the case for art museums and orchestras.

Levine (1988) studied the change in the status of art forms that occurred across America in the nineteenth century. He shows that at that time, the plays of Shakespeare were very popular. Most people had a familiarity with Shakespeare and enjoyed seeing the plays staged and hearing the plays read aloud. The plays provided fodder for satire and parody in popular performance repertoires, further suggesting that audiences from all walks of life were familiar with the stories and the language of Shakespeare. But as the work of Shakespeare was institutionalized as a high art form – made sacred, in Levine's terms – the popularity of Shakespeare dropped off precipitously. Shakespeare was cast as too complex for the "common man" to understand, and as a result, ordinary people stopped consuming Shakespeare.

The arts in nineteenth-century America were not uniform and monolithic – there were many varieties based on class, ethnicity, race, and religion; and cultural practices varied from region to region. The public presentation of art was eclectic, drawing from a variety of forms, and early nineteenth-century Americans "shared a public culture less hierarchically organized, less fragmented into relatively rigid adjectival boxes than their descendants were to experience a century later" (Levine, 1988: 9). Since the division between serious art and popular entertainment was not sharply drawn, Shakespeare – and many other writers, composers, and visual artists from the fine arts – enjoyed a wide audience. But, according to Levine, as the high arts were cast into a sacred realm, the emerging cultural hierarchy in America not only deprived the lower classes of high art but also separated the higher classes from more popular forms.

Both DiMaggio and Levine show that new rules for decorum helped keep the working classes away from the new high arts. The theater in nineteenth-century America, as in Shakespeare's time, were raucous places where audiences talked to each other and ate meals and snacks. They cheered, or booed and hissed, at appropriate moments, and shouted comments to the actors. The sacralization of the theater, however, meant that audiences were supposed to sit quietly throughout the entire performance and applaud only at the end.[9] Art museums resembled churches, in that a quiet demeanor was required, as was appropriate dress (also see Zolberg, 1992; Meyer, 1979). For instance, in 1897, a workman in overalls was refused entry to the Metropolitan Museum of Art in New York. The Museum's director, Louis di Cesnola

> reminded the city that the museum was "a closed corporation" that had the right and obligation to monitor behavior: "We do not want, nor will we permit a person who has been digging in a filthy sewer or working among grease and oil to come in here, and, by offensive odors emitted from the dirt on their apparel, make the surroundings uncomfortable for others." He reiterated the great progress the museum had made in training its visitors: "You do not see any more persons in the picture galleries blowing their noses with their fingers; no more dogs brought in openly or concealed in baskets. There is no more spitting tobacco juice on the gallery floors, to the disgust of all other visitors. There are no more nurses taking children to some corner to defile the floors of the Museum. . . . No more whistling, singing, or calling aloud to people from one gallery to another." (Levine, pp. 185–6)

Lopes (2000) suggests that while the institutionalization of high culture occurred, for the most part, in the late nineteenth century, the institutionalization of popular arts occurred later. Using jazz music as a case study, he suggests that only after fine arts were split off from "everything else," did creators and producers of the popular arts begin to develop clear views on popular art as a distinct category.

In recent years, the distinction between high and low arts has eroded (Zolberg, 1990). This is due to a number of different factors, such as the rise of mass education, artistic movements (e.g. pop art) which explicitly borrow from popular culture or that call into question the distinction between high and popular, assertions made by ethnic and social minorities that their art forms are worthy of respect, postmodernist questioning of grand narratives, including notions of "great works," the shift towards more commercialized funding of nonprofit cultural organizations, and even the inclusion of the art of outsiders (for instance, the mentally ill) in the genre of high art (Zolberg and Cherbo, 1997).

Art Objects and Social Boundaries

An important aspect in the constitution of the category "high art" is the process by which particular art objects come to be included in the canon of the best that has ever been expressed. The *canon* is the body of great works in art and literature that scholars have deemed better or more important than others. *Canon formation* refers to how works get into the canon. Today, scholars rarely assert that art objects are canonized based on unbiased scholarship. Instead, current thinking suggests that the canonization is the result of a political contest: "the emergence of [novels with canonical status is] a process inseparable from the broader struggle for position and power in our society, from the institutions that mediate that struggle, as well as from legitimation of and challenges to the social order" (Ohmann, 1983: 200).

Ohmann (1983) shows that in order for contemporary novels to be considered for canonical status, they must first be published, and then sell well enough to receive critical attention in elite publications which, in turn, leads to their adoption on university syllabuses. Publication is an obvious precursor to canonical status. Sales may be less obvious, but Ohmann shows that poor sellers do not get enough attention to come onto the horizons of the literary elite. Moreover, Ohmann shows that, in the United States, the *New York Times Book Review* is the key publication that helps generate sufficient sales. Perhaps not surprisingly, publishers who advertise more in this publication garner more column-inches of reviews than those that advertise less.[10] Ohmann argues that all of the actors involved in canonizing contemporary novels – literary agents, publishers, literary critics, and university professors – are members of the professional-managerial class, and they favor novels that address concerns that arise from their own class position.[11]

Corse (1995, 1996) shows that the interests of the nation-state are important in the formation of national, canonical literatures. Works that make up the canons of "Canadian literature" and "American literature" reflect certain aspects of national cultures because elites select, for university syllabi or literary prizes, those novels by Canadian or American nationals that address these themes. Corse found that a greater proportion of novels on Canadian syllabi were by women than on American syllabi, and that the two female novelists (Kate Chopin and Harriet Beacher Stowe) in her sample of American canonical literature published their books in the nineteenth century but were not added to the canon until late in the twentieth.

Similar processes are involved in canonizing the visual arts and in creating museum displays (Dubin, 1999). For instance, Metcalf (1986) discusses the rise of American folk art, in the 1930s, as objects for collection and display, and a topic of scholarship. He argues that these objects were institutionalized on a high-art model in which they are taken away from their original, functional context and considered only for their aesthetic properties. This conception of American "primitivism" matched the needs of elite collectors and the rough, hand-made quality of the work assuaged their fears of urbanization, mechanization, and social change that were occurring at that time.

In contrast, Corse and Griffin (1997) demonstrate how minority groups have recently been able to make claims for inclusion of their cultural works in canons of high art. They study the reception of a single novel (Zora Neale Hurson's *Their Eyes were Watching God*) to show how the process of cultural validation works. This book initially received mediocre reviews, but was subsequently reevaluated and validated as worthy of entry into the canon of African-American literature, as well as the larger, "mainstream" canon. In order for the novel's reception to change, a cultural space for African-American fiction had to be opened up through social changes that made it possible for people previously outside the literary hierarchy to make claims for the inclusion of works they admired. Institutional factors, such as the growth of African-American studies programs in universities, helped in this, but so too did the availability of new interpretive strategies that receivers were able to draw upon in evaluating the work. Power continues to play a role in the canonization of literature. The presence of works by women and minorities in the contemporary canon reflects the increasing influence of formerly excluded groups; in contrast, the traditional canon represented the power of privileged ones.

The contents of artistic canons is a political issue, as witnessed by the "culture wars" in the United States.[12] Political movements to include books written by women and people of color alongside, or instead, of the novels of "dead, white males" of the traditional literary canon, and to study art forms from popular and folk cultures, are fiercely resisted by such authors as Bloom (1987) who argue that such multicultural practices dilute cultural heritage by including second-rate authors and genres, and undermine the cohesiveness of society by fragmenting the cultural experiences of Americans. The literature on high-status omnivores, however, suggests that the broadening of canons might result not only from the political claims of excluded groups – or from a sense of political correctness on the part of canonizers – but from a genuine interest in, and taste for, a broad array of art objects, from Bach to bhangra, as it were.

DiMaggio (1987a) enumerates a number of processes by which art objects are classified into genres. "Ritual classification" is based on views that are widely shared in society. Other classifiers include commercial interests, artists, and governments. Canon formation, then, is but one of several classification processes found in art worlds. DiMaggio suggests that the different types of classification schemes may or may not coincide in their results. Commercial classification, for instance, tends to work against ritual classification, eroding it. This is because commercial organizations seek broad, inclusive audiences whereas ritual classification requires smaller, more differentiated audiences.

Conclusion: The Honorific Title of "Art"

This chapter has shown that artistic taste, the institutionalization of notions of high versus low art, and the canonization of art are related to the status order in society. Art is situated in social systems and it provides a resource that, in addition to producing aesthetic appreciation and enjoyment, allows social groups to draw boundaries between themselves and others, or to make links to other social groups. The appreciation of art, of whatever form, requires knowledge of the conventions that underlie the art (Becker, 1982) and the perception of art relates to the human capacity to categorize – and rank – elements in their environment (Douglas, 1966; Alsop, 1982). Children of higher status families are given more training in high art appreciation precisely because higher status groups have been successful in defining high art as more worthy than low art. In this way, high art is power.

To say that the cultural hierarchy is a historical invention or that the distinction between high and low art is socially constructed does not, however, imply that all art objects are of equal value. Some paintings, novels, television shows, and movies qualify for greatness (with respect to particular sets of standards), in that they are rich with what Griswold (1987a) calls "cultural power" – they have the ability "to linger in the mind" and have a durability that makes them meaningful in posterity. Other art objects are powerful because they resonate closely with the audience in a particular time and place, what Cawelti (1976: 300) calls "artistry of the moment." These may be forgotten by history, but are no less the product of genius than more enduring works. Other works range from good to mediocre (or worse), even those which use high art materials. A work is not necessarily great just because it is painted in oils, and is not necessarily rubbish just because it is filmed in Hollywood.

Works in the canons of great art, in literature, visual art, and other genres, may, indeed, be great. Certainly, they are worthy of serious consideration.[13] The problem with canons is that as they screen out the unworthy, they also exclude much that is good, or even great, especially those works created or appreciated by social groups who are not among the elite tastemakers.

The findings of the studies presented in this chapter are robust and important. In sharp contrast to the two previous chapters, however, these studies do not examine the experience of consuming art. Art may indeed reinforce social boundaries, but studies of cultural capital do not explain why people enjoy art or what meanings they may get from it. Most people who go to the symphony or art museums do so because they enjoy it. They probably do not think, "I'll go to the Opera this weekend because it will help me get ahead in my career, or help me meet my future spouse," even if such attendance may have these effects. Art objects, and one's taste for them, have become black boxes that explain intergroup relationships.

NOTES

1   Halle argues that these findings on abstract art undermine Bourdieu's ideas of cultural capital. But Halle's argument, in this respect, is not convincing. First, he suggests that elites are interested in the decorative quality of the works. About 15 percent of upper and upper-middle-class respondents do mention how their abstract works fit with their decor. But about 35 percent say they like the works because of the colors, lines, or shapes in the work. Halle says that these respondents should be counted among those who favor the decorative qualities of the work. But it is hard to imagine how to discuss aesthetic factors with respect to abstract works without discussing formal elements such as color, line, or shape. Second, about one-quarter to one-third of the respondents suggest that abstract works allow one's imagination to wander. And when pressed, these respondents say that their paintings remind them of "clouds" or "waves in the sea," that is, of landscapes. In this way, Halle argues, elites are not much different from anyone else who hangs a landscape on the wall. While Halle's work makes the interesting suggestion that different social classes enjoy some of the same underlying aesthetic preferences, he goes too far in using this as a critique of Bourdieu. The fact is, as he points out, that abstract art is an elite taste. His working-class respondents did not like abstract art. A proportion of his elite respondents did not like it, either. But the point is that only elites display abstract pieces. Furthermore, unless the work was painted by a family member or friend, only his elite respondents knew the names of the artists who painted the works. And the quoted excerpts from his respondents demonstrate that the higher-class respondents discussed their artworks much more knowledgeably. This ability to speak knowledgeably and to display an interest in esoteric art forms is exactly the basis of cultural capital which Bourdieu describes. (Note that, aside from this point, I find Halle's study to be well-designed, well-executed, and enlightening, as my discussion of it in chapter 11 demonstrates.)

2   The term "highbrow" was first used in the 1880s, and "lowbrow" around 1900 (Levine, 1988: 221). The term "middlebrow" did not appear until much later, when it was coined by Lynes (1954). The invention of these terms parallels developments in the establishment of the American cultural hierarchy. Interestingly, my *New Oxford Dictionary of English* (1998) does not include pretensions under the definition of "highbrow." Instead, it defines the term as "scholarly or rarefied in taste," and, unlike the *American Heritage Dictionary* (1976), it suggests that both the term highbrow and the term middlebrow are "often derogatory." The *New Oxford Dictionary* does not indicate that "lowbrow" is a derogatory term, but defines the word as "not highly intellectual or cultured" rather than "uncultivated."

3   *The New Oxford Dictionary of English* reports that the use of the term for an uncultivated person stems from a conflict in seventeenth-century Germany between some townspeople and university professors; a sermon given to the professors quoted "the Philistines are upon you" (Judges 16), and a metaphor was born.

4   DiMaggio (1987a) suggests that one reason for the persistence of the stereotypes is that arts consumption patterns attach to *roles* in society, rather than individuals. Because individuals fill different roles at different times, their consumption patterns are complex, even though the patterns for the roles may be similar to the stereotyped perceptions of them.

5   Halle's (1992, 1993) work supports this contention in that he found many similarities in taste across social groups, for instance, a liking of landscapes. And even among wealthy respondents, a liking for a highbrow art form, abstract art, was not universal.

6   Anheier, Gerhards, and Romo (1995) demonstrate the applicability of Bourdieu's ideas in Germany, by showing that the social structure of German writers is divided into two different spheres, one of elite writers who had high social and cultural capital, and the other of marginal writers who did not. Economic capital did not play much of a role in demarcating the writers.

7   Dubin (1987a) suggests that lower-class whites have traditionally been in a "buffering" position in the social hierarchy between higher classes and ethnic minorities, and therefore, more strongly act to "control" minority groups than the middle and upper classes (p. 136). Dubin studies the "symbolic violence" inherent in working-class knickknacks that portray black people but were used by whites. For instance, a drawer sachet in the shape of a black woman came with a tag that instructs the user to "Hang me up or lay me down." These directions suggest that the sachet can be used in a closet or in a drawer, but "they also symbolically represent the acts of lynching and rape – the two most violent means of social control used against blacks" (p. 133). While many of the objects he examined – toaster covers, paper towel dispensers, "lawn jockeys" that hold lanterns – were not as explicit in their violence as the sachet, they all symbolically reproduced blacks in servile roles. These tchotchkes were common in pre-war America, but are no longer mass-produced.

8   The process DiMaggio describes by which the museum and the orchestra separated out different genres, and especially how the museum eventually purged the plaster casts and reproductions of famous paintings that made up the bulk of its collections makes for fascinating reading.

9   See Sennett (1978: 205–8) on the development of concert manners in Europe.

10 This may reflect the size of the publisher – larger presses both produce more books and have bigger advertising budgets – rather than the possibility that the newspaper favors books of its best customers.

11 In relationship to class-based taste and the content of novels, Long (1985) traces changes in bestsellers from the early 1950s, when the American readership of fiction was general and middle class, to the 1980s, when it had become more highly educated and professional. The change in audiences led publishers to select novels that were more critical, or even nihilistic, over those presenting more

upbeat middle–class values, as the former related more closely to the kind of fiction the well–educated audience wanted to read.

12 Recent controversies in the visual arts, for instance the *Sensation* exhibition in Brooklyn, also highlight the political nature of art (Halle, 2001; Halle et al., 2001; Dubin, 1999; 1992) and memory (Lowenthal, 1985). (See also, Heinich, 1997, on public arts controversies in France.)

13 In this comment, I do not wish to reconstruct the Arnoldian position that the canon contains only undisputed greats. My point is that, even by the standards of the day, the canon excludes works for reasons beyond artistic merit. Though all canonical works hold their value across decades, and some across centuries or even millennia, many works are dropped from the canon, and no work can be said to be valuable from within all interpretive strategies for all times.

Case Study 12.1
Framing Heavy Metal and Rap Music

Based on Amy Binder (1993), "Constructing Racial Rhetoric: Media Depictions of Harm in Heavy Metal and Rap Music" (*American Sociological Review*, 58 (6): 753–67).

Points for Discussion

1   What is a frame?
2   What frames did Binder find applied to the two musical genres she studied? How were the frames applied differently to heavy metal and rap music?
3   How do these frames construct a "racial rhetoric"? How do they reinforce social boundaries in society?
4   How would Bourdieu's theory (from chapter 12) explain Binder's findings? How might Bryson's approach (to musical dislikes) explain them?
5   What effect might the difference in lyrics between the two styles make to how they are framed? Does it matter that, as rap became commercially successful, it was consumed by white audiences as well as black ones? What other factors, in addition to racism, might explain the different frames applied to the two music styles?

Case

Binder (1993) observed two "moral panics" about popular music that occurred in the United States. The first started in 1985 and revolved around heavy metal music. The second commenced in 1990 and centered on rap music. A moral panic, as discussed in chapter 3, occurs when elites worry about the moral disintegration of society (and challenges to their own position in it), and accuse "degenerate" cultural objects of creating the situation.

Binder examined articles in newspapers and magazines that discussed the effects of rap and heavy metal music. Binder shows "that rap music – with its evocation of angry black rappers and equally angry black audiences – was simultaneously perceived as a more authentic and serious art form than was heavy metal music, and as a more frightening and salient threat to society as a whole than the 'white' musical genre" (p. 754).

Binder argues that the media "actively construct the events they report . . . by providing the available means through which audiences make sense of events or objects" (p. 754). Media do this by *framing* the events they portray so that certain interpretations are suggested over others. A frame is composed of orienting ideologies that organize perceptions into recognizable patterns. The specific frames used to present an event or a cultural object connect to more general frames in the wider society. The specific frames "resonate when they can be confirmed, bolstered, or otherwise reinforced by the interpretive schemata of larger cultural frames" (p. 755). A media account is framed in such a way as to encourage readers to accept its suggested interpretation, but, of course, readers can reject the framing as well as accept it.

Binder examined 118 opinion pieces that discussed the lyrical content of the two music styles. These articles were explored through a content analysis. Most of the articles came from five "nationally distributed mainstream publications that target a range of audiences" (p. 756). The periodicals were: *The New York Times, Time Magazine, Newsweek, U.S. News and World Report*, and *Reader's Digest*. They reach largely white readerships, and vary both in their political orientation (ranging from left-of-center and liberal to conservative) and in the income and education level of their readership (ranging from upper-middle class to lower-middle and working class). In addition to the mainstream publications, Binder looked at articles in two middle-class publications targeted toward black readers (*Ebony* and *Jet*), which provided ten opinion pieces on the lyrical content of rap music. (Neither of these publications published opinion pieces on heavy metal music.) In addition, she read, as background, more than one-thousand articles in these publications that discussed rap or heavy metal in a more general way.

In total, Binder found that nine different frames were used in the opinion pieces. Some of the frames react against other frames. Binder calls these counterframes. The nine frames include:

1 The *corruption* frame. This frame presents music as a threat to individual children and teenagers. Listening to it might corrupt their morals or induce them to hurt themselves, by rebelling at school, engaging in early or promiscuous sex, or even by committing suicide.
2 The *protection* frame. This frame is related to the first in that it suggests parents must protect children from the harmful and corrupting effects of music by making the music unavailable to them.
3 The *danger to society* frame. This frame suggests that music is dangerous to the whole society because it incites acts of violence that hurt innocent victims who might not listen to the music themselves.

These three can be clustered together as "music is harmful" frames.

4 The *no harm* frame. This counterframe is used against the first and third frames. It suggests that music causes no harm to either individuals or society because (a) even youthful listeners know the difference between music and real life and/or (b) graphic and violent lyrics occur in only a small proportion of the songs in a given genre of music.
5 The *generation gap* frame. This counterframe suggests that all youth styles contain an element of rebellion. It is natural that parents might dislike current musical styles because they are meant to shock parents. But the music should not be taken seriously beyond its fulfillment of the need for youngsters to differentiate themselves from their elders. This counterframe particularly engages with the second frame in discussing the role of parents in the debate.

6   The *threat to authorities* frame. This counterframe suggests that parents, and elite groups in general, are threatened by musical styles because they undermine their authority and their position in society. If people dislike a musical style to the point of taking political action, what they are really saying is they do not like the social groups who produce the music or they are not ready for their own children to grow up yet. They do not want youths to have any power, even cultural power.

7   The *freedom of speech* frame. This counterframe suggests that actions taken to limit the dissemination of the musical genres infringe on the rights of musicians (and listeners) to freedom of speech. This counterframe is used particularly against the second frame when actions such as banning music and labeling albums with codes to indicate their levels of violence or sexual explicitness are proposed to protect youth.

8   The *important message/art* frame. This counterframe is used against the first and third frames by suggesting not only that the music is not harmful, but that it contains important social messages. Music is an art form, even when it expresses its message in coarse, sexually explicit, or violent terms.

These five (frames numbered 4–8) can be clustered together as "music is not harmful" frames.

9   The *not censorship* frame. This frame could be called a counter-counterframe, because it is used against the seventh frame. It suggests that limiting children's access to explicit music is not censorship and does not infringe on freedom of speech. Children are seen as distinct from adults, and limiting their exposure to undesirable materials is a natural role for their parents. Various schemes suggested to do this are analogous to those which restrict access to pornographic magazines or movies that contain violence, swearing, or sex.

Binder considers this frame to be part of the "music is harmful" bundle of frames. It is the only frame in the "harmful" group that refers to other frames.

Binder finds that these frames and counterframes were applied differently to heavy metal and rap music. Both genres were considered to be harmful, but were framed differently. Heavy metal was discussed from the *corruption* and the *protection* frames. Rap, on the other hand, was discussed from the *danger to society* frame. The *no harm*, *freedom of speech*, and the *threat to authorities* counterframes were used about equally with respect to the two genres as was the *not censorship* frame, but the *generation gap* frame was applied primarily to heavy metal music. The *important message/art* counterframe was applied primarily to rap music.

Binder suggests that the different application of the three harm frames is telling. The *corruption* frame was applied to heavy metal music, but not to rap music. "In an article titled 'How Shock Rock Harms Our Kids,' one writer argued, '[heavy metal] lyrics glamorize drug and alcohol use, and glorify death and violent rebellion, ranging from hatred of parents and teachers to suicide, the ultimate violence to oneself'" (p. 758). The *corruption* and the *protection* frames, taken together, suggest a relationship between parents and children. These two frames appear in two-thirds of articles that consider heavy metal harmful. Writers discussed the corruption of "our children" and the need to protect them. (This predominant framing of heavy metal explains why the *generation gap* counterframe was used for heavy metal, but not for rap which was framed differently.) The key point is that opinion writers using the *corruption* frame discussed the relationship of the music to their own offspring: "The frame's implicit message to the reader was that even privileged children from good homes were at risk from the lyrical content of heavy metal music" (p. 762).

The *danger to society* frame was used much more prominently with respect to rap (in two-thirds of "harmful" frames) than heavy metal (in ten percent of "harmful" frames). When it was used to discuss heavy metal, the danger referred to potential satanic influences that might lead deranged individuals to become serial killers. It was noted, for instance, that the Son of Sam, who murdered eight people in New York City, listened to the band Black Sabbath. But instead of "focusing on the dangers of one-in-a-million devil-worshipping mass killers, the *danger to society* frame as applied to rap much more pointedly emphasized that rap music created legions of misogynistic listeners who posed a danger to women, particularly, because rap music depicted rape and other brutality. Providing a short inventory of women-harming abuses, one writer argued, 'What we are discussing here is the wild popularity (almost 2 million records sold) of a group that sings about forcing anal sex on a girl and then forcing her to lick excrement. . . . Why are we so sure that tolerance of such attitudes has no consequences?' " (p. 760). It is logically possible to view rap music from a *corruption* frame, but this frame was not applied to rap in Binder's sample.[1] "[R]ather than warning the American public that a generation of young black children was endangered by musical messages, the writers argued that the American public at large would suffer at the hands of these listeners as a result of rap music. Clearly, the listener's welfare was no longer the focus of concern" (p. 762).

The "not harmful" counterframes were also applied differentially to rap and heavy metal music. Notably, the *important message/art* frame was used disproportionally for rap music. None of the opinions published in the black magazines used any of the "harm" frames. They all drew upon the "no harm" counterframes, and deployed the *important message/art* counterframe in about half of the articles. In the mainstream press, about 60 percent of articles that drew on "not harmful" frames used the *important message/art* one for rap. This frame suggested that rap represented a true innovation in musical expression. Rap music is seen to embody important social messages and to reflect gritty, urban reality. Rap musicians are seen as positive role models for black youth. For example, "one media writer stated: 'In its constantly changing slang and shifting concerns – no other pop has so many anti-drug songs – rap's flood of words presents a fictionalized oral history of a brutalized generation'" (p. 760). The contrast with heavy metal was striking. "Mainstream opinion writers described heavy metal music as exaggerated, cartoonish buffoonery that posed no danger to listeners . . . while they legitimated rap as an authentic political and artistic communication from the streets. . . . [Elites] exerted a pervasive effort to adopt rap as an 'authentic' cultural form . . . but to dismiss heavy metal as inconsequential – the politically empty macho posturing of white males" (p. 763).

Binder also performed a content analysis of the lyrics of ten controversial heavy metal songs and ten controversial rap songs. She discovered, as one might expect, that both genres contained both violent and sexual references, but that the rap songs were more explicit than heavy metal songs in terms of graphic sex, violence towards police or women, and the use of profanity. Consequently, it is possible that some of the difference in framing could stem from a difference in the songs themselves.

The frames provided the readers of opinion pieces with "a map for understanding what was wrong with the younger generation – whether it was their 'own kids' or urban, poor black kids. This map portrayed a causal relationship between music and behavior. . . . [But it] made no reference to such existential conditions as teen's feelings of hopelessness or powerlessness, or to material concerns like diminishing economic prospects" (p. 766). Further, the map seems to relate to larger "racial rhetorics" embedded in the wider society. Binder concludes, "the discourse about these cultural objects reflected not only the symbolic meanings residing in the cultural objects themselves, but also the social context in which the objects were produced and received. . . . Mainstream writers . . . were concerned about the danger these black youths posed to the society at large. The societal belief that black kids pose more of a threat to society than 'our kids' was reflected in the [frames applied to] 'black' teen-ager's cultural objects" (p. 765).

Note

1   The *corruption* frame was not applied even once in any articles that discussed only rap music. It was applied in articles that discussed only heavy metal music and also in articles that discussed both rap and heavy metal together.

Part III
Art in Society

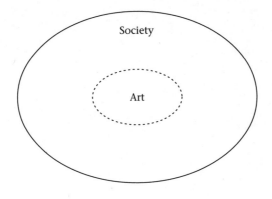

13

The Art Itself

In the beginning was the Word.

(John 1.1)

This chapter discusses a variety of ways to study art works. These approaches all rest on textual analysis. That is, they focus on the art works (the "texts") themselves. Elements within the text – the particular words or plot devices in a novel, the color, line, or form in a painting, the binary oppositions in an advertisement, or the melody and harmony in music – are considered first and foremost. It is these elements, textual analysts argue, that give the work its meaning. This approach was, initially, applied only to the fine arts. More recently, as popular arts have become recognized either as genuine forms of creative expression or as carriers of ideologies in need of deconstruction, popular texts have also been subject to textual analysis, albeit of a different kind.

The approaches in this chapter focus on researchers' analyses of the art objects, and their elucidation of the characteristics of the work that help shape the perceptions of the audience. I start by presenting the concept of formal analysis, and then discuss the concept of the "author." I show how formalist theories of music, formula fiction, and visual art conceive of the text's relationship to its receivers. I also discuss approaches from semiotics and structuralism, drawing on studies of advertisements and pulp fiction. I will also consider how art works "position" readers and how genres and contexts "frame" readers' interpretations.[1]

The studies in this chapter start, and often finish, with an analysis of the art work itself. They tend not to address the production context of the work, except to the extent that scholars may consider authorial intent along with traditional formal analysis. They also tend not to address reception, beyond the mention of receivers. The studies in this chapter provide historical background for the more inclusive studies found in the next chapter. They can be insightful and interesting, but, in their assertion that they uncover meaning, they are more easily criticized than studies that examine people, the ultimate meaning-makers, directly.

The Text

Formal analysis

A *formal analysis* of an art work considers its internal structure and the relation-ship among its constituent points.[2] It may stop at the art work itself or it may consider the development of the work with respect to the formal qualities of art works that preceded it. Formal qualities of an art work would include those aspects of the painting, the book, or the music that are internal to it: the arrangement of forms, stylistic devices, literary or art-historical references, symbols, and the like. Formal analysis also considers the techniques used, the content of imagery or language, and the aesthetic influences from works created in the same or a similar tradition. These elements work together to create the meaning of the work. (See box 13.1 for an example of a formal analysis of a painting.) The intentions of the work's creator are often con-sidered, alongside the formal elements, as the key to unlocking the meaning of a text. Formal analysis, however, does not necessitate a consideration of authorial purpose.

In drama, a formal analysis would consider such literary devices as the soliloquy. Soliloquy is distinguished from the device of the direct address, where the actor speaks directly to the audience, and from standard dialogue. It embodies only those speeches in which the character speaks aloud to him- or herself. Williams (1981) identifies four functions of soliloquy in drama:

> (i) for the expression of *secret* thoughts, which other characters must not know.
> ... (ii) for speech *to the self as to another*, in a form of self presentation. ... (iii) for the expression of *inner conflict*, the process rather than the product of thinking.
> ... [and] (iv) for the expression of certain ultimate conflicts, in *an enforced indirection of address*, where, in a given situation, adequate speech to any particular other is not available. (pp. 140–1, emphasis original)

In using this device, playwrights develop the convention of the soliloquy and use it in their relationship with audiences who "accept its modes: at the simplest level, the convention of accepting that a man speaking on stage in full hearing of an audience cannot be heard by another actor who has moved a

Box 13.1 A Formal Analysis of Piero's *Baptism of Christ*

Baxandall (1985) analyses the composition of a Renaissance painting from a formal perspective.[11] *The Baptism of Christ* was painted by Piero della Francesca in about 1450 (see plate 7). The painting was unusual in a number of respects, and Baxandall explains these. He notes, to start, the pictorial centrality of Christ, who is front and center in the painting. Clearly, Christ is placed this way to highlight his importance in the painting and to emphasize its religious message. The very center of the picture is privileged,

Plate 7 Piero della Francesca, *Baptism of Christ*, 1450s, National Gallery, London, UK/Bridgeman Art Library.

and includes a dove (symbolizing the Trinity), a bowl and water (the sacrament of cleansing), and the head of Jesus, with downcast eyes (for humility). John the Baptist is portrayed towards the right side of the painting. A trio of angels is on the left.

One puzzle in the painting involves the fact that there are a number of ornately dressed figures in the background and there is only one other person to be baptized. Traditionally, paintings of the Baptism include onlookers. Piero faced a challenge in making this altarpiece. The required shape was strongly vertical, rather than a horizontal, making it difficult to fit in all the characters traditionally included in the Baptism. Piero solved this problem by referring to the original Bible story using what we could call a pictorial space–time narrative. The background figures are emblematic of part of the story, portraying people to whom John the Baptist had been speaking just before Christ turned up. The single figure waiting to be baptized, on the far right, stands as a representation of all those waiting to be baptized. There was not room in the picture plane to include others.

There are three Angels to the left of the painting. The tradition in Piero's day was to include an angel in paintings of the Baptism, to hold Christ's clothes, even though an angel is not mentioned in the Gospel. Some observers of Piero's painting have suggested that the angels are not fulfilling their traditional purpose, but this is "an error of observation" (p. 129). One angel appears to wear a rose-colored over-the-shoulder drape. None of Piero's other paintings show angels with similar drapery. Moreover, in other works Piero used rose tints to indicate important elements in the painting and had dressed Jesus in a rose-colored coat. Therefore, Baxandall concludes, the drape is actually Christ's robe, and the angel is doing his duty. Also in fifteenth-century iconography, angels were there for intellectual inspiration: "cueing us to devotion..., referring us by direct gesture to what we should attend to, or reminding us of specific points about the particular mystery [sometimes] with a scroll and text" (p. 129). These angels point us toward the central action. One catches our eye and another gestures toward the center. The angels are set outside the important, central element of the picture by a tree. This keeps them from competing with the central focus of the painting, the Baptism itself. The central angel completes "a triplet of whites" (his own clothes, Christ's undergarment, and the shirt of the man awaiting baptism). The angel could have been carrying a scroll saying, "Wash me and I shall be whiter than snow" (Psalm 51:7), but Piero's painting pictoralizes this message, instead (p. 130). Baxandall also believes that the angels make an art-historical reference. Some art historians have suggested that they are based on the image of Classical graces. Baxandall disagrees and points out that in Piero's early career he was an apprentice to Veneziano. In this capacity, he worked on finishing Donatello's great Cantoria "with its extraordinary frieze of dancing and singing angels, with off the shoulder drapery and wreaths" (p. 131). This is the source of the three angels in the Baptism.

Baxandall's analysis is richer and more detailed than this summary, and discusses some additional points not covered here.[12] But, you get the picture.

few paces a way; at more complex levels, that he is not even addressing the audience, but is being overheard by or is in some sense speaking for them" (p. 141). A formal analysis studies how the device of the soliloquy enables certain kinds of meaning to be embodied in performances.

Similarly, the critic Emile Zola discussed the formal characteristics of light and shadow of Manet's painting, "Luncheon on the Grass" (*Le Déjeuner sur l'Herbe*), a work which was controversial because it portrayed nude and clothed figures together (see plate 8).[3] The public found this mix a bit too risqué for their tastes, but Zola suggests that the painting is valuable on its artistic merits alone.

> The public has taken good care not to judge "Le Déjeuner sur l'Herbe" as a true work of art. The only thing it has noticed is that some people are eating seated on the grass after bathing. It was considered that the artist's choice of subject was obscene and showy, whereas all the artist had sought to do was to obtain an effect of strong contrasts and bold masses. Artists, especially Manet, who is an analytical painter, do not have this preoccupation with subject matter which, more than anything else worries the public. For example, the nude woman in "Le Déjeuner sur l'Herbe" is undoubtedly only there to give the artist an opportunity of painting flesh. What you have to look for in the picture is not just a picnic on the grass, but the whole landscape, with its bold and subtle passages, its broadly painted solid foreground, its light and delicate background and that firm flesh modelled in broad areas of light, those supple and strong materials, and, particularly that delicate splash of white among the green leaves in the background. (Zola, 1867 [1982]: 35)

Not mentioned by Zola is the fact that Manet based the central trio in his painting on a trio of figures in a work by Raphael (see Janson, 1986: 14–15). Looking for such art-historical references is also part of a formal analysis.

Stylistic developments can be explained by their formal (rather than social) elements. A formal history of western art would tell a story along these lines: In the middle ages, paintings were flat, not just literally, but in the illusions they present. Backgrounds were simple or non-existent and they did not portray a sense of depth. People were depicted in rigid poses, and children as miniature adults with the same bodily proportions as their elders. Human figures did not appear very life-like. This style of portrayal provided certain aesthetic possibilities, but also posed some aesthetic problems. During the Renaissance, artists

Plate 8   Edouard Manet, *Le Déjeuner sur l'Herbe*, 1863, Musée d'Orsay, Paris/Bridge-
man Art Library.

solved one of the problems of medieval art by discovering perspective. They
used this device to give their images the illusion of depth. They also learned to
portray people more naturalistically, with life-like gestures. Children, and the
chubby baby angels called *putti*, were shown with the shorter legs and arms and
larger heads of real children. Perspective allowed artists more easily to incorporate backgrounds (landscapes or interiors) in a realistic way. These developments continued into the Baroque, which "solved" the problem of the stark
look of Renaissance paintings, but which eventually took decorative effects to
excess. A new style, Neo-Classicism, pared this down to make less decorative
but more powerful artistic statements. Jumping ahead in time, a formal analysis
would view Impressionism as an advance over the more rigid academic styles
that preceded it. Impressionist artists also learned to use the play of light and
shadow to better effect than in previous styles. Each style of painting, then, is
seen as a development that solves problems in previous styles, and also opens up
avenues for future development by posing problems of its own.[4]

Formal analysis, when it stands on its own and is not combined with other
forms of analysis, rests on the notion that art is *autonomous*. The autonomy of

art implies that art inhabits a separate social sphere and cannot be reduced to production, reception, and reflection effects. This view of art is often termed the *ideology* of autonomous art, and it implies that art is not only separate, but somehow sacred.

Traditionally, only the fine arts were analyzed in a formal way, and formal analysis was used to explicate the "correct" interpretation of the object. The search for the true meaning was often coupled with the study of its creator's intention, as each great work was seen as a unique, meaningful expression of its creator's being.

The idea that one can understand art from its formal characteristics only, perhaps assisted by a look at the artists' intentions, implies that art develops independently of social conditions. This is not very sociological, and is also not true (as Williams, 1981, argues persuasively). Most contemporary art history is concerned with the social history of art as well as the formal characteristics of art works. This is the case, as well, for the analysis of literature, dance, and other art forms. Formal analysis continues to play a part in these disciplines, either on its own or mixed with other analyses, and can even appear when analysts explicitly disavow formalism as a doctrine (Peterson and Corse, 2001). It remains useful, not just for its historical interest, but in what it can tell us about how texts create meaning. The core idea in virtually all analyses of art objects as texts is that *conventions create meaning*. These conventions, whether semiotic codes, literary devices, pictorial composition, or the arrangement of sounds, make meaning possible by enabling art to be communicative.

The Author

We all know that a book has an author, someone who put the words down on the page. This is its commonsense meaning. In the sociology of the arts, the *author* is construed broadly to refer not only to the author of a novel, but also to the painter, the composer, and, in general, the sole creator of the work. In the traditional analysis of the fine arts, and especially in literary criticism, scholars tended to privilege the meaning making capacities of the author. That is to say, analysts paid attention to the author's presumed intention in creating the work. Texts can be ambiguous, and therefore, they can be interpreted in many different ways. It was the job of scholars to explicate the *true* meaning of the text, and a key to finding this was to figure out what the author meant to say.

The death of the author

Barthes (1969 [1977]) declares that the Author has died. In other words, meaning is not seen to reside in authorial intentions. Barthes suggests that once the author pens the words, he or she is no longer relevant to the meaning the text contains. The author is a blip on the screen at the moment of writing, and then disappears. In Barthes words, "the author is never more than the instance writing" (p. 145). Rather than privileging the author, Barthes privileges the text, and the reading of texts, in the meaning making process. (We will examine his semiotic approach below.) He suggests that the true author of a text is the reader, not the text's creator. The reader is the "author" of meaning. In other words, meaning is not seen to reside in authorial intentions, but rather in the readings, re-readings, and re-workings of the text by its readers. He writes, "We know now that a text is not a line of words releasing a single 'theological' meaning (the 'message' of the Author-God) . . . [T]he birth of the reader must be at the cost of the death of the Author" (p. 146, 148).

Barthes also argues that texts are drawn from their social environment, and that by decoding texts, we can learn about the myths encoded in that environment. Texts are not an author's message, rather they are "a multi-dimensional space in which a variety of writings, none of them original, blend and clash. The text is a tissue of quotations drawn from the innumerable centres of culture" (p. 146). In other words, the author creates a text by drawing on pre-existing cultural ideas and mixing them in the text. The particular combinations of cultural "quotations" may be more or less novel, but the ideas are not. They are the historically and situationally contingent codes and signs from the society's meaning system.

Foucault (1979b) also discusses the concept of the author from a poststructuralist perspective. He points out the individualizing process involved in the traditional concept of the author, which suggests both that meaning belongs to the author and that meaning has some kind of stability and coherence. To Foucault, neither of these propositions is true. Meaning is a process, not a fixed entity, and occurs through discourse. Some discourses are endowed with an "author-function" in which someone is given the privileged status as author. However, for Foucault, the concept of the author serves a power-knowledge function in limiting possibilities in the creation of meaning.

Texts and Receivers

The research presented in this section discusses different types of texts and how they create meaning for the audience. The theorists who develop this research are more closely tied to formal analysis than to the approach of Barthes or Foucault, in that their view of meaning is more traditional and they see meaning as relatively stable.

Music and listeners

Meyer (1956) discusses how music creates emotional meaning for listeners. His analysis rests on the music, not on the audience. It is a textual analysis, but it takes one step away from a purely formal analysis by considering how music might move those who hear it. He discusses mainly western symphonic music, but the ideas he presents apply to many other types of music. He suggests that "Emotion or affect is aroused when a tendency to respond is arrested or inhibited" (p. 14). To illustrate this, Meyer gives the example of a frustrated desire:

> [If] a habitual smoker wants a cigarette and, reaching into his pocket, finds one, there will be no affective response.... If, however, the man finds no cigarette in his pocket, discovers that there are none in the house, and then remembers that the stores are closed and he cannot purchase any, he will very likely begin to respond in an emotional way. He will feel restless, excited, then irritated, and finally angry. (pp. 13–14)

Unlike the situation of the nicotine addict, however, in music "the same stimulus, the music, activates tendencies, inhibits them, and provides meaningful and relevant resolutions" (p. 23). This is how music generates emotion.

Music is characterized by a set of conventions which suggest certain sounds are harmonious or expected. For instance, in western music, which is based on diatonic scales, a piece in the key of C major should end on a C (or a tonic, C major chord). When sounds do not follow the expectations of harmony, the music creates a tension in the listeners as they wait for the resolution of the dissonance. So, when we expect the piece to end, but instead of a C, we hear a B or a D, our expectations are foiled and we anticipate the resolution and are satisfied when it occurs. The emotions this tension and resolution arouse are pleasant because we know that the resolution is to occur. That is, we know both the conventions that dictate the harmonious sounds and we also know that other sounds will occur in music which will give way to the harmonious ones.

Music that does not create enough suspense by breaking our expectations with unexpected notes, changes in rhythm, or variations in repetitive phrases, is bland and boring. But music that creates too much tension or does not resolve it properly sounds discordant or cacophonous. Importantly, the conventions of music and the ways of generating tension within it are specific to musical genres. People learn the conventions of the music played in their society, and thus, learn to enjoy it. They gain a richer and more powerful experience of music, from both familiar and unfamiliar traditions, as their knowledge deepens. Music does not create meaning in isolation, but in inter-action with the listener. As Meyer puts it, "this analysis of communication emphasizes the absolute necessity of a common universe of discourse in art. For without a set of gestures common to the social group, and without common habit responses to those gestures, no communication whatsoever would be possible. Communication depends upon, presupposes, and arises out of the universe of the discourse which in the aesthetics of music is called style" (p. 42).

Formula and fiction readers

Meyer's discussion of meaning as coming from tension and its resolution is echoed in studies of formulaic fiction (Wright, 1975; Radway, 1984). Cawelti (1976) examines formula fiction, in particular, Westerns, crime and detective stories, and best-selling social melodrama. He argues that formulaic novels allow people to explore contemporary social issues. Their relevance is what makes them popular. They also fulfill important needs for escape and enjoy-ment, but this is the reason why literary scholars have devalued them. Popular novels help people escape by taking them away from themselves while still "confirming an idealized self-image" (p. 18). The emotional experience in-volved in reading formulaic works can be great, because the reader knows that the story will resolve in the end. The feelings of suspense and fear that are generated in reading horror novels (or seeing horror films) are enjoyable precisely because we know they are not really happening. Reading about characters stalked by a hatchet-wielding mad man, as in Stephen King's *The Shining*, is pleasurable because the illusion is realistic, but it is not real, and we know that the story will end with the heroes, for the most part, intact and victorious. It would be no fun to be the victim of such a lunatic, of course, nor is the experience the same upon reading about actual victims in a newspaper.

Cawelti posits four functions which formulas fulfill, and which explains their popularity:

> 1. Formula stories affirm existing interests and attitudes by presenting an imagin-ary world that is aligned with these interests and attitudes. . . . 2. [They] resolve tensions and ambiguities resulting from the conflicting interests of different groups within the culture or from ambiguous attitudes toward particular values. . . . 3. [They] enable the audience to explore in fantasy the boundary between the permitted and the forbidden and to experience in a carefully controlled way the possibility of stepping across this boundary. . . . [And] 4. [L]iterary formulas assist in the process of assimilating changes in values to traditional imaginative constructs. (p. 36)

Cawelti believes that there is a greater artistry in formulaic works than is generally credited. In order to invent stories that are interesting, formula authors must be able to "give new vitality" to the stereotypical characters that make up formula stories, and be able to create new plot twists or other story elements that, while novel, do not exceed the limit of the formula (p. 10). The movie *Star Wars*, for instance, set the classic Western formula in a science-fiction universe. Successful formula writers artistically use three literary devices: "suspense, identification, and the creating of a slightly removed, imaginary world" (p. 17). He suggests that some formulaic works will be remembered by posterity – he mentions Raymond Chandler and Dashiell Hammett – but that others will be forgotten, not for lack of artistry (although this may sometimes be the case) but because the specific formula of their stories will no longer resonate with the public. The social conflicts they address have either been resolved or have shifted. In other cases, the formula will be remembered, but the stories will be forgotten because they become too far removed from present-day experience. For instance, contemporary formula fiction rarely revolves around knights on a quest who fight dragons and rescue fair maidens. However, the formula has been adapted to contemporary adventure and spy thrillers (p. 41; see also Eco, below). In making his argument, Cawelti distinguishes between "artistry of universality" and "artistry of the moment," both of which are of value and should not be reduced simply to the categories of superior and inferior art.

Art and beholders

Gombrich (1960) studied the psychology of pictorial representation, especially in illusionistic paintings. He suggests that artists had to invent ways to represent reality in convincing ways. Paintings by children, primitive artists, and even medieval masters often do not look very realistic because they rely on representations of the knowledge of an object rather than what it actually looks like in space. So, for instance, a face is shown frontally, a horse is shown in profile, and a lizard is shown from the top, because these views best symbolize the essence of the object represented. Gombrich argues that this is not due to the childish mentality of adults from earlier time periods (as some authors have suggested), but because the portrayal of reality had to be invented. More accurately, conventions for the portrayal of reality had to be invented. Artists start with a series of understandings – schema – of what reality looks like and deploy these, more or less successfully, in their own work. Great artists may improve upon the schemata they learned, correcting them, as it were, and these improved schemata then become available for the newer generation of artists. Importantly, for Gombrich, the development of illusionistic art is not a matter of artists learning to cast a more pure gaze on reality, thus making paintings that capture the "seen" of illusion rather than the "known" schemata of children's art. Rather, all paintings are based on schematic knowledge, but, over time, the schemata are improved to allow the representation of horses from an oblique angle, say, or the receding of roads, fences, and trees through the application of perspective. Certainly, everyone who has seen a face, horse, or lizard has seen it, and recognized it, from a variety of angles. "It is precisely because all art is 'conceptual' that all representations are recognizable by their style" (p.87). "But we have seen that in all styles the artist has to rely on a vocabulary of forms and that it is the knowledge of this vocabulary rather than the knowledge of things that distinguishes the skilled from the unskilled artist. . . . What accounts for the ease or difficulty in rendering a given building or landscape is not so much the intrusion of knowledge as the lack of schemata" (p. 293).

The creation of an illusion does not happen in the isolation of the artist's studio, however. The beholders of a painting need to be able to interpret the artist's schema. Some of the beholders' ability to understand pictorial illusion comes from the way the human brain processes visual information. Optical illusions, for instance, show that human cognitive structure tends to see three dimensions on two-dimensional surfaces.[5] Beholders, moreover, learn about visual representation from their own interaction with reality, and painters must rely on these experiences to make their paintings convincing. For instance, painters may use the rendering of texture to create an illusion:

> But the trick certainly could not work without our contribution to the illusion. Where we have no knowledge of the type of surface represented, our interpretation may still go very wrong. Writing of his experience when he came to England from South Africa, Roy Campbell says, "The strange, crisp, salty consistency of snow was another puzzle. From paintings I had imagined it to be like wax, and snowflakes to be like shavings of candle grease." Few artists who have painted snow scenes can have realised that they relied on . . . our knowledge of snow . . . for the illusion to work. (Gombrich, 1960: 221)

Gombrich highlights the importance of interpretation for both image making and image reading, both of which create the illusion found in painting. "In our study of the language of art we have come . . . to stress one fact – the power of interpretation. We saw it at work in . . . the beholder's share in the readings of images, his capacity, that is, to collaborate with the artist and to transform a piece of colored canvas into a likeness of the visible world. We had seen it in . . . the artist who interpreted the world in terms of the schemata he made and knew" (p. 291). In this, Gombrich moves away from a purely formal analysis of the development of illusion and representation, and towards a contextualized analysis of the pictorial elements in painting that formal analysis considers to exist in isolation.

Semiotic and Structural Analysis

Both semiotics and structuralism derive from ideas in structural linguistics first discussed by Saussure (1915 [1959]). Saussure was interested in how language creates meaning. He distinguished, first, between *langue* and *parole*. *Langue* embodies the structure of a language, its grammar and rules, whereas *parole* is spoken or written language, in which the structure is manifest. In order to learn about *langue*, researchers must study *parole*. From *parole*, they can infer *langue*, which cannot be observed directly. Furthermore, words are signifiers that point to a signified, the concept referred to by the signifier. Together, the signifier and the signified make up the *sign*. The relationship between signifier and signified in language is arbitrary. We call a furry, four-legged thing that barks a "dog" and we call an omniscient, transcendent being a "god," but if everyone were to agree, we could easily exchange their names. The point is that the letters in "dog" and the utterance of the word do not have any necessary relationship to animals that bark, except that speakers of English have agreed on the term. Finally, meaning in language is built up through binary oppositions. An opposition – good–evil, us–them, human–animal – creates meaning through contrast, and clear meanings come from sharp contrasts. If I speak of a hawk and a tiger you are likely to notice that one animal is air-borne and the other is land-bound, and think of sky and earth. You are less likely to think that they are both carnivores, unless I also mention predators and prey. This shows that meaning can be built up by juxtaposing a series of opposites.

Semiotics

Semiotics is the science of signs. (See Hawkes, 1977 [1992] and Bignell, 1997 for reviews). It suggests that when studying a cultural object – or more accurately, a number of cultural objects from the same "language" – a researcher should look for structures, codes, oppositions, and grammars that underlie text or images. The semiotics of art uses Saussure's ideas on language by analogy. Cultural objects from a particular style or genre share a set of codes which can be decoded like language. These codes work not only within a given object, but also *intertextually* across objects in the genre. They take meaning from each other, not only through direct references, but by the sheer existence of the other objects which, taken as a whole, embody a system of rules that structure individual texts.

Barthes (1957 [1993]), an influential scholar of semiotics, argues that a first-order semiological system in cultural objects relate to a second-order semiological system that he terms *myth*. Myths, he argues, naturalize history and are the true, hidden meanings in texts. In a famous example, he analyzes a magazine cover:

> I am at the barber's, and a copy of *Paris-Match* is offered to me. On the cover, a young Negro in a French uniform is saluting, with his eyes uplifted, probably fixed on a fold of the tricolour. All this is the meaning of the picture. But, whether naively or not, I see very well what it signifies to me: that France is a great Empire, that all her sons, without any colour discrimination, faithfully serve under her flag, and that there is no better answer to the detractors of an alleged colonialism than the zeal shown by this Negro in serving his so-called oppressors. I am therefore again faced with a greater semiological system: there is a signifier, itself already formed with a previous system (*a black soldier is giving the French salute*); there is a signified (it is here a purposeful mixture of Frenchness and militariness); finally, there is a presence of the signified through the signifier . . . [the myth of French imperiality]. (p. 116)

Thus, by attending to both the semiotic system, and the mythic system in society, the researcher can find the latent meaning of texts.

In a well-known study, Williamson (1978) conducted a semiotic analysis on a large number of British print advertisements to learn about the codes they employed. She concentrates on the way advertising as a whole creates, semiotically and intertextually, the meaning inherent in individual ads. She states, "We can only understand what advertisements mean by finding out *how* they mean, and analysing the way in which they work" (p. 17, emphasis original). A simple strategy is to align the product with a desirable symbol. So, for instance, a bottle of Chanel No. 5 appears in the corner of a picture of Catherine Deneuve. This "correlative sign work" associates Deneuve's traits, chic, beautiful, and glamorous, with the perfume. Similarly, another ad shows Margaux Hemmingway, dressed in a karate outfit, with Babe cologne. This advertisement suggests that the fragrance has the same characteristics as Hemmingway, youthful and energetic. Further, Williamson suggests that the two advertisements work intertextually, through the opposition of Deneuve and Hemmingway. Hemmingway is *not-Deneuve* and this makes the meaning of the Babe advertisement, and its particular view of femininity ("liberated" and "American"), distinct from the meaning of the Chanel advertisement which presents a more sophisticated and elegant "French" style of femininity. In this way, it serves to differentiate the two fragrances.

Williamson discusses a number of binary opposites that she finds in the advertisements. One of these is natural–artificial. Binary opposites not only create meaning through contrast, but also tend to "privilege" one of the binaries, by suggesting that one is more valuable than the other. Natural, then, is valued over the unnatural or artificial. Within the natural, Williamson finds a secondary binary, cooked–raw, which means, approximately, finished, processed, or improved, versus rough, unprocessed, or unimproved. "Cooked" nature is privileged over "raw" nature, so a product, say orange juice in a carton, is better than unprocessed oranges. This semiotic trick, Williamson argues, encourages consumers to buy products.

Williamson also discusses techniques advertisers employ to draw readers into the advertising narrative. One technique, for instance, is the "looking glass" in which the viewer sees an image that could be himself or, more usually, herself – but it is an improved version of the viewer, the one where wrinkles have disappeared after the application of a skin cream. Another is the "absent participant." The viewer takes the place of this absent person, becoming part of the scene depicted by the advertiser. The viewer, then, might be invited to bring a glass of "Dry Sacks on the Rocks" to a beautiful woman in the picture.

The semiotic codes of advertisements are encoded by the advertiser but must be decoded by the viewer.[6] Williamson suggests that viewers bring their own knowledge to advertisements and this allows them to understand the messages in them. But she argues that the knowledge viewers bring to advertising is itself created by advertising: "the subject drawn into the work of advertising is *one who knows*. To fill in gaps we must know *what* to fill in, to decipher and solve problems we must know the rules of the game. Advertisements clearly produce knowledge . . . but this knowledge is always produced from something already known, that acts as a guarantee, in its anteriority, for the '*truth*' in the ad itself." (p. 99, emphasis original). In this way, advertisements create and perpetuate the ideology of consumption.

More recently, Goldman and Papson (1998) analyze television commercials, shown in America, for the athletic wear company Nike. They suggest that contemporary American culture is a "sign culture" where image is everything. Nike successfully created consumers through its advertisement campaign, which contained two types of advertisements. The first type included sunny, inspirational, multiracial images of people who "just do it" through sports. The second type were amusing, hip, and irreverent, and engaged their viewers' sense of media savvy. In the latter case, Nike commercials seem to deconstruct commercial culture, through the technique of the "knowing wink," while at the very same time, actually reinforcing it.[7]

Narrative structure

Structuralism has influenced the analysis of stories as well, especially through the idea of narrative structure.[8] Stories, especially mythic and formulaic ones, rely on clear binary oppositions (often good versus evil). "When a man is contrasted to a jaguar in a myth, this can represent humanity as opposed to animality, culture as opposed to nature. The symbolism is derived form their differences" (Wright, 1975: 23). Myths, and formula stories, are both general and easy-to-understand because of the simplicity involved in a binary structure. A genre of stories rely on a standard unfolding of the story that highlights the oppositions. The plot of a story, when seen this way, is called its "narrative structure" and can be summarized in a series of plot "functions." Stories from the same genre will have the same narrative structure, although the details of setting, the particulars of the plot complications, and the traits of the characters will clearly differ. In fact, stories with the same narrative structures can end quite differently. Classic love stories, for instance, can end happily (in comedies or fairy tales) or sadly (in tragedies). The different endings obviously make a difference in the reader's (or hearer's) experience of the story, but stories with quite different endings can still embody the same set of oppositional codes; for instance: man–woman, active–passive, rescuer–victim, rich–poor.

Eco (1979) analyzes the narrative structure and oppositions inherent in the James Bond novels by Ian Flemming. All the stories share a similar narrative structure, like a series of moves in a game. They unfold, from book to book, in the same way:[9]

  A. M [Bond's boss] moves and gives a task to Bond;
  B. Villain moves and appears to Bond . . . ;
  C. Bond moves and gives a first check to Villain or Villain gives a first check to Bond;
  D. Woman moves and shows herself to Bond [in the movies, often literally!];
  E. Bond takes Woman . . . ;
  F. Villain captures Bond . . . ;
  G. Villain tortures Bond . . . ;
  H. Bond beats Villain . . . ;
  I. Bond, convalescing, enjoys Woman, whom he then loses. (p. 156)

The binary opposites in the Bond stories can encompass Bond–Villain (good versus evil; free world versus communist world; liberalism versus totalitarianism) or Bond–Woman (male versus female; active versus passive; effective versus ineffective). The stories are different from each other because they rely on different permutations of the basic binaries, not all of which are activated in each story. The characters and their interrelations can bring up a number of subsidiary oppositions, for instance, "cupidity–ideals, love–death, chance–planning . . . perversion–innocence, loyalty–disloyalty," but are in each case, both "immediate and universal" (p. 147).

Eco suggests that the narrative structure of the 007 stories draws upon earlier chivalric myths. Bond is analogous to the knight in shining armor who sets out at the behest of the King (M), who fights monsters (the villain) and rescues the lady (the woman). Both James Bond stories and the earlier fairy tales represent the eternal struggle between good and evil, and as such, are universal and immediate (p. 161).

Frames and Context

The formal elements of a text do not exist in a vacuum. They require a context in order to make them meaningful. Take, for instance, an inverted triangle. It could be a sign, literally, on a highway indicating the need for caution or to yield to other traffic. On a lapel, it might be a sign of gay pride. And on a sheet of music for a jazz saxophonist, it indicates a "tongue slap." The inverted triangle needs to be *framed* in order for the receiver to interpret it and to make it meaningful. Frames create expectations on the part of the audience that set them up to experience the cultural object in particular ways.

Formula can function as a frame, as for instance, in Cawelti's description of the enjoyment and stimulation audiences receive from situations that would be unbearable in life and tragic as news. Bordwell (1985) describes the basic formula of Hollywood films as a stable situation, a disturbance, a struggle, the elimination of the disturbance, and a return to a stable state. Most films use a variety of devices to position audiences to receive the stories they tell as if they were portraying real life. They tell a story, usually in chronological sequence, and make it clear how each scene in the movie follows from the previous and leads to the next. Directors who use different devices create a different set of expectations in their audiences.

McLuhan (1964) suggests that the medium of a cultural object serves as a frame. Print requires different cognitive skills of readers than watching does of viewers or listening does of hearers. This goes beyond the obvious need for literacy (for reading) or visual literacy (for looking) and affects how people think about the material. In McLuhan's famous phrase, "the medium is the message," he suggests that societies based on written culture think in a slow, linear manner, whereas visual cultures think in a non-linear, multiply-linked way. Thus, we expect a James Bond novel to be longer, more involved and, perhaps, more linear, than a James Bond movie. Further, audiences react differently to a Bond movie shown in a cinema than they might to the same film broadcast on television, if only because the level of attention the two media require are different.

Williams (1981: 131) suggests that fine art is signaled by *occasion* and by *place*. These two factors help determine what audiences consider art and non-art. Ballet, for instance, is an art form and is usually signaled by the performers wearing familiar costumes such as tutus, tights, and toe-slippers, moving in certain conventionalized ways to symphonic music. It also tends to take place in a theater. Other kinds of dance, ballroom dancing, folk dancing, and break dancing, for instance, are usually considered social activities rather than art. But if they are performed in a theater, they are more likely to be seen in the context of art than as a leisure pursuit. The importance of context is especially notable in terms of avant-garde art. Modern dance, performed in street clothes to contemporary music, or to silence, requires a context that places it into the category of art. A pile of bricks at a building site is just that. But a pile of bricks in the Tate Gallery in London (as with Carl André's bricks) is received – or proffered for reception – as a work of art, and at least some members of the audience will approach the works with a degree of seriousness that the high arts have traditionally demanded.

Ways of seeing

Berger (1972) looks at the ways that our social system affects the way we look at art works. Drawing on (uncited) work in literary, cultural, and film theory, he specifically examines how we receive visual images. Two of his ideas concern us here. The first, and more general, concerns the notion that a text "positions" the reader; that is, that art works set up certain understandings to which the viewer must adjust. One of these is called the "male gaze." In this, a visual representation is made assuming that the viewer is male; thus, both men and women viewing the object (a female nude, for instance) will be positioned as men (see, e.g. Mulvey, 1975). As Berger summarizes the concept, "*men act* and *women appear.* Men look at women. Women watch themselves being looked at. This determines not only most relations between men and women but also the relation of women to themselves. The surveyor of woman in herself is male. . . . Thus she turns herself into an object – and most particularly an object of vision: a sight" (p. 47, emphasis original).

Berger's second key point has to do with originals and copies. Drawing on the idea of intertextuality from semiotics and Walter Benjamin's (1968) work on the mechanical reproduction of art works, he shows how the reception of a work of art in contemporary society is strongly influenced by the proliferation of images. If our reception of objects is affected by the objects which relate to it, Berger argues, our own reception of art works will be uniquely personal. People have pictures in their homes, often reproductions of famous works. The fact that the image is received amongst one's own possessions, rather than in a museum or the original location (like a cathedral or a mansion), makes a difference. People may even have pinboards that personalize their favorite art works, placing them next to mementos like a Valentine's day card or a photo of their cat. Compare this to the situation before art works were easily reproduced for mass consumption. Art works were received reverentially, because they existed in just one place. To see a particular painting, the viewer had to travel and could not easily compare two different works side-by-side. We can do this readily today, with the help of digitized images, photographs, or, with a little more effort on the part of curators, in museum exhibitions where works have been borrowed from other museums worldwide. In Berger's words:

> The uniqueness of every painting was once part of the uniqueness of the place where it resided. Sometimes the painting was transportable. But it could never be seen in two places at the same time. When the camera reproduces a painting, it destroys the uniqueness of its image. As a result, the meaning changes. Or, more exactly, its meaning multiplies and fragments into many meanings. (p. 19)

Berger also argues that copies affect our viewing of the original. They embody the image of an original, and the original becomes a physical object whose value is increased by our familiarity with the image. Berger mentions *The Virgin of the Rocks* by Leonardo da Vinci. "Having seen this reproduction, one can go the National Gallery [of London] to look at the original and there discover what the reproduction lacks. Alternatively, one can forget about the quality of the reproduction and simply be reminded, when one sees the original, that it is a famous painting of which somewhere one has already seen a reproduction. But in either case the uniqueness of the original now lies in it being *the original of a reproduction*. It is no longer what its image shows that strikes one as unique; its first meaning is no longer to be found in what it says, but in what it is" (p. 21, emphasis original). Berger, following Benjamin, argues that the authority (or aura) of art is stripped from it in splitting the image from the object. This allows for a democratic use of the meanings of art, as in the example of pinboards. But such a use is blocked by elites who hold cultural authority in society. Thus, Berger suggests that art has become a political issue: "The real question is: to whom does the meaning of the art of the past properly belong? To those who can apply it to their own lives, or to a cultural hierarchy of relic specialists?" (p. 32).

Critique

Studies that focus on the text alone are today's straw person. When they leave aside reception, these studies leave out half the meaning-making process, a fact which is recognized by most contemporary theorists. A number of the authors mentioned above consider the audience in a limited way. Gombrich and Meyer, for instance, suggest that meaning results from the interaction of the beholder or listener in relationship to the painting or music. Williamson postulates how readers might decode advertisements, and Cawelti hypothesizes how audiences might enjoy formula fiction. They focus on texts and the formal elements of the text, arguing that these work in concert with the receiver's knowledge and expectations. These authors recognize the importance of reception, but they discuss audiences only as an implied entity.

The problem with leaving out the receiver can be illustrated with Williamson's work. In her interpretation of advertisements, she makes claims about their meaning that sometimes seem arbitrary or farfetched. For instance, in a British ad for chips (french fries), there is an image of hands holding a potato, cracked in half like an egg, with fries falling out. The caption reads, "What nature did for eggs... McCain have done for chips." To me, the appeal of this ad is its visual pun on potatoes and eggs. But there are, apparently, deeper meanings. For instance, seeing the "potato reminds us how different potatoes and chips are, how annoying potatoes are to clean and peel; in seeing the difference between the two we have become aware of all that must be done to turn one into another – cutting up and frying. All this gives chips a superior status since they are the result of this process, they eliminate it for us" (p. 104). This, then, more strongly encourages us to buy frozen french fries. The problem in Williamson's work is that she appears to assume that everyone who reads the ad, or who glances at it while flipping through a magazine, will take the same reading she does.

Scott (1990) suggests that there are three kinds of meaning, the intended meaning (what the author meant to produce), the received meaning (what audiences actually take from the object) and the internal meaning that semioticians, content analysts, and scholars of formal content have tried to identify. Following Giddens (1979), Scott suggests that a search for a separate, objective internal meaning "is a search for a chimera" (p. 33), because as soon as the researcher approaches a text, he or she becomes a part of the audience. Further, the formal elements, codes, and structures of a text are part of a historical context and must be seen in this way. Rather than searching for a disembodied internal meaning, researchers should study texts as "socially situated products" (p. 34). Texts can and do become separated from their author's intention, but nevertheless it is possible to study the intended meaning as well as the received meaning, as both situate the text in social contexts.

The crucial role of the audience (or author), however, does not render useless the analysis of texts. Audiences that do not understand the conventions of a genre can do a number of things. They may find the work incomprehensible. Or they may dislike it. They may read it in terms of conventions from other genres, and take a different meaning. For instance, Bennett and Woollacott (1987) speculate that some readers of James Bond might see the stories through the conventions of detective fiction rather than adventure stories in general or the British imperialist spy thriller in particular, and Denning (1987) suggests that the starting point for Bond stories are codes of tourism and pornography. In an earlier time, cultural authority would have said that if the receiver chose any of these strategies, the receiver was wrong. Today, most theorists recognize that there are a variety of responses that individuals can have to a work of art, and they do not necessarily privilege one interpretation over another. We say that everyone's response is valid. And so it is. But the audience is not completely autonomous. The text does contribute to the meaning people create. The structure and content of the text opens up some potential meanings and closes off others.[10]

Research that posits the important relationship of texts to audiences, situating it in the receiver's knowledge of schema, conventions, or semiotic codes can, along with an analysis of the text, help us learn how the structure of texts can create meaning for receivers. Moreover, conventions *do* create meaning, but the conventions must be shared between audience members and the creators of art. A ballerina can generate emotion through the movement of her body because her audience is steeped in the conventions of ballet. Movies do the same through depictions of houses burning down, or parents searching for stolen babies, or the epic struggle between good and evil. Movies cannot rely on conventions shared only among a small elite, as ballet can, but must appeal to a large number of people who have in common only the most basic human experiences. In sum, meaning cannot be separated either from audiences and their presuppositions or from texts and their structures. The wider consequences of this inability to separate art from society are discussed in the next chapter.

NOTES

1   Content analysis can be considered a form of textual analysis. I do not cover it in this chapter. It is discussed in chapter 2, however. Indeed, most of the studies in the reflection approach rely on a form of textual analysis for their arguments; however, not all textual analyses make reflection arguments.

2   Here, I simplify the concept of formal meaning and gloss over different ways that the term has been used in different disciplines. For instance, Meyer (1956) uses the term "formal" to mean both that meaning comes from the interrelationships among the musical elements of a piece *and* that this meaning is intellectual, in contrast to "expressionist" which implies emotional meaning in music.

3   I am grateful to Karin Peterson and Sarah Corse for pointing this example out to me.

4   Here I have dramatically oversimplified the rich and subtle arguments of such writers as Gombrich (1964) and Kubler (1962). See Hockney (2001) for a radical reinterpretation of such stylistic developments.

5   Gombrich discusses these optical illusions at length. For a discussion of the cognitive tendency to perceive three dimensions, see Hoffman (1998).

6   See also the discussion of encoding/decoding and preferred meanings, as presented in chapter 10, which is relevant here as well.

7   It is interesting to note that advertisements seem to be a magnet for semiotic analysis. In addition to Williamson, and Goldman and Papson, Barthel (1988) and Cortese (1999), among others, incorporate a semiotic component in their work on advertising. In contrast, there are very few studies that look at the actual audience reception of advertisements (but see Schudson, 1986). Perhaps this is related to Turnstall's (1983) idea, presented in chapter 11, that hegemonic messages are most successful when receivers accept them without much attention. Once one's critical faculties are engaged, viewers may more readily avoid advertising's effect. That is, in discussing advertisements with people, an uncertainty principle obtains, in that the observation changes the reception of the advertisements. (This is, of course, true about studies of the reception of all types of culture, but might be particularly heightened for advertisements.)

8   See Wright (1975: ch. 2) for a clear summary.

9   Eco reports that sometimes the plot unfolds in a slightly different order than what he has presented, but all the plot elements he mentions are present in all of the stories.

10 See Eco's (1979) discussion of closed versus open texts.

11 Baxandall's purpose is larger than just formal analysis. His goal in analyzing Piero's painting, and several other pieces of work, is to provide a method, which he calls inferential criticism, for the historical understanding of art, especially with regard to the painter's intentions. Baxandall does not argue that this is the only way to study paintings, but rather, that it is an instructive one.

12 One of the key puzzles Baxandall discusses is why the river, reflective in the background, becomes transparent (or dries up) at Christ's feet. Baxandall tells us that at one point, the painting was gilded, and Christ was bathed in a heavenly, golden, light emanating from the dove, "a kind of divine spotlight" (p. 128). This light would make the water under it transparent. But as the gilding wore off, the reason for the transparent water was no longer evident in the picture itself.

Case Study 13.1
The Renaissance Way of Seeing

Based on Michael Baxandall (1988), *Painting and Experience In Fifteenth Century Italy* (Oxford: Oxford University Press, 2nd edition).

Points for Discussion

1   What is the "period eye" (as a general concept)?
2   What are the specific elements of the period eye during the Italian Renaissance, as described by Baxandall?
3   How does an understanding of the period eye help us to understand paintings from the Italian Renaissance?
4   To what extent does Baxandall's approach fit into the consumption approach to art? How fully can we learn understand audiences who lived in times past?

Case

Michael Baxandall (1988), an art historian, studied the world of Italian Renaissance painting. He was interested in both the production and the reception of painting during this time. In the first part of *Painting And Experience In Fifteenth Century Italy*, he looks at the conditions under which painters worked, and how the patronage system in place at the time affected the content of work. He shows how a change in the social world (from a gaudy style of displaying wealth to a more restrained one) facilitated the shift in the role of the painter from a craftsman to an artist. In the second part, Baxandall reconstructs for the modern reader how a person living in an Italian city during the Renaissance might view the paintings. He calls the particular way of seeing during an era the *period eye*. It is the second part of the book that concerns us here.

Baxandall explores how people are able to take meaning from the two-dimensional representations that form the basis of paintings. He starts with the idea that representations can be ambiguous. When people come to a drawing, they bring along a certain set of skills and habits, what Baxandall calls a *cognitive style*. Take, for instance, figure 13.1. In order to interpret this figure, a person must be used to the idea of shapes like squares or circles, and understand that two-dimensional drawings can represent three-dimensional objects.[1] With these skills, a viewer "will be less likely to see it just as a round thing with projections [a bug with four legs, say], and more likely to see it primarily as a circle imposed on a rectangle" (p. 30). But it could as easily be interpreted as a belt with a large buckle or a wristwatch with no face. So we must add the *context* to the illustration. The original woodcut comes with a caption: "This is the shape of the Holy Sepulchre of Our Lord Jesus Christ" (p. 30). This information tells us that the

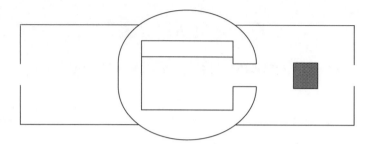

Figure 13.1 Drawing after a woodcut in Santo Brasca's *Itinerario di Gerusalemme* (Milan, 1481).

drawing does represent something; it is not just a random doodle. Furthermore, it belongs to the "ground-plan convention – lines representing the course walls would follow on the ground if one were looking vertically down at a structure" (p. 30); it is a bird's eye view of a building. In order to interpret the drawing, then, a viewer must be familiar with the ground-plan convention. But, Baxandall says, this still is not enough. An experience of buildings is also necessary in order to read the drawing correctly. "A man used to fifteenth-century Italian architecture might well infer that the circle is a circular building, with a cupola perhaps, and that the rectangular wings are halls. But a fifteenth-century Chinese, once he had learned the ground-plan convention, might infer a circular central court on the lines of the new Temple of Heaven at Peking" (p. 31). In other words, to understand a drawing, one needs to share a basic visual vocabulary with the artist (in terms of shape, perspective, and the like), be able to understand the particular conventions the artist drew upon (in this case, a ground plan, as opposed to a line drawing of some other sort), and also understand some of the wider cultural understandings that the artist might draw upon. In other words, one needs to understand the cognitive style prevalent at the time the picture was made.

An understanding of the period eye of the Italian Renaissance allows us more fully to appreciate its paintings. Most readers of this book, as westerners, already understand the basic building blocks of shape and perspective that Renaissance paintings drew upon. But we have a much weaker understanding of the various conventions of the paintings, and also lack many of the cultural tools that the Renaissance painter would take for granted in his viewers.

The first thing that Baxandall does to uncover the Renaissance period eye is to look at the Catholic Church's writings on the purpose of religious paintings, as the majority of Renaissance paintings were of this type. The Church suggests that images should be "lucid, vivid and readily accessible stimuli to meditation on the Bible and the lives of Saints. If you convert [these ideas] into a brief for the painter, they carry an expectation that the picture should tell its story in a clear way for the simple and in an eye-catching and memorable way for the forgetful, and with full use of all the emotional resources of the sense of sight" (p. 41). In this way, then, Renaissance painters try to tell a story from the Bible that will be clear to all viewers. They do not attempt to express their private feelings or personal visions in their works. This means that we do not have to try to uncover the interior world of the painter's mind to learn what he hopes to convey in his work.

Renaissance viewers were deeply familiar with the Bible. As a consequence, painters rendered faces and locations more as generalized types than as identifiable instances, so as to lessen any contrast between their representations and those imagined by the viewers. Biblical stories were told, and known, in much greater detail than is generally the case today. For instance, in the Annunciation story, in which the Virgin Mary learns that she will carry the child Jesus, there are three distinct steps, or "mysteries." A Renaissance viewer would be able to discern the precise stage in the story more readily than today's viewers (some of whom might not even know the story or why an angel is speaking to Mary). Most viewers, however, will know that the Angel Gabriel is kneeling before Mary because something special and sacred is happening. When viewing Piero della Francesca's *Annunciation*, they will not make the mistake of thinking that the Angel is kneeling to worship the pillar that stands between him and Mary. In the third mystery, Mary goes through five distinct reactions (disquiet, reflection, inquiry, submission, and merit) upon learning that she will give birth to Christ. When a painter sets out to depict the Annunciation, he will illustrate not just a single mystery, but one particular sub-theme, and his public will recognize it.

Painters also were able to convey meaning in their paintings by using certain colors or portraying characters with certain gestures. Early in the fifteenth century, paintings were often gilded. Since gilt (gold foil) was expensive, painters used this to highlight the most important or holy elements of their work. For instance, Piero della Francesca used a shower of golden light to highlight the moment of Christ's baptism.[2] Piero also used a certain rose color to indicate sacred elements in his work, for instance, the robes worn by Jesus. Some blue pigments were richer and much more expensive than others, so patrons often specified which blue to use. One, for instance, required that "the ultramarine used for Mary is to be of the quality of two florins to the ounce, while for the rest of the picture ultramarine of one florin to the ounce will do" (p. 11). As the value of this rich violet-blue, as opposed to the cheaper "German blue," was widely recognized in the society, painters could use it to convey important information: "the exotic and dangerous character of ultramarine was a means of accent that we, for whom dark blue is probably no more striking than scarlet or vermilion, are liable to miss. . . . In Masaccio's expensively pigmented *Crucifixion*, the vital narrative gesture of St. John's right arm is an ultramarine gesture" (p. 11). Later in the century, when the use of gilding had declined, the "relative splendour of hues" remained an important tool for painters (p. 82). "There were expensive colours, blues made from lapis lazuli or reds made from silver and sulphur, and there were cheap earth colours like ochre and umber. The eye was caught by the former before the latter" (p. 83).

Renaissance painters also draw upon commonly understood gestures. Some of these are readily accessible to modern viewers. For instance, when an angel points to the central scene (which may be the Baptism, or the Madonna and Child), we recognize the gesture as one that says, "look there, where the action is." Some of this body language, however, is no longer used and has been forgotten. No dictionaries of Renaissance gestures currently exist to help us understand unfamiliar gestures. Still, there are clues to Renaissance gestures, for instance in the language of signs used by Benedictine monks during periods of silence. These for instance, encourage us "to read Masaccio's *Expulsion from Paradise* . . . in a more precise way, as combining in the paired figures two inflections of emotion: it is Adam [covering his eyes with his fingers] who expresses shame, Eve [pressing her breast with the palm of her hand] only grief" (p. 61).

Armed with research on Biblical stories, knowledge of the cost, value, and meaning of various colors, and an understanding of quattrocento gestures, modern viewers would be able to wrest a much richer insight from their encounter with Renaissance paintings. Nevertheless, these elements of the period eye uncovered by Baxandall relate fairly well to a modern viewer's understandings of paintings. We realize that we do not know some of the conventions, but many of them (color indicating importance, gestures as meaningful) make sense to us. Even the painter's brief – to depict a story clearly – might sound more like illustration to us than the inspired greatness that we attribute to fine art (including Renaissance paintings), but we understand the concept. In discussing the next facet of the period eye, Baxandall shows how truly different the cognitive style of Renaissance viewers was from our own.

One of the goals of a religious painting was to capture the attention of the viewer, so that he (or she) would contemplate it closely. One way painters did this, Baxandall agues, was to encourage the viewer to engage playfully with the picture's elements. One skill of the time, common among the classes who patronized art, involved the calculation of volume. This was important because merchants traded and agreed on prices for goods in the absence of standardized containers. A shipment of grain, for instance, might come in a variety of bags and barrels of various odd shapes. If merchants were unable to come up with fairly accurate estimates of the size of shipments, they might unwittingly pay too much or sell for too little. A science of "gauging" existed to help solve this problem. It taught merchants how to decompose odd shapes into regular shapes – spheres, cubes, cylinders, cones, and the like – whose volumes were calculable by geometric formulae.

Painters took advantage of the habit of gauging by painting the key figures in their works, and the landscapes and piazzas they inhabited, in such a way that they could be decomposed into various three-dimensional solids. In this way, they literally made their paintings "en-gauging" to a segment of the population that was particularly important to them. To be sure, the merchants and professionals did not actually calculate the volume of the Virgin Mary, say, but they were sensitive to those pictorial elements that used quattrocento mathematical principles and found in them particular immediacy and force.

We no longer see the conspicuous skills exercised by Renaissance painters when they incorporated the concepts of gauging into their works. Viewers from other contexts, with specialties, say, in physiology and musculature, might find the draped, volumetric figures of fifteenth-century Italian paintings less powerful than styles that depict nudes. As Baxandall puts it, "Much of what we call 'taste' lies in this, the conformity between discriminations demanded by a painting and the skills of discrimination possessed by the beholder. We enjoy our own exercise of skill, and we particularly enjoy the *playful exercise* of skills which we use in normal life very earnestly. If a painting gives us opportunity for exercising a valued skill and rewards our virtuosity with a sense of worthwhile insights about that painting's organization, we tend to enjoy it: it is to our taste" (p. 34, emphasis added).

Notes

1 Baxandall suggests that these basic skills are learned. More recent theorists of visual perception (e.g. Hoffman, 1998) suggest that these most basic skills are genetically determined and exist in all people. This research does not conflict with Baxandall's discussion of more complex perceptions, however.

2 The painting is *Baptism of Christ*, ca. 1440–50, in the National Gallery of London. The guilding mentioned, however, has now worn off. (This example is taken from Baxandall, 1985, which explores the historical understanding of pictures in a more general way.)

3 Baxandall credits the Warburg Institute for the image; however, they do not hold an original edition of the book, but rather a 1966 scholarly edition by Anna Laura Momigliano Lepschy. I thank Paul Taylor of the Photographic Collection, Warburg Institute for pointing this out to me.

14

The Constitution of Art in Society

From earliest times, the riddle of the world's origins has been explained, symbolically, in terms of an act of artistic creation. The Teutonic tribes of Northern Europe held that Wotan carved the first human beings out of the trunk of fir trees with his sword. According to Hindu tradition, the universe is created and destroyed by the dance of Shiva. And many myths tell how man was first shaped out of a lump of clay: by Lao-Tien-Yeh, the Heavenly Father, in early Chinese legends; by Prometheus in the Greek creation stories; and by Jehovah in the Bible. It is not surprising, therefore, that an aura of mysterious power has always surrounded the practitioners of art, and that the artist has been often seen as the creative person par excellence.

(Jacob W. Getzels and Mihaly Csikszentmihalyi, 1976: v)

This chapter argues that art and aesthetics, even the questions of artistic value and the genius of artists, can be topics for sociological inquiry. The research presented in this chapter is focused not only on the art itself, but also on how it is embedded in society. Moreover, it recognizes that art is constituted in society, and conversely, that art itself plays a constitutive role with respect to social actors.

In some ways, the research described in this chapter hearkens back to the aims of the "grand" tradition of sociology and theorists such as Adorno. His aims were to connect music to broad historical trends, to modes of consciousness, and to cognitive habits (Witkin, 1998). The grand approach fell into disfavor due to weaknesses in its methods and to changes in intellectual currents in the discipline of sociology (positivists accused Adorno of asserting his claims without testing them empirically). Nevertheless, Adorno's scholarly reach encompassed the music itself and even extended to aesthetic judgments. The research that replaced the grand tradition – theories from both the production side and the consumption side of the cultural diamond – usually relegated the art itself to the background, as it focused on, and privileged, the intricacies of the production system or the actions of the audience. Indeed, these approaches can render the art epiphenomenal; it becomes merely a byproduct of production or the inconsequential site of independently generated audience resistance or identity construction. As Bowler (1998: 32) puts it, neither production nor consumption traditions have yielded much "insight into the specificity or distinctiveness of aesthetic-cultural forms and practices."[1]

The Fabrication of Meaning

Griswold (1987a) argues that meaning exists in the relationship between the reader and the message in the text. Meaning is a fabric "woven from the warp of the cultural object and the woof of those human presuppositions that are evoked by the context in which the cultural discourse takes place" (p. 1080). An art object embodies a range of symbolic capacities, which the reader selectively draws upon to generate meaning. Presuppositions can be intensely personal, but they are also social, exhibiting regular variation across social categories such as class, gender, occupation, generation, or nationality.

To test her idea empirically, Griswold studied the reception of the works of a single author, George Lamming, in three different settings: the United States, Great Britain, and the West Indies.[2] Lamming, who wrote in the postwar period, was born in Barbados and educated in the British style in Trinidad. His status as a "scholarship boy" alienated him from his past life in the village, but also from his more wealthy classmates. As an adult, he moved to London, where he started to write, and later in his life spent some time in the United States. His career as a novelist was successful, and he was "modestly lionized on both sides of the Atlantic" (p. 1086). The context of his writing included the immigration of Afro-Caribbean nationals into the UK to help with the post-war labor shortage, and the rise of West Indian fiction in Great Britain, which was due, in part, to the availability of Arts Council funding and the attention given by the British intelligentsia to their "exotic brethren." In the US, the context was the rise of the civil rights movement following a number of Supreme Court decisions on racial issues in the mid-1950s. And in the Islands, anglophone Caribbean nations were asserting their independence and leaving the British Empire.

The choice of Lamming as a subject was motivated by the fact that his novels appeared in all three settings simultaneously. Most fiction which sells inter-nationally is published in one country first and then, when successful, else-where. Prior success in one setting would be likely to affect the reception of the book in another. Since Lamming's fiction was published at the same time in all three settings, Griswold could determine the readings of each book independently of influence from the other countries.

Griswold studied six Lamming novels, published between 1953 and 1972. To capture the reception of these novels, Griswold examined published book reviews from a variety of sources. In total, she examined 95 reviews, 30 from the West Indies, 28 from Britain, and 37 from the United States. Griswold notes that the reviews are written by the literary elite for educated, middle-class audiences, and thus are representative of these groups rather than the wider society. The West Indies provided a slightly higher proportion (67 percent) of favorable reviews, as compared to the US (41 percent) and the UK (39 percent). Beyond that, the reviewers in the three countries focused on very different aspects of the novels and presented different meanings. For instance, Lamming's first book, *In the Castle of My Skin*, was a semi-autobiographical story about a boy growing up in the 1930s and '40s in Barbados. "West Indian readers said [the novel] was about the ambiguities of identity; the British readers said it was about how a youth, any youth, comes to maturity; American readers said it was about race" (Griswold, 1994: 84).

In general, American reviewers thought all Lamming's books were primarily about race. They displayed an "obsession" with the topic, by talking about those aspects of the novels which involved racial conflict, racial memory, and racial harmony. Three-quarters of American reviews mentioned race as a theme, as compared to one-quarter of the West Indian reviews, "and even less of the British" (p. 1096). The American reviewers reported the author's race in many reviews. They also discussed themes of nation building, independence, and social change, but to a lesser extent than race. American reviewers did not talk much about the literary style of the books. Griswold found it striking that they did not comment on the humor in Lamming's novels, even though a number of very funny scenes were interspersed within the mostly tragic stories. Americans, then, took books by a black artist quite seriously, to the point of missing (or failing to report) the humor in them.

British reviewers, on the other hand, focused on the literary style of the books. They discussed the characters, characterization, and other elements of literary form, such as the writing style and the plot development. In this, Griswold argues, the British attempted to coopt the postcolonial literary movement into their own tradition of fiction; they used the literary tools from the "great tradition" and applied them to new material from the old empire. Interestingly, although Lamming's works involve stories about the immigration of Afro-Caribbean people to Great Britain, and the relationships among black and white people in both the UK and the Caribbean, British reviewers were "conspicuously silent" on the issues of race and, especially, colonialism. Griswold attributes this to the "preoccupation" in Britain with colonialism, and a stereotypical "British reticence about sensitive and unpleasant" topics (p. 1103).

Reviewers in the Caribbean took still different readings of what the novels were about. They thought that the books were about building and finding one's identity, and mentioned ambiguity – the "impossibility of ever knowing the truth" (p. 1098) – as a theme. They particularly focused on the characters, dialect and the representation of spoken language in the novels. Griswold suggested that individual and national identity were issues particularly salient in the West Indies, especially in literature, where images from England ("daffodils") and images from Africa ("dashikis") were both "outside" the local experience.

Griswold argues that "cultural works are 'tools' used by people to grapple with present and pressing problems" (p. 1104). Each social group she studied faced different problems and issues (civil rights in America, the end of the empire in Great Britain, and nation building in the Caribbean), as well as different presuppositions, and this led them to interpret the texts in different ways. Not all works, however, can sustain the multiple interpretations found in reviews of Lamming's work. Griswold argues that art objects vary in their *cultural power*, "the capacity of certain works to linger in the mind and . . . to enter the canon" of great works (p. 1105). The best art is able to sustain rich meanings and a variety of interpretations, it is multivocal – this is its power. These works rely on a set of conventions, and yet they play with the conventions in a way that "intrigues or disturbs recipients, without utterly mystifying or frustrating them" (p. 1105).

In presenting her idea of fabrication – the interplay of text and presupposition that generates meaning – Griswold takes issue with theorists who suggest that meaning resides wholly in the text. Studying the literary and stylistic devices, narrative structures, binary structures, or multivocality alone cannot render the meaning of the text. Audiences must receive the work, against their horizon of expectations, for meaning to emerge. But Griswold also takes issue with theorists from the active audience approach who believe that people can create whatever meaning they like from just about anything. She argues that meaning does not reside wholly within the mind of the reader. Both the text and the reader contribute to the creation of meaning.

Art and Everyday Life

DeNora (2000) studied music and human action. She sought to understand how music constructs daily life; or more accurately, how individuals construct daily life using music. DeNora believes that the power of music is inseparable from its use; thus, she argues that researchers need to study music-in-action in social contexts. DeNora, along with interactionist sociologists, suggests that social order is constructed and reconstructed on a daily basis by individual actors; it is an "achievement" (p. 109), not an external fact. Her approach

> orbits around action-as-practice. It is less concerned with depicting actors as "knowing", that is deliberate or instrumentally rational subjects, and more concerned with exploring the matter of how forms of social life are established and renewed, albeit at the often subconscious levels of practice, habit, passion and routine. (p. 110)

DeNora, in a broad sense, is interested in the "aesthetic dimensions of social organization" which have been largely ignored by sociologists. Music, an aesthetic material, plays a role in the constitution of order and can be connected to "modes of action, feeling and embodiment" (p. 110).

DeNora carried out a series of ethnographies to get at her questions. In the first phase of her research, she interviewed fifty-two women about their musical life. She found that nearly all respondents "were explicit about music's role as an ordering device at the personal level," and regardless of their ability to describe music in formal terms, they were articulate about what type of music they "needed" in different contexts (p. 49). The women often used music, while alone, to change or enhance their moods, energy levels, or cognitive state; they "used music to facilitate concentration, to vent unpleasant emotions, to manage and modulate emotional states, and to relive past emotional states" (p. 160). For instance, when depressed, respondents said they might choose to listen to sad music to match their mental state, or they might choose cheerful music to pull themselves out of their blues. They might play loud, rhythmic music before going out to a party, club, or job interview, to gear themselves up. In this way, "music is both an instigator and a container of feeling" (p. 58).

DeNora's respondents also used music to construct social interactions. Some women, especially the younger ones, choose certain pieces of "'romantic', 'relaxing' or 'smoochy' music" (p. 116) to accompany intimate encounters, to "decorate the auditory space in which relaxing and being intimate...occurs" (p. 117). Many women, from across age groups, used music to set the tone of parties, perhaps choosing classical or jazz for a sophisticated dinner party, folk music for an informal one, and latin, disco, or rock numbers for a drinks party or barbecue.

DeNora also studied aerobics classes. These provide a "totalizing" environment (p. 103) in which instructors choose music with certain characteristics of tempo, rhythm, orchestration, and melody to structure participants' cognitive awareness. With the music thumping, they literally forget fatigue and exercise more vigorously; the music empowers bodies. In this way, "music works as a prosthetic technology of the body, heightening and extending bodily capacities" (p. 159–60).

Music appears in settings where respondents have not chosen to listen. To study the effects of music in such situations, DeNora studied retail shops in a British high street. The head office of many store chains provide approved tapes for their branches, and most shops, chains or independents, play background music. In the stores, "musical materials serve as 'welcome mats' or a 'keep out' notices, depending on how they are received" (p. 136). Young shoppers liked the current hits played in clothing shops geared toward hip, chic consumers, whereas elderly shoppers preferred stores that were silent or, at least, had less intrusive music. Store managers chose different music for different times of the day or year.

The managers believed that the type of music they played affected purchases. DeNora cited two studies of wine stores, which support this assertion. Wine stores are useful settings in which to study purchase decisions because most customers have only a vague notion of what they will buy when they enter the store. In one study, customers bought more expensive wines when the store played classical music than when it played pop music (Arenti and Kim, 1993). In a second, more customers bought French wine when French music played near a display of same-price French and German wine. The opposite effect occurred when German music was played (North and Hargreaves, 1997). Interestingly, most of the customers in the second study, interviewed after purchase, said that they had not noticed the music.

In her own ethnography, DeNora followed "volunteer shoppers" around stores. Both she and the research subject wore portable microphones and made comments into them about the shopping experience. Most notably, the music affected the tone of voice used by both the subject and researcher. DeNora also observed shoppers engaged in "'brief body encounters with music'. These were moments – sometimes of only a second's duration – where shoppers could be seen to 'fall in' with the music's style and rhythm and where music was visibly profiling consumers' comportment, where it had an impact on the mundane choreography of in-store movement" (p. 144). These structuring effects of music occurred mainly at pre-conscious or unconscious levels.

DeNora's work brings up interesting issues about the "commercial dominance of the public sonic sphere" (p. 162): "if music is a device of social ordering, . . . if it can be seen to have effects upon bodies, hearts and minds, then the matter of music in the social space is . . . an aesthetic–political matter" (p. 129). It matters who controls the music we hear in public because the music has power in our interaction with it.

Notably, DeNora's work never moves far away from the music itself. For example, she describes a Bach cantata:

Underpinned by dotted – agitated? – rhythms, the sopranos sing the three-syllable message ("Wachet auf" [wake up]) on three sustained notes of the E flat major triad, and this tonally centered, authoritative "call" is underpinned by a busy counter point of the altos, tenors, and basses and a "rushing", forward-moving obbligato in the treble instrumental accompaniment. (The opening is illustrated in [DeNora's own] figure 7.) (p. 153)

(DeNora's figure 7 shows the musical score of the first few measures of the piece.) In her sophisticated descriptions of musical pieces, along with her respondents' untrained ones ("a nice juicy chord" with "a lot of notes, and usually, perhaps in a lower register," p. 68), DeNora is interested in how particular musical properties become salient to people in certain places and times and how these translate into action. She describes such musical properties as "affordances": "Objects 'afford' actors certain things; a ball, for example, affords rolling, bouncing and kicking in a way that a cube of the same size, texture and weight would not" (p. 39). DeNora argues that music affords human agency:

Music is active within social life, it has "effects" then, because it offers specific materials to which actors may turn when they engage in the work of organizing social life. Music is a resource – it provides affordances – for world building. (p. 44)

In talking about affordances, DeNora wishes to point out that each piece of music holds out certain possibilities to listeners; it offers tools, in effect, for them to construct reactions of mood, cognitive awareness (or forgetfulness), and embodied energy or calm.[3] But it is crucial to note that listeners may choose to take up these tools or they may not. In other words, affordances suggest, but do not compel, forms of action. Music does not "cause" the behavioral responses; it is not a mere "stimulus" like a strong cup of coffee or a sleeping potion that, once ingested, creates uncontrollable bodily reactions in the user. Not all listeners will get up and dance to lively music, for instance, even though lively music affords toe-tapping, finger snapping, and whole-body dancing. As DeNora puts it, "no music will reliably move all listeners" (p. 161).

DeNora's thesis shares two basic ideas with Griswold's approach. First, researchers must never forget the art itself. DeNora's concept of affordances is similar to Griswold's idea that the text offers multivocal, but not unlimited, meaning possibilities to the reader. Second, the human use of art involves an active interaction with it. For Griswold, meaning is fabricated by readers. DeNora's approach goes further; her "theorization of cultural power extends

well beyond the usual concern with the meanings of art objects as it concep-
tualizes their power at a more existential level of human being where body,
consciousness and feeling intersect" (p. 77). Both DeNora and Griswold draw
on interdisciplinary expertise, blending insights from musicology and literary
criticism with sociology.

Artistic Fields

Bourdieu (1993) proposes a model of artistic *fields*. Though this model has
many similarities to Becker's idea of art worlds – the two terms can often be
taken as synonymous[4] – Bourdieu emphasizes both power relations and the
social construction of ideas within a field more strongly than does Becker.[5]
Bourdieu's ideas are historically rich, complex, and spread across a number of
books.[6] Fyfe (2000: 24–5) writes:

> The key to Bourdieu's sociology of art is that modernization has been a long-
> term process of differentiation which transformed societies into networks of
> specialist fields of action: economics, politics, sport, intellectual life, art and so
> forth. Each field is a social space ordered according to its distinctive rules and
> offering its own prizes. . . . *Modern society* refers to a web of interconnected spaces
> or areas which together form a field of power. The field of power is where
> different elites compete with one another for economic, political, and cultural
> assets and for hegemony over subordinated classes.

Artistic fields, then, are one set of many institutions that together constitute
society. Some fields are more autonomous than others. That is, some are able
to set out their own rules and rewards with relatively little interference from
outside influences. But the level of autonomy is always relative, since all fields
are interpenetrated to some extent by other fields, and they all are smaller
arenas within the overarching field of power.

Bourdieu (1993) suggests that artistic fields are divided into different poles or
sectors. The particular divisions of artistic fields in a given society are conditioned by the nature of class relationships there; they are historically constructed, as are the ideologies which are constituted in them. Artistic fields
have an autonomous pole where the arts are mostly left to their own devices,
and a "heteronomous" one where the arts are interpenetrated by other fields,
notably the commercial.

The autonomous pole of artistic fields relies on the "pure gaze": participants
value "art for art's sake" and display a notable disinterestedness in economic value. As a result, the most highly autonomous sectors of the artistic
field are rich in cultural capital, though not economic capital. Artists derive

prestige from their art to the extent they are held in high esteem by the field's members. Intellectuals, perhaps, might discuss their work and its significance. The pay-off artists seek, then, is recognition. Autonomous artists do not sell works on a grand scale, however, and generally do not become rich through it. The field provides rewards for this, too, through disdain for anything commercial. So commercial failure can be a badge of honor in autonomous fields. Autonomous artists produce art for audiences who share the same aesthetic goals, at the same time as they strive to avoid outside interference.

In contrast, the "heteronomous," or commercial, pole is open to outside influence. Artists in the commercial fields are judged by how well they meet audience demands; that is, by how well they sell. Commercial art brings in substantial financial capital. However, it is held in low regard by members of society who derive their prestige through an association with and knowledge of high culture. Bourdieu subdivides heteronomous art into a higher status "bourgeois art," which has some pretensions of art-ness and is popular with the middle classes, and the lower status "industrial art," which unabashedly panders to commercial requirements, either of companies (as in greeting card or advertising art) or of the vast low-brow, mass tastes (as in motel and tourist art, unironic kitsch, and the popular arts). To Bourdieu, only a few of the fine arts are truly autonomous. Lopes (2000) points out, however, that just as fine arts have two poles (bourgeois and pure), so do the popular arts. There are baldly commercial sectors, but also sectors where participants value "authenticity" and look down on "sell-outs."

Two features of Bourdieu's work are relevant here. The first is that he takes seriously the fact that fields carry ideologies. The pure gaze was historically constructed as part of the romantic myth of the artist (see box 8.1), and expressed in the philosophy of Kant. The second is that he pays attention to both production and consumption, offering a sustained theoretical synthesis of the two. The acts of production and consumption, shaped by the field, also continually reproduce it. Taste is tightly tied to power struggles and status arrangements in the wider society (see chapter 12). Importantly, Bourdieu discusses the existence of both a pure aesthetic and a popular aesthetic in contemporary society. Audience members relate to art through one of these general aesthetic approaches. The popular aesthetic, which is sentimental and values pictorial realism, is the aesthetic of the dominated. The pure aesthetic, on the other hand, values art for its *form*, not for its subject matter. Consequently, the pure aesthetic does not look to art for an accurate representation of reality or for the glorification of history, the state, or the church. Indeed, it looks down on these features, just as it rejects the commercial. It is, Bourdieu argues, the aesthetic of the dominant. These aesthetics exist in relationship to one another. Significantly, the pure aesthetic is a *refusal* of the popular.

Constructing Art and Aesthetics

Authors such as Bowler (1994), Wolff (1988), and Zolberg (1990) have called for sociological attention to be paid to art works and to the social construction of aesthetics.[7] Zolberg points to the "lack of clearly bounded conceptual categories in the arts themselves" and argues that these "ambiguities of definition and genre boundaries ... [leave] sociologists who chose to study the arts no alternative but to examine the conceptions and formulations of its subject matter" (p. 193).

Understanding aesthetics and society

Bowler's work (1998; 1997; 1991) is deeply engaged with questions of how art is constituted in society. Bowler's (1998) argument is consistent with Bourdieu's: Artistic fields may be autonomous, but they are autonomous from other institutions such as the church, the state, the social elite, and market forces, not from society. Thus, she shifts the sociological question from the relationship of art *and* society to the constitution of art *in* society, or, more accurately, the interrelationships among art and other social institutions (p. 38).

Bowler (1997) examined the social construction of asylum art during the early twentieth century. She argues that the elevation of expression by asylum patients (mere "artifact") into the category of "art" must be contextualized by "three inter-related shifts: (i) an epistemological shift in the definition of insanity and mental functioning more generally; (ii) an aesthetic shift centering on artists' rejection of traditional modes of representation; and (iii) a social-institutional shift involving twentieth-century avant-garde artists' appropriation of the art of the insane as a device in their attack on modern society and the institution of art" (p. 23). A crucial point in the construction of asylum art as a new aesthetic category was that some aspects of the inpatients' art dovetailed with burgeoning views in the avant-garde about "pure" creativity: "Free of exterior influence, free of the contaminating effects of the market, the madman seeks neither profit nor prestige. The asylum artist thus casts an aura of authenticity on an avant-garde whose own self-proclaimed 'outsider' status became increasingly difficult to sustain as one vanguardist gesture after another was absorbed into the modernist canon" (p. 29). Asylum art also "appears as part of a field of socially debased objects (the 'primitive,' the scatological, the perverse) cultivated by the avant-garde for shock value" (p. 28). In this study, then, Bowler shows the interpenetration of developments in psychology, aesthetics, and the avant-garde, and the content of art. She also describes changes in the social production of art, a factor often missing from art historical accounts of "the art of the insane."

Bowler (1991) also argues that social movements can have an aesthetic. She looks at the Fascist movement in Italy and its inter-relationship with the aesthetic movement, Futurism. She argues that discussing Italian Fascism without a consideration of the aesthetic issues of Futurism is inadequate; indeed, she argues one cannot explain the social movement without also discussing the aesthetic one. Bowler did *not* attempt to explain fascism by recourse to Futurism, rather her project was to map the complex and historically shifting relations between politics and art.[8]

In an important book, Parker and Pollock (1981) discuss the ideologies, particularly gendered ones, that are embedded in our understandings of visual art. Their book's title, *Old Mistresses*, is a reference to the fact that we do not have a description of historically important female artists. Drawing on their work, and that of Pollock (1988) and Wolff (1990), Bowler (1998) examines the marginalization of Mary Cassatt (1844–1926) in art history. Cassatt, an American who became an active member of the French Impressionists, enjoyed critical success during her lifetime. But until the 1970s, she was largely ignored in books on Impressionism and in museum exhibitions.

The theme of public space played a central role in Impressionist painting, but Cassatt "whose canvasses shared the stylistic orientation and formal characteristics of her peers but who consistently depicted interior, domestic spaces *fell outside the definition . . .* of what 'counted' as modernist" (Bowler, p. 43, here drawing on Wolff, 1990: 56, emphasis added). Cassatt is especially known, and especially derided, for her maternal scenes. Interestingly, only one-third of her paintings are of mothers and children. The public spaces she painted, however, are "confined to the settings and subjects of polite society: elegant, bourgeois families in the park, debutantes at the theater" and the like (p. 43). The other (male) Impressionists painted these subjects too, but they also produced "backstage scenes of dances, courtesans, mistresses, and kept women in settings like the café, cabaret, or brothel" (p. 43). Thus, Cassatt's work did not meet a key criterion in the a nascent ideology of the avant-garde – that one's work should press social and moral boundaries, as well as aesthetic ones – thus her work was not seen as avant-garde, despite her contemporary success and the then cutting-edge formal qualities of her work.

Fyfe (2000) also discusses how aesthetic definitions prevent certain social groups from claiming the title of artist. He examines struggles, in the eighteenth century, over the definition of originality, focusing on reproductive etchers in England. These etchers copied already existing works for wide-scale distribution. Today, we consider these etchers to be "unoriginal" or "mere" copyists. At the height of their art, however, they considered their work to be original. They made many decisions in translating works in oils or watercolors to etchings which involved *interpreting* the copied works. In addition, they took many liberties with the content of paintings to improve them in reproducing them. They were able to claim to be original artists, despite an uneasy relationship with the painters whose work they reproduced, because the eighteenth century was "aesthetically heterogeneous, and the divide between arts and crafts was still in the process of being institutionally secured" (p. 108).

The aesthetic scheme of the reproductive etchers was challenged by painters whose rival aesthetic carried a more stringent definition of originality. In essence, painters built their own reputations at the expense of those of the reproductive etchers. This conflict was highlighted when the Royal Academy was founded in Britain in 1768. Reproductive etchers were denied full membership, and they were also effectively "denied originality" as the concept came "to mean one who makes a cultural difference" (p. 111). Reproductive etching went into decline after this, due in part to the changing definitions of originality, but also as a result of the deskilling of printmaking through new techniques and the use of assistants which, in effect, turned printmaking into a manufacturing process, and the development of photography for reproductive purposes.

Constructing genius

Genius is seen as ineffable, and therefore, not amenable to systematic study. Nevertheless, genius can be influenced by social factors, and the concept of genius is a social construct, so it should be possible to develop a sociology of genius. This is not to say that great talent does not exist; it patently does. But what society looks for in genius, how it defines it and recognizes it, are part of the social construct. The particular ideology held within society or an art world will render some highly talented individuals as geniuses, but not others, equally talented. As DeNora (1995: 191) puts it, an "existential fact of life" is that the social constructs that constitute modern life, and that are essential to it, simultaneously enable social interaction *and* "perpetrate symbolic violence: what is facilitating for some may be constraining for others."

Along these lines, Sydie (1989) argues that the concept of artistic genius that existed during the Italian Renaissance (and which was influential for some centuries after this time) excluded women from artistic genius *by definition*. Creativity in the arts or sciences was seen, at that time, as akin to God's creativity, though on a human scale. God was also clearly gendered; He is male, and so by analogy, human creativity was seen as a masculine trait. The Renaissance theory of creativity was buttressed by the fact that patrons and collectors of the arts were also men. Patrons, especially, were seeking to reinforce their prestige and power in the public realm (as opposed to the private realm of women). Moreover, the great public commissions of religious art brought a recognition of genius primarily to the *patron*, whose vision caused the creation of the art, not to the artist who executed the patron's orders. Thus, the lack of women artists during the Renaissance was not due to a lack of craft skills alone (though women were not given such training), but the fact that creativity was defined as God-like (and masculine), and it was judged by men.

In related work, Battersby (1994) delves deeply into the historical construction of genius, demonstrating its gendered nature. She traces the etymology of the word to the *genius* of ancient Rome. A "genius" was a guiding spirit that protected *male* power and fertility. She follows the development of the concept, noting that everywhere, the idea of genius was reserved for men. The Greeks did not have the idea of genius, in today's sense. They did have a concept of creativity, but one that lacked the idea of creation *out of nothing*. Instead, creative men tried to reproduce the most beautiful forms created by the gods. In doing this, reality provided only a rough guide of the ideal, since reality always contained blemishes and faults. The contemporary concept of genius started to develop, as we have seen, during the Renaissance, culminating in the romantic conception of the artist. The concept is based on the ideal of male creativity and excludes women from participation. The standards used to determine genius are slippery and contradictory, and thus can exclude women from the classification in any number of "objective" ways. The case of Mary Cassatt illustrates just one.

Battersby's work reminds us that the image of the artist as the god-creator of the epigraph has not existed from time immemorial. Rather it was constructed in the Renaissance and developed into the romantic conception of genius. Moreover, as Battersby would note, the "*aura of mysterious power*" surrounding artists, as the epigraph unintendedly but powerfully illustrates, is gendered. It is male.

Battersby suggests that feminists should create their own aesthetics by nominating a pantheon of great artists. Currently existing (gendered) aesthetics are deeply embedded in society, making Battersby's project a difficult one. Nevertheless, Parker and Pollock (1981) take steps in this direction. One artist they discuss is Artemesia Gentileschi (1593–1652/3) who has recently become well-known for her paintings of Judith and Holofernes (see plate 9). The story is from the Bible, and tells how Judith, accompanied by her servant woman, was sent as a hostage to the tent of the enemy general Holofernes. In a brave act, she decapitated him in his sleep. This subject, and even its violent climax, was a common subject at the time, also portrayed by Caravaggio, among others.

Gentileschi's life and reputation demonstrate the barriers faced by female artists. Gentileschi was initially trained by her father, who was also a painter.

Plate 9 Artemisia Gentileschi, *Judith Beheading Holofernes*, ca. 1620, Galleria degli Uffizi, Florence, Italy/Bridgeman Art Library.

During her lifetime, she had to reassure her patrons that her ideas were her own and not copied from someone else (Parker and Pollock, p. 20). She was forgotten for some centuries – a self portrait, for instance, moldered in a storeroom, thought to be merely an allegory by an unknown painter. As she was rediscovered, some critics attempted to pigeon-hole (and thus dismiss) her:

> writers have been unable to fit her paintings into the usual feminine stereotype: they cannot trace the expected signs of femininity, weakness, gracefulness or delicateness. Thus, unable to put her work into a stereotype, they turn instead to the dramatic events of her life. . . . Her repeated rape by her teacher . . . and her torture at the trial to ascertain the truth of her allegations are frequently cited in sensationalized accounts of her life. . . . [M]any have been tempted to read her paintings as evidence of dislike of men, a notion contradicted by the same writers' gleeful accounts of her "amours" which produced four daughters, also

painters. It is only when we escape this disturbing fascination with her life and return to her work in its context within a specific time and place and school of painting that we can fully appreciate her activities as a painter. (Parker and Pollock, p. 21)

As Parker and Pollock (p. 20) put it, Gentileschi's "works conform to the dominant stylistic mode of Caravaggist realism and dramatic subject matter and are a distinctive contribution to that tradition." Some writers have hailed Gentileschi as offering "a banner for Women's Lib" (see Nochlin, 1971 [1973]: 11).[9] While better than dismissing or sensationalizing her, Parker and Pollock suggest this also misses the point:

Gentileschi's paintings of celebrated heroines should not be seen as evidence of an individual woman's proto-feminist consciousness reflected in art, but rather as her intervention in an established and popular genre of female subjects through a contemporary and influential style. It is only against this specific background, this prevailing climate, that the particular character of Gentileschi's work can be distinguished. It is by relating the contradictions inherent in the seventeenth-century's fascination with confrontations between male and female protagonists to this woman's treatment of those stories and styles that we can begin to produce useful insights into a theory of how women have fully participated in and altered dominant forms of art practice.

In asserting this, Parker and Pollock point out that women have been more successful as artists at some historical points than others, and that some artistic styles are more amenable to appropriation by women than are others.[10] Moreover, they remind us that art is situated in a social world.

Conclusion

This chapter has argued that art is embedded in society; it is deeply interwoven with other aspects of the social world. Authors writing from this point of view argue that the art itself, often ignored in sociology, deserves careful examination, not as an isolated entity, but in its interaction with society. They also suggest that aesthetic systems, and even genius itself, can be topics for sociological inquiry.

The chapter has implicitly critiqued the cultural diamond model. The heuristic simplicity of separate, abstract categories of art, creator, consumer, and society has a flaw; it separates in theory what can never be separable in life: art, artists, consumers, and ideological beliefs *are* society; they do not stand apart from it, but rather, are part of it. As Bowler (1998: 33) forcefully argues, [the absence of the work of art from sociological analysis] unwittingly subverts what is arguably our most significant achievement: demonstrating that the work of art is ... a *social* object. For if the contribution of sociology to the study of art has been to demystify traditional art-historical and literary-critical conceptions of the artist as isolated genius, to pose serious challenge to unreflexive classifications of timeless "great work" through a demonstration of the degree to which canon formation represents a series of historically-contested processes, why does the *work of art* continue to be so systematically excluded from the *sociology of art*? [emphasis original]

Many production and consumption studies focus on the social conditions of production or consumption of art, without reference to the matter ostensibly underlying the inquiry, the art itself. Much research that focuses on the art itself, however, amputates art from its social context. Relatively few studies have convincingly examined the interpenetrations of art, audience, artists, and the social world. In this, however, the chapter has presented some exemplars.[11]

A key argument of this chapter is that our commonsense views of creativity and genius are socially constructed ideas. These ideas shape the conditions under which artists work and underlie our judgments of artistic value. Sometimes students make the mistake of believing that arguments about socially constructed ideas imply that such ideas are false or unreal. This is not the case. Indeed, socially constructed ideas about art and artists are extremely important and they have real consequences in the social world. The point is, however, that the ideas are historically contingent and not inevitable. Art and artists can be, and have been, constructed differently in other times and places.

Genius may, indeed, be ineffable, but it is amenable to sociological inquiry. Genius is not an innate category untouched by human hands, but neither is it a discourse and nothing more. As Csikszentmihalyi (1996: 47) writes:

Certain [theorists] claim that creativity is all a matter of attribution. The creative person is like a blank screen on which social consensus projects exceptional qualities. Because we need to believe that creative people exist, we endow some individuals with this illusory quality. This ... is an oversimplification. For while the individual is not as important [to creative discoveries] as it is commonly supposed, neither is it true that novelty could come about without the contribution of individuals [nor] that all individuals have the same likelihood of producing novelty.

Meaning, expressive content, and aesthetics, then, are proper domains for sociological inquiry. But what of aesthetic judgments? Zolberg (1990) critiques the aesthetic neutrality that underlies the sociology of the arts, and calls on sociologists to engage with aesthetic debates.[12] Wolff (1988: 106) concurs:

The sociology of art involves critical judgments about art. The solution to this, however, is not to try even harder for a value-free sociology and a more refined notion of aesthetic neutrality; it is to engage directly with the question of aesthetic value. This means, first, taking as a topic of investigation that value already bestowed on works by their contemporaries and subsequent critics and audiences. Secondly, it means bringing into the open those aesthetic categories and judgements which locate and inform the researcher's project. And lastly, it means recognizing the autonomy of the question of the particular kind of pleasure involved in past and present appreciation of the works themselves.

And, of course, aesthetic judgments cannot be made "neutrally." They must be made with reference to some aesthetic system. Judgments may be made from within the existing system, based on prevailing ideologies, or they may be made from outside, based on critical, feminist, or queer aesthetics, to name a few. Such analyses can tell us who the winners and losers within the scheme are likely to be. Aesthetic judgments are relative, then, but that does not mean that all art is equal. Many works are "better" only with respect to their own system, but some works seem to transcend their aesthetic boundaries. We can draw on Griswold's concept of cultural power to suggest that these works, rich and evocative across different systems, may be the truly great works of art.

NOTES

1   The English translations of Bowler's Italian text were provided to me by Bowler herself.
2   Griswold notes the colonial overtones in using the term "West Indies" to describe the English-speaking Caribbean islands. She employs the term, nevertheless, as the one most frequently used during the time that Lamming wrote and in the reviews of his work.
3   For a clear statement of the use of culture as a tool-kit, see Swidler (1986).
4   An art world and an artistic field both refer to domains which encompass art. Both Becker and Bourdieu believe that combined actions within these domains, rather than lone artists, create art; both argue that conventions, ideologies and aesthetics reside in art worlds and are created by participants within the domain, and that legitimating ideologies make art and art worlds possible. And both theorists believe that the domains are multiple, shifting, and overlapping. Both terms, then, appear to refer to the same social phenomenon. The theories of Bourdieu and Becker broadly agree on the conception of the phenomenon, but they differ in many of the arguments they make, in their theoretical focus, and in their metatheoretical background.
   Bourdieu himself (1993: 34–5) suggests that Becker's conception is "reducible to a *population*, i.e. a sum of individual agents" whereas his, Bourdieu's, is not. This is a

very narrow, and I believe, incorrect view of Becker's work. (However, in claiming this reading, Bourdieu cites two of Becker's older articles [1976; 1974a] rather than Becker's book. This may partly account for Bourdieu's underselling of Becker's contribution.)

Ferguson (1998) takes up Bourdieu's idea of this difference between art worlds and artistic fields by highlighting the art world's focus on cooperative networks and arguing that they "can exist only in fairly circumscribed social or geographical settings endowed with mechanism that promote connection" (pp. 635–6). (This is not my reading of Becker's work.) In contrast, Ferguson says that a field rests on the idea of "acute consciousness of positions . . . in a circumscribed social space" (p. 634) and is "structured by a largely textual discourse that continually (re)negotiates the systemic tensions between production and consumption" (p. 637). But, as Baumann (2001: 405) argues,

> the differences between field and world are differences of degree rather than of type. Bourdieu (1993) illustrates his concept of field through a study of the *French* literary field – fields, too, need to be bounded both geographically and socially to be analytically useful . . . Ferguson (1998) seems to emphasize the ideological foundation of a field and the organizational foundation of a world. However, in their original formulations, both field and world allow for ideological and organizational elements, albeit to varying degrees.

Baumann opts to use the terms interchangeably.

5 I strongly agree with Baumann (2001) that the differences between Becker and Bourdieu are a matter of emphasis, rather than substance. Nevertheless, I introduce Bourdieu here as his concept, and especially his theorization of it, engages more fully with constitutive approaches to art. In addition to discussing power relations (essentially, class-based ones) absent from Becker, Bourdieu's formulation more fully integrates production and consumption within the artistic field.

In terms of differences, Becker fails to discuss how art worlds are connected to wider social processes, and to each other, and in effect, he severs art worlds from the society in which they are embedded. Bourdieu goes to the opposite extreme, laudably theorizing such connections, but at the same time, sometimes giving his theories a deterministic flavor. Becker discusses conflict; conflict occurs among audiences located in different layers of the art world, between core and support personnel, and among art world insiders (and between insiders and outsiders) over a host of aesthetic issues. But Becker does not discuss, as Bourdieu does, larger class or power struggles. Becker and Bourdieu both believe that audiences are crucial members of artistic realms, but Becker leaves it at that, whereas Bourdieu discusses audiences and their role in fields in great depth.

Bourdieu's work, written in a dense French academic style, has an intellectual patina absent from the intelligent, but clear and easy-to-read Becker. I believe that this leads some readers to devalue the richness of Becker's arguments. Moreover, I think Becker's argument is a constitutive one, especially in his discussion of conventions, aesthetics, reputation, and the like. Becker is usually cast as a production of

culture person, and this is, indeed, the best box in which to fit him, but his field of
vision is wider than the box.

6 See Bourdieu (1996, 1993, 1992, 1990, 1984); Bourdieu and Darbel (1991);
   Bourdieu and Passeron (1977); and Bourdieu and Waquant (1992). It may be
   worth noting that at the same time as Bourdieu's work has made an enormous
   contribution to the sociology of culture, it has attracted a concomitant level of
   criticism (for a tip of this critical iceberg see, J. Alexander, 1995; Fowler, 1997).

7 Wolff and Zolberg also suggest that sociologists can benefit from the tools
   humanists use to understand art. We have already seen the benefits of this
   suggestion in the work of Griswold and DeNora. This chapter also presents the
   work of art historians Parker and Pollock and the philosopher Battersby.

8 Along these lines, Guillén (1997) argues that organizational theories also have
   aesthetic components, and that understanding these contributes to an understanding of adoption patterns of organizational theories and the interpenetration of such
   intellectual realms as organizational theory and architecture.

9 It is not clear whether this phrase should be attributed to Nochlin or to her
   editors, Hess and Baker.

10 Battersby (1994 pp. 35–6) points out that women artists were much more
   prevalent and successful during the middle ages than they were for several subsequent centuries. This was because medieval philosophy insisted that creativity
   belonged solely to God. Consequently, the artist, of whichever gender, was
   unimportant. Women, notably nuns, produced paintings, frescos, embroidery,
   and illuminated manuscripts. (See also, Parker, 1996.)

   Tuchman's (1989) idea of the empty field seems particularly relevant in explaining the disempowerment of women artists during the Renaissance. Women were
   active in medieval guilds, but hostility toward women artists increased only when
   artists began to gain status during the Renaissance (Battersby, p. 36).

11 The views presented in this chapter are perhaps more eclectic than those presented
   in others. But as Crane (1987: 148) notes, "Systematic analysis of visual materials
   by social scientists has rarely been done and few guidelines exist for a sociological
   examination of aesthetic and expressive content in art objects." Recently, more
   sociologists have paid attention to these issues. It may also be worth mentioning
   that to be convincing, constitutive approaches must examine many issues in depth;
   consequently, such studies are less common than analyses of production, consumption, or the text.

12 Zolberg (1990: 199) points out that sociology has, for the most part, ignored the
   arts (although this had been changing in the decade before Zolberg published her
   book). She suggests, in a way reminiscent of Bourdieu's ideas of the field of power,
   that in choosing to overlook the arts, the discipline of sociology has implicitly
   drawn on value judgments, indeed, aesthetic ones. She suggests that sociologists
   have not studied the popular arts (as instances of valid creative expression) due to
   anti-commercial values deeply embedded in sociology, and they have not studied
   the fine arts (practically at all) due to anti-elitist values in the discipline.

Case Study 14.1

A Strange Sensation: Controversies in Art[1]

Points for Discussion

1 What factors played into the controversy over the *Sensation* exhibition? To what extent was the controversy about the art itself and to what extent was is about social factors?
2 Should the artist's intentions make a difference to the reception of the work of art? Not everybody was willing to accept Ofili's or the Chapman brothers' statements on their goals in producing certain art works. Why might more people have been willing to accept Ofili's word than that of the Chapman brothers?
3 Should controversial art ever be censored? Under what conditions? Why or why not?
4 How do aesthetics play a role in controversies?
5 Do you like Ofili's painting (or the Chapman brother's sculpture)? Why or why not?

Case

The show *Sensation* at the Brooklyn Museum of Art, October 1999 to January 2000, came to the attention of the general public in the United States when New York City Mayor Rudolph Giuliani tried to keep the show from opening. He argued that one particular painting – *The Holy Virgin Mary* by Chris Ofili – was a disrespectful, even blasphemous, portrayal of the Mother of God, and thus, was offensive to Catholics. The City of New York provides the Brooklyn Museum with funding for infrastructure costs such as for heating and lighting, but it did not directly fund this exhibition. Nevertheless, the Mayor thought it was appropriate to stand in judgment, stating: "These public funds are being used to aggressively bash the religious views of a significant number of people in this city and state and country. And the question is, can taxpayer dollars be used for this kind of disgusting, anti-religious . . . demonstration?" (quoted in Halle, 2001: 140). The ensuing controversy was rich with ironies and brings up many issues in the sociology of art.

The Mayor attacked the painting after reading a review in the *New York Daily News* (a tabloid paper) two weeks before the exhibition was to open. His office already knew about the show, but the Mayor did not pay much attention until the press did. When the exhibition opened as planned and despite his objection, the Mayor withdrew city funds from the Brooklyn Museum and took steps to evict it from its city-owned premises. The museum obtained an injunction against the Mayor's actions, and funds were temporarily restored. But the city appealed and planned to fight the museum in court. The city dropped its lawsuit, however, when the police shooting of an unarmed black man ignited another controversy.

The painting that became the center of the controversy in the American showing of *Sensation* – it was also shown in London and Berlin – is difficult to describe without taking an implicit evaluative stance (see back cover illustration). Indeed, how to describe the painting was part of the controversy. One could say that it is a collage of paper, oil paint, glitter, polyester resin, and elephant dung on linen, but that, of course, does not capture it.

The painting is large, eight feet high by six feet wide. The subject, the Madonna, is black. She is wearing robes of deep blue, opened to reveal a breast. And she is situated on a yellow background, surrounded by what look like butterflies, or as many critics put it, like *putti* (little angels). But closer inspection provides a surprise; they are the pictures of female genitalia and buttocks snipped from naughty magazines (a pun on hole/holy?). The exposed breast and two supports at the bottom of the painting are made of elephant dung. The dung may be seen as a decorative feature. As Ofili insists, elephant dung is not smelly, wet, and disgusting. Instead, as elephants are herbivores, their excrement is not particularly offensive. Ofili dries clumps of it thoroughly before carefully attaching them to a canvas. Furthermore, the dung is then coated in several layers of resin. Ofili uses elephant dung regularly, and it featured on pieces shown at the Tate Gallery in London when Ofili won the Turner Prize. The dung played a key role in the Manhattan debate. As Halle (2001: 140) put it:

> [The] *New York Daily News* article [which sparked the debate] . . . said the Virgin was "splat-tered" with elephant dung. Several of the early critics repeated this description, with its implication that the artist had desecrated the Virgin. Ofili's defenders quickly moved to correct this description . . . Some defenders also stressed the fact that the Virgin was set in a glittering gold background whose effect was to beautify the image.

Ofili's proponents repeatedly pointed out Ofili's status as a practicing Catholic and highlighted his statements that in Africa, elephants represent power, and dung, fertility. Ofili's painting is of a black Madonna, and Ofili, a British citizen, is himself black of Nigerian origin. Thus, Ofili's painting potentially brings up issues of race, as well as religion. One interesting feature of the conflict was that it centered mainly on the latter.

Another interesting feature of the controversy was that the show conspicuously displayed contentious, challenging art. Advertisements for the show used humor to bring this out (and to bring crowds in). The text on one poster read:

Health Warning:
The content of this
exhibition may cause
shock, vomiting, confusion,
panic, euphoria, and
anxiety. If you suffer
from high blood pressure,
a nervous disorder, or
palpitations, you
should consult your doctor before viewing
this exhibition.

(quoted in Halle, 2001: 146)

The telephone line for exhibition tickets was 1-87-SHARKBITE – obliquely referring to a work in the show, by Damien Hirst, of a large shark suspended in formaldehyde. But of all the pieces in the show, Ofili's collage seems an odd one to have provoked controversy. Many other pieces appeared to be more shocking or confrontational. For instance, Damien Hirst's work included not only the shark, but also a pig sliced in half (*This Little Piggy Went to Market, This Little Piggy Stayed at Home*), in which the separately-housed lengthwise halves of pig moved in different directions on a track and then moved back together again, and a dead cow infested with real maggots which "gave off a foul odor" (Halle, 2001: 158). *Zygotic acceleration, biogenetic desublimated libidinal model (enlarged × 1000)* by Jake and Dinos Chapman (see plate 10), "is a sculpture made up of life-size and life-like mannequins of children with penis noses and anus mouths all grotesquely joined together. The girls are wearing nothing else but identical black and white Fila sneakers" (Halle, 2001: 158–9). In the London showing of *Sensation*, the most controversial piece was by Marcus Harvey, titled *Myra*. It is a large portrait of the British serial child killer Myra Hindley made from the handprints of children. Finally, the show contained another piece on religion that, on the face of it, might seem controversial. By Sam Taylor Woods, *Wrecked* includes a portrait of the artist herself "at the center of a large banquet table, naked from the waist up displaying her large bosom and striking a pose with upraised arms reminiscent of Jesus Christ. She is surrounded by twelve of her artist friends who are all clothed, but...drunk [i.e. 'wrecked']" (Halle, 2001: 160). With over 100 works on display, the show also had a reasonable number of pieces that did not become controversial and that, in style, were not particularly confrontational.

To gauge audience reactions, Halle and colleagues at the LeRoy Neiman Center conducted 860 exit interviews of a systematic sample of people who had attended *Sensation*. A key finding of the poll, though not a surprising one, was that people self-select when they go to exhibits. The demographic profile of the exhibition's audience showed that a disproportionate number identified as Democratic (few Republicans came to the show) and about 37 percent (as compared to 13 percent in the general population) said they had no religious affiliation (Halle, 2001: 156). Though it is not surprising that people self-select, the finding suggests an important consideration in the debates over censorship: art placed inside private buildings like museums, even if they are open to the public, pose less of a danger than art shown in public settings, such as parks. Those likely to be offended will stay away. About half the respondents were first-time visitors to the Brooklyn Museum (p. 176), confirming the maxim that "controversy sells."

Halle asked respondents what they thought of the show and a number of pieces in it. Most respondents were not offended by the show. About 60 percent said they found the show "not at all offensive," and only about four percent said they found it very offensive (p. 163). Notably, most of Halle's respondents liked Ofili's work. Comments included:

"I thought that the picture was very beautiful. I loved the artist's interpretation of the Virgin Mary."
"Beautiful – I love all his work. Felt that it was extremely incorrectly portrayed in the media."
"I think it is beautiful. I love the single dung breast, it's classic."

(Halle, pp. 169–70)

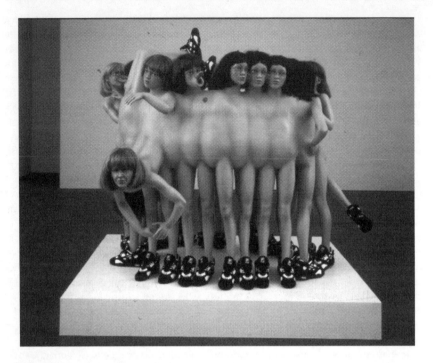

Plate 10 Jake and Dinos Chapman, *Zygotic Acceleration, Biogenetic Desublimated Libidinal Model (Enlarged × 1000)*, 1995. Jake and Dinos Chapman. Courtesy Jay Jopling/White Cube, London.

Black audience members also, on the whole, liked Ofili's painting, especially for its portrayal of the black Madonna. Nevertheless, a few African Americans took an opposite reading and found it offensive.

> "I loved it! The hip hop version of the Virgin Mary is great. His explanation of why he chose this should be enough to be accepted."
> "Beautiful. After hearing about how offensive it was, I was surprised at how beautiful it was. I like the fact that the Virgin was depicted with Afro-centric features."

[But]

> "This [elephant dung] was very offensive on a black Mary. I can't understand the artist. The Virgin Mary represents holiness, godliness, cleanliness, not elephant dung and porno clips. This is an abomination to me."

(Halle, pp. 166–7)

Even though the audience was very tolerant of all the pieces in the show, the one that they disliked the most was the Chapman Brother's "depictions of naked, sexually mutated girls" (Halle, p. 170). Only half of the respondents said it was not at all offensive; more than 10 percent said it was very offensive (p. 163). The work "is supposed to be a comment on genetic engineering and cloning" (Halle, p. 159), and the artists claimed that it would make viewers laugh. But audiences did not always see it that way. People who found the piece offensive said:

"I hated all their work. It was disgusting and pornographic. The children seemed like a molester's fantasy."

"It just bothers me. I see no real reason behind what they make. I don't find it funny and they don't really seem interested in the issues they propose."

"Very offensive. Reminded me of pedophilia, which has NO place in the art world!"

(Halle, p. 171)

On the other hand, other viewers had positive things to say:

"Amazing! A revelation. Goes beyond anything I've seen in challenging attitudes on sex, childhood, and the cult of beauty and physicality."

"Addresses issues that people would rather not discuss or be exposed to . . . sexuality, death, pornography, 'the perfect female.'"

(Halle, Tiso, and Yi, 2001: 142)[2]

The fact that many more viewers were offended by the Chapman brothers' piece than Ofili's, however, suggests that a single person, like a mayor, cannot decide what does or does not offend the public.

The roots of controversy

Many factors are at play in the development of an arts controversy. To list some crucial points: The Mayor appeared to be using the controversy for political advantage, specifically, for currying favor among Catholics while maintaining a pro-choice stance on abortion. Charles Saatchi, who owns the collection and provided funding for the exhibition, appeared to be using the exhibition to increase the market value of his collection. The media also played a key role in sparking the controversy.

This controversy drew on themes from other, recent arts controversies. In these, the conflicts were not just about offensive art, but also about the public funding of it. A common public sentiment seems to be, as Senator Dick Armery (Republican, Texas) put it, "If you want to show [art] in such a tasteless way, do it on your own dime and your own time" (cited in Dubin, 1992: 241). The connection to public funding in the *Sensation* case was tenuous, however, as the show had received no government support, and was underwritten by corporate donations and admission charges. Nevertheless, one theme in the controversy was public funding and offensive art. The wider arts controversies have an aspect of moral panic to them, with art standing in for other social conflicts. The ideological dimensions of the controversies mix, in complex combinations, aesthetic values, political ideologies (identity politics, democracy, religion, and the role of government), and the intersection of culture and class.

One issue, that of the conflicting aesthetics implicit in reactions to the show, deserves further comment. Dubin (1992: 5–6) draws on Douglas's (1966) ideas of purity and danger, suggesting that art objects that provoke negative reactions are usually those that violate symbolic boundaries by combining what is usually separate or by challenging what seem to be "natural categories." Ofili's work falls into this category with its mixing of the Madonna (sacred) with pornography (profane) and with elephant dung (ambiguous). His work also may shock, as it is decorative and pretty from a distance; only up close do the rude elements stand out. Indeed, Ofili's intentions seem to be to play with the issues of piety and disrespect, mixing a symbol of chastity with pornographic images. (The Chapman brothers' piece also mixes categories, adult genitalia with children's faces, which seems to viewers to be more shocking than Ofili's juxtapositions).

In contemporary society, there is no single, established, consensual definition of "art," its functions, or its aesthetics. Should art be intellectual, complex, and challenging? Should it glorify the best in society? Should it be beautiful? And, if so, what is "beautiful"? One common view is that art should uplift the viewer who will find pleasure in looking at it. Art might focus on high moral or spiritual sentiments, or in a more pedestrian vein, it might be pretty or cheerful; but in any case, it should be well-executed by someone who has "more skill than a five-year-old." This is not the definition of art held in the avant-garde scene. The cognoscenti of this art world prefer work that is thought-provoking and striking, whether visually, intellectually, or emotionally. Being "deeply moved" by a work can mean being enraged, shocked, or repulsed, rather than charmed or awed. Both models of art, the aesthetics of soothing beauty and the aesthetics of disquieting stimulation, are valid ways of looking at art works. But they rest on fundamentally different premises.[3]

Debates about art, of course, encompass more than two views. The *Sensation* show, however, situated itself squarely in the avant-garde discourse, pressing the boundaries of what is acceptable morally, politically, and socially. Its catalogue stated:

> Artists must continue the conquest of new territory and new taboos. The greatest images are those that invoke both reality and sensation . . . We now all love the Impressionists because we have come to know and feel comfortable with them. But the chief task of new art is to disturb that sense of comfort. (Norman Rosenthal, quoted in Halle, p. 145)

Not all art critics agreed. Phillippe de Montebello, director of the Metropolitan Museum of Art, for instance, did not like the exhibition:

> [W]hat remains terribly disturbing to me is that so many people, serious and sensitive individuals, are so cowed by the art establishment that they do not speak out and express their dislike for works that they find either repulsive or unaesthetic or both. (quoted in Halle, p. 162)

Critics also varied in their interpretation of Ofili's work. While very few found it offensive, many thought that it was mediocre and "merely" decorative. In other words, many art critics did not find Ofili's work challenging enough!

Artists create with an audience in mind. For avant-garde artists, art is aimed at a small art world of peers, critics, curators, collectors, and well-socialized audience members who judge their artistic reputation. They do not aim their work at a wider public. The public at large does not like avant-garde art, or as the avant-garde would put it, they do not "understand" it. But for some proponents of the avant-garde, this is precisely the point. People who are not hip to the movement will not get it, thereby displaying their "inferiority." As Michael Kimmelmann writes:

Like a lot of contemporary art, [Ofili's] "Holy Virgin Mary" is ultimately aimed at the art world. Savvy viewers are meant to feel superior to anyone who would find the dung and the pornography offensive by recognizing how Mr. Ofili means to turn what is shocking into something sweet. Both shock and whatever you might call its reverse reaction are crucial to the mechanics of the picture. (*New York Times*, October 5, 1999)

Avant-garde aesthetics are not merely one among many ways to view art, they also represent a status claim.

Notoriety opens up an artist's work to a wider audience. This audience may not share the conventions of the artist's milieu, and is thus more likely to misunderstand the work. This is a crucial point. The conflicting aesthetics of the avant-garde art world and the much larger art world inhabited by most Americans is a central component in arts controversies. The controversies reflect larger issues and represent struggles that go beyond art, but they are also about the fundamental nature of art.

Notes

1   This case draws on Halle (2001) for substantiation of details of the exhibition and the controversy, as well as for his excellent audience survey. See also Halle, Tiso, and Yi (2001). The collections in which Halle's articles appear also provide very useful discussions of art and religion (Arthurs and Wallach, 2001), and of the *Sensation* show itself (Rothfield, 2001). C. Becker (2001) also discusses Ofili's work and issues that grew out of the *Sensation* controversy.
2   Halle did not report any positive comments on the Chapman Brothers' work in his sole authored piece. These comments, from people who were not offended, come from his co-authored piece.
3   In a related argument, Williams (1961: 30) has written:

> In many societies it has been the function of art to embody what we can call the common meanings of the society. The artist is not describing new experiences, but embodying known experiences. There is great danger in the assumption that art serves only on the frontiers of knowledge. It serves on these frontiers . . . Yet it serves, also, at the very centre of societies . . . [I]n our own complex society, certain artists seem near the centre of common experience while others seem out on the frontiers, and it would be wrong to assume that this difference is the difference between "mediocre art" and "great art". Not all "strange" art, by any means, is found valuable, nor is all "familiar" art found valueless.

Part IV
Conclusion

15

Studying Art Sociologically

[T]he sociology of [the arts, as an intellectual field] is more like a field of flowers than a field of battle. It [has] produced impressive theoretical assertions, brilliant but isolated insights and rich veins of research findings, but [it has not coalesced] as a proper field. . . .

(Wendy Griswold, 1993: 455)

In this book, my aim has been to show you the richness of the sociology of the arts. Through a sociological lens, we have learned much about art, and much about society. A sociological approach has helped us understand the degree to which art reflects society, and how it can shape society. It has shown us the complexity of the production of art and the mechanisms of its distribution. Through this, we have learned about the ways the production and distribution systems mold art. The production of culture approach has taught us about artists and their careers. We have also learned more about art and about organizational behavior, through studying for-profit and not-for-profit cultural organizations. The study of cultural industries has also enlightened us about industry systems and about globalization. We have seen how people use culture, for aesthetic pleasure, to construct meanings, and to constitute their identities, their moods, and their bodies. We have seen that art plays a role both in reinforcing social barriers and in making links across social divides. And we have learned that contemporary understandings of art, aesthetics, and genius are socially constructed and historically contingent – and that these are also powerful and real.

Art is best studied holistically. Though many authors agree that this is desirable, most focus entirely on aspects of either production or consumption. And both of these approaches tend to shuffle the art work to one side. Even those authors who consider more than one aspect of the art world – the art itself, its production or consumption, or its constitution in society – often concentrate on only one or two aspects. It is quite difficult to do otherwise. A few extraordinary books deserve mention for their success in bridging the gaps. For instance, Becker's (1982) magnum opus has profoundly influenced this book. Although Becker is often considered a "production of culture" author, he does consider that audiences are part of the art world, and he argues in favor of a constitutive view of the role of artists, artworks, reputation, and genius in the art world. He also discusses the actual content of many art works. In her project on romance novels, Radway (1984) discusses audiences and their readings of the novels. She also describes the production context of romance novels in a chapter on publishers, and considers novels themselves in two chapters on the narrative structure of successful and failed romances.

Becker's argument is a rich analysis of a broad spectrum of arts; it skims across the surface of multiple examples rather than studying any one in depth. Becker, however, does not provide a sustained discussion of the audience, beyond their socialization into the art world's conventions. Radway's emphasis is on the reception of romances. Hers is a deep study of the reception of art, but focuses on a small and homogenous group of readers. Baxandall (1988) is another rare author who has managed to look at three aspects of the art world – production, consumption, and art work – in Italian Renaissance painting. His work is excellent, but he presents each aspect in a separate chapter (as does Radway). This implies that different methodological tools are needed for each type of analysis, and inadvertently suggests that the different approaches are not easily reconciled, and might even be incompatible. Bourdieu's *oeuvre* (e.g. 1993, 1992, 1990, 1984) is enormously important in the sociology of art. He has considered the constitution of artistic fields, and has attempted to find a balance between production and reception. His ideas on audiences – that they use art and its associated cultural capital to create distinctions – is a central one. But to appreciate Bourdieu's arguments, you need to read not just several chapters in a book, but several books.

The divisions in the literature have been made evident through the organization of chapters in this book. Griswold (1993: 455) suggests that the field of sociology of literature (and by extension, the sociology of the arts) is "not really a field at all" because it is not "organized around key questions or debates the way a proper field ought to be." I disagree that fields of research necessarily have to be coherent (though individual studies should be). Nevertheless, Griswold is correct in pointing out that many of the central issues in the sociology of the arts are not presented as debates to be evaluated through research. Instead, they separate the field into niches, in which experts speak more to their close colleagues than to those in other subfields. While it might be useful for scholars to address issues that cut across the divisions (which may lead to the empirical and intellectual battles that Griswold desires), the field of flowers, to which Griswold compares the sociology of art in the epigraph, can be delightful and inspiring.

Most of the studies I have reviewed are exemplary. They are also, for the most part, relatively narrow in scope. I agree with Griswold (1994) that, ideally, studies of art consider all the points in the cultural diamond. I also agree with Bowler (1998) that abstracting art from society can distort the understanding of it, or render it epiphenomenal. Nonetheless, I do *not* wish to suggest that studies that focus on only one or two points on the cultural diamond, or that set aside art, or that separate it analytically from society are, for these reasons, inferior studies. On the contrary, it is impossible for any study – in any discipline, sociology included – to examine all aspects of a phenomenon. Studies may be broad (but shallow) or they may be deep (but narrow), but studies which are both broad and deep are extremely rare. Studies may focus on production over consumption, or vice versa. They may focus on the constitutive nature of art, but then necessarily ignore something else. This is why academic disciplines rest on a multitude of studies from a variety of approaches or traditions. Each study, if excellent, contributes in its own way to the knowledge of the field.

Not all sociologists will agree that a field of knowledge either can be advanced or is best advanced by the accumulation of research with such profoundly different starting points as the studies reviewed in this book. Not everyone will appreciate my pragmatic and constructive review of each of the approaches in the field. Much of the heat in scholarly debate – in sociology of art, in sociology in general, and in most other academic disciplines – comes from debates over what is the right question, not what is the right answer. Some sociologists believe that the only worthy question in the sociology of art is what meaning individuals take from art; only the active audience approach will do. Others believe that only objective, measurable phenomena ought to be studied, and that meaning – not to mention creativity, genius, and other socially constructed ideas – are not appropriate topics. To them, positivism is the only true road to enlightenment. Scholars steeped in postmodernism may wish only to deconstruct the discourse, and view any attempts to study what is "really there" as merely attempts to reinforce the grand narratives they wish to dismantle. In suggesting that a variety of questions and methods are valid in sociology, I will step on the toes of those sociologists who wish me to criticize all but their own favorites.

I believe that research should be judged on its own merits: Is it an excellent study, given its own aims, objectives, and metatheory? If so, then it can make a valuable contribution to knowledge. If not, then we may feel free to ignore it. This does not mean that we cannot criticize even the best studies for their shortcomings – they all will have some. We should certainly ask if studies are wrong, and notice if they contain errors or flaws. But, as Becker (1974b: 15) notes, we should not expect studies to find *the* complete and whole truth, but rather *a* truth: "The answer lies in distinguishing between the statement that X is true about something and the statement that X is all that is true about something." No study will ever have the last word. We can borrow from Goldthorpe's (2000) distinction between real versus spurious debate. Real debates are over what studies found and how they found it; that is, debates over the answers. Spurious debates are over what questions are right. Nevertheless, this is easier said than done. Goldthorpe himself suggests that sociology's two great contributions are rational choice theory and statistical modeling based on probability sampling, and thus he would dismiss a majority of the research presented in this book as irrelevant or trivial.

A further problem inherent in the sociology of art may be absent from (or, in any case, less obvious in) some other branches of sociology. That is, art is an honorific term. Studying art from a sociological viewpoint brings into question the basis for the status-giving nature of art. For instance, I have lumped together fine, folk, and popular arts in this book. While I recognize that different art forms are subject to a variety of different dynamics, my argument is that these manifestations of human creativity are more similar than different and can be understood with the same set of theoretical and methodological techniques. If, however, you draw status honor for yourself from an association with the fine arts (or an "authentic" popular or folk art), this approach will undermine your status claims – or at least, it may shake up your unexamined understandings about the nature of art.

Sociology of art also has an image problem, especially among some humanists. As Graña (1971: v–vi) puts it,

> ever since Flaubert read Auguste Comte with a mixture of amusement and scorn, the *idea* of such a mode of knowledge [sociology] has appeared to literary intellectuals as an ignorant illusion, fostered by pseudo-scientific enthusiasm and incapable of dealing with the intricacies of human behavior.... In the case of sociologists' efforts to offer their understanding of literary and artistic work the suspicion was even deeper and more sour. The anticipation was always that sensitive imaginations would be forced to witness the spectacle of the great testaments of "meaning" – memorable, depth-rich, elusive – subjected to the irrelevant commentaries of brazen and reductionist minds.... W. H. Auden advises humanists "never to commit a social science." ... It would be comfortable to have things Auden's way, with humanist criticism tactful, thoughtful and sensitive on the one hand, and sociology, oppressively and naïvely pretentious on the other. But I hope to show that to think in this fashion is cheap, melodramatic, and false.

It is also useful to remember that just as different approaches to art within sociology vie, sometimes with great rancor, over whose question is best, disciplines also compete with each other for status.

Becker (1970: 72) uses the metaphor of a mosaic in the growth of socio-logical knowledge through methods such as case studies and life histories. He contrasts this metaphor to the idea that a single study needs to be complete and say all there is to say:

> As sociology [rigidified and "professionalized" through the 1960s], more and more emphasis [was] placed on what we may, for simplicity's sake, call the *single study*. I use the term to refer to research projects that are conceived of as self-sufficient and self-contained, which provide all the evidence one needs to accept or reject the conclusions they proffer, whose findings are to be used as another brick in the growing wall of science – a metaphor quite different than that of the mosaic.

As sociology has shifted again to include cultural and postmodern themes, it has moved away (but only in part) from the scientific brick wall metaphor of knowledge construction. A mosaic metaphor for the development of soci-ology, if not superior to the scientific view, is at least a practical one, given sociology's multiple approaches. My goal in giving an overview of the field has been to lay out the best tiles – each brilliant, each necessarily small and limited – in the mosaic. My hope, then, is that this review has created a useful picture of the sociology of art. Beyond that, I hope you find the picture aesthetically pleasing and that it will illustrate the beauty of sociology.

References

Abbott, Andrew and Alexandra Hrycak (1990). "Measuring Resemblance in Sequence Data: An Optimal Matching Analysis of Musicians' Careers," *American Journal of Sociology*, 96 (1): 144–85.

Abercrombie, Nicholas (1996). *Television and Society*. Cambridge: Polity.

Abercrombie, Nicholas (1992). "Pavarotti in the Park," University of Lancaster, Inaugural Lecture Series.

Abercrombie, Nicholas and Brian Longhurst (1998). *Audiences: A Sociological Theory of Performance and Imagination*. London: Sage.

Abercrombie, Nicholas, Alan Warde, Keith Soothill, John Urry, and Sylvia Walby (1994). *Contemporary British Society*, Second Edition. Cambridge: Polity Press.

Adams, Ann Jensen (1994). "Competing Communities in the 'Great Bog of Europe': Identity and Seventeenth-Century Dutch Landscape," in W. J. T. Mitchell (ed.), *Landscape and Power*. Chicago: University of Chicago Press, pp. 35–76.

Adler, Judith E. (1979). *Artists in Offices: An Ethnography of an Academic Art Scene*. New Brunswick, NJ: Transaction Books.

Adorno, Theodor W. (1941 [1991]). *The Culture Industry*. London: Routledge.

Adorno, Theodor W. (1941 [1994]). "On Popular Music," reprinted in John Storey (ed.), *Cultural Theory and Popular Culture: A Reader*. Hemel Hempstead: Harvester Wheatsheaf, pp. 197–209.

Aksoy, A. and K. Robins (1992). "Hollywood for the 21st Century: Global Competition for Critical Mass in Image Markets," *Cambridge Journal of Economics*, 16 (1): 1–22.

Albert, Stuart and David A. Whetten (1985). "Organizational Identity," *Research in Organizational Behavior*, 7: 263–95.

Albrecht, Milton C. (1954). "The Relationship between Literature and Society," *American Journal of Sociology*, 59: 425–36.

Alexander, Jeffrey C. (1995). *Fin de Siècle Social Theory: Relativism, Reduction and the Problem of Reason*. London: Verso.

Alexander, Victoria D. (2001). "Analysing Visual Materials," in Nigel Gilbert (ed.), *Researching Social Life*, Second Edition. London: Sage, pp. 343–57.

Alexander, Victoria D. (1999). "A Delicate Balance: Museums and the Market-place," *Museum International*, 51 (2): 29–34.

Alexander, Victoria D. (1998). "Environmental Constraints and Organizational Strategies: Complexity, Conflict, and Coping in the Nonprofit Sector," in Walter W. Powell and Elisabeth Clemens (eds.), *Private Action and the Public Good*. New Haven: Yale University Press, pp. 272–90.

Alexander, Victoria D. (1996a). *Museums and Money: The Impact of Funding on Exhibitions, Scholarship, and Management*. Bloomington: Indiana University Press.

Alexander, Victoria D. (1996b). "Pictures at an Exhibition: Conflicting Pressures in Museums and the Display of Art," *American Journal of Sociology*, 101: 797–839.

Alexander, Victoria D. (1996c). "From Philanthropy to Funding: The Effects of Corporate and Public Support on American Art Museums," *Poetics: Journal of Empirical Research on Literature, the Media and Arts*, 24: 89–131.

Alexander, Victoria D. (1994). "The Image of Children in Magazine Advertisements from 1905 to 1990," *Communication Research*, 21: 742–65.

Alexander, Victoria D. and Marilyn Rueschemeyer (forthcoming). *Art and the State in Comparative Perspective*. Manuscript.

Allmendinger, Jutta and J. Richard Hackman (1996). "Organizations in Changing Environments: The Case of East German Symphony Orchestras," *Administrative Science Quarterly*, 41: 337–69.

Allmendinger, Jutta, and J. Richard Hackman (1995). "The More the Better? A Four-Nation Study of the Inclusion of Women in Symphony Orchestras," *Social Forces*, 74 (2): 423–60.

Allmendinger, Jutta, J. Richard Hackman, and Erin V. Lehman (1996). "Life and Work in Symphony Orchestras," *Musical Quarterly*, 80 (2): 194–219.

Alsop, Joseph (1982). *The Rare Art Traditions*. London: Thames & Hudson.

Alvarado, Manuel, ed. (1988). *Video Worldwide: An International Study*. London: John Libbey.

Anand, N. and Richard A. Peterson (2000). "When Market Information Constitutes Fields: Sensemaking of Markets in the Commercial Music Industry," *Organization Science*, 11 (3): 270–84.

Ang, Ien (1991). *Desperately Seeking the Audience*. London: Routledge.

Ang, Ien (1985). *Watching Dallas: Soap Opera and the Melodramatic Imagination*. London: Routledge.

Anheier, Helmut K., Jürgen Gerhards, and Frank P. Romo (1995). "Forms of Capital and Social Structure in Cultural Fields: Examining Bourdieu's Social Topography," *American Journal of Sociology*, 100 (4): 859–903.

Appadurai, Arjun (1990). "Disjuncture and Difference in the Global Cultural Economy," in Mike Featherstone (ed.), *Global Culture: Nationalism, Globalization and Modernity*. London: Sage, pp. 295–310.

Arenti, C. S. and D. Kim (1993). "The Influence of Background Music on Shopping Behaviour: Classical versus Top-forty in a Wine Store," *Advances in Consumer Research*, 20: 336–40.

Arian, Edward (1971). *Bach, Beethoven and Bureaucracy: The Case of the Philadelphia Orchestra*. University, AL: University of Alabama Press.

Arnold, Matthew (1869 [1960]). *Culture and Anarchy*. London: Cambridge University Press.

Arthurs, Alberta and Glenn Wallach, eds. (2001). *Crossroads: Art and Religion in American Life*. New York: The New Press.

Astley, W. Graham and Andrew H. Van de Ven (1983). "Central Perspectives and Debates in Organization Theory," *Administrative Science Quarterly*, 28: 245–73.

Bacon-Smith, Camille (1992). *Enterprising Women: Television Fandom and the Creation of Popular Myth*. Philadelphia: University of Pennsylvania Press.

Baker, Wayne E. and Robert R. Faulkner (1991). "Role as Resource in the Hollywood Film Industry," *American Journal of Sociology*, 97 (2): 279–309.

Ball, Michael S. and Gregory W. H. Smith (1992). *Analyzing Visual Data*, Qualitative Research Methods Series, 24. London: Sage.

Bandura, Albert, Dorthea Ross, and Sheila A. Ross (1963). "Imitation of Film-Mediated Aggressive Models," *Journal of Abnormal and Social Psychology*, 66 (1): 3–11.

Banks, Marcus (2001). *Visual Methods in Social Research*. London: Sage.

Barthel, Diane L. (1988). *Putting On Appearances: Gender and Advertising*. Philadelphia: Temple University Press.

Barthes, Roland (1969 [1977]). "The Death of the Author," in *Image Music Text*. London: Fontana Press, pp. 142–8.

Barthes, Roland (1957 [1993]). *Mythologies*. London: Vintage.

Bator, Paul M. (1982). "An Essay on the International Trade in Art," *Stanford Law Review*, 34 (2): 275–384.

Battersby, Christine (1994). *Gender and Genius: Towards a Feminist Aesthetics*. London: Women's Press.

Baudrillard, Jean (1970 [1998]). *The Consumer Society: Myths and Structures*. London: Sage.

Bauman, Zygmunt (1998). *Globalization: The Human Consequences*. Cambridge: Polity.

Baumann, Shyon (2001). "Intellectualization and Art World Development: Film in the United States," *American Sociological Review*, 66: 404–26.

Baumol, William J. and William G. Bowen (1966). *Performing Arts: The Economic Dilemma*. New York: Twentieth Century Fund.

Baxandall, Michael (1988). *Painting And Experience In Fifteenth Century Italy*, 2nd edition. Oxford: Oxford University Press.

Baxandall, Michael (1985). *Patterns of Intention: On the Historical Explanation of Pictures*. New Haven: Yale University Press.

Baxandall, Michael (1980). *The Limewood Sculptors of Renaissance Germany*. New Haven: Yale University Press.

Bayton, Mavis (1998). *Frock Rock: Women Performing Popular Music*. Oxford: Oxford University Press.

Becker, Carol (2001). *Surpassing the Spectacle*. New York: Rowman & Littlefield Publishers.

Becker, Howard S. (1989). "Ethnomusicology and Sociology: A Letter to Charles Seeger," *Ethnomusicology*, 33: 275–85.

Becker, Howard S. (1982). *Art Worlds*. Berkeley: University of California Press.

Becker, Howard S. (1976). "Art Worlds and Social Types," *American Behavioral Scientist*, 19 (6): 703–19

Becker, Howard S. (1974a). "Art as Collective Action," *American Sociological Review*, 39 (6): 767–76.

Becker, Howard S. (1974b). "Photography and Sociology," *Studies in the Anthropology of Visual Communication*, 1 (1): 3–26.

Becker, Howard S. (1970). *Sociological Work: Method and Substance*. Chicago: Aldine.

Becker, Howard S. (1963). *Outsiders: Studies in the Sociology of Deviance*. New York: Free Press.

Becker, Howard S. (1951). "The Professional Dance Musician and his Audience," *American Journal of Sociology*, 57: 193–209.

Belting, Hans (2001). *The Invisible Masterpiece*. London: Reaktion Books.

Belting, Hans (1994). *Likeness and Presence: A History of the Image Before the Era of Art*. Chicago: University of Chicago Press.

Benjamin, Walter (1968). "Art in the Age of Mechanical Reproduction," in Hannah Arendt (ed.), *Illuminations*. New York: Harcourt, Brace & World, pp. 217–51.

Bennett, Andy (2001). *Cultures of Popular Music*. Buckingham: Open University Press.

Bennett, Andy (2000). *Popular Music and Youth Culture: Music, Identity and Place*. London: Macmillan.

Bennett, Andrew (1997). " 'Going Down the Pub!': The Pub Rock Scene as a Resource for the Consumption of Popular Music," *Popular Music*, 16 (1): 97–108.

Bennett, David H. (1980). "Malangi: The Man Who Was Forgotten Before He Was Remembered," *Aboriginal History*, 4 (1): 42–7.

Bennett, T. and J. Woollacott (1987). *Bond and Beyond: The Political Career of a Popular Hero*. London: Macmillan.

Berger, John (1972). *Ways of Seeing*. New York: Viking Penguin, Inc.

Berezin, Mabel (1991). "The Organization of Political Ideology: Culture, State, and Theater in Fascist Italy," *American Sociological Review*, 56 (5): 639–51.

Bielby, Denise D. and William T. Bielby (1996). "Women and Men in Film: Gender Inequality Among Writers in a Culture Industry," *Gender and Society*, 10 (3): 248–70.

Bielby, Denise D. and William T. Bielby (1993). "The Hollywood 'Graylist'? Audience Demographics and Age Stratification Among Television Writers," *Current Research in Occupations and Professions*, 8: 141–72.

Bielby, William T. and Denise D. Bielby (1994). " 'All Hits are Flukes': Institutional-ized Decision Making and the Rhetoric of Network Prime-Time Program Development," *American Journal of Sociology*, 99 (5): 1287–313.

Bielby, William T. and Denise D. Bielby (1992). "Cumulative versus Continuous Disadvantage in an Unstructured Labor Market: Gender Differences in the Careers of Television Writers," *Work and Occupations*, 19 (4): 366–86.

Bignell, Jonathan (1997). *Media Semiotics*. Manchester: Manchester University Press.

Binder, Amy (1993). "Constructing Racial Rhetoric: Media Depictions of Harm in Heavy Metal and Rap Music," *American Sociological Review*, 58 (6): 753–67.

316 REFERENCES

Blaikie, Andrew (1999). *Ageing and Popular Culture*. Cambridge: Cambridge University Press.

Blair, Helen (2001). " 'You're only as Good as Your Last Job': The Labour Process and Labour Market in the British Film Industry," *Work, Employment and Society*, 15 (1): 149–69.

Bloom, Allan (1987). *The Closing of the American Mind: How Higher Education Has Failed Democracy*. New York: Simon and Schuster.

Blumler, Jay G. (1991). "The New Television Marketplace: Imperatives, Implications, Issues," in Curran, James & Michael Gurevitch (eds.), *Mass Media and Society*. London: Methuen.

Blumler, Jay G. and Elihu Katz, eds. (1974). *The Uses of Mass Communication*. London: Sage.

Boorstin, Daniel J. (1964). *Image: A Guide to Pseudo-Events in America*. New York: Harper & Row.

Bordwell, David (1985). *Narration in the Fiction Film*. Madison: University of Wisconsin Press.

Bourdieu, Pierre (1998). *On Television and Journalism*. London: Pluto Press.

Bourdieu, Pierre (1996). *The State Nobility: Elite Schools in the Field of Power*. Oxford: Polity Press.

Bourdieu, Pierre (1993). *The Field of Cultural Production*. Oxford: Polity.

Bourdieu, Pierre (1992). *The Rules of Art: The Genesis and Structure of the Literary Field*. Stanford, CA: Stanford University Press.

Bourdieu, Pierre (1990). *Photography: A Middle-Brow Art*. Stanford, CA: Stanford University Press.

Bourdieu, Pierre (1984). *Distinction: A Social Critique of the Judgement of Taste*. Cambridge: Harvard University Press.

Bourdieu, Pierre and Alain Darbel (1991). *The Love of Art: European Art Museums and their Public*. Cambridge: Polity Press.

Bourdieu, Pierre and Jean-Claude Passeron (1977). *Reproduction in Education, Society and Culture*. Beverly Hills: Sage.

Bourdieu, Pierre and Loïc J. D. Waquant (1992). *An Invitation to Reflexive Sociology*. Oxford: Polity Press.

Bowler, Anne E. (1998). "Teoria e Metodo nella Sociologia dell'Arte," ["Theory and Method in the Sociology of Art"] in Danila Bertasio (ed.) *Immagini Sociali Dell'Arte*. Bari, Italy: Edizioni Dedalo.

Bowler, Anne E. (1997). "Asylum Art: The Social Construction of an Aesthetic Category," in Vera L. Zolberg and Joni Maya Cherbo (eds.), *Outsider Art: Contesting Boundaries in Contemporary Culture*. New York: Cambridge University Press, pp. 11–36.

Bowler, Anne E. (1994). "Methodological Dilemmas in the Sociology of Art," in Diana Crane (ed.), *The Sociology of Culture Emerging Theoretical Perspectives*. Oxford: Blackwell, pp. 247–66.

Bowler, Anne E. (1991). "Politics as Art: Italian Futurism and Fascism," *Theory and Society*, 20: 763–94.

Bryson, Bethany (1996). "'Anything but Heavy Metal': Symbolic Exclusion and Musical Dislikes," *American Sociological Review*, 61: 884–99.

Buckingham, David (1987). *Public Secrets: EastEnders and its Audience*. London: British Film Institute.

Buckingham, David (1993). *Children Talking Television: The Making of Television Literacy*. London: Falmer Press.

Burell, Gibson and Gareth Morgan (1979). *Sociological Paradigms and Organisational Analysis*. Portsmouth, NH: Heinemann.

Cantor, Muriel (1989). "The Artist's Condition: Comment and Discussion," in C. Richard Swaim (ed.), *The Modern Muse: The Support and Condition of Artists*. New York: ACA Books, pp. 59–61.

Cantor, Muriel G. and Joel Cantor (1992). *Prime-Time Television: Content and Control*. Beverly Hills: Sage.

Carney, Raymond (1986). *American Vision: The Films of Frank Capra*. Cambridge: Cambridge University Press.

Cawelti, John G. (1976). *Adventure, Mystery, and Romance: Formula Stories as Art and Popular Culture*. Chicago: University of Chicago Press.

Centerwall, Brandon S. (1993). "Our Cultural Perplexities: Television and Violent Crime," *The Public Interest*, 111 (Spring): 56–71.

Chamberlin, Russell (1983). *Loot! The Heritage of Plunder*. London: Thames & Hudson.

Christopherson, Susan and Michael Storper (1989). "The Effects of Flexible Specialization on Industrial-Politics and the Labor-Market – The Motion Picture Industry," *Industrial and Labor Relations Review*, 42: 331–47.

Cintron, Leslie (2000). *Preserving National Culture: The National Trust and the Framing of British National Heritage, 1895–2000*. Ph.D. Thesis, Harvard University.

Cohen, Stanley (1972 [1980]). *Folk Devils and Moral Panics: The Creation of Mods and Rockers*. New York: St. Martin's Press.

Collett, Peter (1987). "The Viewers Viewed: Reprinted from *The Listener*" *Et Cetera* 44 (3): 245–51.

Collins, Randall (1979). *The Credential Society: An Historical Sociology of Education and Stratification*. New York: Academic Press.

Cook, B. F., ed. (1997). *The Elgin Marbles*, second edition. London: British Museum Press.

Cooper, Geoff (2001). "Conceptualising Social Life," in Nigel Gilbert (ed.), *Researching Social Life*, second edition. London: Sage, pp. 1–13.

Corradi, Juan E. (1997). "How Many did it Take to Tango? Voyages of Urban Culture in the Early 1900s," in Vera L. Zolberg and Joni Maya Cherbo (eds.), *Outsider Art: Contesting Boundaries in Contemporary Culture*. New York: Cambridge University Press, pp. 194–214.

Corse, Sarah M. (1996). *Nationalism and Literature: The Politics of Culture in Canada and the United States*. New York: Cambridge University Press.

Corse, Sarah M. (1995). "Nations and Novels: Cultural Politics and Literary Use," *Social Forces*, 73 (4): 1279–308.

Corse, Sarah M. and Saundra Davis Westervelt (2002). "Gender and Literary Valorization: The Awakening of a Canonical Novel," *Sociological Perspectives*, 45: 139–61.

Corse, Sarah M. and Monica D. Griffin (1997). "Cultural Valorization and African-American Literary History: Re-Constructing the Canon," *Sociological Forum*, 12: 173–203.

Cortese, Anthony J. (1999). *Provocateur: Images of Women and Minorities in Advertising*. New York: Rowman & Littlefield Publishers, Inc.

Coser, Lewis A., ed. (1978). Special issue on "The Production of Culture", *Social Research*, 45 (2).

Coser, Lewis A., Charles Kadushin, and Walter W. Powell (1982). *Books: The Culture and Commerce of Publishing*. Chicago: University of Chicago Press.

Couch, Carl J. (1996). *Information Technologies and Social Orders*. New York: Aldine de Gruyter.

Crane, Diana (2000). *Fashion and Its Social Agendas: Class, Gender, and Identity in Clothing*. Chicago: University of Chicago Press.

Crane, Diana (1992). *The Production of Culture: Media and the Urban Arts*. London: Sage.

Crane, Diana (1987). *The Transformation of the Avant-Garde: The New York Art World, 1940–1985*. Chicago: University of Chicago Press.

Crane, Diana (1976). "Reward Systems in Art, Science, and Religion," in Richard A. Peterson (ed.), *The Production of Culture*. Beverly Hills, CA: Sage, pp. 57–72.

Crane, Diana, Nobuko Kawashima, and Ken'ichi Kawasaki, eds. (2002). *Global Culture: Media, Arts, Policy, and Globalization*. London: Routledge.

Craven, R. R., ed. (1987). *Symphony Orchestras of the World: Selected Profiles*. Westport, CT: Greenwood Press.

Critcher, Chas (2003). *Moral Panics and the Media*. Buckingham: Open University Press.

Cronin, Anne M. (2000). *Advertising and Consumer Citizenship: Gender, Images and Rights*. London: Routledge.

Crouch, S. R. (1983). "Patronage and Organizational Structure in Symphony Orchestras in London and New York," in Jack B. Kamerman and Rosanne Martorella (eds.), *Performers and Performances: The Social Organization of Artistic Work*. South Hadley, MA: Bergin and Garvey, pp. 109–22.

Csikszentmihalyi, Mihaly (1996). *Creativity: Flow and the Psychology of Discovery and Invention*. New York: Harper Collins.

Csikszentmihalyi, Mihaly and Rick E. Robinson (1986). "Culture, Time and the Development of Talent," in Robert J. Sternberg and Janet E. Davidson (eds.), *Conceptions of Giftedness*. New York: Cambridge University Press, pp. 264–84.

Curran, James (1990). "The New Revisionism in Mass Communication Research: A Reappraisal," *European Journal of Communication*, 5: 135–64.

Davies, Máire Messenger (1989). *Television is Good for Your Kids*. London: Shipman.

Dayan, Daniel and Elihu Katz (1992). *Media Events: The Live Broadcast of History*. Cambridge, MA: Harvard University Press.

Denisoff, R. Serge (1986). *Tarnished Gold: The Record Industry Revisited*. New Brunswick, NJ: Transaction Books.

Denning, Michael (1987). *Cover Stories: Narrative and Ideology in the British Spy Thriller.* London: Routledge.

DeNora, Tia (2000). *Music in Everyday Life.* Cambridge: Cambridge University Press.

DeNora, Tia (1995). *Beethoven and the Construction of Genius: Musical Politics in Vienna, 1792–1803.* Berkeley: University of California Press.

DeNora, Tia (1991). "Musical Patronage and Social Change in Beethoven's Vienna," *American Journal of Sociology,* 97: 310–46.

Desan, Philippe, Priscilla Parkhurst Ferguson, and Wendy Griswold, eds. (1988). "Editors' Introduction: Mirrors, Frames, and Demons: Reflections on the Sociology of Literature," in *Literature and Social Practice.* Chicago: University of Chicago Press, pp. 1–10.

Diebert, Ronald J. (1997). *Parchment, Printing, and Hypermedia.* New York: Columbia University Press.

DiMaggio, Paul (1992). "Cultural Boundaries and Structural Change: The Extension of the High Culture Model to Theater, Opera, and Dance, 1900–1940," in Michèle Lamont and Marcel Fournier (eds.), *Cultivating Differences: Symbolic Boundaries and the Making of Inequality.* Chicago: University of Chicago Press, pp. 21–57.

DiMaggio, Paul (1991a). "The Museum and The Public," in Martin Felstein (ed.), *The Economics of Art Museums.* Chicago: University of Chicago Press, pp. 39–50.

DiMaggio, Paul (1991b). "Constructing an Organizational Field as a Professional Project: U.S. Art Museums, 1920–1940," in Walter W. Powell and Paul J. DiMaggio (eds.), *The New Institutionalism in Organizational Analysis.* Chicago: University of Chicago Press, pp. 267–92.

DiMaggio, Paul (1987a). "Classification in Art," *American Sociological Review,* 52: 440–55.

DiMaggio, Paul (1987b). "Nonprofit Organizations in the Production and Distribution of Culture," in Walter W. Powell (ed.), *The Nonprofit Sector: A Research Handbook.* New Haven: Yale University Press, pp. 195–220.

DiMaggio, Paul (1986). "Can Culture Survive the Marketplace?" in Paul DiMaggio (ed.), *Nonprofit Enterprise in the Arts: Studies in Mission and Constraint.* New York, Oxford University Press, pp. 65–92.

DiMaggio, Paul (1982a). "Cultural Entrepreneurship in Nineteenth-Century Boston: The Creation of an Organizational Base for High Culture in America," *Media, Culture and Society,* 4: 33–50.

DiMaggio, Paul (1982b). "Cultural Entrepreneurship in Nineteenth-Century Boston, Part II: The Classification and Framing of American Art," *Media, Culture and Society,* 4: 303–22.

DiMaggio, Paul (1982c). "Cultural Capital and School Success: The Impact of Status Culture Participation on the Grades of U.S. High School Students," *American Sociological Review,* 47: 189–201.

DiMaggio, Paul (1977). "Market Structure, The Creative Process, and Popular Culture: Toward an Organizational Reinterpretation of Mass-Culture Theory," *Journal of Popular Culture,* 11: 436–52.

DiMaggio, Paul and John Mohr (1985). "Cultural Capital, Educational Attainment and Marital Selection," *American Journal of Sociology,* 90: 1231–61.

DiMaggio, Paul and Francie Ostrower (1990). "Participation in the Arts by Black and White Americans," *Social Forces*, 68 (3): 753–78.

Dimaggio, Paul and Kristen Stenberg (1985). "Why Do Some Theatres Innovate More Than Others? An Empirical Analysis," *Poetics: Journal of Empirical Research on Literature, the Media and Arts,* 14: 107-22.

DiMaggio, Paul and Michael Useem (1978). "Social Class and Arts Consumption," *Theory and Society*, 5: 141–61.

Dines, Gail and Jean M. Humez, eds. (1995). *Gender, Race, and Class in Media.* London: Sage.

Douglas, Mary (1966). *Purity and Danger: An Analysis of Pollution and Taboo.* London: Routledge.

Douglas, Mary and Baron Isherwood (1979). *The World of Goods: Towards an Anthropology of Consumption.* New York: Norton.

Dowmunt, Tony, ed. (1993). *Channels of Resistance: Global Television and Local Empowerment.* London: BFI Publishing in association with Channel Four Television.

Dubin, Steven C. (1999). *Displays of Power: Memory and Amnesia in the American Museum.* New York: New York University Press.

Dubin, Stephen C. (1992). *Arresting Images: Impolitic Art and Uncivil Actions.* New York: Routledge.

Dubin, Steven (1987a). "Black Representations in Popular Culture," *Social Problems*, 34: 122–40.

Dubin, Steven C. (1987b). *Bureaucratizing the Muse: Public Funds and the Cultural Worker.* Chicago: University of Chicago Press.

Durkheim, Emile (1895 [1982]). *The Rules of Sociological Method.* New York: Free Press

Dutton, Denis, ed. (1983). *The Forger's Art: Forgery and the Philosophy of Art.* Berkeley: University of California Press.

Eagleton, Terry (1983). *Literary Theory: An Introduction.* Minneapolis: University of Minnesota Press.

Eco, Umberto (1979). *The Role of the Reader: Explorations in the Semiotics of Texts.* Bloomington: Indiana University Press.

The Economist (2000). "Ventriloquism: Engastrimythos for Dummies," December 2, p. 145.

The Economist (1998). "Aboriginal Art: Drawing from the Mists of Time," June 6, p. 124.

Edwards, Richard (1979). *Contested Terrain.* New York: Basic Books.

Eisenmann, Thomas R. and Joseph L. Bower (2000). "The Entrepreneurial M-Form: Strategic Integration in Global Media Firms." *Organization Science*, 11 (3): 348-55.

Eisenstein, Elizabeth L. (1979). *The Printing Press as an Agent of Change*, Volumes 1 and 2. New York: Cambridge University Press.

Elia, Ricardo J. (1995). "Greece v. Ward: The Return of Mycenaean Artifacts," *International Journal of Cultural Property*, 4: 119–28.

Entman, Robert M. and Andrew Rojecki (2001). *The Black Image in the White Mind: Media and Race in America*, with a new preface. Chicago: University of Chicago Press.

Ewen, Stuart and Elizabeth Ewen (1992). *Channels of Desire: Mass Images and the Shaping of American Consciousness*, second edition. Minneapolis: University of Minnesota Press.

Ewen, Stuart (1988). *All Consuming Images: The Politics of Style in Contemporary Culture.* New York: Basic Books.

Ewen, Stuart (1976). *Captains of Consciousness: Advertising and the Social Roots of the Consumer Culture.* New York: McGraw-Hill.

Faulkner, Robert R. (1973). "Career Concerns and Mobility Motivations of Orchestral Musicians," *Sociological Quarterly*, 14: 334–49.

Faulkner, Robert R. and Andy B. Anderson (1987). "Short-Term Projects and Emergent Careers: Evidence from Hollywood," *American Journal of Sociology*, 92 (4): 879–909.

Featherstone, Mike (1990). "Global Culture: An Introduction," in Mike Featherstone (ed.), *Global Culture: Nationalism, Globalization and Modernity.* London: Sage, pp. 1–14.

Felson, Richard B. (1996). "Mass Media Effects on Violent Behavior," *Annual Review of Sociology*, 22: 103–28.

Ferguson, Priscilla Parkhurst (1998). "A Cultural Field in the Making: Gastronomy in 19th-Century France," *American Journal of Sociology*, 104 (3): 597–641.

Fine, Gary Alan (1996). *Kitchens: The Culture of Restaurant Work.* Berkeley: University of California Press.

Fish, Stanley (1980). *Is There a Text in this Class? The Authority of Interpretive Communities.* Cambridge: Harvard University Press.

Fiske, John (1989). *Reading the Popular.* New York: Routledge.

Fitz Gibbon, Heather M. (1987). "From Prints to Posters: The Production of Artistic Value in a Popular Art World," *Symbolic Interaction*, 10 (1): 111–28.

Foucault, Michel (1979a). *Discipline and Punish.* New York: Vintage.

Foucault, Michel (1979b). "What is an Author?" in Josue V. Harari (ed.), *Textual Strategies: Perspectives in Post-Structuralist Criticism.* Ithica: Cornell University Press, pp. 141–60

Fowler, Bridget (1997). *Pierre Bourdieu and Cultural Theory: Critical Investigations.* London: Sage.

Friedman, Jonathan (1990). "Being in the World: Globalization and Localization," in Mike Featherstone (ed.), *Global Culture: Nationalism, Globalization and Modernity.* London: Sage, pp. 311–28.

Frith, Simon (1978 [1981]). *Sound Effects: Youth, Leisure, and the Politics of Rock 'n' Roll.* New York: Pantheon.

Fyfe, Gordon (2000). *Art, Power and Modernity: English Art Institutions, 1750–1950.* London: Leicester University Press.

Galenson, David W. and Bruce A. Weinberg (2000). "Age and the Quality of Work: The Case of Modern American Painters," *Journal of Political Economy*, 108 (4): 760–77.

Gans, Herbert J. (1982). "Preface," in Michèle Lamont and Marcel Fournier (eds.), *Cultivating Differences: Symbolic Boundaries and the Making of Inequality.* Chicago: University of Chicago Press, pp. vii–xv.

Gans, Herbert J. (1974). *Popular Culture and High Culture: An Analysis and Evaluation of Taste.* New York: Basic Books.

Gans, Herbert J. (1962). *The Urban Villagers.* New York: Basic Books.

Geertz, Clifford (1983). *Local Knowledge: Further Essays in Interpretive Ethnography.* New York: Basic Books

Geertz, Clifford (1973). *The Interpretation of Cultures*. New York: Basic Books.

Gerbner, George (1995). "Marketing Global Mayhem," *The Public*, 2 (2): 71–6.

Gellner, Ernst (1988). *Plough, Sword and Book: The Structure of Human History*. Chicago: University of Chicago Press.

Getzels, Jacob W. and Mihaly Csikszentmihalyi (1976). *The Creative Vision: A Longitudinal Study of Problem Finding in Art*. New York: Wiley.

Giddens, Anthony (1993). *Sociology*, second edition. Oxford: Polity.

Giddens, Anthony (1979). *Central Problems in Social Theory*. London: Macmillan.

Gilbert, Nigel (2001). "Research, Theory and Method," in Nigel Gilbert (ed.), *Researching Social Life*, second edition. London: Sage, pp. 14–27.

Gilmore, S. (1987). "Coordination and Convention: The Organization of the Concert World," *Symbolic Interaction*, 10: 209–27.

Gilroy, Paul (1993). *The Black Atlantic: Modernity and Double Consciousness*. Cambridge: Harvard University Press,

Gitlin, Todd (1983). *Inside Prime Time*. New York: Pantheon.

Giuffre, Katherine (1999). "Sandpiles of Opportunity: Success in the Art World," *Social Forces*, 77 (3): 815–32.

Glynn, Mary Ann (2000). "When Cymbals become Symbols: Conflict over Organizational Identity within a Symphony Orchestra," *Organization Science*, 11 (3): 285–98.

Goffman, Erving (1979). *Gender Advertisements*. Cambridge, MA: Harvard University Press.

Goldin, Claudia and Cecilia Rouse (2000). "Orchestrating Impartiality: The Impact of 'Blind' Auditions on Female Musicians," *The American Economic Review*, 90 (4): 715–41.

Goldman, Robert and Stephen Papson (1998). *Nike Culture*. London: Sage.

Goldmann, Lucien (1964). *The Hidden God: A Study of Tragic Vision in the Pensées of Pascal and the Tragedies of Racine*, Tr. Philip Thody. London: Routledge.

Goldthorpe, John H. (2000). "The Present Crisis in Sociology: A Way Beyond Spurious Pluralism," *Sociologisk Forskning*, 37 (3–4): 6–19.

Golomshtok, Igor (1985). "The History and Organization of Artistic Life in the Soviet Union," in Marilyn Rueschemeyer, Igor Golomshtok, and Janet Kennedy (eds), *Soviet Émigré Artists: Life and Work in the USSR and the United States*. New York: M. E. Sharpe, Inc., pp. 16–59.

Gombrich, E. H. (1964). *The Story of Art*. London: Phaidon Press.

Gombrich, E. H. (1960). *Art and Illusion*. London: Phaidon Press.

Goody, Jack and Ian Watt (1968). "The Consequences of Literacy," in Jack Goody (ed.), *Literacy in Traditional Societies*. Cambridge: Cambridge University Press, pp. 27–68.

Graham, Gordon (2000). *Philosophy of the Arts: An Introduction to Aesthetics*, second edition. London: Routledge.

Gramsci, Antonio (1930s [1971]). *Selections from the Prison Notebooks*. London: Lawrence and Wishart.

Graña, César (1971). *Fact and Symbol: Essays in the Sociology of Art and Literature*. New York: Oxford University Press.

Graña, César (1964). *Bohemian versus Bourgeois: French Society and the French Man of Letters in the Nineteenth Century.* New York: Basic Books.

Gray, Ann (1992). *Video Playtime: The Gendering of a Leisure Technology.* London: Routledge.

Griswold, Wendy (1999). "The Cultural Consequences of Cowbirds," paper presented at the 1999 annual meeting of the American Sociological Association (Chicago).

Griswold, Wendy (1994). *Cultures and Societies in a Changing World.* London: Pine Forge Press.

Griswold, Wendy (1993). "Recent Moves in the Sociology of Literature," *Annual Review of Sociology*, 19: 455–67.

Griswold, Wendy (1992a). "Mushroom in the Rain: The Uses of Culture in Comparative and Historical Sociology," *Culture*, (Newsletter of the Sociology of Culture Section of the American Sociological Association), 7 (1): 9–12.

Griswold, Wendy (1992b). "The Writing on the Mud Wall: Nigerian Novels and the Imaginary Village," *American Sociological Review*, 57: 709–24.

Griswold, Wendy (1990). "A Provisional, Provincial Positivism: Reply to Denzin," *American Journal of Sociology*, 95: 1580–3.

Griswold, Wendy (1987a). "The Fabrication of Meaning: Literary Interpretation in the United States, Great Britain, and the West Indies," *American Journal of Sociology*, 92: 1077–117.

Griswold, Wendy (1987b). "A Methodological Framework for the Sociology of Culture," *Sociological Methodology*, 17: 1–35.

Griswold, Wendy (1986). *Renaissance Revivals: City Comedy and Revenge Tragedy in the London Theatre, 1576–1980.* Chicago: University of Chicago Press.

Griswold, Wendy (1981). "American Character and the American Novel," *American Journal of Sociology*, 86: 740–65.

Griswold, Wendy and Misty Bastian (1987). "Continuities and Reconstructions in Cross-Cultural Literary Transmission: The Case of the Nigerian Romance Novel," *Poetics: Journal of Empirical Research on Culture, the Media and the Arts*, 16: 327–51.

Guillén, Mauro F. (1997). "Scientific Management's Lost Aesthetic: Architecture, Organization, and the Taylorized Beauty of the Mechanical," *Administrative Science Quarterly*, 42: 682–715.

Gunter, Barrie (2000). *Media Research Methods.* London: Sage.

Hall, Stuart (1993). "Culture, Community, Nation," *Cultural Studies*, 7 (3): 349–363.

Hall, Stuart (1980). *Culture, Media, Languages.* Hutchinson.

Hall, Stuart and Tony Jefferson, eds. (1975). *Resistance through Rituals: Youth Subcultures in Post-War Britain.* London: Hutchinson.

Halle, David (2001). "The Controversy Over the Show 'Sensation' at the Brooklyn Museum, 1999–2000," in Alberta Arthurs and Glenn Wallach (eds.), *Crossroads: Art and Religion in American Life.* New York: The New Press, pp. 139–87.

Halle, David (1993). *Inside Culture: Art and Class in the American Home.* Chicago: University of Chicago Press.

Halle, David (1992). "The Audience for Abstract Art: Class, Culture, and Power," in Michèle Lamont and Marcel Fournier (eds.), *Cultivating Differences: Symbolic*

Boundaries and the Making of Inequality. Chicago: University of Chicago Press, pp. 131–151.

Halle, David, Elisabeth Tiso, and Gihong Yi (2001). "The Attitude of the Audience for 'Sensation' and of the General Public toward Controversial Works of Art," in Lawrence Rothfield (ed.), *Unsettling "Sensation": Arts-Policy Lessons from the Brooklyn Museum of Art Controversy*. New Brunswick, NJ: Rutgers University Press, pp. 134–52.

Hannerz, Ulf (1990). "Cosmopolitans and Locals in World Culture," in Mike Featherstone (ed.), *Global Culture: Nationalism, Globalization and Modernity*. London: Sage, pp. 237–51.

Hannerz, Ulf (1989). "Notes on the Global Ecumene," *Public Culture*, 1 (2): 66–75.

Hauser, Arnold (1951 [1968]). *The Social History of Art*, Vol. 2. London: Routledge.

Hawkes, Terence (1977 [1992]). *Structuralism and Semiotics*. London: Routledge.

Hebdige, Dick (1979). *Subculture: The Meaning of Style*. New York: Methuen.

Heckathorn, Douglas D. and Joan Jeffri (2001). "Finding the Beat: Using Respondent-Driven Sampling to Study Jazz Musicians," *Poetics: Journal of Empirical Research on Culture, the Media and the Arts*, 28: 307–29.

Heinich, Nathalie (1997). "Outside Art and Insider Artists: Gauging Public Reactions to Contemporary Public Art," in Vera Zolberg and Joni Maya Cherbo (eds.), *Outsider Art: Contesting Boundaries in Contemporary Culture*. Cambridge: University of Cambridge Press, pp. 118–27.

Held, David, Anthony McGrew, David Goldblatt, and Jonathan Perraton (1999). *Global Transformations: Politics, Economics and Culture*. Cambridge: Polity Press.

Helsinger, Elizabeth (1994). "Turner and the Representation of England," in W. J. T. Mitchell (ed.), *Landscape and Power*. Chicago: University of Chicago Press, pp. 103–25.

Herman, Edward S. and Robert McChesney (1997). *The Global Media: The New Missionaries of Corporate Capitalism*. London: Cassell.

Hillman-Chartrand, Harry and Claire McCaughey (1989). "The Arm's Length Principle and the Arts: An International Perspective – Past, Present, and Future," in Milton C. Cummings, Jr. and J. Mark David Schuster (eds.), *Who's to Pay for the Arts? The International Search for Models*. New York: ACA Books, pp. 43–80.

Hirsch, Paul M. (2000). "Cultural Industries Revisited," *Organization Science*, 11 (3): 356–61.

Hirsch, Paul M. (1972). "Processing Fads and Fashions: An Organization-Set Analysis of Cultural Industry Systems," *American Journal of Sociology*, 77: 639–59.

Hitchens, Christopher (1987). *The Elgin Marbles: Should They be Returned to Greece?*, with essays by Robert Browning and Graham Binns. London: Chatto & Windus.

Hobson, Dorothy (1982). *Crossroads: The Drama of a Soap Opera*. London: Methuen.

Hockney, David (2001). *Secret Knowledge: Rediscovering the Lost Techniques of the Old Masters*. London: Thames & Hudson.

Hodge, Bob and David Tripp (1986 [1994]). "Ten Theses on Children and Television," in *The Polity Reader in Cultural Theory*. Cambridge: Polity Press, pp. 174–9.

Hoffman, Donald D. (1998). *Visual Intelligence: How We Create What We See*. New York: W. W. Norton.

Hoggart, Richard (1957). *The Uses of Literacy*. London: Essential Books.

Hoynes, William (1994). *Public Television for Sale: Media, the Market and the Public Sphere*. San Francisco: Westview Press.

Humphrey, Ronald and Howard Schuman (1984). "The Portrayal of Blacks in Magazine Advertisements: 1950–1982," *Public Opinion Quarterly*, 48: 551–63.

Iyer, Pico (1989). *Video Nights in Kathmandu*. New York: Vintage.

Jameson, Fredric (1984). "Postmodernism, or The Cultural Logic of Late Capitalism," *The New Left Review*, 146: 53–92.

Janson, H. W. (1986). *History of Art*, third edition, revised and expanded by Anthony F. Janson. New York: Harry N. Abrams, Inc.

Jauss, Hans Robert (1982). *Toward an Aesthetic of Reception*. Minneapolis: University of Minnesota Press.

Jeffri, Joan and Robert Greenblatt (1989). "Between Extremities: The Artist Described," *Journal of Arts Management and Law*, 19 (1): 5–14.

Jeffri, Joan, Joseph Hosie, and Robert Greenblatt (1987). "The Artist Alone: Work-Related, Human, and Social Service Needs – Selected Findings," *Journal of Arts Management and Law*, 17 (3): 5–22.

Jenkins, Henry (1992). *Textual Poachers: Television Fans and Participatory Culture*. London: Routledge.

Jhally, Sut and Justin Lewis (1992). *Enlightened Racism: The Cosby Show, Audiences, and the Myth of the American Dream*. San Francisco: Westview Press.

Jones, Colin (2000). "Pulling Teeth in Eighteenth-Century Paris," *Past and Present: A Journal of Historical Studies*, 166 (February): 100–145.

Kanter, Rosabeth Moss (1989). *When Giants Learn to Dance*. New York: Simon & Schuster.

Kanter, Rosabeth Moss (1977). *Men and Women of the Corporation*. New York: Harper & Row.

Katz, Elihu and George Wedell (1977). *Broadcasting in the Third World: Promise and Performance*. Cambridge: Harvard University Press.

Klein, Gillian (1985). *Reading into Racism: Bias in Children's Literature and Learning Material*. London: Routledge.

Klein, Naomi (2000). *No Logo*. London: Flamingo

Kubler, George (1962). *The Shape of Time: Remarks on the History of Things*. New York: Yale University Press.

Lachmann, Richard (1988). "Graffiti as Career and Ideology," *American Journal of Sociology*, 94: 229–50.

Lai, Chia-Ling (2002). "The Transformation of Museum Field on the Transnational Scale and the Intensification of International Travelling Exhibitions," paper presented at the British Sociological Association's Annual Conference, 25–27 March, University of Leicester.

Lamont, Michèle (1992). *Money, Morals and Manners: The Culture of the French and the American Upper-Middle Class*. Chicago: University of Chicago Press.

Lamont, Michèle and Marcel Fournier (1992). "Introduction," in Michèle Lamont and Marcel Fournier (eds.), *Cultivating Differences: Symbolic Boundaries and the Making of Inequality*. Chicago: University of Chicago Press, pp. 1–17.

Lampel, Joseph, Theresa Lant, and Jamal Shamsie (2000). "Balancing Act: Learning from Organizational Practices in Cultural Industries," *Organization Science*, 11 (3): 263–69.

Lang, Gladys Engel and Kurt Lang (1990). *Etched in Memory: The Building and Survival of Artistic Reputation*. Chapel Hill: University of North Carolina Press.

Lang, Gladys Engel and Kurt Lang (1988). "Recognition and Renown: The Survival of Artistic Reputation," *American Journal of Sociology*, 94 (1): 79–109.

Laslett, Peter (1976). "The Wrong Way through the Telescope: A Note on Literary Evidence in Sociology and in Historical Sociology," *British Journal of Sociology*, 27 (3): 319–42.

Laurence J. and J. Mace, (1991). *Television Talk and Writing*. Cambridge: National Extension College.

Leal, Odina Fachel and Ruben George Oliven (1988). "Class Interpretations of a Soap Opera Narrative: The Case of the Brazilian Novella 'Summer Sun,'" *Theory, Culture and Society*, 5 (1): 81–99.

Lealand, G. (1984) *American Television Programmes on British Screens*. Broadcasting Research Unit.

Leavis, Q. D. (1932 [1978]). *Fiction and the Reading Public*. London: Chatto and Windus.

Levine, Lawrence W. (1988). *Highbrow, Lowbrow: The Emergence of a Cultural Hierarchy in America*. Cambridge: Harvard University Press.

Lévi-Strauss, Claude (1967). *Structural Anthropology*. New York: Anchor Books.

Lewis, Justin (1991). *The Ideological Octopus*. London: Routledge.

Lieberson, Stanley (2000). *A Matter of Taste: How Names, Fashions, and Culture Change*. New Haven: Yale University Press.

Liebes, Tamar and Elihu Katz (1993). *The Export of Meaning*. Oxford: Oxford University Press.

Liebow, Elliot (1967). *Tally's Corner: A Study of Negro Streetcorner Men*. Boston: Little, Brown.

Long, Elizabeth (1986). "Women, Reading, and Cultural Authority: Some Implications of the Audience Perspective in Cultural Studies," *American Quarterly*, 38 (4): 591–612.

Long, Elizabeth (1985). *The American Dream and the Popular Novel*. London: Routledge.

Lopes, Paul (2002). *The Rise of a Jazz Art World*. New York: Cambridge University Press.

Lopes, Paul (2000). "Pierre Bourdieu's Fields of Cultural Production: A Case Study of Jazz," in Nicholas Brown and Imre Azeman (eds.), *Pierre Bourdieu: Fieldwork in Culture*. Lantham, MD: Rowman and Littlefield, pp. 165–85.

Lopes, Paul D. (1992). "Innovation and Diversity in the Popular Music Industry, 1969–1990," *American Sociological Review*, 57: 56–71.

Lowenthal, David (1985). *The Past Is a Foreign Country*. Cambridge: Cambridge University Press.

Lowenthal, Leo (1961). "The Triumph of Mass Idols," in *Literature, Popular Culture, and Society*. Palo Alto, CA: Pacific Books, pp. 109–36.

Lull, James (2000). *Media, Communication, Culture: A Global Approach*, second edition. Cambridge: Polity.

Lull, James, ed. (1988). *World Families Watch Television*. London: Sage.

Lynes, Russell (1954). *The Taste Makers*. London: Hamish Hamilton.

MacCannell, D. (1976). *The Tourist: A New Theory of the Leisure Class*. London Macmillan.

MacDonald, Dwight (1957). "A Theory of Mass Culture," in Bernard Rosenberg and David Manning White (eds.), *Mass Culture: The Popular Arts in America*. New York: Macmillan.

Macdonald, Keith (2001). "Using Documents," in Nigel Gilbert (ed.), *Researching Social Life*, second edition. London: Sage, pp 194–210.

Mace, J. (1992). "Television and Metaphors of Literacy," *Studies in the Education of Adults*, 24 (2): 162–75.

Malinowski, Bronislaw (1948). *Magic, Science, and Religion and Other Essays*. Glencoe, IL: The Free Press.

Marchand, Roland (1985). *Advertising the American Dream: Making Way for Modernity, 1920–1940*. Berkeley: University of California Press.

Marcuse, Herbert (1972). *One Dimensional Man*. London. Abacus.

Martorella, Rosanne (1982). *The Sociology of Opera*. South Hadley, MA: J. F. Bergin.

Martorella, Rosanne (1977). "The Relationship between Box Office and Repertoire: A Case Study of the Opera," *Sociological Quarterly*, 18: 354–66.

Marx, Karl (1859 [1963]). *Selected Writings in Sociology and Social Philosophy*, T. Bottomore and M. Rubel (eds.). Harmondsworth: Penguin.

Marx, Karl (1846 [1978]). "The German Ideology," in Robert C. Tucker (ed.), *The Marx-Engels Reader*, second edition. New York: W. W. Norton, pp. 146–200.

McChesney, Robert W. (2000). *Rich Media, Poor Democracy: Communication Politics in Dubious Times*. New York: The New Press.

McKinley, E. Graham (1997). *Beverly Hills, 90210: Television, Gender and Identity*. Philadelphia: University of Pennsylvania Press.

McLuhan, Marshall (1964). *Understanding Media: The Extensions of Man*. New York: McGraw-Hill.

McNeely, Connie and Yasemin Nuhoglu Soysal (1989). "International Flows of Television Programming: A Revisionist Research Orientation," *Public Culture*, 2 (1): 136–44.

McPherson, Miller, Lynn Smith-Lovin, and James M. Cook (2001). "Birds of a Feather: Homophily in Social Networks," *Annual Review of Sociology*, 27: 415–44.

McQuail, Denis (1997). *Audience Analysis*. London: Sage.

Meislin, R. J. (1983) "...And in Mexico, Latin Values Will Be Stressed," *New York Times*, September 29.

Menger, Pierre-Michel (2001). "Artists as Workers: Theoretical and Methodological Challenges," *Poetics: Journal of Empirical Research on Culture, the Media and the Arts*, 28: 241–54.

Menger, Pierre-Michel (1999). "Artistic Labor Markets and Careers," *Annual Review of Sociology*, 25: 541–74.

Merelman, Richard M. (1992). "Cultural Imagery and Racial Conflict in the United States: The Case of African-Americans," *British Journal of Political Science*, 22: 315–42.

Merryman, John Henry (1985). "Thinking about the Elgin Marbles," *Michigan Law Review*, 83 (8): 1881–923.

Metcalf, Eugene W., Jr. (1986). "The Politics of the Past in American Folk Art History," in John Michael Vlach and Simon J. Bronner (eds.), *Folk Art and Art Worlds*. Ann Arbor, MI: UMI Research Press, pp. 27–50.

Metropolitan Museum of Art (1997). *Annual Report for the Year 1996–1997*.

Meyer, Karl E. (1979). *The Art Museum: Power, Money, Ethics*. New York: William Morrow and Co., Inc.

Meyer, Karl E. (1973). *The Plundered Past: The Story of the Illegal International Traffic in Works Of Art*. New York: Atheneum.

Meyer, Leonard B. (1956). *Emotion and Meaning in Music*. Chicago: University of Chicago Press.

Mezias, John M. and Stephen J. Mezias (2000). "Resource Partitioning, the Founding of Specialist Firms, and Innovation: The American Feature Film Industry, 1912–1929," *Organization Science*, 11 (3): 306–22.

Modleski, Tania (1984). *Loving with a Vengeance: Mass Produced Fantasies for Women*. London: Methuen.

Monaco, James (1979). *American Film Now: The People, The Power, The Money, The Movies*. New York: Oxford University Press.

Morgan, Gareth (1986). *Images of Organization*. London: Sage.

Morgan, Michael (1989). "Television and Democracy," in Ian Angus and Sut Jhally (eds.), *Cultural Politics in Contemporary America*, London: Routledge.

Morley, David (1980). *The "Nationwide" Audience: Structure and Decoding*. London: British Film Institute.

Morley, David (1986). *Family Television: Cultural Power and Domestic Leisure*. London: Comedia Publishing Company.

Moulin, Raymonde (1987). *The French Art Market: A Sociological Review*. New Brunswick: Rutgers University Press.

Mulvey, Laura (1975). "Visual Pleasure and Narrative Cinema," *Screen*, 16 (3): 6–18.

The National Commission on the Causes and Prevention of Violence (1969). *To Establish Justice, To Ensure Domestic Tranquility*. Washington, DC: U.S. Government Printing Office.

Neuman, W. Lawrence (2000). *Social Research Methods: Qualitative and Quantitative Approaches*, fourth edition. Boston: Allyn and Bacon.

Nicholas, Lynn H. (1994). *The Rape of Europa: The Fate of Europe's Treasures in the Third Reich and the Second World War*. New York: Vintage.

Nochlin, Linda (1971 [1973]). "Why Have There Been No Great Women Artists?" in Thomas B. Hess & Elizabeth C. Baker, eds., *Art & Sexual Politics: Women's Liberation, Women Artists, and Art History*. New York: Macmillan. [Originally published in *Art News* 69 (2): 22–39; 67–71.]

North, Adrian C. and David J. Hargreaves (1997). "Music and Consumer Behaviour," in David J. Hargreaves and Adrian C. North (eds.), *The Social Psychology of Music*. Oxford: Oxford University Press, pp. 268–82.

Ohmann, Richard (1983). "The Shaping of a Canon: U.S. Fiction, 1960–1975," *Critical Inquiry*, 10: 199–223.

Oliver, Mary Beth and G. Blake Armstrong (1998). "The Color of Crime: Perceptions of Caucasians' and African-Americans' Involvement in Crime," in Mark Fishman and Gray Cavender (eds.), *Entertaining Crime: Television Reality Programs*. New York: Aldine de Gruyter.

O'Sullivan, Tim, Brian Dutton, and Philip Rayner (1998). *Studying The Media: An Introduction*, second edition. London: Arnold.

O'Toole, John (1985). *The Trouble with Advertising: A View from Inside*. New York: Times Books.

Paik, Haejung and George Comstock (1994). "The Effects of Television Violence on Antisocial Behavior: A Meta-Analysis." *Communication Research*, 21 (4): 516–41.

Parker, Rozsika (1996). *The Subversive Stitch: Embroidery and the Making of the Feminine*. London: The Women's Press.

Parker, Rozsika and Griselda Pollock (1981). *Old Mistresses: Women, Art and Ideology*. London: Pandora.

Payne, Bruce L. (1989). "Support for Older Artists," in C. Richard Swaim (ed.), *The Modern Muse: The Support and Condition of Artists*. New York: ACA Books, pp. 67–80.

Penkakur, M. & R. Subramanyam (1996). "Indian Cinema Beyond National Boarders," in John Sinclair, Elizabeth Jacka, and Stuart Cunningham (eds.), *New Patterns in Global Television: Peripheral Vision*. Oxford: Oxford University Press.

Pescosolido, Bernice A., Elizabeth Grauerholz, and Melissa A. Milkie (1997). "Culture and Conflict: The Portrayal of Blacks in U.S. Children's Picture Books through the Mid-and Late-Twentieth Century," *American Sociological Review*, 62 (3): 443–64.

Peterson, Karin (1997). "The Distribution and Dynamics of Uncertainty in Art Galleries: A Case Study of New Dealerships in the Parisian Art Market, 1985–1990," *Poetics: Journal of Empirical Research on Literature, the Media and Arts*, 25: 241–63.

Peterson, Karin and Sarah M. Corse (2001). "Artistic Definition in a Postmodern Age: Formalism, Aesthetics, and the Expansion of Value," unpublished paper, Department of Sociology, University of Virginia.

Peterson, Richard A. (1997). *Creating Country Music: Fabricating Authenticity*. Chicago: University of Chicago Press.

Peterson, Richard A. (1994). "Culture Studies Through the Production Perspective: Progress and Prospects," in Diana Crane (ed.), *The Sociology of Culture Emerging Theoretical Perspectives*. Oxford: Blackwell, pp. 163–89.

Peterson, Richard A. (1986). "From Impresario to Arts Administrator: Formal Accountability in Nonprofit Cultural Organizations," in Paul DiMaggio (ed.), *Nonprofit Enterprise in the Arts: Studies in Mission and Constraint*. New York, Oxford University Press, 161–83.

Peterson, Richard A. (1979). "Revitalizing the Culture Concept," *Annual Review of Sociology*, 5: 137–66.

Peterson, Richard A., ed. (1976). *The Production of Culture*. Beverly Hills, CA: Sage.

Peterson, Richard A. (1972). "A Process Model of the Folk, Popular, and Fine Art Phases of Jazz," in C. Nanry (ed.), *American Music: From Storyville to Woodstock*. New Brunswick, NJ: Rutgers University Press, pp. 135–51.

Peterson, Richard A. and David G. Berger (1975). "Cycles in Symbol Production: The Case of Popular Music," *American Sociological Review*, 40: 158–73.

Peterson, Richard A. and Roger M. Kern (1996). "Changing Highbrow Taste: From Snob to Omnivore," *American Sociological Review*, 61: 900–7.

Peterson, Richard A. and Albert Simkus (1992). "How Musical Tastes Mark Occupational Status Groups," in Michèle Lamont and Marcel Fournier (eds.), *Cultivating Differences: Symbolic Boundaries and the Making of Inequality*. Chicago: University of Chicago Press, pp. 152–86.

Pevsner, Nikolaus (1940). *Academies of Art: Past and Present*. New York: Macmillan.

Phillips, J. D. (1982). "Film Conglomerate Blockbusters: International Appeal and Product Homogenization," in Gorham Kindem (ed.), *The American Movie Industry: The Business of Motion Pictures*. Carbondale: Southern Illinois University Press, pp. 325–35.

Philo, Greg (1998). *Message Received: Glasgow Media Group Research, 1993–1998*. Harlo: Longman.

Philo, Greg (1990). *Seeing and Believing: The Influence of Television*. London: Routledge.

Philo, Greg (1982). *Really Bad News*. London: Writers and Readers.

Piore, Michael J. and Charles F. Sabel (1984). *The Second Industrial Divide: Possibilities for Prosperity*. New York: Basic Books.

Plattner, Stuart (1996). *High Art Down Home: An Ecomomic Ethnography of a Local Art Market*. Chicago: University of Chicago Press.

Pollock, Griselda (1988). *Mary Cassatt*. New York: Harper & Row.

Postman, Neil (1986). *Amusing Ourselves to Death*. New York: Penguin Books.

Powell, Walter W. (1988). "Cultural Production as Routine: Some Thoughts on 'America's Bookstore,'" in Philippe Desan, Priscilla Parkhurst Ferguson, and Wendy Griswold (eds.), *Literature and Social Practice*. Chicago: University of Chicago Press, pp. 177–81.

Powell, Walter W. and Rebecca Jo Friedkin (1986). "Politics and Programs: Organizational Factors in Public Television Decision Making," in Paul DiMaggio (ed.), *Nonprofit Enterprise in the Arts: Studies in Mission and Constraint*. New York, Oxford University Press, pp. 245–69.

Press, Andrea L. (1994). "The Sociology of Cultural Reception: Notes towards an Emerging Paradigm," in Diana Crane (ed.), *The Sociology of Culture Emerging Theoretical Perspectives*. Oxford: Blackwell, pp. 221–45.

Press, Andrea L. (1991). *Women Watching Television: Gender, Class, and Generation in the American Television Experience*. Philadelphia: University of Pennsylvania Press.

Price, Sally (1989). *Primitive Art in Civilized Places*. Chicago: University of Chicago Press.

Radway, Janice A. (1991). "Writing Reading the Romance," Introduction to the second edition of *Reading the Romance: Women, Patriarchy and Popular Literature.* Chapel Hill: University of North Carolina Press.

Radway, Janice (1988a). "The Book-of-the-Month Club and the General Reader: On the Uses of 'Serious' Fiction," in Philippe Desan, Priscilla Parkhurst Ferguson, and Wendy Griswold (eds.), *Literature and Social Practice.* Chicago: University of Chicago Press, pp. 154–76.

Radway, Janice (1988b) "Reception Study: Ethnography and the Problems of Dispersed Audiences and Nomadic Subjects," *Cultural Studies,* 2: 359–76.

Radway, Janice A. (1984). *Reading the Romance: Women, Patriarchy and Popular Literature,* first edition. Chapel Hill: University of North Carolina Press.

Reed, Adam (forthcoming). "Henry and I: An Ethnographic Account of Men's Fiction Reading," *Ethnos.*

Ritzer, George (1993). *The McDonaldization of Society.* Thousand Oaks, CA: Sage.

Robertson, Roland (1995). "Glocalization: Time-Space and Homogeneity-Heterogeneity" in Mike Featherstone, Scott Lash and Roland Robertson (eds.), *Global Modernities.* London: Sage, pp. 25–44.

Robinson, Deanna Campbell, Elizabeth B. Buck, and Marlene Cuthbert, eds. (1991). *Music at the Margins: Popular Music and Global Cultural Diversity.* London: Sage.

Robinson, Walter (1990). "Art Careers Still Pay Poorly, Surveys Find," *Art in America,* 34 (February): 35.

Root, Jane (1986). *Open the Box: About Television.* London: Comedia.

Rose, Gillian (2001). *Visual Methodologies.* London: Sage.

Rosen, Sherwin (1981). "The Economics of Superstars," *American Economic Review,* 75 (December): 845–58.

Ross, Andrew (1989). *No Respect: Intellectuals and Popular Culture.* London: Routledge.

Rothfield, Lawrence, ed. (2001). *Unsettling "Sensation": Arts-Policy Lessons from the Brooklyn Museum of Art Controversy.* New Brunswick, NJ: Rutgers University Press.

Rueschemeyer, Marilyn (1993). "State Patronage in the German Democratic Republic: Artistic and Political Change in a State Socialist Society," in Judith Huggins Balfe (ed.), *Paying the Piper: Causes and Consequences of Art Patronage.* Chicago: University of Illinois Press, pp. 209–33.

Ryan, John (1985). *The Production of Culture in the Music Industry: The ASCAP-BMI Controversy.* New York: University Press of America.

Ryan, John and Richard A. Peterson (1993). "Occupational and Organizational Consequences of the Digital Revolution in Music Making," *Current Research on Occupations and Professions,* 8: 173–201.

Ryan, John and Richard A. Peterson (1982). "The Product Image: The Fate of Creativity in Country Music Songwriting," *Annual Review of Communication Research,* 10: 11–32.

Ryan, John and William M. Wentworth (1999). *Media and Society: The Production of Culture in the Mass Media.* Boston: Allyn and Bacon.

Sahlin, Marshall (1985). *Islands of History.* Chicago: University of Chicago Press.

Saussure, Ferdinand de (1915 [1959]). *Course in General Linguistics.* New York: Philosophical Library.

Schiller, Herbert I. (1989). *Culture, Inc.: The Corporate Takeover of Public Expression.* New York: Oxford University Press.

Schiller, Herbert I. (1969). *Mass Communication and American Empire.* Boston: Beacon Press.

Schudson, Michael (1986). *Advertising: The Uneasy Persuasion: Its Dubious Impact on American Society.* New York: Basic Books.

Scott, Allen J. (2000). "French Cinema: Economy, Policy and Place in the Making of a Cultural-Products Industry," *Theory, Culture and Society,* 17 (1): 1–38.

Scott, John (1990). *A Matter of Record: Documentary Sources in Social Research.* Cambridge: Polity.

Seaman, William R. (1992). "Active Audience Theory: Pointless Populism," *Media, Culture and Society,* 14: 301–11.

Seiter, Ellen (1995). "Different Children, Different Dreams: Racial Representation in Advertising" in Gail Dines and Jean M. Humez (eds.), *Gender, Race, and Class in Media.* London: Sage, pp. 99–108.

Sennett, Richard (1978). *The Fall of the Public Man.* New York: Vintage.

Shipler, D. K. (1983). "In Israel, Tolerance a Goal of 'Sesame Street' . . . ", *New York Times,* September 29.

Shively, JoEllen (1992). "Cowboys and Indians: Perceptions of Western Films among American Indians and Anglos," *American Sociological Review,* 57 (6): 725–34.

Shrum, Wesley (1991). "Critics and Publics: Cultural Mediation in Highbrow and Popular Performing Arts," *American Journal of Sociology,* 97 (2): 347–75.

Silverstone, Roger (1994). *Television and Everyday Life.* London: Routledge.

Simpson, Charles R. (1981). *SoHo: The Artist in the City.* Chicago: University of Chicago Press.

Simpson, Elizabeth, ed. (1997). *The Spoils of War. World War II and Its Aftermath: The Loss, Reappearance, and Recovery of Cultural Property.* New York: Abrams.

Smith, David W. E. (1988). "The Great Symphony Orchestra: A Relatively Good Place to Grow Old," *International Journal of Aging and Human Development,* 27 (4) 233–47.

Stacey, Jackie (1993). *Star Gazing: Hollywood Cinema and Female Spectatorship.* London: Routledge.

Starr, Paul (1999). "Cheap Culture," paper presented at the annual meeting of the American Sociological Association (Chicago).

Stinchcombe, Arthur L. (1959). "Bureaucratic and Craft Administration of Production," *Administrative Science Quarterly,* 4: 168–87.

Storey, John (1996). *Cultural Studies and the Study of Popular Culture: Theories and Methods.* Edinburgh: Edinburgh University Press.

Storey, John (1993). *An Introductory Guide to Cultural Theory and Popular Culture.* London: Harvester Wheatsheaf.

Strinati, Dominic (1995). *An Introduction to Theories of Popular Culture.* London: Routledge.

The Surgeon General's Scientific Advisory Committee on Television and Social Behavior (1972). *Television and Growing Up: The Impact of Televised Violence.* (Report to the Surgeon General, United States Public Health Service). Washington, DC: U.S. Government Printing Office.

Swidler, Ann (2001). *Talk of Love: How Culture Matters*. Chicago: University of Chicago Press.

Swidler, Ann (1986). "Culture in Action: Symbols and Strategies," *American Sociological Review*, 51: 273–86.

Swidler, Ann, Melissa Rapp, and Yasemin Soysal (1986). "Format and Formula in Prime-Time Television," in Sandra J. Ball-Rokeach and Muriel G. Cantor (eds.), *Media, Audience and Social Structure*. Newbury Park, CA: Sage, pp. 324–37.

Sydie, R. A. (1989). "Humanism, Patronage and the Question of Women's Artistic Genius in the Italian Renaissance," *Journal of Historical Sociology*, 2 (3): 175–205.

Taylor, Laurie and Bob Mullan (1986). *Uninvited Guests: The Intimate Secrets of Television and Radio*. London: Chatto and Windus.

Thibodeau, Ruth (1989). "From Racism to Tokenism: The Changing Face of Blacks in *New Yorker* Cartoons," *Public Opinion Quarterly*, 53: 482–94.

Thompson, Kenneth (1998). *Moral Panics*. London: Routledge.

Thurston, Carol (1987). *The Romance Revolution: Erotic Novels for Women and the Quest for a New Sexual Identity*. Chicago: University of Illinois Press.

The Times [of London] (2000). "Portrait Let High Society Grin and Bare Its Teeth," Wednesday, 19 July, p. 10.

Tomlinson, John (1991). *Cultural Imperialism*. London: Continuum.

Trubek, Amy B. (2000). *Haute Cuisine: How the French Invented the Culinary Tradition*. Philadelphia: University of Pennsylvania Press.

Tubb, Kathryn Walker, ed. (1995). *Antiquities Trade or Betrayed: Legal, Ethical and Conservation Issues*. London: Archetype Publications.

Tuchman, Gaye (1989). *Edging Women Out: Victorian Novelists, Publishers, and Social Change*. New Haven: Yale University Press.

Tuchman, Gaye (1982). "Culture as Resource: Actions Defining the Victorian Novel," *Media, Culture and Society*, 4 (1): 3–18.

Tuchman, Gaye (1978). "Introduction: The Symbolic Annihilation of Women by the Mass Media," in Gaye Tuchman, Arlene Kaplan Daniels, and James Benét (eds.), *Hearth and Home: Images of Women in Mass Media*. New York, Oxford University Press, pp. 3–38.

Tuchman, Gaye, Arlene Kaplan Daniels and James Benét, eds. (1978). *Hearth and Home: Images of Women in Mass Media*. New York: Oxford University Press.

Tuchman, Gaye and Nina E. Fortin (1984). "Fame and Misfortune: Edging Women Out of the Great Literary Tradition," *American Journal of Sociology*, 90 (1): 72–96.

Turnstall, Jeremy (1983). *The Media in Britain*. London: Constable.

Turow, Joseph (1997). *Breaking Up America: Advertisers and the New Media World*. Chicago: University of Chicago Press.

Tylor, Edward B. (1871 [1924]). *Primitive Culture*. Glouster, MA: Smith.

Urquia, Norman (forthcoming). "Doin' It Right: Contested Authenticity in London Salsa Clubs", to appear in Andy Bennett and Richard A. Peterson (eds.), *Popular Music Scenes: Anglo-American Perspectives on Contemporary Music in Europe and America*, [working title]. Nashville: Vanderbilt University Press.

Urry, John (1990). *The Tourist Gaze: Leisure and Travel in Contemporary Societies*. London: Sage.

USA Today (1998). http://www.usatoday.com/life/enter/movies/lef104.htm (downloaded 28 September, 1998).

Van Deberg, William L. (1984). *Slavery and Race in American Popular Culture*. Madison, WI: University of Wisconsin Press.

Varis, Tapio (1985). *International Flow of Television Programmes*. Paris: UNESCO.

Varis, Tapio (1974). "The International Flow of Television Programs," *Journal of Communication*, 34 (1): 143–52.

Vidmar, Neil and Milton Rokeach (1979). "Archie Bunker's Bigotry: A Study in Selective Perception and Exposure," in Richard P. Adler (ed.), *All in the Family: A Critical Appraisal*. New York: Praeger Special Studies. pp. 123–38.

Wallerstein, Immanuel (1974). *The Modern World System*. New York: Academic Press.

Watson, Tony J. (1995). *Sociology, Work and Industry*, third edition. London: Routledge.

Watt, Ian (1957). *The Rise of the Novel: Studies in Defoe, Richardson and Fielding*. Berkeley: University of California Press.

Weber, Max (1946). "The Social Psychology of the World Religions," In H. H. Gerth and C. Wright Mills (eds.), *From Max Weber*. New York: Oxford University Press, pp. 267–301.

Weber, William (2000). "From Miscellany to Homogeneity in Concert Programming," paper presented at the *States of the Arts: Aesthetic Media in Europe Across the Millennia* conference, University of Exeter, UK, 1–2 September.

Weber, Robert Philip (1990). *Basic Content Analysis*, second edition. London: Sage.

WGBH Educational Foundation (1991). *The Fine Art of Faking It*, from the television series *Nova* for the Public Broadcasting System (video). Princeton: Films for the Humanities & Sciences.

White, Harrison C. and Cynthia A. White (1965 [1993]). *Canvases and Careers: Institutional Change in the French Painting World*. Chicago: University of Chicago Press.

White, Cynthia and Harrison White (1964). "Institutional Change in the French Painting World," in Robert N. Wilson (ed.), *The Arts in Society*. Englewood Cliffs, NJ: Prentice-Hall.

Whyte, William Foote (1943). *Street Corner Society: The Social Structure of an Italian Slum*. Chicago: University of Chicago Press.

Wildman Steven S. and Stephen E. Siwek (1988). *International Trade in Films and Television Programmes*. Cambridge, MA: Ballinger.

Williams, Raymond (1981). *The Sociology of Culture*. New York: Schocken Books.

Williams, Raymond (1973). "Base and Superstructure in Marxist Cultural Theory," *New Left Review*, 82 (November/December): 3–16.

Williams, Raymond (1961). *The Long Revolution*. London: Chatto & Windus.

Williams, Raymond (1959). *Culture and Society, 1789–1950*. London: Chatto & Windus.

Williamson, Judith (1978). *Decoding Advertisements: Ideology and Meaning in Advertising*. London: Marion Boyars.

Willis, Paul (1978). *Profane Culture*. London: Routledge.

Winn, Marie (1977). *The Plug-In Drug.* Harmondsworth: Penguin.

Witkin, Robert W. (1998). *Adorno on Music.* London: Routledge.

Wolff, Janet (1990). *Feminine Sentences: Essays on Women and Culture.* Berkeley: University of California Press.

Wolff, Janet (1988). *Aesthetics and the Sociology of Art.* London: George Allen and Unwin.

Wolff, Janet (1981). *The Social Production of Art.* New York: New York University Press.

Wolff, Janet and John Seed, eds. (1988). *The Culture of Capital: Art, Power and the Nineteenth-Century Middle Class.* Manchester: Manchester University Press.

Wright, Will (1975). *Sixguns and Society: A Structural Study of the Western.* Berkeley: University of California Press.

Wuthnow, Robert and Marsha Witten (1988). "New Directions in the Study of Culture", *Annual Review of Sociology,* 14: 49–67.

Zola, Emile. (1867 [1982]). Selections of his work, in Francis Frascina & Charles Harrison (eds.), *Modern Art and Modernism: An Anthology.* London: Harper & Row, pp. 29–38

Zolberg, Vera L. (1992). "Barrier or Leveler? The Case of the Art Museum," in Michèle Lamont and Marcel Fournier (eds.), *Cultivating Differences: Symbolic Boundaries and the Making of Inequality.* Chicago: University of Chicago Press, pp. 187–209.

Zolberg, Vera L. (1990). *Constructing a Sociology of the Arts.* New York: Cambridge University Press.

Zolberg, Vera L. (1986). "Tensions of Mission in American Art Museums," in Paul DiMaggio (ed.), *Nonprofit Enterprise in the Arts: Studies in Mission and Constraint.* New York: Oxford University Press, 184–98.

Zolberg, Vera and Joni Maya Cherbo, eds. (1997). *Outsider Art: Contesting Boundaries in Contemporary Culture.* Cambridge: University of Cambridge Press.

Zukin, Sharon (1982). *Loft Living: Culture and Capital in Urban Change.* New Brunswick, NJ: Rutgers University Press.

Index

Barthel, Diane L., 54*n*, 272*n*
Barthes, Roland, 181, 191, 258, 259,
 263–4
base *see under* Marxism
Bastian, Misty, 164
Bator, Paul M., 167
Battersby, Christine, 290, 296*n*
Baudrillard, Jean, 162
Bauman, Zygmunt, 157
Baumann, Shyon, 104, 226, 295*n*
Baumol, William J., 118–19
Baxandall, Michael
 formal analysis, 253–5, 272*n*
 guild suppression of innovation, 136
 Renaissance Italy, 143, 273–6, 277*n*,
 308
Bayton, Mavis, 140, 149
BBC, 107*n*
The Beatles, 109
Becker, Carol, 303*n*
Becker, Howard
 art worlds, xv–xvi, 2–3, 67, 68–75, 76,
 77, 78, 79, 80–1, 113, 285, 294–6*n*,
 308
 artistic reputation, 147
 artists, 79, 131–4, 137, 150*n*
 audiences, 308
 conventions, 72–4, 132, 240
 effects of distribution system, 90
 governments and the arts, 121
 innovation, 149
 meanings of social groups, 182, 197*n*
 mosaic metaphor, 18*n*, 311
 quilt circles, 115
 romantic myth of the artist, 143
 symbolic interactionism, 82*n*
 truth, 310
Beethoven, Ludwig van, 118, 145–6,
 151*n*, 227
belief systems, 38
Belting, Hans, 143
Benjamin, Walter, 268, 269
Bennett, Andrew, 115, 124*n*, 161, 163–4
Bennett, David H., 167, 168
Bennett, T., 270

Berezin, Mabel, 121
Berger, David G., 78, 97, 108–11
Berger, John, 268–9
Beverly Hills, 90210, 187, 188–90
Bielby, Denise D.
 age discrimination, 141
 gender discrimination, 139–40, 150*n*,
 155
 racial discrimination, 141, 155
 television pilots, 102–3, 107*n*
 union data, 138
Bielby, William T.
 age discrimination, 141
 gender discrimination, 139–40, 150*n*,
 155
 racial discrimination, 141, 155
 television pilots, 102–3, 107*n*
 union data, 138
big band music, 234
Bignell, Jonathan, 263
bikeboys, 185
Billingham, Richard, 17*n*
binary oppositions, 263, 264–6
Binder, Amy, 244–8
biographies, as popular icons, 25–6
Birmingham School, 197*n*
black boxes concept, 9
black civil rights movement, 37, 39
Black Sabbath, 247
Blaikie, Andrew, 220*n*
Blair, Helen, 152, 153–5
Blenheim, Oxfordshire (Turner), 24
blockbusters, 124
 art museums, 96, 119, 166, 169
 movies, 91, 96, 99, 153
 publishing industry, 96
Bloom, Allan, 239
The Blue Danube, 230
blues music, 141, 233, 234
Blumler, Jay G., 101, 182
BMI (Broadcast Music Incorporated),
 141
bodice-ripper genre, 96, 218
Bollywood, 162
Book of the Month Club, 93, 106*n*

representation of race, 29–31
rise of folk art, 238–9
social control of artists, 143–4
study of popular icons, 25–6
television show imports, 159–60
see also Americanization
Universal Studios Hollywood, 89, 100
Universe Symphony, 132
univores, 232
upper classes
  art in private settings, 206–7, 241*n*
  audience reception of TV programs,
    211–12
  control of minority groups, 242*n*
  fears of mob violence, 24
  in France, 84
  musical dislikes, 233
  social Darwinism, 228
  social roles, 233
  tastes, 229–30
  women's hobbies, 141
  see also elites
urban dance music, 115
urbanization, 48
Urquia, Norman, 116
Urry, John, 169
U.S. News and World Report, 245
USA Today, 89
Useem, Michael, 228
uses and gratifications approach, 182–3,
  195, 210
utilitarian economics, 127

V-chip, 59
Van de Ven, Andrew H., 18*n*
Van Deberg, William L., 37
Van Gogh, Vincent, 227
vanguard culture, 144
Varis, Tapio, 160, 162
Vatican, 167
Veneziano, Domenico, 254
Venezuela, 183
vertical integration, 108–9
video mode, 215
videos, 106*n*, 159

see also music videos
Vidmar, Neil, 191–2
Vigée-Lebrun, Elizabeth, xxi, 21, *22*
violence
  media effects literature, 49, 50–1
  and television, 55–9
The Virgin of the Rocks, 269
visual arts
  age at which artists achieved success,
    148
  age discrimination, 141
  canonization of, 238–9, 240
  Chicago Artists-in-Residence (AIR)
    program, 143–4
  in German Democratic Republic, 122
  as international art forms, 166
  market system, 121
  in private settings, 206, 220*n*, 241*n*,
    268
  reliance on art museums, 71
  success rate in New York, 134
  see also engravings; etchings; paintings
visual images, 60, 268
volunteer shoppers, 283

wage slaves, 11
Wallach, Glenn, 303*n*
Wallerstein, Immanuel, 158
Waquant, Loïc J.D., 296*n*
Warburg Institute, 277*n*
Warhol, Andy, 148
Water Lilies, 169, 227
Waterstone's, 90
Waterworld, 89, 99–100
Watson, Tony J., 14–15, 18*n*
Watt, Ian, 54*n*, 139
Wayne, John, 223
Weber, Max, 8, 10, 182, 224, 235
Weber, Robert Philip, 36*n*
Weber, William, 236
Wedell, George, 163
Weinberg, Bruce A., 142, 148
The Well-Tempered Clavier, 230
Wentworth, William M., 48, 53*n*, 58, 96
West End theaters, 166, 169